The Aging Intellect

Douglas H. Powell

Routledge
Taylor & Francis Group
New York   London

Cover image: "Icarus", plate VIII of the illustrated book "Jazz" by Henri Matisse. © 2011 Succession Henri Matisse/Artists Rights Society (ARS), New York. Photo: Archives Matisse.

Routledge
Taylor & Francis Group
711 Third Avenue
New York, NY 10017

Routledge
Taylor & Francis Group
27 Church Road
Hove, East Sussex BN3 2FA

© 2011 by Douglas H. Powell
Routledge is an imprint of Taylor & Francis Group, an Informa business

Printed in the United States of America on acid-free paper
10 9 8 7 6 5 4 3 2 1

International Standard Book Number: 978-0-415-99685-3 (Hardback)

Library of Congress Cataloging-in-Publication Data

Powell, Douglas H.
  The aging intellect / Douglas H. Powell
    p. cm.
  Includes bibliographical references and index.
  ISBN 978-0-415-99685-3 (hardback : acid-free paper)
    1. Cognition in old age. 2. Cognition--Age factors. 3. Aging. 4. Quality of life.
I. Title.

BF724.85.C64P677 2011
155.67'13--dc22   2010043256

Visit the Taylor & Francis Web site at
http://www.taylorandfrancis.com

and the Routledge Web site at
http://www.routledgementalhealth.com

With love to my wife, Jo,
who knows about writers,
for her understanding and support,
encouraging me to be the best I can be

Contents

Acknowledgments vii
Introduction xi

1 Maximizing Intellectual Powers in the Third Age of Life 1

2 How Health Affects the Intellect 19

3 How the Mind Ages 39

4 Healthy Lifestyle Habits Benefiting the Aging Body and Mind 63

5 Direct Actions That Benefit the Intellect 89

6 Optimal Cognitive Aging 111

7 Normal Cognitive Aging 133

8 High-Risk Cognitive Aging 157

9 Writing and Learning About the Aging Intellect 183

   Glossary of Frequently Used Terms 203

   Notes 209

   Index 283

Acknowledgments

First in line to receive my thanks are the women and men who volunteered to help with this project. These are the participants in the 3rd Age Study from the Florida Geriatric Research Program, the relatives and friends of my students, and the scores of members from the Harvard University Retirees Association who filled out a lengthy health survey and made themselves available to be interviewed. They taught the students, and their teacher, a great deal about the aging process. Special appreciation goes to Malcolm Hamilton for helping recruit the Harvard volunteers and to Bob Kelly at Phillips Brooks House for providing the students with a place to interview subjects.

The 3rd Age Study was made possible because of the support of William E. Hale, MD, Director Emeritus of the Florida Geriatric Research Program of Morton Plant Mease Health Care in Clearwater, Florida, and then Director of Clinical Research Carol Weideman, PhD. Robert Woodside and Eleanor Reuters managed the recruitment, scheduling, and data storage. Interviews with more than 300 subjects and the necessary staff support were provided by Barbara Bonda, Robert Chellberg, Noel Hedrick, Edmund Herman, Suzanne Hornbuckle, Margaret Kennedy, Nina Krueger, Mary Moynihan, Roberta Pearce, Donna Simcoe, Barbara Sleicher, Carol Venherm, and June Wilbur. Dr. Felix Nwokolo provided medical oversight and recruited underrepresented minority group subjects. Additional male subjects were obtained at the Tarpon Cove Yacht and Racquet Club of Naples, Florida; the Somerville, Massachusetts, YMCA; and Porter Hill Presbyterian Village of Grand Rapids, Michigan.

The analysis of the 3rd Age data was greatly helped by William H. Bossert, the David B. Arnold Jr. Professor of Science at Harvard University, who shared his considerable wisdom about data interpretation and tutored me in the rudiments of using Python for statistical analysis of the data sets. Dr. Charles D. Spielberger, Distinguished Research Professor Emeritus and Director of the Center for Research in Behavioral Medicine and Health Psychology at the University of South Florida, generously permitted us to use a research version of his State-Trait Personality Inventory [Spielbeger, C. D. (2005). *State Trait Personality Inventory.* Menlo Park, CA: Mind Garden].

As the data from the 3rd Age Study were analyzed, presented, and discussed with students from several classes in the Harvard Summer School, they contributed ideas to the three-level theoretical models that became optimal, normal, and high-risk cognitive aging. Later classes of students at Harvard and Florida Gulf Coast University contributed papers based on interviews with volunteer subjects. These interviews provided support, or lack of it, for elements of the model and resulted in modifications to the lists of characteristics linked to optimal, normal, and high-risk cognitive aging. These papers and subsequent discussions were the inspiration for many of the ideas as well as most of the cases and clinical observations contained in this book.

Thank you all: Javed Ali, Patrick Avanessian, Jane Baker, Lauren Barraco, Ashley Best, Betty Bishop, Joseph Bruno, Amanda Caplan, Marisol Carmona, Joseph Carvajal, Kayla Cauthon, Tianna Christiano, Lorraine Chu, Robert Conway, Quenton Craddock, Rita Cutroni, David Davis, Steven DeWolf, Tara DiCarlo, Melina DiPolina, Joan Emison, Ewa Erdman, Matthew Foreman, Kathleen Foster, Dorothy Friendly, Johann Gadson, Courtney Gales, Kristina Gallo, Elizabeth Ghannam, Nancy Granert, Jamie Haag, McKenzie Halvick, David Harris, Joel Hernandez, Frank Herrera, Mary Heth, Ilana Hodson, Anin Inglis, Gul Jabbar, George Jewell, Susan Jones, Robert Johnson, Yoon-Keang Joo, Caroline Joyner, Janet Juley, Sara Kellogg, Hope Kepley, Li-Wei King, Perin Kothari, Jennifer Larson, Christen Leen, Kimberly Levin, Dani Levine, Geisa Matos-Machuca, Matthew Madson, Gabriela Marquez, Shirley Marvin, Sheilah Maturo, Richard Maye, Nyola Moore, Ryan Morrow, Jamilla Munford, Ivan Nelson, "Ben" Ngamsuwanjaroen, Martha Nicholson, Marcel Ostrowsky, Sun Sook Park, James Pearson, Raquel Pereira, Gary Philbrick, Emily Pitts, Stacey Pulk, Stacey Reed, Sharon Ricciardi, Ashley Rose, Rachel Rubianes, Yoshiko Sato, Clara Schack, Pia Schmidt, Linda Senecal, Kurtis Shrewsberry, Jennifer Shultis, Diane Tang, Sherman Teng, Jennifer Thomas, Ha Tran, ImeIme Umana, Timothy Vasil, Venkat Vajjhala, Yenny Vazquez, Nicolas Vera, Alex Vermiel, Nicholas West, Stephanie Wilka, and Emaba Zaman.

I am especially grateful to Tom Piper, Baker Foundation Professor and Lawrence E. Fouraker Professor of Business Administration, Emeritus, who accompanied me through the years of this enterprise and listened patiently to my efforts to understand what my students and I were learning together about cognitive aging. Thanks also to Bob Armstrong for bringing Eugene O'Kelly's *Chasing Daylight* to my attention. As the lecture notes, student papers, and research of others were gradually transformed into a manuscript, the process was eased by knowledgeable friends and colleagues who read and critiqued earlier drafts of chapters: Janne Hurrelbrink Bias; Earl Bracker, MD; Donald Davidoff, PhD; Robert Lawson; and Brenda Miller, MSW. The final draft of the book benefited greatly from the perceptive and supportive editorial contributions of Jo Ann Miller.

I appreciate the oversight and gentle direction from Dr. George Zimmar, Publisher of Routledge Mental Health; the management of Senior Editorial Assistant Marta Moldvai, who kept this enterprise on schedule; the skillful copyediting of Joanne Freeman; and the production management of Marsha Hecht.

Introduction

The Aging Intellect has three main purposes. First, it makes a case for including intellectual functioning—especially worries that older adults may have about their mental powers—in the broad definition of what constitutes "health." The second purpose of this book is to describe the characteristics that distinguish three distinct levels of intellectual functioning that are found among older women and men: optimal cognitive aging, normal cognitive aging, and at high risk for cognitive impairment. Each of the dozen or more characteristics of optimal, normal, and high-risk cognitive aging is based on scientific evidence and was verified in interviews with 151 older individuals. The third goal of this book is to present evidence-based healthy lifestyle habits and other behaviors, within the reach of most aging women and men, that are likely to improve their quality of life and minimize the rate of physical and cognitive decline.

This book is written primarily for two groups of readers. The first are those caring for older adults. The second are the nonoptimally aging women and men in the 3rd Age of life, those years from about 60 to 80, who are well aware that they are not doing some of the things they could do to become more physically and intellectually vigorous. They may have tried and failed many times to get more exercise, lose weight, or eat healthier. I will give them a new list of reasons to try again to change one or two behavior patterns that could lead to aging optimally. First on that list is preserving the aging intellect. Several excellent books and scientific articles have appeared in this millennium that identify many of the characteristics of people who are aging optimally. Largely missing in these publications, however, is mention of those lifestyle habits and other actions linked to optimal *cognitive* aging. This is a significant omission because as we grow older an intact intellect is no longer taken for granted. Adults in the 3rd Age increasingly worry that an impaired intellect will rob them of their independence, their ability to connect with loved ones, and the appreciation of other experiences that give their life meaning.

This book will summarize healthy life style habits that also benefit the intellect such as exercise, eating healthily and maintaining satisfying social relationships. It also will illuminate what is known about specific actions that older adults can take that are associated with optimal cognitive aging. Examples are minimizing distractions that disrupt attention; making use of selection, optimization, and compensation; and engaging in attention restoration activities.

At present, less than only about 30% of the factors associated with optimal cognitive aging are known. This book attempts to add to the current understanding of lifestyle habits and other behaviors that distinguish those with optimally aging minds from the majority of their contemporaries who are aging normally and those at high risk for accelerated mental decline.

Chapters 2–5 constitute a "mini-textbook" about factors that indirectly or directly affect cognition. Chapter 2 documents the adverse effects of six different medical conditions on the intellect, including untreated hearing loss, which is often overlooked as a preventable cause of cognitive decline. Chapter 3 describes how the mind ages, focusing especially on the differences between abilities that decline rapidly and those that remain relatively stable. It also presents findings that may be new to the reader, such as the adverse impact on memory of the inability to suppress distracting thoughts, and neuroplasticity—how the aging brain structure is influenced by external stimulation.

Chapters 4 and 5 look at the research evidence supporting the belief that specific behaviors are associated with optimal cognitive aging. Chapter 4 identifies seven modifiable lifestyle habits associated with aging optimally. These include nonathletic leisure activities and compliance with medical instructions. Direct actions that benefit the intellect are the topic of Chapter 5. Among those not often mentioned are attention-restoring activities such as a walk in the woods or appreciating art.

The characteristics of individuals classified as optimal, normal, or high-risk cognitive agers, illustrated by clinical examples, are described in Chapters 6–8. The final chapter is a summary of what I have learned about optimal cognitive aging while writing this book. For example, this process deepened my understanding of the potentially adverse effects of positivity bias on the reasoning of elders. This is the tendency of elders to pay more attention to positive than negative features when choices have to be made. And, my appreciation of the several subtypes of mild cognitive impairment has been expanded, including the recognition that a small group of adults with MCI exist who revert to a nonimpaired state during follow-up.

At the end of all but the final chapter is a section on my reflections on some of the material that was presented as well as thoughts about the potential applications of the material to adults. Like me, some elder care workers are themselves in the 3rd Age of life. One of the benefits of being a little older is that our experiences provide us with a reality-based perspective about the utility of some of the ideas in these chapters. Because I have long been a practitioner who has enjoyed doing clinical research and anticipate that some of you reading this book may share my interests, I have highlighted potentially interesting areas for exploration by aspiring clinician-scientists.

Notes

The notes in this book are written for those interested in learning more about the topic. In addition to the relevant citations, the endnotes elaborate, quantify, or qualify statements made in the chapters and not infrequently reference publications with a contrary view.

The investigations cited favor longitudinal research and larger cross-sectional studies using community-dwelling subjects, those based on multicenter collaborations, those that randomly assigned subjects to treatment and control groups, and meta-analyses or summaries/reviews of the literature. Most of the research reports were published since 2000. During the review of this research, it was striking to me how international gerontological research has become. Nearly every important topic in the field of cognitive aging has been addressed by investigators on two or more continents.

Regarding the references, clinician readers will be aware that it is still a long time from publication to practice. The numerous discoveries about cognitive aging made in the past decade have yet to become part of the knowledge base of many providers. I am well aware of how difficult it is to remain current in a clinical specialty when the demands of patients, clients and colleagues leave so little time for reading current research and keeping up to date with the most recent findings on problems common to 3rd Agers.

Books such as this one are an effort to close this gap. The time lag also may be diminishing because newspapers, the Internet, online publications, TV, and other media sources now regularly provide the lay public with information about important health care findings, sometimes even before scientific journals carrying these new findings arrive in the professional's mail. A positive feature of this development is that it may improve patient-provider collaboration. Some laypeople, who often have more time to read, will be able to inform their providers about findings in recent publications relevant to their condition that may benefit both of them.

A Note About Cases

To illustrate most of the major points in the pages ahead, *The Aging Intellect* contains case studies, examples, anecdotes, and brief quotations. Most were inspired by student papers and discussions, and the rest were drawn from my clinical practice and research. All of the longer pieces, and many of the shorter ones, were rewritten by me. The longer cases in Chapters 6–8 are based on a combination of at least three real people, one of whom was known to me. Other than age, the specific details about the subjects have been altered to guard the identity of the subjects and the students. Only the references to me or my own experiences are true. Other similarities in the book are coincidental.

Provenance

This book began life as a series of lecture notes given to the students in my courses on aging at Harvard and at Florida Gulf Coast University in Ft. Myers. The course examined qualities linked to optimal, normal, and high-risk aging. In the beginning, these lecture notes were based on the findings from two large research projects involving nearly 2,000 subjects and from the publications of other researchers.

The motivation to write *The Aging Intellect* came unexpectedly, when early in the course I added the requirement that each student write papers based on their interviews with older subjects. Six classes of students at Harvard and at Florida Gulf Coast University interviewed an assortment of grandparents, teachers, neighbors, coworkers, customers, and in one case, an elderly felon at a prison where a student worked.

Perhaps because the first papers were handed in early in the course, with the writing largely based on spontaneous observations, unfiltered by previous learning, and unencumbered by professional formatting, the student descriptions were especially vivid and perceptive, filled with stories and candid comments that fleshed out the picture of these aging individuals well beyond the lists of qualities we had assembled.

From these student papers, I drew quotes, descriptions, case fragments, and inspiration to write longer cases illustrating the key points of the next generation of lecture notes. Before long, it was apparent that these real-life examples from the student papers not only enlivened the reading but also provided confirmation, or lack of it, for the characteristics related to the theoretical list associated with optimal, normal, and high-risk cognitive aging. Since no other book, to my knowledge, addressed this topic from both a clinical perspective and an empirical footing, it seemed to me that these findings were worth sharing with others interested in this topic. Several years ago I began to convert the lecture notes to book chapters. I hope that *The Aging Intellect* will add some new ideas to those seeking to learn more about those factors that do and do not contribute to optimal cognitive aging.

The empirical data on which this book is based come from two large cross-sectional studies. The first was based on the analysis of the cognitive test scores of 1,002 physicians aged 25–92.[1] On the basis of test scores, we identified a small percentage of optimally aging doctors who had test scores comparable to those in the prime of life.

The second research project was the 3rd Age Study in Clearwater, Florida. Its purpose was to extend the pilot study of physicians to a nonphysician population, with the aim of identifying lifestyle patterns, health practices, and other behaviors that correlated with optimal cognitive aging. Usable health survey and brief interview data were collected from 287 older members of the Florida Geriatric Research Program.

Papers and discussions with the students about their interviews with 151 subjects (age range 54–88) contributed findings bearing on the characteristics of optimal, normal, and high-risk cognitive agers. Eleven other subjects were excluded because of missing information. The proportion of subjects in the 55–59 age group was 5%, in the 60–69 age group it was 35%, in the 70–79 age group it was 34%, and in the 80+ age group it was 26%. While the overwhelming majority of the subjects interviewed were classified as optimal cognitive agers, not all were aging optimally. Thirty-five volunteers exhibited behaviors that were consistent with our understanding of normal cognitive aging. Ten of the subjects exhibited lifestyle behaviors and attitudes that put them at high risk for cognitive impairment. Although few in number, these nonoptimally aging subjects allowed us to confirm or reject qualities we thought were associated with normal or high-risk cognitive aging. For elder caregivers, these lists suggest places to begin when assessing older adults or when advising those aspiring to age optimally.

The limitations of the research based on interview data are apparent. One obvious drawback is that it is a clinical study based on a small number of subjects, with optimal cognitive agers overrepresented. Another is that this research began as a teaching exercise, so that some of the initial interview data were incomplete because questions were added to the later interviews as our understanding grew about the characteristics of optimal cognitive aging. These caveats acknowledged, I believe that the healthy lifestyle habits and other behaviors we found to be associated with optimal cognitive aging verify, and may add a variable or two, to the list of characteristics exhibited by older adults aging well. It also may be that the qualities we identified in elders not aging optimally are the greater contribution.

The Aging Intellect is intended to be informational and is not a substitute for professional advice. Should the reader become motivated to develop healthier lifestyle habits (e.g., starting an exercise program or new diet), it is important to consult with a physician or other health care provider before beginning.

Douglas H. Powell
Concord, Massachusetts

1

Maximizing Intellectual Powers in the Third Age of Life

The *Aging Intellect* is a book about the growing differences in mental ability among those in the 3rd Age of life and the behaviors that influence the quality of the aging intellect. The focus of this book is women and men who are approximately 60–80 years of age and those who care about and for them. My goal is to present evidence-based strategies for helping older adults who are under our care or on their own live more fully.

This book not only is written for professionals and others caring for 3rd Agers but also is directed at adults looking after their aging parents and grandparents, who may wonder what actions their loved ones can take to get the most out of life for as long as possible. And, because we live in a world where all of us are increasingly responsible for managing our own care, I have tried to make this book accessible to those older adults who are interested in learning what they might do to improve the quality of their advancing years. They also might want to judge how they match up with the physical and cognitive characteristics of their optimally aging peers and, if necessary, plan changes in their daily routines to maximize their potential.

50th Reunion

Imagine you are at your 50th reunion. It has been a long time since you have seen most of your classmates. Looking around at the opening picnic supper, you cannot help but be surprised by the remarkable physical differences among men and women who attended school with you. A few stand out as trim and vigorous as they were at graduation a half century ago. The majority of your classmates look about the way you expect people your age to look—perhaps a few dozen pounds stouter and several steps slower than at graduation but still feeling pretty good. A few catch your attention because of their diminished energy and physical limitations.

Less obvious, but just as impressive, would be the variation in the intellectual powers among the 50th reuniongoers. A few are as quick and clever as ever. Among several, you notice "senior moments"—tip-of-the-tongue problems and difficulty recalling the names of people, things, and numbers. Stories of not remembering why they opened the refrigerator door or of losing track of their cars in parking lots abound. Nearly everyone has an Alzheimer's joke. But also among your classmates is a small group for whom the possibility of having Alzheimer's disease is not amusing. These classmates now seem slowed mentally, have trouble maintaining their attention, and drift to the fringes of conversation.

If you could compare the current physical and mental state of the class with a half century ago, odds are you would find that intellectual decline during those years has followed about the same downward slant as heart, lung, kidney, and other physical functions.

I attended a 50th reunion like this one not long ago. And in fact, I was struck by the dramatic physical and mental dissimilarities among my classmates. On the flight home from the reunion, my wife and I talked about the substantial differences there seemed to be in the mental acuity among the 50th reunioners and others we know in this age group. We speculated about which behaviors and attitudes might be linked to aging optimally, normally, or being at high risk for impairment at this time of life.

Since I was supervising trainees in a geriatric setting at the time and teaching a course on aging, I looked for a book that would provide a better understanding of the factors that contribute to the dramatic differences in the mind and body that I had just witnessed. While the shelves bulged with books about aging successfully, optimally, and well, nothing had been published about the remarkable intellectual differences among these older women and men. My disappointment at the inability to find such a book resulted in a 4-year research study that led to writing *The Aging Intellect*.

In this book, we take a close look at the cognitive and physical changes and challenges confronting women and men in the 3rd Age[1] of life—that period of the life span beyond the first season of preparation and maturation and the second season of necessary concentration on work and child rearing, but prior to the final stage of old age and death. Now free of the major obligations of work and family, still in relatively good health, and rich in discretionary time, people in the 3rd Age can enjoy the renewed potential to live life much more on their own terms.

Because it is defined by adequate health, reasonable energy level, and capacity for social engagement as well as by chronological age, the 3rd Age is full of possibilities for nearly everyone. Most 3rd Age women and men are still in the mix, engaged by choice in working, loving, and playful activities that bring satisfaction. A few continue in an occupation full or part time or pursue demanding learning experiences. Others help care for grandchildren and sometimes elderly loved ones. Many enjoy those pleasurable leisure activities they never had time for during those years of hectic employment and while caring for their children. 3rd Agers comprise the core of volunteers whose regular commitments of time and talent enable many community organizations to function.

If the 3rd Age were a season, it would be autumn. Just as in a grove of maple trees where some lose their leaves more rapidly than others in the fall, the boundaries of this stage of the life cycle are elastic. Most 3rd Agers are found in the decades between 60 and 80, but they may enter this era any time between the mid-50s and early 70s, while some remain well into their 80s. When the first decade of the 21st century opened, more than 36 million women and men were in this age group, the largest number in history. In 2010, the 3rd Age population exceeds 45 million; a decade later women and men aged 60–80 will number well over 60 million, approaching one in every five Americans.[2]

The Growing Importance of the Intellect

When we judge the overall quality of life, we include the mind as well as the body. This is what the World Health Organization intended in its classic definition of health as "complete physical, mental, and social well-being, not merely the absence of disease or infirmity."[3] In addition to the presence or absence of disease, this definition includes the importance of social networks, psychological state, and the intellect.

Until relatively recently, however, the intellect has been largely ignored by nationwide health surveys and by medical care providers in the United States. For instance, three national health surveys asked more than 100,000 Americans about the effect of numerous medical conditions on their quality of life but did not ask about the impact of diminished mental acuity short of dementia.[4]

Also rare is the health care provider who includes questions about the intellect during a medical visit. Think about your last physical exam. This checkup may have included a review of your medical history, a top-to-bottom physical inspection, and lab tests. In addition, the doctor or nurse may have asked other questions: How much do you smoke, drink, or use other drugs? Are you bothered by depression or anxiety? Do you feel safe at home? But the practitioner probably did not ask a question about a topic that is much more likely to be on your mind—namely, how are you holding up mentally? Many of us would not mind sharing our worries about our little mental lapses—about those times a child's zip code takes a temporary leave of absence from memory, or yesterday when we suddenly couldn't remember the word for that thing you put over your head when it rains. But, if the doctor does not ask, are we unlikely to bring it up?

Failure to assess the intellect is a crucial omission because most older adults share my worries. When health researchers in San Diego, California, summarized the factors people most often mention as important to successful aging, they found that the top two were absence of physical disability and cognitive impairment.[5] The importance to optimal aging of an intact intellect was mentioned more often than a sense of well-being or social engagement.

Peter Ditto and his research team at Kent State University in Ohio asked 3rd Agers to imagine what their life would be like if they had to endure seven chronic medical conditions, including coma, severe pain, and the inability to reason or remember. Then, they instructed the volunteers to rate on a scale of 1–9 what the quality of their life would be with these maladies. After coma and being in a chronic vegetative state, cognitive impairment was ranked as less desirable than the other medical conditions.[6] Furthermore, 3rd Agers more often indicated that they would prefer death to life if they were compromised intellectually.[7]

Summarizing the importance of the intellect to older adults, Ditto wrote the following:

> People may believe their cognitive activities can still be enjoyed in the presence of even severe physical impairment. Severe cognitive impairment, however, is seen by most people as having a much more basic and pervasive disruptive effect on the ability to enjoy even purely physical activities. People fear cognitive dysfunction because they expect it to rob them of the ability to engage in virtually any activity that gives life meaning.[8]

The first decades of the 21st century may be remembered as a time when the aging intellect began to receive the attention it deserves. The reason is that the third millennium opened with a rapidly growing understanding of how the brain functions. In part, this was the result of the running start provided by the U.S. Congress that designated 1990–2000 as the Decade of the Brain. The momentum also came from the expanding field of neuroscience, which provides an intellectual home and collegial stimulation for a diverse group of academics, professionals, and research scientists who share an interest in the workings of the mind. A group of these neuroscientists is proposing a new 10-year project called the "Decade of the Mind."[9] This book intends to contribute to a greater understanding of the variations in the aging mind by providing evidence in support of health-related behaviors and intellectual activities associated with optimal, normal, and high-risk cognitive aging.

Three Levels of Intellectual Functioning in the 3rd Age

When we are with a large group of older people who are about the same age (such as the 50th reunioners), it is easier to tell the differences in mental acuity among them because we can compare them with one another. But, suppose you are a caregiver to a 75-year-old man who says he is having increasing trouble remembering people's names and phone numbers, and that yesterday he mistakenly turned his car onto a one-way street going in the opposite direction. Fortunately, there was no one coming the other way, so he avoided an accident. But does this mean, however, that he should think about giving up his driver's license? Or, imagine you are the adult child of your recently widowed 3rd Age mother, who lives half a country away. Since your father's death, she has become increasingly withdrawn, inactive, and isolated. Your mother says she is fine, but the last time you saw her she looked 10 years older than a few months earlier. How worried should you be about these individuals? And, how might you clinically assess their overall intellectual abilities?

These examples introduce the second purpose of the book, which is to describe the three levels of intellectual functioning observed among independently living, older adults: optimal cognitive aging, normal cognitive aging, and at high risk for cognitive impairment. These classifications themselves are not new, but the standards used to define each of these states differ slightly from those in other studies.[10]

The estimated proportion of optimal cognitive agers, normal cognitive agers, and those at high risk for cognitive impairment in a population of

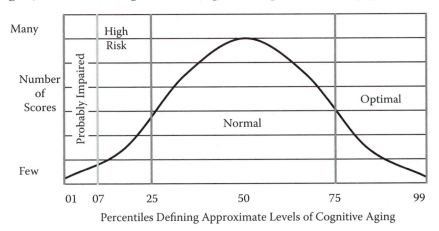

Percentiles Defining Approximate Levels of Cognitive Aging

Figure 1.1 Theoretical model for percentages of optimal, normal, and high-risk cognitive agers.

community-dwelling, nondisabled older adults in the United States is shown in Figure 1.1. Chapters 6, 7, and 8 provide the evidence for these estimations, along with more detailed examples of the characteristics that distinguish these levels of intellectual functioning.

Optimal Cognitive Aging

Optimal cognitive aging is characterized by avoiding risky lifestyle habits that endanger the intellect and practicing behaviors associated with maintaining or slowing the decline of mental skills. These individuals are mentally vigorous and regularly focus their intellectual powers on activities that interest them. While the majority are physically energetic as well, a few are physically disabled. Optimal cognitive agers are getting most of what is possible for each of them whether their IQs are average or exceptional. While many seem bright, optimal agers are not uniformly the best educated, and not all were standouts in school. A number had undistinguished academic records and worked at ordinary jobs. Between 20 and 30% of 3rd Agers fall into the optimal cognitive aging category.

Optimal cognitive agers are very different from those aging normally and those at high risk for cognitive impairment. As a group, their most striking features are high energy and activity levels—three to four times greater than those in the middle of the pack. Most optimal cognitive agers say their physical status is as good as or better than 5 years previously, and they are far more vigorous than their peers. Another distinguishing feature of these optimal cognitive agers is that they are proactive about medical checkups. They do not wait until they are symptomatic to schedule a physical exam. Optimal cognitive agers also are compliant with medical advice.

Being open to new experiences and to the new communication technologies characterizes these optimal cognitive agers. They also recognize that they will lose some of their mental acuity as they grow older, so they monitor how they are doing and take constructive action. Nearly all have reasonably large and diverse social networks, with friends across generations. An unanticipated finding was that appearance matters to most optimal cognitive agers. These women and men were more often described as younger looking, well dressed, and well groomed.

Normal Cognitive Aging

As used in this book, "normal cognitive aging" is synonymous with "average" or "usual" cognitive aging. It refers to older adults who may have experienced minor physical problems and whose intellectual abilities have declined as expected on the basis of their age and educational background. Normal cognitive agers comprise about 50–60% of those in the 3rd Age of life.

Their primary characteristic is a moderate energy level. That is still plenty of pep to do the things they want to do, but we do not marvel at their vigor. Most normal cognitive agers say that their energy level is the same or less than 5 years earlier and about on a par with that of their peers. Typically, their energy and activity levels are less than half that of optimal cognitive agers.

As a group, the men and women aging normally do not consistently monitor their physical and mental status. They typically are not proactive about medical care; instead, they often wait for symptoms to appear before consulting a physician. They may or may not be aware of activities that influence their health, but whether aware or not, they do not consistently act on this knowledge. Emotional problems cut into their usual sense of well-being 2 to 3 days a month.

Normal cognitive agers say that they are aware that some of their mental skills are holding up and some are falling off, but they do not worry much about the process. They seem to have accepted their limitations and are letting nature take its course. Normal cognitive agers make little apparent effort to evaluate how they are functioning mentally and make the necessary accommodations. Unaware that visuospatial abilities are among the first aptitudes to decline with age, they resign themselves to having trouble locating their cars at the mall rather than developing a strategy for remembering.

With normal cognitive agers, there is a much greater sense that they are letting life come to them rather than seeking it out. They have not given up entirely on preserving their intellect, however, and when encouraged, they open their minds to new experiences.

High Risk for Cognitive Impairment

Among the 3rd Agers are a small number whose several medical conditions and poor lifestyle habits put them at a higher risk for cognitive impairment. Some already exhibit worrisome chronic memory and other persistent cognitive problems. One of their most visible characteristics is an energy deficit. Many seem as dramatically deficient in energy as the optimal agers seem to overflow with it. Nearly all of those at high risk for cognitive impairment say that their physical and intellectual powers have declined in the past 5 years, and they are less vigorous than their contemporaries. Older adults classified among those at high risk for cognitive impairment make up 10–20% of the 3rd Age population.

Many high-risk cognitive agers live with five or more chronic medical conditions or exhibit behaviors that have potentially serious physical and cognitive consequences. A large minority of high-risk cognitive agers who are symptomatic deny that there is anything seriously wrong with them and often resist seeking professional care until they have an adverse medical event like a heart attack. Even when they are diagnosed and given written prescriptions, many of those in the high-risk group resist filling their prescriptions or fail to follow the instructions.

Friends melt away, and there is a feeling of being a burden to others. Little of their life occurs outside their homes or their immediate families. High-risk cognitive agers have a limited range of activities they enjoy, and some dwell on what they cannot enjoy anymore.

Cognitively, those at risk are a mixed bag. Although most seem slower than average mentally, they are not suffering from dementia. Some have high IQs, but their capacity to use their intellectual powers is impaired by depression or other psychological problems. A small proportion may have age-associated cognitive decline or mild cognitive impairment but are able to function independently with the support of family and friends. Persistent and frustrating cognitive difficulties with attention and memory are most common, but some also have problems with spatial orientation, especially getting lost repeatedly or exhibiting poor judgment. They are particularly vulnerable to being swindled.

Healthy Lifestyle Habits That Minimize Decline and Maximize Intellectual Capability

My host at a recent brunch in Cambridge, Massachusetts, who knew I was working on a book about cognitive aging, asked who the intended audience was. After saying that the book was for those caring for elders, my reply went something like this:

> Older readers, too, but especially the overlooked majority of 3rd Age women and men who know they are not aging well but haven't given up. If they are obese, they know it's because they eat too much and exercise too little. They may have high blood pressure and know they should take their medication but don't on a regular basis. Even though they have been diagnosed with type 2 diabetes, they don't consistently monitor their blood sugar level or watch their diet. Some still smoke or drink too much and know they shouldn't, but haven't been able to maintain a concerted effort to stop. They know they are not aging optimally and periodically try to live more healthily, but they lose momentum. They would like to improve but don't see how they can do it.

Then I added, "I want to reach these people with this book to try to help them." A long, uneasy silence followed. Finally, one of my friends said gently, "But they don't read, do they?" Others at the table nodded, silently agreeing.

My reaction to what seemed to me at first to be an inaccurate and condescending response was irritation, followed quickly by the recognition that these friends were trying to help me avoid writing a book that no one would read. So, I decided I had better be able to express clearly and concisely the reasons that nonoptimally aging adults might pick up a book like this. Here is what I wish I had said:

> It is not accurate to assume that because people don't practice healthy lifestyle habits that they have given up. This is like arguing that smokers don't periodically think again about trying to give up cigarettes and aren't open to reasons that might encourage them to make another try. Ditto for those who are obese or drink too much. Also, believe it or not, things are improving. In the past 10 years, a growing percentage of 3rd Agers are taking better care of themselves: Fewer are smoking, drinking, or are sedentary, while more report lower cholesterol, have had Pap smears, flu shots, and say they are in good or excellent health. And, by the way, disability rates are dropping for women and men who are over 65, and active life expectancy is at an all-time high. Since individuals who aren't aging optimally make up the majority of older Americans, many of them must have contributed to these improved numbers. They have not given up nor are they unreachable. These are the people I especially am writing for.

My aim is to encourage normal and high-risk women and men to make realistic small changes in their health practices that could minimize cognitive decline as well as improve their health. I have no illusions that this is an easy task. But, having been a longtime member of this large group might give me an edge. Now well into my 70s, I know from personal, as well as professional, experience what it is to struggle to give up bad habits that feel as though they have bored into your bone marrow. I lost the battle dozens of times before I was finally able to let go of smoking. Then, miraculously effort number 50 worked after 49 failures, and I was at last free of this addiction. Because I have been overweight most of my adult life, I can still feel some of the disbelief and shame that was triggered when my doctor told me that it was time to begin taking blood pressure medication. It was weeks before I filled the prescription, and another month passed before I regularly started taking those little orange pills. But it was this upsetting confrontation that finally motivated me to shed some of my excess fat.

Also apparent is how desensitized to good advice that we who need to replace some of our bad habits with healthy ones have become. Hardly a day passes without a newspaper, blog, magazine, or TV report urging those of us who are not aging optimally to reform our ways. Many of us tune out this well-intentioned advice because we are sick of hearing it, especially when we are pretty sure we cannot do anything about it—at least not right now—unless there is a good reason.

Actually, there are two good reasons to try again. First, other 3rd Agers have started doing it, with promising results. The best example has been the success of the antismoking campaign. Close to a half-million Americans die prematurely each year as a result of tobacco use, and more than 8 million Americans live with smoking-related chronic illnesses. Despite the addictive nature of tobacco and the powerful economic forces that have promoted its use, nearly half of all living adults who ever smoked have quit. Antismoking programs have been a major success, with few parallels in the history of public health.[11]

In addition to fewer of their numbers smoking, the last two decades have seen a decrease in the percentage of 3rd Agers engaging in risky lifestyle habits (e.g., being sedentary) and an increasing proportion exhibiting healthy behaviors—for instance, controlling cholesterol levels and getting flu shots. This evidence, taken together with declining disability rates and a greater proportion of 3rd Age adults saying they are in good health is convincing evidence that more older adults have gotten the message and are living healthier lives.[12]

No one knows for certain why these changes have occurred since the mid-1990s, but it is likely that the continuous flow of media reports about things we can do to live more healthily has played a major role. And, no one knows who these older women and men were who stopped smoking, began exercising, started watching their diets to manage their cholesterol, or opted to get their flu shots. No doubt many of these were already aging optimally. But, it is a good bet that many of these positive changes also were due to the efforts of the nonoptimally aging majority of 3rd Agers for whom the light suddenly went on and found it within themselves to change their ways.

The second reason to begin another effort to build healthy habits into our lives is that these actions benefit our minds along with our bodies. Table 1.1 lists four groups of healthy lifestyle habits that are linked to optimal cognitive aging. The first group of healthy routines is based on reports from three prospective studies that looked at the effects of these four and other lifestyle habits on the risk of disease and death in 3rd Age subjects.[13] Also, each of these factors—being a non-smoker, getting regular exercise, avoiding obesity, and eating healthily—has beneficial effects on the aging intellect.

Our grandparents would not have been surprised by these findings benefitting us physically, but it might have been news to them that these same actions minimize their cognitive decline. What is less obvious is that lifestyle habits that benefit the body also almost always enhance the mind. Individuals who practice these healthy routines will not only have less

Table 1.1   Examples of Healthy Lifestyle Habits Linked to Optimal Cognitive Aging

Form healthy lifestyle routines:
  Do not smoke
  Get exercise
  Fight obesity
  Eat healthily
Comply with evidence-based medical advice:
  Take prescription medication
  Use medical technology
Maintain psychosocial adjustment:
  Repopulate social networks
  Manage stress
Maximize intellectual powers:
  Apply selection, optimization, and compensation
  Engage in attention restoration activities

probability of heart disease and other medical conditions as they grow older but also these actions slow cognitive decline and lower the risk of dementia. Take exercise: It is no secret that older adults who work out regularly reduce their chances of developing coronary disease or other medical conditions. What is not as well known is that exercise also improves most intellectual functions among those who work out compared to those who do not break a sweat. This is just as true for older adults as it is for their children and grandchildren.[14]

No matter how hard we work to maintain a healthy lifestyle, chances are that each of us will have to cope with chronic medical conditions in the 3rd Age. Examples of conditions afflicting a substantial proportion of Americans aged 55–74 are hypertension, sleep apnea, and type 2 diabetes. All are associated with lower scores on mental tests and greater probability of dementia. The good news is that doctors' prescriptions that keep chronic medical conditions such as high blood pressure under control also help us maintain our mental acuity and lessen the chance of cognitive impairment. This applies to medical devices as well. For instance, when researchers compared patients with sleep apnea who used the continuous positive airway pressure (CPAP) mask to those who did not use the mask, they found that the treated patients had keener attention, better short-term memory, and a faster response time.[15]

These are important facts to keep in mind because only about half the people prescribed medication for all conditions comply with the directions of the health care provider. Either they do not bother to fill the prescription or do not take the medication as prescribed.[16] Noncompliant patients with chronic medical conditions need to remind themselves that they are putting their minds at risk along with their bodies.

Maintaining a satisfactory psychosocial adjustment by filling gaps in social networks and coping adequately with life stresses is correlated with optimal cognitive aging. A vulnerability that all we 3rd Agers share is losing people important to us, so repopulating our social networks contributes to keeping a keen mind. Feeling satisfied with the number of people we can count on in our life contributes to our physical well-being and to maintaining mental ability.[17]

Also crucial to physical and mental health is management of stress. As we grow older, most of us become more adept at sidestepping distasteful people and unpleasant circumstances that create stress. But, the 3rd Age of life brings with it a number of unavoidable changes, losses, opportunities, and unexpected developments. How well we are able to control stressful feelings influences both our physical health and our intellectual powers.[18]

Finally, optimal agers minimize the negative effects of age-related cognitive decline by putting into action strategies that maximize their intellectual powers. Imagine that you are planning a long drive to visit your daughter and her family at their new home in St. Louis, Missouri, which is about 1,500 miles from where you live. Before you start, you recognize that your energy level and navigational skills are not what they once were. What can you do? Two useful strategies are shown in Table 1.1.

Here's how selection, optimization, and compensation[19] might help you remain intellectually capable during the trip. For instance, you might select a longer but less heavily traveled highway to lower the driving stress. You can optimize your performance on the road by starting the trip when you are at the peak of your diurnal (or day-night) cycle. If you are a "lark" and at your best in the morning, you can try to start the drive early in the morning and try to get off the highway by mid-afternoon. In addition to studying the maps carefully, you can compensate for your aging navigational skills by investing in a global positioning system (GPS) to help you find your way. You also can decide to accommodate your diminished energy level by driving fewer miles each day and spending an extra night on route.

Also, you can engage in attention restoration activities while on the road, take a break every three hours or so to give your concentration skills, which wear down more rapidly with age, a respite, or pull into a wooded rest area instead of the parking lot of a fast food restaurant and take a short stroll. As a result your concentration is likely to be sharper during the next leg.

Five Working Principles

My goal in this book is to present tested strategies for helping older adults use their mental capabilities as fully as possible. Five working principles, illustrated by the cases presented in this book, guide this work.

First, keep in mind that generations of researchers have agreed that what affects the body for good or ill has the same influence on the mind. When assessing the quality of the aging intellect, begin by paying attention to physical health. A healthy lifestyle usually is associated with cognitive behaviors typical of optimal agers. It also predicts less cognitive decline. A group of 3rd Age women classified as optimal agers was followed for 15 years. Those who had fewer chronic diseases such as diabetes and hypertension and practiced healthy lifestyle habits (e.g., not smoking, getting regular exercise, and maintaining enjoyable social networks) were more likely to remain functioning optimally. Even more to the point is that little exercise and having fewer friends link to lower IQ scores.[20]

Another reason to keep aware of the mind–body connection is to reinforce compliance with medical advice. The hypertensive man who does not bother to take his blood pressure medication and the woman still smoking in spite of chronic bronchitis both "know" they are putting themselves at risk for a stroke or pulmonary disease "someday" in what they hope will be the distant future. Because they are not yet symptomatic, their denial is reinforced. But, what they may not know is that they are putting their minds at risk today. Untreated hypertension and smoking are tied to lower scores on mental ability tests and a higher probability of developing dementia. I have had cases for which simply pointing out these facts provided the incentive for a man to start taking his medication daily or for a woman to try again to become a nonsmoker.

Second, assume that the intellect is an important subject to those elders in your care. So bring it up. Assume that how your clients and patients are getting along mentally is as important to them as their physical health. Anxieties about whether their mental lapses are merely expressions of benign age-related forgetfulness or are first indications of dementia, increase with accumulating birthdays. The majority of older adults want to continue to lead active lives and be able to keep up mentally with their younger friends, children, and grandchildren. They know that their continued mental acuity is not only a key determinant of their quality of life but is also essential to the capacity to remain independent as they grow older.

The third belief that has guided my work with others is that small changes can make a big difference in health and in slowing mental decline. This principle was first noted by psychologist-philosopher-physician William James a century ago. He observed: "There is very little difference between one man and another: but what difference there is, is very important."[21]

Here is an example. Studies that followed adults over time found that those who declined the least mentally as well as physically practiced several healthy lifestyle habits. Most were non-smokers, moderate drinkers, and regular exercisers. What was interesting about these findings was the powerful effect of changing just one habit on the likelihood of developing a serious illness such as a heart condition. For instance, eating cereal for breakfast once a week reduced the probability of heart failure by 14%.[22]

Other small changes benefitted the intellect. Consider that inactive elders who volunteer just once a week in their community increased the chances of maintaining their mental skills by 24%. 3rd Agers who eat fish only once a week reduce their likelihood of dementia by 19%. That is a lot of protection for a little bit of effort.[23]

Among 3rd Age individuals in our care who aspire to age optimally it can be more than a little daunting to look at all of the factors associated with optimal aging and think about how much effort it would take to modify their lifestyle. After all, they have been trying to lose 10 pounds for a decade without success. How can they hope to change a half dozen of their habits? One answer is to appreciate that making only one small change in their daily routine can make a difference in their cognitive functions as well as their health.

Number four on my list of working principles is anticipate that 3rd Agers experience many of the same challenges and passions as younger adults, and most benefit from the ability to talk with a professional about their concerns. It is fair to say that a clientele of adults old enough to be our mothers or grandfathers may have on their mind as rich an array of topics as their children and grandchildren.

For more than two decades, I have supervised clinicians in training to work with geriatric patients. Time after time, young clinicians have made observations like this one:

> Who could have known this 80-year-old widow, who just moved into a retirement home because she is wheelchair bound with muscular dystrophy, would be so feisty, so energetic, and so passionate? Yesterday, I talked to her because she was furious that the home doesn't allow people in wheelchairs to sit at the tables with the nondisabled residents in the big dining room. She thinks that's discriminatory and is starting a petition demanding equal seating rights. She's a ball of fire, a deacon in her church, who spends a morning a week reading to kindergartners who don't speak English. She says her biggest frustration now is sex. The muscular dystrophy makes it harder for her to have an orgasm with her boyfriend as they used to. But the cuddling is good.

The 3rd Age can be a time of dramatic changes. Consider the baby boomers currently leaving the workforce. Not since their teenage years have there been so many changes that may need to be confronted in a period of 5 to 10 years, and not since their adolescence have the differences among contemporaries been so noticeable. In the next decade, boomers are likely to see more alterations in their lives than in the past 20 years. Quite a few find that their identity, which was defined by preretirement work and child care, will need to be refocused. "I used to be …" is not much of an identity. Many will find that their bodies are changing, and that their formerly stable social circle is losing members as they move to warmer climates or to be closer to their children. Many wonder how long they should stay in a house that is twice as large as they need.

Working clinically with 3rd Agers can be as interesting and challenging as working with young and middle-aged adults. Moreover, they are just as responsive to clinical intervention as those decades their junior.

A final principle that has influenced my practice is that some of our most important work with our clients and patients results from activating "the doctor within." It was Dr. Albert Schweitzer (1875–1976) who first brought to our attention the value of activating the doctor within for those in our care. Dr. Schweitzer was a brilliant theologian, musician, philosopher, and physician, among whose remarkable accomplishments were the founding and sustaining of the Albert Schweitzer Hospital in Lambaréné, in west central Africa.

Dr. Schweitzer was often visited by journalists. One such visitor was Norman Cousins, then editor of *The Saturday Review,* an influential literary magazine of his day. Early in his visit, Cousins commented that the natives were fortunate to have access to Dr. Schweitzer and modern medicine rather than having to depend on witch doctors. The following day, Dr. Schweitzer invited Cousins to join him at the medical clinic in the jungle. There Schweitzer introduced Cousins to an elderly witch doctor, whom they watched treat patients. To some, the witch doctor gave herbs; with others, he filled the air with incantations; a third group he sent to Dr. Schweitzer.

Afterward, Cousins asked Dr. Schweitzer how anyone could become well after being treated by a witch doctor. Dr. Schweitzer replied: "The witch doctor succeeds for the same reason all of the rest of us succeed. Each patient carries his own doctor inside him. They come to us not knowing that truth. We are at our best when we give the doctor that resides within each patient a chance to go to work."[24]

How do we go about activating that doctor within our nonoptimally aging clientele? Most of them know they are not living healthily, and some may even be aware that they are endangering their intellect as well as their bodies. In their minds, they have tried everything, and it has not worked. A number tell us they have given up hope. Yet, there they are in our office.

Sometimes it is because someone listens to them and takes their problem seriously, two components of a therapeutic alliance[25] that wakes up their doctor within. Evan is an example.

Evan

Married last spring at 74, Evan felt so lucky to have found love again with Amy, who was just a few years younger. Things were not always smooth between them since both were strong-minded individuals, the alpha personalities in their families. Amy was a retired lawyer, and Evan had sold his software business. Just before they were married, they discussed their problems with the minister, who referred them to a social worker in the community. Evan described their relationship from his point of view as akin to sailing the coast of Maine in the fog without a map; he had to find out the hard way where the submerged rocks lay.

Amy summarized their problems this way: "I love him, but sometimes he's impossible." They continued to talk to the therapist about once a month after their marriage. When things went well between them, they were wonderful. They enjoyed their first New Year's Eve together—at home with a superb dinner followed by dancing to their favorite music with the lights turned down and feeling very much in love. Since he had marginal hypertension, Evan took his blood pressure every morning. Bright and early on January 1, it was 126/78, within normal limits.

About 10:00 a.m. that morning, while Amy was out for a jog, Carl, an old friend of Evan's but unknown to Amy, called to wish them both a happy new year and to let Evan know that he and his wife were in town. Could they stop by to meet Amy? Evan invited them to come for lunch.

This is when things started to spiral downhill. Amy told Evan that he should have asked her first before saying it was okay for Carl to come for lunch. She had hoped for a romantic morning together instead of preparing lunch for strangers. Evan replied he didn't think that he needed to ask her permission when an old friend wanted to visit, and by the way, wasn't it just last Wednesday night that she invited friends of hers for dinner without checking with him? Evan didn't understand why she wasn't more welcoming. Both stewed.

Abruptly, Evan called Carl back and arranged to have lunch at a nearby fast food restaurant. On the way home, Evan stopped to buy flowers for Amy. When he gave them to her, she threw them in the trash. Nasty things were said. They stopped speaking and did not share a bed that night. Evan did not sleep well. While tossing and turning, he wondered if he had made a mistake getting married again. That morning, he was not surprised by the blood pressure reading of 162/99, clearly hypertensive.

Then, he went for a long walk around a nearby pond by himself. While Evan walked, he felt the resentment still embedded in him as he went over the exact words Amy had used that were so hurtful and that made him feel so justified in his ire. No doubt about it, he was the wronged party. As he started the second lap around the pond, Evan found that the anger he felt began to melt away. He began to think about the fun he and Amy had together, how well they worked as a team, and how much he loved her.

Then, out of nowhere, Evan recalled a fragment from a Sunday morning sermon in church a few months earlier. It had to do with the importance of forgiving others for the hurt they inflict on us and then also forgiving yourself for holding on to righteous indignation that usually makes things worse. Evan had never tried forgiving people who had been hurtful to him in the past, but he thought it was worth a try. So, he concentrated on forgiving Amy and then himself.

It took him another lap around the pond, but gradually Evan could feel the tension leaving his body, most noticeably in his neck and shoulders. After he came home, Evan made his wife a cup of coffee, apologized, and told her that he loved her and that they should start the New Year again that day. They made up. An hour later, Evan had to go to the clinic for some lab tests. His blood pressure was 110/74, quite a change from 6 hours earlier.

A week later, they discussed this event with the therapist, especially that valuable sermon that Evan recalled about forgiveness. The next day, the therapist was talking to the minister about another case and mentioned that one of his parishioners had been greatly helped by a sermon he had given recently on the subject of forgiveness. The minister replied that he has not given a sermon on that topic in years.

How exactly Evan was able to solve the problem on his own remains a mystery. The minister was sure he had not mentioned forgiveness, and the therapist knew the topic had never come up in their work together. Did this idea of forgiveness of his spouse come from something Evan read, heard on a talk show, or came across on the Internet? Or, was Evan's doctor within on duty that morning during the walk around the pond?

2

How Health Affects the Intellect

Among the major components of optimal cognitive aging is avoiding for as long as possible chronic medical conditions that adversely affect the body and mind.[1] This chapter examines the evidence that several chronic medical conditions frequently found among 3rd Agers have a negative effect on the intellect. It also presents some unexpected findings about disability and the relationship of healthy lifestyle factors to optimal cognitive aging.

Chronic Medical Conditions and the Intellect

Like many older adults, I suffer from several chronic medical conditions. The most troublesome one so far has been atrial fibrillation (AFib). Characterized by a rapid and irregular heartbeat, this condition has been my live-in companion for over a decade. Until 3 years ago, my doctors limited the outbreaks of AFib to a few days every couple of months with combinations of medication and cardioversion (shocking the heart). For most people, this is a progressive disease, so treatments that worked earlier in my life have gradually lost their effectiveness. I was not an exception and for nearly a year I lived with a hurried, erratically beating heart.

During this period, I started this book. Or rather, I tried to begin writing it without success because I found it impossible to focus my attention and shut out distracting thoughts. At first, I joked grimly that I must have developed a late-onset attention deficit disorder. Then I began to wonder if the uncontrolled AFib could be disrupting my concentration. Perhaps the erratic blood flow to my brain was responsible for my inability to pay attention and block out distractions.

When I asked my cardiologist about this theory, he said that he had not heard of an association of these symptoms with AFib but thought it was possible and encouraged me to look further. A PubMed search yielded more than a dozen studies worldwide demonstrating adverse consequences of AFib on the intellect.

Eventually, my AFib was brought under control by surgery. This experience caused me to wonder about the cognitive consequences of other physical afflictions common to 3rd Age women and men. This chapter pulls together studies from around the globe that show the unfavorable cognitive effects of six chronic medical conditions found among older adults in the United States and most developed countries. These conditions include two cardiovascular diseases (hypertension and atrial fibrillation), two pulmonary conditions (chronic obstructive pulmonary disease and sleep apnea), and diabetes and hearing loss.[2] These diseases were selected because of their negative consequences for increased rates of dementia and reduced mental acuity and because the progression of these diseases can often be arrested or reversed by medical interventions that help slow the rate of decline in cognitive function.[3]

In the studies, investigators used many different types of tests to assess mental ability. Because the research was concerned with the relationship between chronic disease and dementia, the most frequently used test was a brief cognitive measure—the Mini Mental State Exam (MMSE).[4] Many times clusters of abilities or single aptitudes also were assessed. Examples of these global, clustered, and specific mental abilities are listed in the Glossary.

Cardiovascular Disease

Cardiovascular disease encompasses most diseases afflicting the heart and circulatory system. These include congestive heart failure, coronary artery disease, heart attacks, arterial aneurysms, and conditions that impede the blood flow through circulatory systems such as atherosclerosis, arteriosclerosis, and stroke.

It is not difficult to imagine the negative mental effects of heart failure, myocardial infarctions, and stroke. Less obvious is the cognitive decline caused by two other forms of cardiovascular disease with which many in the 3rd Age live. These are hypertension and atrial fibrillation.

Hypertension

The frequency of high blood pressure increases with age. Just over two thirds of people in the 65–74 age bracket have been diagnosed with hypertension.[5] Hypertension is considered to be present when a person's systolic blood pressure (the top number, when the heart is beating) consistently reads 140 mmHg or greater and their diastolic blood pressure (bottom number, when the heart is at rest) is 90 mmHg and above. Recent research indicates that people with blood pressure between 120/80 and 139/89, called pre-hypertension, face greater health risks than those with lower readings.[6]

Because high blood pressure is not often accompanied by symptoms obvious to a layperson, the first inkling that someone has hypertension may come during a routine medical visit. Early diagnosis and treatment of this condition yield large benefits because chronic hypertension is a major risk factor for cardiac problems, stroke, and arterial aneurysms, as well as a leading cause of kidney failure.

Also serious are the adverse consequences of hypertension for the intellect. Among the most convincing findings are those from three different longitudinal studies of more than 6,000 older subjects: Japanese Americans in Honolulu; Whites in Boston; Blacks in Indianapolis. These studies, which followed the diverse group of volunteers for decades, correlated hypertension with scores on mental tests.[7]

When these investigations began, all subjects received a medical screening, which included blood pressure readings, and took a battery of cognitive tests. Several years later, the medical screening and mental tests were repeated. When the follow-up test results were compared with the baseline scores, investigators from all three studies reached similar conclusions: Older subjects with elevated systolic and diastolic blood pressure showed a greater decline in global cognitive ability and were at greater risk for dementia than their nonhypertensive contemporaries. These differences remained after controlling for age, education, and medical history.

Besides a more rapid general cognitive decline among hypertensives, other researchers on three continents[8] reported that people with high blood pressure had lower test scores on nearly every aptitude measured. This includes executive functions (e.g., blocking out distractions, planning, and mental flexibility), processing speed, visuospatial aptitude, psychomotor skills, memory, and verbal fluency.

Hypertension affects adults of all ages. The negative effect of high blood pressure on the intellect may be more serious for younger people than their parents and grandparents.[9] One report found that the differences in mental test scores between hypertensives and those with normal blood pressure are greater among younger adults than among 3rd Agers. Compared to 3rd Age subjects, whose scores on mental tests showed relatively small differences between those with and without hypertension, 23- to 40-year-olds without high blood pressure outperformed their hypertensive contemporaries by a relatively larger amount on tests assessing executive functions, working memory, and attention.[10] This study suggests that long before high blood pressure causes physical damage, it could put younger hypertensives at a competitive disadvantage compared to their peers. For these young and midlife individuals, a minor problem with memory, difficulty paying attention, or working a little more slowly because of hypertension could make the difference between one person getting an honors grade or a promotion and someone else getting neither.

Medical researchers have made considerable progress in understanding why the mental skills of hypertensives fall off more sharply than their age mates with normal blood pressure. A Dutch research team found that high blood pressure is associated with hypoperfusion of the connective tissue of the brain called white matter.[11] Restricted blood flow is associated with atrophy of the white matter, resulting in less-efficient thinking. Findings from studies of older Japanese and American Midwesterners with hypertension agreed that those subjects with lower intelligence test scores had the greatest shrinkage of the white matter of the brain.[12]

Pharmacological interventions that successfully treat hypertension benefit the intellect. Follow-up studies of treated and untreated older hypertensives regularly find that those taking high blood pressure medication have only 60% of the risk of developing cognitive impairment compared with their contemporaries who are not compliant.[13] This may be because the brains of those with high blood pressure who take their medications have only 40% of the white matter shrinkage of those who choose not to take their prescribed medication.[14]

Atrial Fibrillation

Atrial fibrillation (AFib) is the most common of the cardiac arrhythmias. About 110,000 Americans over 65 experience this condition. Caused by a disruption in the electrical system of the heart, the distinctive symptoms of AFib are a rapid, fluttery, irregular heart rate.[15] The heart may beat so lightly and quickly that it may be impossible for a lay person to find a pulse. During an episode of atrial fibrillation, the person may sweat, may feel lightheaded and fatigued, and may have chest pain and difficulty breathing normally. Anyone who has two or more episodes of irregular heartbeat is thought to be at risk for AFib.

The primary risk for patients with untreated AFib is stroke. Because the blood is not pumped completely out of the left atrium, one of the two upper chambers of the heart, it may pool and create blood clots. Should these clots lodge in an artery of the brain, they can cause a stroke. Having AFib also increases the risk of developing dementia. Three longitudinal investigations in Italy and the United States found that patients with AFib were three to five times more likely to have a stroke or develop cognitive impairment than those with normal heart rates.[16]

Atrial fibrillation can impair the intellect even without a stroke or dementia. When investigations in five different countries asked if older adults with AFib were more likely to have lower mental ability scores than those with normal sinus rhythm, the answer was largely "yes." Studies in Italy, the Netherlands, Sweden, the United Kingdom, and the United States all reported that patients with AFib performed below those with normal heart function on most of the aptitude tests used in their investigations.[17] These differences held up when adjusted for age, education, health, and other variables.

So far, the negative cognitive effects of AFib have more often been found to be global than specific. To some extent, this reflects the interests of the investigators who explored the association between AFib and more serious cognitive impairment, including dementia. Nearly all of the reports found that older adults with AFib had lower scores on global, multiaptitude tests. When specific aptitude tests were given, those abilities most frequently affected by AFib were attention and mental flexibility.[18]

In the absence of stroke, why would AFib be associated with a downturn in mental acuity? The prevailing theories suggest that AFib causes either tiny strokes or inadequate blood to the brain. Microemboli form in the left atrium, which results in small, "silent" cerebral infarctions when the blood is pumped into the brain. The theory of inadequate blood supply to the brain posits that the irregular heartbeats result in hypoperfusion of brain cells. This leads to ischemia and white matter lesions in the brain.[19] German neuroscientists using magnetic resonance imaging (MRI) scans of patients in their early 60s with AFib confirmed elements of this theory. They found poorer attention, memory, and executive functions as well as smaller hippocampal volume in people with AFib compared to those without it.[20]

Anticoagulating medications reduce the risk for stroke in patients with AFib by 50–80%.[21] Blood-thinning medication also improves the chances of avoiding cognitive impairment. London researchers discovered that scores for verbal fluency and mental flexibility were substantially higher among more than 400 men taking antithrombotic medications than those in the placebo group.[22]

Unfortunately, only about half of patients with AFib using anticoagulation drugs are able to maintain their blood level in the narrow therapeutic range.[23] Dutch scientists wondered what the cognitive effect might be for patients with AFib who were able to use the medication to thin their blood to the recommended level compared to those who did not. They studied the records of older patients with AFib who had been prescribed anticoagulants and who had their blood levels checked regularly to determine if they were maintaining the recommended therapeutic level. The investigators gave a large sample of these volunteers with AFib a dementia screening test. Then, they compared the test scores with their INR (international normalized ratio, a measure of blood clotting times) level for the previous year. They discovered that those older adults who were less able to keep their INR within a therapeutic range were three times as likely to be cognitively impaired as those who consistently maintained a proper anticoagulant level.[24]

Chronic Pulmonary Disease

One in eight Americans 65 and older has a chronic pulmonary disease.[25] COPD and obstructive sleep apnea (OSA) are two forms of lung disease that compromise intellectual functioning.[26]

Chronic Obstructive Pulmonary Disease

COPD refers to two lung diseases: chronic bronchitis and emphysema. Both are characterized by airflow obstruction that interferes with normal breathing. Because these conditions frequently coexist, physicians often use the term COPD. Nine of ten people who die of COPD were smokers.

Chronic bronchitis occurs when the bronchial tubes have been irritated over a long period of time. Excessive mucus is produced constantly, and the lining of the bronchial tubes becomes thickened. An irritating cough develops, the lungs become scarred, and airflow is hampered. Emphysema destroys the air sacs (alveoli) in the lungs, where oxygen from the air is exchanged for carbon dioxide in the blood. Damage to these air sacs is irreversible. As they are destroyed, the lungs are able to transfer less and less oxygen to the bloodstream, causing dyspnea or shortness of breath.

Physicians have long observed that older patients with lung diseases have a greater risk for cognitive impairment than contemporaries without it. Among the first to report lower cognitive scores by patients with COPD was Igor Grant and a team of neuropsychologists at the University of California San Diego School of Medicine.[27] They found that three times as many 3rd Age patients with COPD had moderate-to-severe mental impairment compared to people the same age without the disease. Hardest hit were higher-level mental functions such as mental flexibility, reasoning, and solving puzzles.

These California neuroscientists speculated that the lower levels of intellectual functioning were because the blood transported to the brain from the lungs of patients with COPD contained lower-than-normal levels of oxygen and a greater percentage of carbon dioxide. This is called *hypoxemia*. Subsequent investigations demonstrated that increased hypoxemia was correlated with decreased cognitive functions.[28]

Research in Europe and the Middle East confirmed the theory that oxygen-desaturated blood flowing into the brain is likely to be the cause of lower mental aptitude among those suffering from COPD. Investigators in

Turkey and Italy used SPECT (single-photon emission computed tomography) scans to compare blood perfusion of the brain in normal older adults and COPD patients with and without hypoxemia.[29] They discovered that the COPD patients had reduced blood circulation in the prefrontal and parietal regions of the brain compared to normal subjects. COPD patients with hypoxemia, however, showed much lower scores on tests of attention and memory than either the normals or COPD patients without hypoxemia.

Nonsurgical treatments for COPD aim at the reduction of physical symptoms through medications as well as external interventions—most commonly exercise and long-term oxygen therapy (LTOT).[30] Elizabeth Kozara and a team of investigators at the National Jewish Medical Center in Denver, Colorado, compared the cognitive test scores of a group of normal older subjects and patients with COPD with mild hypoxemia, most of whom were on LTOT. The researchers found that the patients with COPD differed from those with normal lung function only on a measure of verbal fluency.[31] In Norway, medical scientists gave a dozen mental skills tests to a smaller number of patients before and after 3 months of LTOT. Every aptitude score improved after the 3 months of LTOT.[32]

Because exercise is often prescribed for mild COPD, behavioral scientists wondered if regular, carefully controlled workouts might benefit these patients since it increases blood oxygenation. At Wake Forest and Ohio State universities, research teams compared groups of older adults with mild COPD who exercised regularly for short (10–12 weeks) or longer (12–15 months) periods with other, more sedentary patients.[33] After the short period of exercise, the older subjects in both the short and longer exercise groups showed improvement in spatial reasoning and verbal fluency. In many ways, however, it was the changes in some noncognitive areas that were interesting. Those who worked out rated their endurance and quality of life as much improved. They also reduced their scores on stress and depression. No improvement occurred in the group of nonexercising 3rd Agers.

What was even more interesting was a follow-up study a year later of some of the patients with COPD who had continued to exercise. Although all were encouraged to continue their workouts, only 4 in 10 complied. The remainder returned to their sedentary lifestyle. When the two groups were tested again after 12 months, the differences were striking. The test results for the subjects who continued to exercise did not improve, but the scores of the sedentary former exercisers declined substantially.[34]

Obstructive Sleep Apnea

OSA is a condition in which individuals have repeated episodes of blocked breathing during sleep. This often occurs when the throat muscles relax and block the airway. One in five older adults has at least moderate OSA.[35] It is about twice as common in males, and more than half of those who suffer from sleep apnea are obese.

The primary symptoms are pauses in breathing during sleep. Each of these episodes, called *apneas* (literally "no breath"), lasts long enough for one or more inhalations to be missed. When the brain senses the lack of oxygen in the blood, it briefly rouses the person so that he or she will resume breathing. Often, the result is a night of fragmented sleep. When they wake up in the morning, people with OSA may feel sleepy and fatigued. Many are unaware that they had trouble breathing during the night. The condition is most often first recognized by those who share the OSA sufferer's bed. OSA is usually diagnosed with an overnight test in a sleep lab at a medical clinic. Clinically significant levels of apnea are defined as five or more events of any type per hour of sleep. People with severe OSA may have as many as 15–20 apneas per hour.[36]

To understand better the effects of sleep apnea on intelligence, medical researchers in Tempere, Finland, and Cincinnati, Ohio, analyzed the results of 65 separate reports from 1990 through 2005.[37] They agreed that there were two types of moderate-to-severe cognitive decrements attributable to OSA. These involved (a) complex mental operations such as executive functions and reasoning; (b) the sort of abilities that are affected by a poor night's sleep, such as mental alertness and response speed.[38]

While experts agree that sleep apnea is associated with reduced mental powers, some disagreement exists regarding the cause. Because executive functions, working memory, and reasoning are associated with the prefrontal cortex, many believe that nocturnal hypoxemia and excessive carbon dioxide in the blood result in damage to that region of the brain. French and German sleep experts offered a more parsimonious explanation. They interpreted these findings to mean that the cognitive impairment attributed to OSA is simply because people with this condition do not sleep well. Sleepiness is the reason for inattentiveness, working slowly, and difficulty coping with complicated mental challenges. In their minds, a good night's sleep may be all it takes to restore mental keenness.[39]

So, we have two groups of experts who disagree on what, and how serious, the negative effects of sleep apnea are on the intellect. Investigators in several countries addressed this puzzle. They theorized that the negative cognitive impact was probably greatest among those people with sleep apnea-induced hypoxemia. Those subjects whose OSA did not result in reduced oxygen content in the blood to the brain would show less cognitive impairment.

In the United States, Nancy Adams and her colleagues in the Midwest tested this theory by comparing the mental ability scores of OSA sufferers with and without hypoxemia.[40] They found that men and women with hypoxemia had poorer memories than those without oxygen-desaturated blood. Sleepiness only predicted diminished attention. In Grenoble, Switzerland, and Montreal, Canada, research teams concurred about the role of hypoxemia as a cause of lower scores on measures of executive function and working memory. The subjects also rated themselves as high or low on a sleepiness scale. Sleepiness was only associated with lessened attentiveness and short-term memory.[41]

To my knowledge, there are no widely accepted pharmacological treatment alternatives available. Because a large proportion of adults with sleep apnea are also obese, which plays a role in obstructing breathing, one prescription is weight loss. A Wisconsin study found that midlife adults who lost weight also reduced the frequency of their apneas.[42]

Another treatment for patients with OSA is the continuous positive airway pressure (CPAP) mask. This device, which fits over the face or nose, delivers a constant stream of oxygen that enables unobstructed breathing by opening the airways. This reduces the frequency of apneas and in many cases eliminates disturbed sleeping entirely. A Spanish medical team demonstrated the effectiveness of CPAP by administering authentic CPAP to a group of patients with OSA and sham CPAP to other volunteers with OSA.[43] In addition to feeling less drowsy and more energetic, the authentic CPAP device helped OSA patients think more clearly. Canadian, Italian, and Mexican patients with OSA treated with the CPAP were found to have better attention, improved short-term memory, and faster processing speed.[44]

Other Chronic Conditions

A number of other medical maladies affect the intellect. Two chronic conditions found among increasing numbers of 3rd Agers are diabetes and hearing loss. Left untreated, both are associated greater cognitive decline.

Diabetes

Close to one American in four over the age of 65 has diabetes, and increasing numbers of older adults are being diagnosed in nearly all developed countries.[45] Nine of ten diabetics were diagnosed after the age of 40. Diabetes diagnosed in adulthood is called type 2 diabetes or NIDDM (non-insulin-dependent diabetes mellitus). The hormone insulin is responsible for signaling the muscle, fat, and liver cells to absorb glucose from the blood. Type 2 diabetes most often occurs when insufficient insulin is secreted by the pancreas or the cells resist the insulin, leading to excessive amounts of glucose and triglycerides circulating in the bloodstream.

The physical health risks for diabetics are substantial. Elevated blood sugar and fatty acid levels, which elevate cholesterol readings, can cause hypertension and raise the risk of heart attacks, peripheral neuropathy, kidney disease, and other serious medical conditions.

Diabetes can harm the intellect as well. Investigators worldwide who compared patients with type 2 diabetes to healthy contemporaries consistently reported that diabetic subjects performed below normal volunteers on most memory tests.[46] Neuroscientists have presented convincing evidence that when the cerebral cortex and the hippocampus are not able to receive enough nutrition because the cells lack the insulin to absorb glucose, the outcome is accelerated cognitive decline. Using MRI scanning, European and Japanese investigators have produced evidence linking greater white matter atrophy to reduced mental ability in older individuals with type 2 diabetes.[47]

Taking care of yourself matters to your mind if you have been diagnosed with diabetes. Researchers in New York found that those middle-aged patients who best controlled their blood glucose levels had the least cognitive decline and loss of brain volume. Health care providers have long wondered whether their older patients with type 2 diabetes who are less consistent in controlling their glucose levels are at a greater risk for greater cognitive decline than those diabetics who usually are able to keep their blood sugar within normal limits.

That concern has turned out to be largely correct. Diabetic patients in three states were studied intensively for 4 weeks. During that period, they were asked to take brief aptitude tests when they checked their glucose levels several times a day. Just over half of the patients recorded lower working memory scores when they had elevated glucose readings.[48]

Giving up long-established patterns of eating behavior and establishing new self-care habits is hard work, so compliance is a problem with type 2 diabetes. Efforts to encourage diabetes patients to comply with medical instructions to manage their condition through various interventions have been reasonably successful if the criterion of compliance at least two thirds of the time is used. These interventions have taken many forms—outreach by health care facilitators in the Netherlands, dietary instruction in two towns in southern India, and improving provider communication with patients in a Seattle, Washington, health maintenance organization.[49]

Hearing Loss

Hearing loss is one of those medical conditions with an incidence that increases dramatically in the 3rd Age; 50% more Americans aged 65–74 report impaired hearing than those a decade younger. By contrast, the number of people with impaired vision in these two age groups increased less than 1% in the same time span.[50]

One of every four 3rd Agers suffers from hearing loss; that is, their hearing ranges from slightly compromised to deafness. Most often, progressive hearing loss among older adults is the result of degenerative changes in the auditory nerve of the inner ear. This condition results in a reduced ability to hear faint and high-pitched sounds. Reduced auditory capacity also is caused by conductance hearing loss due to the sounds not being transmitted through the outer ear into the middle ear. Reasons for this condition include earwax, infections, fluid buildup, perforated eardrums, and damage from loud noises or from other sources. Many of these conductance problems can be resolved by medical interventions.[51]

The psychosocial costs of auditory impairment are not hard to imagine. Even those 3rd Agers who are mildly hard of hearing report a declining quality of life.[52] The social distance widens between them and their friends, and they are more likely than their contemporaries with normal hearing to feel left out and increasingly lonely. Psychological distress rises, and mental health declines. Hearing loss leads to problems paying attention and to diminished mental ability as well.

Paul Baltes and his colleagues at the Max Planck Institute in Munich, Germany, found a powerful link between auditory acuity and intelligence. In a series of investigations with older volunteers, they discovered that those with the best hearing also had the highest scores in mental ability tests. These were unusually strong correlations, about the same magnitude as the relation between age and IQ.[53] Moreover, good hearing grows more important to the intellect as the years pass. Among the older Germans, the correlation between less hearing loss and higher mental aptitude was more than twice as strong as the association between audition and cognition in younger subjects.[54]

Why does hearing loss reduce our intellectual powers? One reason is that socially active hard-of-hearing listeners must invest considerable effort in concentrating to hear the words being spoken, comprehending conversations, sometimes replaying the conversation in their minds—including the gaps created by the missing words—and using the context to guess at the meaning, all the while missing chunks of incoming information. These actions leave fewer resources to encode the material. The result is that later it will be harder to remember the content of the conversation because it was not loaded into memory.[55]

Some investigations have found that hearing difficulties may precede or accelerate cognitive decline in older adults. Speculation is that the memory problems of hearing-impaired older adults, which have been attributed to normal age-related decline, in fact may be more a consequence of the hearing loss itself.[56]

Although estimates vary, only one in five older adults with hearing loss is using or has used some type of sound amplification device.[57] These days, hearing aids come in a variety of shapes and sizes, including those that fit behind the ear and in the ear canal. Miniature omnidirectional microphones are the most common. Based on analog technology, they pick up sound waves, amplify them, and send them through the ear canal. Many kinds can be switched to directional when it is important to hear sounds coming from the front rather than from the sides or rear. Omnidirectional microphones may be preferred in those situations when it is important to be able to hear people talking on the left or right, front and back. Most have manually operated volume controls. A limitation of omnidirectional hearing aids is that they amplify all sounds, including unwanted ones. Another type of hearing aid employs digital technology, which enables the user to amplify some sounds, such as conversation with friends in a noisy restaurant, while simultaneously dampening the background babble.[58]

Not everyone with hearing loss wants to wear a hearing aid. A number of 3rd Agers view the appliance as esthetically unappealing as well as evidence that they are getting old. Estimates worldwide are that only one in five potential older users actually purchases a hearing aid. And, perhaps because no external device has yet been created that completely overcomes the limitations of an impaired ear, many who have been fitted with the device wear the hearing aid irregularly or stop using it entirely.[59]

Do hearing aids improve the intellect of elders with impaired audition? The answer is that it is too early to tell. No one has given a group of adults with hearing loss a mental ability test at the beginning of a longitudinal study and then followed them for a decade or so to see whether those who wore hearing aids consistently were stronger intellectually at the end of the project than those without sound amplification devices. The few results that have accumulated showed that some measures of memory are improved by auditory assistance because being able to hear more clearly makes it easier to recall what was said.[60]

With or without hearing aids, 3rd Agers with impaired audition will benefit from applying defensive listening. Awareness that some settings will make it difficult to hear normal conversations, which will stress comprehension and memory, is the first step in coping with impaired hearing.[61] In addition, try to avoid those settings in which listening is likely to be effortful. Whether for business or pleasure, people with impaired audition should choose a setting that is quiet, without significant background noise, and where it is possible to look directly at the persons with whom they are having a conversation. If this is impossible and it is necessary to listen to people in a crowded setting with distracting background noise, pick a peripheral spot where the likelihood of hearing the conversation is greater. If necessary, ask the speaker to talk more slowly if it is still difficult to pick up what is being said.

Declining Disability: An Unanticipated Event

Today's newborns in the United States and other developed countries can expect to live longer than at any other time in history. The dramatic lengthening of life expectancy is the good news. The bad news is that some health professionals have said, "So what? These extra years of life expectancy are not being added to middle age when we are vigorous. The additional time occurs at the end of life when we are likely to be frail, disabled, and cognitively impaired." This pessimistic view of the impact of medical advances that extend life expectancy without simultaneously maintaining the quality of life has been dubbed "the failure of success."[62]

The 1960s and 1970s provided plenty of support for the "failure-of-success" theory. For workers over the age of 50, longer life expectancy resulted in longer periods of disability.[63] Alarmed at the rising rates of disability for midlife adults, the U.S. Congress instructed the Census Bureau to carry out large-scale health surveys at regular intervals to gather information about the rates of chronic disease and physical disability for all adults,[64] including those older than 65. This information was critical for estimating the probable numbers of disabled elderly and the costs for the care they would require.

When the survey results were analyzed, the researchers were surprised, pleased, and then puzzled by the results. When the survey began, 26.2% of Americans 65+ suffered from one or more disabilities.[65] In the next two decades, the percentage of older women and men reporting some degree of disability steadily declined every 5 years to 19% in 2004–2005. This means that about 2,855,468 women and men who were 65 or older in the year 2004 avoided medical conditions that would have disabled them two decades earlier.[66] That is quite a gain in a little over 20 years.

If we were to guess that the lower disability rates among older people are because they have fewer chronic diseases, we would be wrong. In fact, the incidence of these conditions among 3rd Agers has actually increased slightly. Investigators looking at the changes in subjects aged 65–69 from other health surveys found that from 1997 to 2004 the percentage of these subjects reporting a chronic condition rose for nearly every infirmity.[67] Those with the greatest increases were people suffering from arthritis/joint pain (+6.1%), obesity (+5.6%), hypertension (+5.0%), and diabetes (+4%). Findings like this have been reproduced in Sweden and Spain.[68]

No one knows for certain what the reasons are, but surely some of the contributors are effective emergency procedures (e.g., medication to dissolve blood clots for stroke victims), more effective pharmaceuticals to slow the progression of chronic diseases such as hypertension, improved medical technology (ranging from sophisticated diagnostic instruments to portable treatment devices), and advances in surgical procedures that restore eyesight, replace nonworking joints, and normalize blood flow to the heart.

As medical advancements have made a substantial contribution to declining disability, they have been accompanied by an improvement in health related lifestyle habits. During these two decades many older adults have stopped smoking, started exercising, and begun to take better care of themselves. The changes increase the odds of minimizing the adverse effects of a chronic medical condition. One report estimates that such optimally aging people have 25% of the disability of those with the most risk factors and postpone the onset of initial disability for more than 7 years.[69]

How Is Your Health Compared With Five Years Ago? Some Unexpected Findings

Several years ago I became interested in the activities in which 3rd Agers engage that help them cope with the age-related challenges that accompany growing older. Of particular interest were those psychosocial factors that correlated with maintaining a vigorous body and mind. As part of this 3rd Age Study, my colleagues and I interviewed 287 volunteers from the Florida Geriatric Research Program in Clearwater.[70]

The volunteers were asked to rate their health. Their choices were "excellent," "very good," "good," "fair," or "poor." Then, we asked them how their current health was compared to 5 years earlier. Was it "much worse," "worse," "same," "better," or "much better?"[71] Before we analyzed the results of this survey, a colleague and I anticipated that the majority of the subjects would judge their health to be the same or worse/much worse than when they were a half-decade younger.

When we looked at the results, my coworker exclaimed, "Were all of these volunteers demented?" He was joking, of course, but what prompted his involuntary reaction was the tabulation of the subjects' responses shown in Figure 2.1, which compares present health with health 5 years earlier. Figure 2.1 makes it clear that our prior assumptions about the inevitability of a decline in self-rated health over half decades in the 3rd Age were wrong. The largest number of subjects who rated their present health as good to excellent said that they were in better health now than a half decade earlier.

The unexpected result was that the people who said their current health was as good or better than 5 years earlier were not limited to those in the best health. Almost two thirds of those who judged their current health as poor or fair said that they felt physically the same or better than 5 years previously. This was surprising because most of those in the less-healthy

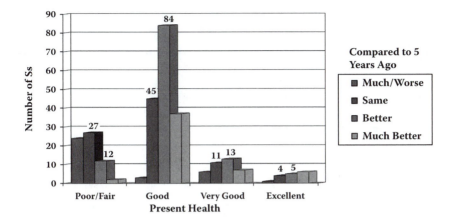

Figure 2.1 The present health of 3rd Agers compared with 5 years earlier. (From Powell, 2002. *Psychosocial correlates of stable or improved health among 3rd Agers.* Paper presented at the annual meeting of the Gerontological Society of America.)

group had experienced serious physical, social, or psychological challenges in the past 5 years. Just a few examples are cancer, heart disease, and stroke; blindness, osteoporosis, and Parkinson's disease; abuse, divorce, and physical or mental impairment of spouse; and death or serious illness of loved ones, including children and grandchildren.

Since there was so much difference in ages among these volunteers, we wondered whether those on the younger side of the 3rd Age years were the ones largely responsible for saying that their health was the same or better than 5 years ago. Our analysis found that the proportion of women and men saying that their health was better today than 5 years ago was about the same in each group, from 65–69 (19.2%) to 80+ (17.6%).

How do we explain these findings? Since we had not anticipated these results, we did not include questions about why the subjects thought that they were in as good or better health today than they were years earlier. But, we did ask them, "Overall, what has worked best for you to cope with the stresses in your life since age 55?" We looked at the responses of those subjects whom we thought would have been least likely to say that their overall health was the same or better now than a half decade ago. These were the 41 subjects currently in poor/fair physical condition, who ranged in age from 69 to 86. We found that the ways of coping mentioned by those in poor or fair health overlapped considerably with those subjects in better physical condition. By health, they were not referring to the sum of their medical diagnoses but rather their overall health-related quality of life.

Table 2.1 What Has Worked Best to Help You Cope With Stresses in Your Life From age 55? Subjects in Poor/Fair Health Who Say Their Health Is the Same or Better Than 5 Years Ago

Medical interventions
"Cataract surgery saved my eyesight."
"Got over my depression with therapy and medication."
"Two new hips and no more pain. I can go dancing again."
"New medication. Breast cancer in remission."
Mental challenges
"Reading nonfiction; doing difficult puzzles."
"Learning to play the organ."
"Oil painting."
"Working on a Ph.D in philosophy."
"Taking my computer programming skills to higher levels."
Living life more on my own terms
"Now that I'm retired, don't feel rushed anymore."
"Live life on my schedule, not somebody else's."
"Freedom to do my things, my activities, to live my life the way I desire."
"Getting my life back together since losing husband to long illness."
Simplified living
"Downsized, simplified, and moved to a trailer park."
"Simplifying my life—getting rid of excess possessions."
Being active
"Able to golf and swim, walk."
"Fishing, skiing, tennis, figure skating."
"Being active. Always having more to do than hours of the day."
Travel
"Our trip to Tahiti."
"Summer in Michigan."
Engaging in community activities
"Volunteering for social justice causes."
"Lots of self-pity after wife died. Thought of those less fortunate. Volunteered at Hospice."
"Got involved in Adopt-a-Grandchild and enjoy new relationships with her and her parents."
Happy with social networks
"Support from friends, family, my cats, and husband."
"Having children, sisters, and mom around and having their support."
More time for loved ones
"Seeing more of my family now than when I worked."
"Am in contact with my kids and grandchildren all the time."

Table 2.1 (Continued) What Has Worked Best to Help You Cope With Stresses in Your Life From age 55? Subjects in Poor/Fair Health Who Say Their Health Is the Same or Better Than 5 Years Ago

"Doing things with my wife. We have learned golf and bridge together from scratch."

Faith

"Rediscovered my faith."

"Pray and go to church regularly."

"I'm not the most devout, but my church is the center of my life."

Positive thinking

"Realize better that each day counts; don't waste time on petty things or events I can't change."

"Taking the positive out of each day and ignoring the negatives."

Financial security

"Can live without too many money worries now."

"Not rich but financially comfortable."

Table 2.1 gives some of the thoughts voiced by the group in poor or fair health regarding why they had been able to deal with the stresses of growing older and maintain a high quality of life.

Not surprising was the mention of specific medical interventions that improved the participants' quality of life. From getting over depression to acquiring new hips to successful cancer surgery, little doubt exists that medical advances helped many of these people regain far better health and improved their outlook.

Frequent reference was made by these older adults in poor and fair health to the importance of mental challenges, another confirmation of the importance of a sound intellect for most older adults. These cognitive activities included pursuing new activities or improving old ones, cultivating new interests, and pushing oneself intellectually by reading and studying.

The wide range of activities that these 3rd Agers found to help them cope with the stresses in their lives was impressive. The ability to live life on their own terms after losing a spouse and to live more simply worked for some. Others found reduction of stress in vigorous activities—sports and walking, travel, and volunteering for hospice or adopt-a-grandchild. Many found invaluable support from friends, family, and even pets. A number were sustained by their religious faith and support from the church community, while others took a resolutely positive view of their life experiences, refusing to let negative experiences bring them down. And, finally, let us not minimize the positive contributions of financial security to our mental and physical health.

What was interesting was that each of these subjects had his or her ways of managing stressful experiences. Everyone seemed to have a slightly different list of things that benefited his or her health-related quality of life, as unique to them as their fingerprints.

Reflections and Applications

The topics in this chapter affect the way I think about my own experience of growing older and influence my work with 3rd Age clients. Understanding the complex nature of health-related quality of life helps me appreciate that when we ask older adults about their health the answer we receive may have less to do with the number of chronic illnesses they are coping with and more to do with their global sense of well-being.

A sense of well-being includes important elements like having an adequate energy level, engaging in satisfying activities, having people close to them whom they can count on, having manageable levels of stress, and maintaining intellectual competence. It is factors such as these that contributed to the unexpected study findings that most 3rd Agers, even those in fair or poor health, regarded their health as the same or better than 5 years earlier. Keeping these many dimensions in mind helps us more fully understand the response when we ask those in our care, "How are you?"

It is nearly impossible not to be aware of the rising rates of chronic disease since 1990 in the United States and in many other economically developed countries. It also was not a surprise to learn that more medical problems in the 3rd Age have not resulted in increased disability. Like many of my generation, I have been the grateful beneficiary of many of the advances in medicine that were developed during my adult years. Without cataract surgery in my 50s, I would be blind; knee replacement surgery in my early 60s has enabled me to walk without assistance; medications in the later 60s for AFib and hypertension reduced the likelihood of a stroke or cardiovascular disease; and a catheter ablation in my 70s restored normal sinus rhythm, enabling me to begin exercising again and to think more clearly.

Right here, I want to stop and remind myself of how fortunate I am. Demographics matter. The greatest negative physical and cognitive effects of these chronic diseases are borne by those members of our society with the least education and lowest income. Studies around the world consistently find that chronic diseases are most prevalent among the poor, minority group members, and those with the least education. As a group, they suffer most from all afflictions, such as hypertension and diabetes, and they also lose more ground intellectually because of their chronic medical conditions than their wealthier, better educated contemporaries.[72] One solution is education. When controlled for educational level, many minority 3rd Agers differ little from Whites in healthy life expectancy at age 30 and at age 65. At lower levels of education, the racial differences are pronounced.[73]

Gender differences continue to be apparent. In 2005, female newborns could expect to see 80 birthdays, while male babies could anticipate 75. As people move into the 3rd Age, these differences widen. Life expectancy at 65 is 85 for women and 77.2 for males. Most of us will not be surprised to learn that gender differences exist in the health of older adults. While women live longer than men, they can also expect more years of life that involve disability. In 2002, the life expectancy at 65 was 19.1 years for women and 16.2 for men. Of these remaining years, about 8 of these were predicted to involve some form of disability for females compared to about 5 for males.[74]

Gender differences also occur in the incidence of chronic medical conditions and bad habits practiced by those in the 3rd Age.[75] Females more often have hypertension (70.8% of women, 64.1% of men) and joint pain (46.2% of women, 36.1% of men). Males more frequently suffer from AFib (9.0% of men, 6.0% of women) and severe hearing loss (11.3% of men, 3.5% of women). No large surveys of the incidence of sleep apnea sorted the results by both gender and age, but one review article estimated that older men with sleep apnea outnumber older women by two or three to one. The breakdown between the genders of five of the bad habits mentioned in this book is as follows: smoking (8.3% of women, 12.6% of men); drinking (38.9% of women, 55.6% of men); sedentary lifestyle (50.7% of women, 45% of men); obesity (36.4% of women, 33.0% of men); high cholesterol (24.2% of women, 10.9% of men). While the percentages varied substantially from one study to another, the direction of the differences between women and men was constant.

The weight of the accumulated research evidence that many medical conditions have such power to dim our intellectual lights was a surprise. When beginning this book, I had no idea that so many of the diseases of older age, so widespread among us, would have an adverse impact on the mind.

Of all of the healthy lifestyle habits that directly benefit the quality of the older age into which we are growing, surely one of the easiest to implement is compliance with professional advice about treatment for chronic disease. Yet, the compliance rate for taking medications as directed ranges from 26% to 59%.[76] Since half or more of the 3rd Agers with whom we deal may be affected, health care providers should find a way to bring up compliance with patients. Is this man with hypertension taking the medication as prescribed by his physician? How consistently is that woman with AFib monitoring her diet, having her blood levels checked regularly, and adjusting her medication? Why doesn't that obviously hard-of-hearing fellow ever wear the hearing aid that he purchased a year ago? If these people are not able to comply, why not? Do they appreciate the benefits, physical and intellectual, of compliance? Do they understand the risks to their mental ability as well as their health of noncompliance? Is there something we can do to help?

It is difficult to read through the studies that have been completed on the association between chronic diseases and lessened mental ability without seeing opportunities for further investigations that would greatly increase our knowledge if carried out by curious practitioner-scientists. Here are just four examples: (a) What else can be done to improve compliance? (b) What contributes to declining disability among those in your care? (c) Do hearing aids enhance intellectual functions? (d) Among older people in poor health who continue to have a positive attitude, what factors influence this outlook?

Clinicians need to keep in mind that gerontological researchers are just beginning to appreciate the adverse cognitive effects of chronic disease. Aside from hypertension, 9 of 10 studies on the link between medical conditions and lower levels of cognition have been reported in the 21st century, and nearly all are cross sectional. The majority of the tests used to measure mental ability are not especially sensitive to subtle intellectual decline. This may partially explain why many of the analyses have discovered small or no effects of medical conditions on mental acuity.[77]

Practically, this means that half or more of the 3rd Agers in our care who have a chronic medical condition may not have symptoms of degraded mental functions. But, odds are that some will. The decline may be small but noticeable to the clients. Reminding ourselves that small changes can make a great deal of difference to some individuals, we need to take seriously the possibility that some 3rd Agers who notice these small changes in themselves will be concerned and receptive to talking about their concerns. This is when the "art" in the art and science of being a health care provider takes center stage.

3

How the Mind Ages

For most adults, mental ability slopes gently downward until age 60. As Figure 3.1 shows, the level of intellectual functioning of the average 60-year-old is only 6% less than that of a 30-year-old.[1] At 70, the overall IQ is 11% less than the average of the young adults. In the next decade, the rate of cognitive decline accelerates, with the average octogenarian's mental ability being about 20% lower than those at 30.

A limitation of these data is that they are cross sectional, not longitudinal. That is, each age group consists of different subjects who were tested at about the same time. It is possible that the differences between the age groups may be caused by factors known to be associated with lower IQ scores (such as health, education, or cohort differences) rather than age.[2]

A challenge when conducting cross-sectional research is matching all of the subjects on variables known to influence cognitive decline. For instance, education and income level influence the rate at which mental abilities diminish. It is not surprising that people with more education and financial resources show less intellectual deterioration in the 3rd Age than those less fortunate.[3] So, when subjects for a cross-sectional study are selected, there is an advantage in their being comparable to one another with respect to education and income level. This makes it more likely that changes in mental ability from one decade to the next are caused by age rather than by other factors that also affect the power of the aging intellect.

We were able to match education and income level when we tested physicians during the development of MicroCog, a computerized test designed to identify professionals with mild cognitive impairment (MCI). We gave the test to 1,002 medical doctors aged 25 to 92. In the process of developing MicroCog, we also tested 581 nonphysician subjects whom we labeled "normals."[4]

Figure 3.2 shows the total scores on MicroCog for the two groups. We can see the value of more education in slowing cognitive decline. In all age groups from 30 to 75+, the medical doctors slightly outscore the normals. However, the downward trajectory of the curves is parallel.

More education gives an edge on mental ability tests that lasts into the 3rd Age of life. The 60-year-old doctors performed at about the same level as

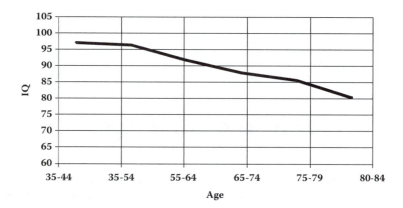

Figure 3.1 Change in full-scale IQ from age 30.

50-year-old normals on MicroCog, while medical doctors aged 65–74 scored about as high as normals a decade younger.[5]

Mental Abilities That Decline Least and Most With Age: Research Findings

Not all mental skills decline at the same rate. Processing speed is the leading indicator of cognitive aging because it is the intellectual function that diminishes most dramatically as we grow older. Our processing speed is how long it takes us to understand what the problem is, decide on the correct response, and give an answer. Tests of processing speed might involve solving analogies or assembling a puzzle under timed conditions. In real life, processing speed can be measured by the length of time it takes to check a credit card statement for errors or memorize the directions to a friend's house.

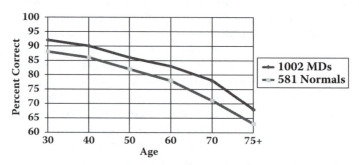

Figure 3.2 Age-associated decline in total mental ability among physicians and nonphysician (normal) individuals.

Advancing years slow processing speed. One investigation, summarized in Figure 3.3, shows the effects of aging on the time required to complete the digit symbol substitution test.[6] This test requires that the subject learn symbols associated with numbers 1–9 (e.g., *n* goes with 1, $\Omega = 2$) and then fill in the correct symbols as possible within the short time allowed when the numbers are presented in random order. Age group differences show up early. The 40-year-olds were 20% slower than those in their 30s. By age 60, it took twice as long to complete the test than for the young adults. The 70-year-olds were nearly three times slower. No other single mental ability declines as rapidly during the adult years as processing speed.[7]

Time pressure is not the only factor that influences how well older people perform. The difficulty level of the problem to be solved also contributes to processing time. Psychologists gave a test of reasoning (analogies test) under strict time limits to adults aged 25 to 75+.[8] The analogies were rated as easy, medium difficulty, or hard. Little difference occurred between the youngest and oldest volunteers on the easy analogies ("Green is to grass as _____ is to sky"). On analogies of medium difficulty, the scores of those aged 75 and older were only 6.5% lower than those a half century younger. The performance of older test-takers fell off noticeably compared to the young adults on the hardest of the analogies (e.g., "Fission is to splitting as fusion is to _____?"). Here, the combination of difficulty and time pressure took its toll even on midlifers at the threshold of the 3rd Age. Those in the 55- to 64-year-old group scored nearly 18% below the 25-year-olds on the hardest analogies.

Of particular interest to 3rd Agers is what happens when the time pressure is removed and younger and older subjects are compared only on the number of correct responses. A body of research by University of Virginia professor Timothy Salthouse has demonstrated that when speed is removed

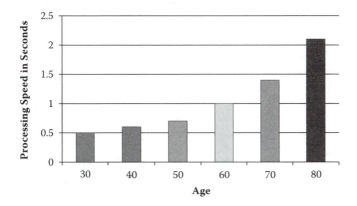

Figure 3.3 Processing speed and aging.

as a variable performance on complex tasks, by scoring the percentage of correct answers to the analogies questions instead of the number of right responses, the decline from age 30 to 75 is reduced by about two-thirds.[9]

As we might anticipate, not all mental abilities decline at the same rate. Some aptitudes, called crystallized abilities, decline gradually with age because they are less dependent on processing speed.[10] Crystallized abilities do not usually involve time pressure and are largely dependent on acquired knowledge and formal education. General information, vocabulary, and calculation are examples.

In contrast, fluid abilities are less dependent on acquired knowledge and education and are more influenced by how quickly the mind works. Commonly used tests to measure fluid aptitudes include visuospatial tasks (assembling puzzles or blocks to match a design), learning and applying a number-symbol code, and reasoning. Most tests of fluid abilities involve working memory and processing speed, which, as we have seen, decline more rapidly with advancing age than other mental skills.

Our own research with both doctors and normal subjects supported the theory that crystallized and fluid aptitudes decline at different rates.[11] Figure 3.4. graphs the average age group scores of physicians aged 30 to 75+ on two crystallized abilities (short-term verbal memory and calculation) and two fluid aptitudes (reasoning and visuospatial abilities) from the MicroCog test battery.

In Figure 3.4, notice that the crystallized abilities slope gently downward from age 30, while the two fluid aptitudes diminish rapidly with each passing decade. At age 70, the average calculation and short-term memory scores were only 8% and 9% lower than at age 30. During that same 40-year interval, fluid abilities-related visuospatial and reasoning scores fell 44% and 28%, respectively.

Comparable findings occur with other tests. The individually administered Wechsler Adult Intelligence Scale consists of two halves: the Verbal

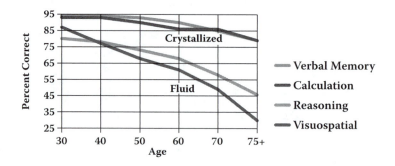

Figure 3.4 Decline in crystallized and fluid abilities: 1,002 physicians.

and Performance IQs. The Verbal IQ is comprised largely of subtests measuring crystallized abilities, whereas the Performance IQ consists mainly of tests of fluid aptitudes. The pattern of the test score differences of subjects from 30 to 70 years of age resembled the MicroCog physician data, although the absolute differences were smaller. The differences in average Verbal or crystallized IQ between the younger and older volunteers was only 3%; however, the mean Performance/fluid IQ for the septuagenarians was 20% lower than those 30 years of age.[12]

Effects of Aging on Working Memory and Multitasking

Advancing age degrades working memory and the capacity for multitasking. Working memory is the ability to store important information while working on a related task.[13] Tests that scientists employ to assess working memory include repeating a series of digits backward. An everyday example is multiplying 78 × 78 without a calculator. Decades of research have found that working memory follows the same downward slope as fluid abilities. The effect is more apparent with mental challenges of greater difficulty.[14]

Working memory is required when complex decisions need to be made. Imagine that you are a 3rd Ager who has to choose among three different health plans. Each has slightly different costs, coverage, copays, breadth of health care providers to choose from, and levels of consumer satisfaction. Making a decision about which plan is best for you requires that you carefully read the prospectus of all three plans and then compare each with the others on the factors that are important to you. For instance, are you willing to settle for generic rather than the more expensive brand name drugs in order pay less for your health insurance?

Studies of complex decision-making competence in selecting health care coverage find that compared to midlifers, older adults work more slowly. In addition, they make more errors in comprehending the differences between key elements in the health plans (such as what is and what is not covered) and make nonoptimal decisions more frequently.[15] The older adults who are better at complex decision making tend to have more education, have greater emotional stability, are more open to advice from others, and are willing to delegate responsibility to those helping them make the decision.

Multitasking is doing two things at one time—the intellectual equivalent of rubbing your tummy and patting your head simultaneously. Other terms for this process, which have slightly different meanings but encompass the same general idea, are dual-task attention and divided attention. You are multitasking when you read your e-mail while talking on the phone or make out a grocery list while sitting in a meeting. People at all age levels have more difficulty when they try to do two things at once compared to working on a single problem. Multitasking also can be dangerous. Consider cell phone use while driving. Whether hands free or not, talking to someone on the cell phone while behind the wheel increases the probability of an accident fourfold for all age groups. This is the same risk as driving drunk.[16]

As people grow older, their multitasking capability wanes.[17] On average, people in their 60s and 70s take about twice as long as younger adults to carry out two tasks at a time. In addition, one of the two is usually not done well. Do experienced older people reduce the differences between them and midlife adults on familiar tasks such as routine household chores?[18] Might their years of doing these chores enable the seniors to compensate for their slower machine speed?

The short answer is "no." Here are two cases in point, both involving cooking: Occupational therapists in Colorado videotaped women in their late 20s and those in their early 70s while they carried out a variety of household chores, including cooking eggs and making toast and coffee.[19] Based on the tapes, the older women were less efficient in carrying out these tasks. In Toronto, psychologists compared the efficiency of younger and older subjects matched for education and IQ in preparing a breakfast consisting of coffee, toast, sausage, eggs, and pancakes. The aim was to cook the foods so that they would all be ready to eat simultaneously. This was a challenge because each had a slightly different cooking time. They found that 3rd Agers worked more slowly, made twice as many overcooking or undercooking errors as the younger chefs, and had more difficulty shifting their attention from one task to the other to monitor the progress of the cooking.[20]

Mental Skills That Decline With Age: Interview Findings

As someone who holds dual citizenship as a clinician and a researcher, I find that the therapist in me is always a little skeptical about whether older people interviewed by students would exhibit the same patterns of cognitive decline as the hundreds of subjects in my own investigations and the research of others. For instance, would the interview subjects notice the same differences in the relative decline of their crystallized and fluid aptitudes that are pictured in Figure 3.4? And, might these clinical interviews turn up unexpected findings about how the mind ages?

I excerpted short descriptions of declining mental skills from some of the student interviews of volunteers who were all classified as optimal cognitive agers. These optimal agers rated their mental abilities as the same or better than 5 years earlier and stronger than those of their age mates. Yet, three of four acknowledged some decline in intellectual functioning. Their comments about the cognitive decline they noticed can be clustered into four groups: slower processing speed; occasional trouble recalling names, numbers, and things; intermittent tip-of-the-tongue (TOT) blockage; and periodic difficulties maintaining attention.

Nancy (age 78) notices that it takes her quite a bit longer to knit sweaters for her great-grandchildren than it did her grandchildren. In addition to her hands moving a little slower, she thinks it takes her longer to figure out the patterns.

According to Gary (78), larger, more difficult projects like making furniture take quite a bit more time to complete than a few years ago. He also admits that he now works mostly on pieces he is familiar with rather than taking on something new.

Sarah (78) reads both fiction and nonfiction, does crossword puzzles, watches the news, and even takes video college courses. However, she sometimes feels a decline of her verbal memory for people's names, including occasionally those of her grandchildren.

Melina (70) has not lost any of her mental abilities, except she notices the occasional temporary blocking of the name of something or a zip code. This frustrates her because it is right on the tip of her tongue.

Nick (74) says that sometimes when he is talking to his friends he loses track of what he is talking about. He starts telling the story, but about halfway through he loses his way and cannot remember the point of the story. The last time this happened, Nick had to ask, "What were we talking about?" As soon as someone reminded him, Nick recalled how the story should go. His buddies told him this happens to them all the time.

Gabriela (69) says she is as sharp as ever, with one exception: Names and numbers are an issue. Sometimes, she calls one grandchild by another one's name.

Peter (79) says he does a lot to stay mentally active. He reads four newspapers a day. The only problems he has are occasional attention problems. An example was getting lost when following a detour off the interstate highway. When he stopped at a gas station to ask for help, Peter could not focus his attention sharply enough to memorize the new direction the first time. "It doesn't always happen but sometimes things don't lock in right away like they used to," he says.

Overall, these clinical interviews partially confirmed the predicted order in which fluid or crystallized aptitudes decline. The research finding that was solidly confirmed was slower processing speed. Among these optimal agers, this was the most frequently mentioned declining aptitude. Most often, this is noticed when carrying out complex tasks (knitting sweaters or building furniture) that demand both working memory and psychomotor speed. Declining visuospatial ability made its presence known in Peter's example of getting lost while driving.

After slower processing speed, working memory, and visuospatial problems, the next most frequently mentioned cognitive difficulty involved moments of inability to remember a name, a number, or what something is called, such as "that covering on the outside of houses that looks like cement" (stucco). These were often experienced as a TOT problem. A TOT memory blockage is the sensation of being on the verge of remembering but being unable to produce a word you are certain you know. Here is a description of the TOT experience written by Harvard psychology professor and physician William James more than a century ago:

> Suppose we try to recall a forgotten name. The state of our consciousness is peculiar. There is a gap therein; but no mere gap. It is a gap that is intensely active. A sort of wraith of the name is in it, beckoning us in a given direction, making us at moments tingle with a sense of our closeness, and then letting us sink back without the longed-for term.[21]

Though less dramatically experienced, TOT memory blockages occur among all adults, and their frequency increases with age. Investigators in California asked groups of subjects in their 20s, 60s, and early 80s to keep a diary of such moments during a 4-week period.[22] Predictably, the oldest subjects recorded the most TOT experiences, averaging one every 3 days, compared to the younger volunteers, who had a memory blockage every 4 or 5 days. However, octogenarians outperformed the younger subjects in the spontaneous recall of the lost word, which was remembered 98% of the time.[23]

An interesting finding from the student interviews was the number of optimal agers who mentioned minor difficulties with maintaining attention: getting sidetracked while telling a story, momentary inability to recall a familiar name or phone number, and at times not being able to instantly assimilate information to be memorized, such as the directions back to the interstate highway when one is lost. The subjects who commented on their difficulties with concentration attributed their problems to "senior moments," by which they meant a lapse in memory.

Neuroscientists in Europe and North America might disagree, arguing instead that the memories of well-functioning seniors are usually relatively strong. Their problem is weakened concentration due to interference created by the growing inability to inhibit or block out previously learned but no longer relevant knowledge. When 3rd Agers were instructed to memorize a list of words, and forget half of them after being learned, they were both slower and less accurate than young adults with similar IQs and memory skills. Since previous testing demonstrated that all of the subjects had similar scores on memory tests, it seems that problems older adults have with remembering are because of the inability to suppress distractions rather than a weakened memory.[24]

For nearly two decades, research psychologist Lynn Hasher and her coworkers[25] have reported the adverse effects of diminished cognitive inhibition among older adults on memory, reading, and solving more complicated problems. They have identified three components of cognitive inhibition that affect learning and problem solving: the *access* function, which denies admission of irrelevant information during new learning; the *restraint* function, which operates when automatic responses are triggered by a familiar cue but are no longer correct; and the *delete* function, which suppresses information that is no longer relevant.[26] Hasher's research helps us understand the examples above: Gabriela's lapse in remembering the name of a granddaughter who walks into her house unexpectedly is because of the momentary difficulty of suppressing the names of her other female grandchildren; lost driver Peter's problem focusing on the instructions back to the interstate is because he has trouble deleting the wrong directions from his mind so that he can memorize the correct ones.

Neuroplasticity

Aging is linked to diminished blood flow to the brain, reduced sensory capability, gray and white matter atrophy, reduced neurotransmitter activity, synaptic shrinkage and dendritic regression, as well as less activation of the hippocampal and occipital areas and the loss of overall brain volume.[27] These changes in the brain are largely responsible for age-related decline in intellectual ability. Using brain-scanning technology, cognitive neuroscientists in the United States, Canada, and Sweden studied the brain activity of older and younger volunteers as they were trying to recall the answers to a series of memory tests.[28] As expected, the younger subjects outperformed their elders. While attempting to recall the correct answer, the older subjects showed weaker activation of portions of the brain associated with memory, especially in the hippocampal and occipital regions. Reduced hippocampal activation during mental tasks causes less-effective encoding of information to be remembered as well as less-efficient recollection at retrieval.

This explains the cognitive decline among most of the aging seniors. But, how do we account for those optimal agers whose intellectual powers remain on a par with men and women in midlife? One explanation is a phenomenon called *neuroplasticity*. Neuroplasticity is the capacity of the human brain to change in response to environmental stimulation. The effects of the external experience may be on the structure, connectivity, and functioning of the brain.[29]

Here is an example of neuroplasticity. In Durham, North Carolina, brain researchers at Duke University tested the theory that older subjects with good memories use more of their brains, specifically both halves of the prefrontal cortex, when taking memory tests than do their peers with weaker recall abilities.[30] In this experiment, the volunteers were asked to memorize several lists, including 24 unrelated word pairs (lawyer-window). Then, while they were being asked to recall this material (e.g., "lawyer-?"), PET (positron emission tomography) scans of the prefrontal cortex were carried out. The PET scans showed that mentally vigorous aging adults used more areas of their brains during memory tasks or other cognitive challenges. Specifically, older subjects with good memories used both hemispheres of the prefrontal cortex, while those with weaker recall relied on just one side. This is viewed as compensation for the age-related diminished functioning in other regions of the cerebral cortex.[31]

What is it that influences one 3rd Ager's ability to activate both halves of his or her prefrontal cortex when trying to recall the word paired with "lawyer," while another cannot mobilize more than one hemisphere? What external behavioral patterns might influence 3rd Agers to use more of their brain to pay attention, to encode and retrieve information, to visualize where in the mall lot the car is parked? The baker's half dozen of healthy lifestyle habits described in Chapter 1 is a good start for such a list: Not smoking, exercising regularly and fighting obesity, eating healthfully, taking prescribed medication, repopulating social networks, and managing stress all link to higher intellectual functioning. To that list of activities, others have added cognitive training, meditation, treatment of mental disorders, and engaging in stimulating activities.[32]

An example is physical exercise. For more than a decade, psychologist Arthur Kramer and his colleagues from the University of Illinois have spearheaded research efforts to demonstrate the power of exercise to improve cognition, enhance neural activity, and increase brain volume. In two recent articles,[33] they reported that 6 months of moderate levels of aerobic activity were sufficient to produce significant improvements in cognitive function—with the most dramatic effects occurring in executive control (in this case, planning, goal maintenance, working memory, and task switching). These improvements are accompanied by altered brain activity and increases in prefrontal and temporal gray matter volume that translate into a more efficient and effective neural system.

Might those seniors who learn a new physical and mental skill also influence the structure of their brains? German neuroscientists taught a group of 3rd Age volunteers to juggle three balls.[34] The subjects were given magnetic resonance imaging (MRI) scans three times: prior to learning to juggle, when they had learned to juggle for at least 60 seconds, and 3 months after the study ended. The MRI scans of the trained group of elders showed an increase in gray matter in the hippocampus, the temporal area, and other regions of the cortex while they were in the process of acquiring this skill. At the 3-month follow-up, when the 3rd Agers were no longer learning a new skill, the gains in gray matter disappeared. With respect to this particular skill, the increase in gray matter throughout the brain occurred only during the initial training and receded when exercise stopped. These cases suggest that neuroplasticity is activity dependent, and the apparent change in brain structure is likely to disappear when the skill is learned.

But, something had changed within these individuals. Even with their reduced gray matter volume, they could still juggle.[35]

Neuroplasticity is one of the exciting new ideas in the field of cognitive aging. The notion that regions of our brain may grow or become more active in response to external activities is encouraging for those aspiring to age optimally. As with most new ideas, however, much remains to be learned about the nature of neuroplasticity before its basic principles can be applied to older adults with confidence.

Here are four questions, drawn from a larger list, that need to be addressed to help us understand how learning about neuroplasticity will improve the lives of older people.[36] Will the proposed linkages be confirmed in longitudinal studies with larger numbers of ordinary community-dwelling older adults? To what extent do changes in brain structure and activation patterns affect cognitive performance on objective measures of intellectual functioning? To what extent are changes in the brain activity dependent on external stimulus, and if the apparent changes in neurobiological structure vanish when the external stimulus ceases (e.g., no more juggling), are the cognitive gains retained? Finally, what is the role of the intricate neural mechanisms that underlie brain plasticity? Regional activations or reductions are unlikely to be the whole story. So, in spite of the wealth of information that has accumulated in the past two decades, a long journey lies ahead to understand the full potential and limitations of neuroplasticity.

The Lower End of the Bell Curve: Age-Related Cognitive Decline, Mild Cognitive Impairment, and Dementia

Apparent in a growing number of older adults are signs of compromised intellectual functioning. These lapses are more severe than intermittent difficulties recalling names, numbers, or things or TOT blockages. They are persistent, debilitating, and worrisome. The following are four illustrations:

Clara (73) always prided herself on her memory. For decades, she did her grocery shopping without a list. Recently, she has noticed that she is beginning to have trouble remembering. Last week, she made a quick trip to the grocery store to pick up four items for dinner and could not think of one of them when she started shopping. This is the third time this has happened in the past month. She wonders if these memory problems might be the first signs of Alzheimer's disease. Both her mother and aunt had Alzheimer's in their 70s. Clara wonders whether she should bring her memory problem up with her doctor at her next checkup. But, he never asks her about how she is doing mentally, so maybe she does not need to worry.

At 83, Bernie still plays a good game of tennis. In fact, he still plays doubles once a week with friends 10 to 15 years his junior. In the past couple of years, however, Bernie has started to have difficulties remembering the score and then whether he was playing in the forehand or backhand court when they changed sides. In the past 6 months, during a break between games, the other players noticed that Bernie was uncertain who his partner was when they resumed the game. After they finished playing, the other players talked among themselves about Bernie's memory problems and whether they should let his wife know about their concerns.

During the past year, Maurice's three children have started to worry that their 76-year-old widower father is starting to lose his driving ability, especially his navigational skills. This has never been his strength, but things are getting worse. Last summer, while visiting his son in New Jersey, Maurice volunteered to do the grocery shopping and became so lost that he had to call 911 to help him find his way back to his son's house. Recently, Maurice admitted to his daughter that he misread a map on the way to visit a friend in Maine and "drove halfway to Canada" before he recognized the mistake and found his way back to the friend's house. When his children bring up their worries about his driving, Maurice ignores them, saying that he is no worse now than he has always been.

Anna's bout with H1N1 flu kept her in the hospital for more than a week before she was well enough to return home. At 84, Anna loved living independently in her cozy two-bedroom condo. When an old friend came to visit Anna about a month after she returned from the hospital, the friend smelled traces of gas when she opened the door. Asked about the odor, Anna admitted that she had forgotten to light one of the gas burners the night before and only noticed the smell when she got up in the middle of the night to go to the bathroom. She immediately shut the burner off and opened the windows. Later, Anna admitted to her friend that she had forgotten to turn the oven off after cooking dinner a week earlier, and several times has left the light on over the stove. Anna tells herself that this will pass when she is fully recovered from the flu. Her friend, a retired nurse, is not so sure.

The 3rd Agers experiencing these mental lapses, and those caring for them, often wonder if they are merely examples of normally decreasing mental acuity or if they are the first stages of Alzheimer's disease (AD). Or, are they symptoms of an "in-between condition," called *mild cognitive impairment* (MCI), in which cognitive deficiencies are greater than would be expected based on age and educational background but fall short of the standards for dementia.

Before discussing MCI, we should define what is meant by the mental conditions on either side of it: age-related cognitive decline and dementia. *Age-related cognitive decline* is a term used by professionals to describe an intermittent pattern of problems with memory, orientation, or reasoning that are essentially benign.[37] These are greater than average for the person's age but are still considered within normal limits. This noticeable age-related weakening of mental skills may be greater in one area such as memory or involve other aptitudes such as visuospatial ability. Age-related cognitive decline is not seen as an early stage of dementia but rather as a nonpathological extreme of normal cognitive aging.[38]

Dementia refers to the loss of mental abilities because of death or damage to brain cells. The most common form of dementia is AD, a devastating condition that takes away the very essence of an individual's identity—their memory of themselves.[39] In addition to memory impairment that gradually increases in severity over at least a 6-month period, five other primary features distinguish AD: (a) a loss of at least one other mental ability, such as attention, calculation, motor skills, orientation, judgment, and problem solving; (b) inability to function normally in self-care, hobbies, and occupational, community, and social activities; (c) noticeable, gradual decline from a previous level of intellectual functioning over a period of 6 months or more; (d) exclusionary criteria, which involves ruling out other causes for the cognitive impairment, such as disease (cancer metastasizing to the brain), other systemic conditions (hypothyroidism), psychiatric disorder (depression), or behavioral problems (alcohol abuse); and (e) lower mental ability confirmed by history and testing.[40]

About one in eight Americans aged 65 or older have moderate-to-severe AD.[41] As we might imagine, the proportion of 3rd Agers with AD increases with age. One estimate of the frequency of moderate and severe cases is that the frequency of AD roughly doubles every half decade after 65, for example, 65–69 (1.4%), 70–74 (2.8%), 75–79 (5.6%), 80–84 (10.5%).[42]

Not everyone with dementia suffers from AD. Other conditions also cause memory problems, inattentiveness, disorientation, and impaired psychomotor skills. Two of the most common are Lewy body dementia and vascular dementia. In their early stages, both of these conditions are difficult to differentiate from one another and from AD. Patients with Lewy body dementia are found among people with Parkinson's disease. This condition shares with AD the gradual unremitting cognitive decline and impaired social and occupational functioning. Among the clinical symptoms that distinguish Lewy body dementia from AD are a relatively intact memory but with episodes of difficulty sustaining attention and handling visuospatial tasks. Other clinical symptoms may include sleep disruptions and visual hallucinations.[43]

Vascular dementia (formerly called multi-infarct dementia) is caused by multiple tiny strokes (or infarcts) in the brain due to transient interruption of blood flow from clogged or burst blood vessels. These accumulated infarcts cause diffuse damage throughout the brain that can lead to vascular dementia. Significant comorbidity with AD is found, including impairment in at least two cognitive domains. Clinical characteristics that may differentiate vascular dementia from AD are spared memory but impaired processing speed and executive functions, as well as emotional lability.[44]

Generations of geriatric clinicians and neuroscientists have agreed that an intermediate stage of cognitive decline exists. This stage is below normal age-based expectations but above the threshold for AD. What these experts have disagreed most about is how likely this in-between stage will lead to AD. Two examples that already have been mentioned are age-associated cognitive decline (AACD) and MCI. AACD is considered to be more likely to remain stable, whereas MCI is viewed as a transitional phase leading to dementia.[45]

Closer inspection of the criteria for AACD and MCI, however, finds a great deal of overlap. For example, the major identifying characteristics of both are symptoms of memory impairment or other weakened mental skills in otherwise healthy normal older adults. Both also stipulate that mental ability tests verify that someone has these conditions by scoring in the lower ranges of normal IQ but above the threshold for dementia.

Longitudinal studies of 3rd Age subjects diagnosed with either AACD or MCI confirmed the impression that there is much overlap between them.[46]

Table 3.1 3–5 Year Follow-up of Subjects Diagnosed With Mild Cognitive Impairment

Author and Year	Country of Study	Age of Subjects	Remained Stable	Reverted to Not Impaired	Progressed to Dementia
Ravaglia et al., 2008	Italy	74	46%	12%	42%
Lopez et al., 2007	USA	80	31	18	51
Tschanz et al., 2006	USA	78	33	12	55
Huang et al., 2005	China	72	43	15	42

Both have higher-than-normal progression rates to dementia. The estimated incidence of all these diagnostic categories increased with greater age and less education.[47] Table 3.1 indicates that the rate of progression to dementia from MCI during the period of the research was between 42 and 55%. In four follow-up studies of AACD, the percentage of subjects who developed dementia ranged from 24.7 to 47%.[48]

On the basis of the research reviewed here, the distinctions between AACD and MCI seem to me, as a working clinician, to be largely of theoretical interest. In practice, they have most of the same diagnostic features, and those who have either of these conditions progress to dementia at a rate two to three times greater than do healthy normals. Therefore, my clinical mind lumps them together as MCIs. So, when discussing MCI, I have in mind a heterogeneous group of older adults whose cognitive skills are below average for their age and educational level but above the threshold for dementia.

We have discussed the probabilities of converting to dementia for 3rd Agers diagnosed with MCI. What happens to the others who do not develop AD? Table 3.1 addresses that question by summarizing the results of four longitudinal studies of subjects diagnosed with MCI.[49] Each study followed these older women and men with MCI for a minimum of 3 years. The progression rate to dementia was 10–15% annually. During the follow-up period, nearly half of the subjects progressed to dementia. Compared to normal 3rd Agers the diagnosis of MCI raises the risk of dementia in the near future 6 to 9 times. A good deal of research has been published about the psychosocial characteristics of those more likely to progress to dementia. These include the expectable demographic factors such as older age, less education, having limited resources, and other medical conditions. MCI based primarily on memory problems, and characterized by apathy, disinhibition, and impulsivity are at higher risk for progression.[50]

Not everyone with MCI, however, progresses to dementia. About a third remain stable during the period of the study and one in seven are assessed as not impaired at follow-up.

How do we understand those that do not progress to dementia during this longitudinal research? When discussing the results of these longitudinal studies of MCI patients the investigators spent little time discussing why some of their mildly impaired subjects did not progress.

Four explanations come to mind. First, making the differential diagnosis between the lower range normal intellectual functioning and MCI is difficult, and experienced experts can disagree about a diagnosis while looking at the same clinical evidence.

A second explanation is that the person diagnosed with MCI may have sought and received successful treatment for his or her condition that restored or stabilized intellectual functioning.

A third possibility is normal intra-individual variation. We do not know how variable or stable MCI is within most patients. The diagnosis could have been made in some subjects when they were having a downward swing in their cognitive variability, and a not impaired evaluation could have been made when the fluctuation in their mental skills moved into positive territory.

Finally, it is possible that being diagnosed with MCI mobilized some patients or loved ones to begin activities associated with not impaired cognitive functioning such as exercise, mental stimulation, and greater social interaction.

Cognitive Aging: How Much Is Hereditary?

How much of our mental ability is determined by heredity and how much by environmental influences? And, to what extent is our intelligence affected by the interaction between our genetic makeup and external factors? For those of us interested in optimal cognitive aging, these are not trivial questions. To make the case that there are things that we can do to affect the quality of the older age we are growing into, we first have to demonstrate that environmental forces play a significant role in shaping our intellect.

Research evidence has been accumulating from studies of identical twins raised apart that provides more precise answers to the contributions of nature and nurture to our mental ability.[51] Of these, the OctoTwin Study is the most interesting. Investigators in Sweden, the United Kingdom, and the United States gave mental aptitude tests to twins aged 80 and older who were adopted by different families as youngsters. Since these twins had lived apart for most of their lives, the thinking here was that the correlation between their IQs would be caused by genetic factors. The researchers found that about 60% of the similarity in their IQs was attributable to heredity and the rest to environmental causes. Reports from the Swedish

Adoption Twin Study, the Minnesota Twin Study, and other investigations found that between 50 and 60% of the factors associated with IQ are related to heredity and the rest to environmental influences.[52]

Among a growing number of neuroscientists today, the debate about the relative contributions to intelligence of nature and nurture is largely moot. This is because genes do not act independently. They are interactive. Every gene needs an environment in which to act.[53] The environment can be external, as when stimuli from the outside world modify the structure of the brain. An illustration is research by Colcombe and his colleagues, who found that adults who exercised regularly lost less brain tissue than less-fit subjects in areas of the cortex related to memory, reasoning, and spatial ability.[54]

It is increasingly apparent that the heredity-environment discussion has moved from nature versus nurture to the integration of nature and nurture. Today, neuroscientists are hard at work studying neuroplasticity, seeking those specific environmental influences that affect particular gene expressions and alter the structure and functions of the brain.

Reflections and Applications

How does this knowledge help those caring for older adults? Begin by taking seriously the findings that certain mental skills will probably diminish with age, even among those aging optimally. This information provides a good starting point when asking 3rd Agers about the quality of their intellectual functions. Even optimal cognitive agers are likely to have some declining skills that concern them, and it may be comforting to know that people who are looking after them appreciate how the mind ages and wouldn't mind hearing their concerns. The likelihood of aging optimally increases when 3rd Agers anticipate these age-related cognitive weaknesses and find ways to compensate for them.

For instance, an argument can be made that people's worst abilities are likely to worsen with age. That is, the weakest aptitudes in midlife (e.g., visuospatial ability or reasoning) are candidates to decline more rapidly than other skills. Looking at Figure 3.4 again, we see that fluid abilities, which are slightly lower at the beginning, trend downward more rapidly than crystallized competencies.[55]

Consider the case of Maurice, described in the vignettes above. His visuo-spatial abilities were not strong in midlife, and his navigational skills have since worsened, especially in the last 5 years. Although he is reluctant to admit it, he knows that he is easily disoriented, has trouble finding his way to unfamiliar places, and is often relieved to arrive at his destination without getting lost. As it turned out, his children confronted him about his difficulty navigating. Before his trip south for the winter, they encouraged him to plan his route carefully using computer-assisted map services. For his birthday in December, they gave him a GPS (global positioning system). Maurice was able to accept his children's help, which solved his navigational problems for now.

For me, the information about the hazards of multitasking was preaching to an already true believer. I learned this lesson the hard way. Just before my 62nd birthday, while I was talking on the telephone with a colleague, a staff assistant brought me a letter to sign. The letter was to Dan Ramsey, then the president of the Harvard Risk Management Foundation, the group that funded our research on aging doctors. I remember scanning the letter and signing it. About a week later, the letter was returned from Dan with the address circled in red with a large exclamation mark. The address of the letter, which I thought I proofed while talking on the phone, read:

Mr. Daniel M. Ramsey
President
The Harvard **Risky** Management Association

Since then, it has been one thing at a time for me.

Figure 3.3 contains useful clinical information for those caring for elders. Slower processing speed affects nearly everyone, including optimal agers. Those optimally aging women and men who continue to function competently in their occupations and families usually know that their mental machine speed is slower than it was a decade or two earlier, and they work around this limitation by allocating more time to checking their credit card charges. When slower processing speed becomes problematic for 3rd Agers is when they have a complex decision to make.

Imagine that a 72-year-old client wants your opinion. Earlier this month, she received a form for renewing her license as a social worker and has put off deciding whether to keep working or retire. She still enjoys part-time clinical practice with developmentally disabled adults, and her coworkers want her to stay. But it has been a long winter, and she is feeling worn out and has been thinking about giving up her job. This is partly because she has been dealing with breast cancer for the last year. Although the disease is now in remission, the chemotherapy and radiation have taken a lot out of her. And, renewing her license requires a hefty payment, along with completing several dozen hours of continuing education. On top of that is the malpractice insurance. The decision has to be made by the end of the week. She wants your opinion. What should she do?

Should you find yourself working with someone who wants to discuss major life issues like this, the research described in this chapter is a place to start. For instance, older adults should not be hurried when decisions are complicated. Making sound judgments about complex matters requiring the consideration of many factors takes longer than in middle age. The likelihood of a high-quality decision improves when a 3rd Ager is encouraged to set aside enough concentrated time to think about the problem, gather the relevant information, talk with confidantes, look objectively at the pluses and minuses of each option, and assess gut feelings.

The student interviews gave examples of optimal agers who experienced other periodic mental difficulties, including name, number, or word retrieval difficulties. In a 3rd Age population, these TOT lapses may occur two to three times a week. How can clinicians help people with TOT blockages? One option is to tell them that nine times out of ten the forgotten word pops up spontaneously within a minute or two. Otherwise, like cures for hiccups, people have their own homemade remedies. Mine is to put the forgotten word in the back of my mind and move on to thinking about something else. The word nearly always returns within a short time. Experts on such occurrences make these recommendations: (a) Try guessing the first or last letter of the TOT word; (b) estimate the number of syllables in it; (c) think of synonyms or homonyms; and (d) if appropriate, reduce stress/preoccupation level so you can concentrate on word retrieval.[56]

The negative effect of distractions on memory was emphasized by the research reviewed in this chapter. Even when elders were as competent on memory tests as younger adults, they had more difficulty with the recall of material they had previously memorized because they were less effective in blocking out incorrect information. Being unable to recall a grandchild's name or a familiar phone number, not being able to focus on information to be memorized such as the names of new neighbors, or getting lost when telling a story is not unusual among adults aging well.

What advice is there for elders who ask what they can do to maintain their concentration skills? Most of the evidence-based recommendations come from the research on age-related decline in the ability to inhibit distractions. After discussing the role of suppressing distractions in memory, here are four simple strategies that 3rd Agers in our study used to retain focus: First, get right to the point. If you are telling a story, keep it short and ignore distracting side roads, no matter how attractive they are. Next, one thing at a time. If you are going to the basement freezer for ice cream, keep your mind on that task and try to block out other interesting thoughts on the way to the freezer. Third, when you cannot recall the name of a granddaughter, silently "call the roll" of grandchildren until her name comes to you. Finally, suppress other competing preoccupations when meeting new people or hearing directions so that you can concentrate on this new information.

For the professional with clinical research interests, this chapter suggests a number of intriguing possibilities. Among them are these: (a) What is the frequency of mental mistakes during a 7-day period among optimally aging groups of 3rd Agers? (b) What contributes to recovery of lost names, numbers, or words? (c) To what extent might healthy lifestyle habits contribute to changes in brain function or structure? (d) What external factors are associated with stability or reversion to normal of individuals diagnosed with MCI?

And, of course, neuroplasticity is one of the exciting new ideas in cognitive aging and will be a major research area for years to come. Today, the application of imaging techniques such as PET and functional MRI scans enables neuroscientists to observe the brain in action as people solve problems, as well as study the changes in brain structure that occur because of healthy lifestyle habits such as exercise.

These accolades given, it is also true that the field is in its infancy. The majority of the research has been with laboratory rodents. Studies of humans have been with small numbers. Longitudinal research with adults is just beginning. Much remains to be discovered and understood.[57] A problem for health care providers is that the enthusiasm for the concept of neuroplasticity has gotten ahead of the science. Extravagant promises about reversing the aging process or remodeling our brains that come from the Internet, 60-second sound bites, and 200-word newspaper stories rarely can do justice to the complexities and to the limitations of promising scientific findings.

After these media reports appear, you can expect to be approached by elders in your care with questions about whether these new mental games, physical exercises, diets, or other endeavors might be helpful to their intellect. Here are several thoughts to keep in mind: Information that activates the "doctor within" is not a bad thing, even if the promising new activity or idea has a limited scientific basis. As long as the activity is safe, I see no harm in encouraging older clients to pay attention to things that may help them sustain their intellectual powers. Moreover, most cognitive skills can be improved through training. Although these enhanced aptitudes may not generalize to other tasks, and they tend to diminish rapidly with disuse, engaging in new challenges is good for our clients if only to prove that they can still do it. And, it does not matter either if the benefits are not long lasting. Life is lived in the short run.

An important application of these findings is making a decision about when a referral to a medical professional should be made to evaluate the mental status of someone in your care who is exhibiting signs of cognitive impairment. Recognizing weakened mental abilities in older adults is not difficult, but it can be extremely difficult to judge accurately how impaired a person is likely to be on the basis of a single symptom such as declining memory or disorientation. In these cases, a referral is necessary to a primary health care provider, who can send the patient for a consultation to a neurologist or neuropsychologist trained to differentiate normal cognitive decline from MCI and dementia. Making these distinctions requires a complete evaluation that usually includes a detailed history, physical examination, cognitive testing, and sometimes brain scans.

For those caring for older adults with worrisome symptoms, the challenge is deciding how to proceed. It is a good bet that many 3rd Agers exhibiting visible signs of mental decline will be unenthusiastic about a referral to a specialist in diagnosing dementia. At the heart of their resistance may be a version of this fear: "Why do I want to know whether I have Alzheimer's disease? It's incurable. Since nothing can help me, why do I want to know?"

Here are two answers to this question: First, the symptoms exhibited by the four subjects described in this chapter do not inevitably result in the diagnosis of dementia. Sometimes, the results are comforting and can be easily resolved. While she has experienced normal cognitive decline, Clara's evaluation and test scores showed her to be above average compared to other septuagenarians. The only recommendation for her is to make a list before she shops. Maurice's diagnosis was age-related cognitive decline, but his navigational problems can be mitigated by more thorough planning and using a GPS.

The second reason a referral to a specialist can be helpful is that early diagnosis leads to a higher probability of a positive outcome. The neurological evaluation of both Bernie and Anna resulted in the diagnoses of MCI. Even with this diagnosis, there is reason for hope. Table 3.1 reminds us that a high percentage of adults diagnosed with MCI did not progress to dementia during a 3- to 5-year follow-up period. And, a small number, about one in seven, return to normal. Also, new psychoeducational and pharmaceutical treatments with the potential for stabilizing or reversing MCI are coming to the market as these words are written. For instance, a 2009 report from a large multicenter study demonstrated that MCI subjects who received 10 sessions of cognitive training gained as much as normal participants in reasoning and processing speed and maintained this improvement for 2 years.[58] So, there is justification for a cautiously positive attitude even when the diagnosis is MCI. Art's story[59] is an example.

Art

I am a retired physician and an emeritus professor of medicine. Also, I have Alzheimer's disease. My diagnosis was suspected by my wife and confirmed by my internist. All the while, I was in total denial (a common failing when doctors are patients). After doing a few tests of my memory in the office, the doctor ordered other tests and a brain scan. The diagnosis was mild Alzheimer's disease.

I was started on a medicine that has been used for many years and has many side effects. I had a few Alzheimer's patients in my practice who had taken this medicine with no benefit. My doctor had me continue it, though I was kicking and screaming, and the side effects eventually disappeared. This drug was continued, and another was added later on, which turned out to be helpful.

In 2 months, I was much better, and I am now close to normal. At my worst, I have difficulty speaking, do not know the names of my grandchildren or my doctor, can neither add nor subtract or find my way home. I am considered one of the rare lucky ones.

Looking back, I now recognize my memory problems arose 10 years ago when I was 76. I chaired a monthly program about medical ethics. I knew most of the speakers and found it easy and enjoyable to introduce them. That year, I began to be more forgetful. I had to read the prepared material to make the introductions. My memory for names started to slip, never faces. "Senior moments," I concluded.

Over the last decade, I had two transitory ischemic attacks or small strokes, and my mental difficulties worsened. The final blow was the occasion 1 year ago when I was receiving a citation for service in my hospital. I stood up to thank them and found that I could not say a word. "Aging brain," I said and sat down. That is when I saw my doctor, and the diagnosis of Alzheimer's disease was made.

For some reason—no one knows why—my condition has improved. I am still not back to normal, and I have bad days, but I can continue to live at home with the help of my wife and the care of my doctor.

I am learning many things since being improved that have helped me. I would like to share with you: When you want to recall things, carry a little note pad and write it down. When you cannot remember a name, make a little joke and ask them to repeat it—then write it down. Read books. Take walks. If you cannot walk, exercise in bed. Draw and paint. Garden, if you can. Do puzzles and games. Try new things. Organize your day. Learn to prepare food, eat, dress, wash, and go to bed in an efficient way. Eat a healthy diet that includes fish twice a week, fruits and vegetables, and omega 3 fatty acids.

Finally, do not be ashamed to talk to your friends and your family. People want to help you.

To my knowledge, no one has compared cases like Art's that do not convert to dementia to those individuals diagnosed with MCI who do progress as expected. What a research project this would be. Certainly, in Art's case the medications played a central role. But, what about some of the suggestions Art has made, as well as other healthy lifestyle habits practiced by people aging optimally that could be examined along with dozens of others? Art was fortunate in having a doctor who was willing to continue working with him when he had to be convinced to take medication he did not believe would help him and who must have encouraged him to come up with ideas of his own to help himself.

Knowing that dementia is not a certainty for everyone with MCI can inspire hope among those in your care. Having a health care provider who has some ideas about activities that might retard the progression to dementia can also stimulate them to come up with ideas of their own that will make a difference in their well-being.

Still, the majority of those diagnosed with MCI or mild AD will progress toward more severe impairment. What you do then depends on your role, your other responsibilities, and your relationship with these clients. Overall, you want to be sure that those with cognitive impairment have someone to care for them. Sometimes, these are professionals with experience working with such cases. Often, however, no one is available. There will be some people newly diagnosed with cognitive impairment who may feel abandoned if you suddenly terminate your relationship with them because you are not an expert. You can provide them a great deal of comfort if you accompany them as they cope with the challenges in this next phase of their lives.

4

Healthy Lifestyle Habits Benefiting the Aging Body and Mind

Healthy lifestyle habits are those activities we engage in routinely that benefit the aging body and mind. Backed by evidence from a decade or more of research by multiple groups of investigators, these healthy lifestyle habits include exercising regularly, engaging in active leisure pursuits, fighting obesity, eating healthily, using alcohol moderately, maintaining satisfying social relationships, and managing stress.[1]

Exercise Regularly

Well established are the health benefits of regular exercise. Less often reported is how beneficial exercise is for the mind. Hundreds of research reports over the past half century pointed to the correlation between working out regularly and higher mental ability. Here's an example. Psychologists in Salt Lake City, Utah, divided older adult volunteers into three groups: those who engaged in moderate aerobic exercise, those who did strength and flexibility exercises only, and those who were sedentary. All three groups took mental ability tests at the beginning and end of the study. The regimen for the aerobic group consisted of fast walking or light jogging for 60 minutes three times a week. The strength training group's routine was to stretch and lift moderate weights for the same period of time. The sedentary group did no exercising. After 4 months, the mental abilities of the sedentary volunteers were unchanged. During that same period, the aerobic exercisers improved their scores 9%, while the abilities of those engaged in strength/flexibility workouts rose 4%. The cognitive skills on which the subjects who exercised scored higher spanned a wide range of aptitudes: faster reaction time, better attention, speedier reading, and greater intellectual flexibility.[2] This is a lot of improvement for just 4 months of moderate exercise.

Disagreement exists regarding how much physical exertion is required to enhance mental ability. For instance, the workouts in Salt Lake City might have seemed undemanding by the scientists studying more than 1,000 volunteers, aged 70–79, from around Boston; New Haven, Connecticut; and Durham, North Carolina.[3] They found that those septuagenarians who engaged in the most strenuous household activity or exercise had the least deterioration of their mental skills.[4]

What is the right amount of exercise for the aging intellect? Scientists in the Midwest addressed this question along with several others about the impact of exercise on the mental skills of older adults. These included[5]

1. How much does regular exercise enhance the cognitive vitality of older people?
2. Does exercise benefit some abilities more than others?
3. What is the effect of the duration of the exercise?
4. Does the type of exercise matter?
5. How much does age or physical condition limit the benefit from exercise?

The researchers carried out a meta-analysis (an analysis of the analyses) of 18 studies of the impact of exercise on the intellectual functioning of older subjects. The cognitive abilities measured included executive functions (planning, reasoning, and multitasking); control (inhibition of distractions); speed (response or reaction time); and spatial (recall or manipulate forms).

Turning back to the first question about whether fitness training enhances the cognitive vitality of older people, the answer is "Yes." Figure 4.1 shows that the improvement in overall mental ability achieved by the exercisers was four times greater than the nonexercising volunteers.

The answer to the second question is also affirmative. Exercise improves some abilities more than others. Executive functions (planning, reasoning, and multitasking) are strongly affected by exercise. Also considered a part of executive functions is control, the ability to block out disrupting thoughts and feelings.

Not surprising is the relatively small effect of exercise on speed of response. This is because processing speed is more strongly influenced by heredity than other aptitudes. It seems reasonable then to assume that problem-solving speed will be less affected by environmental influences such as exercise.

Question 3 asked whether the duration of the exercise influenced changes in mental aptitudes. Considerable difference of opinion exists among experts regarding how long a workout should be. Some believe that short bursts of exercise are as beneficial as a longer workout.[6] In this study, the duration of

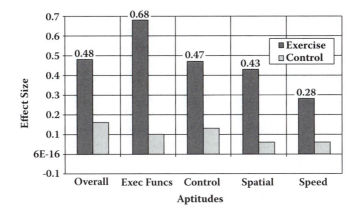

Figure 4.1   Effects of fitness training on the mental ability of older adults.

the workouts was measured in two ways: by the length of the daily exercise and by how long the program of exercise continued. The results showed that the exercise sessions had to be at least half an hour in length, at least three times a week to benefit the intellect of the exerciser.

The answer to the question about how long 3rd Agers should remain in an exercise program to benefit mentally was less obvious. To no one's amazement, the greatest improvement in test scores occurred among those who exercised for 6 months or more. What was surprising was that those who exercised for only 1 to 3 months experienced almost as much positive change in mental ability as those who worked out for a longer period. So, any period of exercise beyond 30 days has a good chance of enhancing the intellect.

The short answer to the question "Does the type of exercise matter [to the intellect]?" is "Yes, it does." Aerobic workouts have about twice the positive influence on mental ability as strength and flexibility training only. But, it does not have to be either/or. Older volunteers whose weekly workout included strength and flexibility training alternated with aerobic exercise had the most improvement in mental ability.

Finally, do older people get as much mental lift from exercise as the younger participants? And, how about older people who are depressed or who are recovering from a heart attack? Again, the answer is positive. Exercisers aged 65 and older improved as much or more on mental aptitude tests as did the younger subjects. In addition, depressed patients and those recovering from heart disease exhibited the same degree of improvement on cognitive tests as their healthy contemporaries.

Would exercise improve the mental functions of older people suffering from cognitive impairment? Once more, the answer is "Yes." University of Texas Medical School investigators selected 30 studies that reported the results of efforts to enhance the intellectual functioning of cognitively impaired older adults through exercise.[7] Although the exercise effects were less dramatic, those who worked out improved more on mental tests than their sedentary contemporaries.

One of the reasons physical activity stimulates mental ability is because it increases blood flow to the brain. Doctors at the Baylor College of Medicine in Houston measured cerebral perfusion in female and male volunteers at age 65 and then annually for the next 4 years.[8] They divided the participants into three groups: (1) those who continued working, (2) those who retired and remained physically active, and (3) those retirees who became sedentary.

At 65, there was no difference in cerebral perfusion in the three groups. Two years later, however, the blood flow to the brains of the working and active retiree groups was no different from the baseline measurements. By contrast, the cerebral perfusion of the retired-sedentary subjects declined. After 4 years, the blood flow to the brain of the retired sedentary individuals was 10% lower than that of the other two groups.[9]

Because the evidence showing that exercise is associated with higher levels of cognition has been so consistent, a University of Illinois research team looked at whether exercise links to less age-related loss of brain tissue.[10] They tested 3rd Age volunteers for aerobic fitness. Each subject also received a magnetic resonance imaging (MRI) brain scan. When their aerobic capacity and brain density were compared, fitter subjects had less loss of brain tissue in three areas of the brain related to reasoning, spatial ability, and memory. A study directed by another member of this team found 6 months of aerobic fitness training was correlated with increased prefrontal and temporal gray matter volume.[11]

Engage in Active Leisure Pursuits

Research around the world confirmed that exercise is good for our health and our intellect. What about other everyday activities, unrelated to sports or formal exercise, that burn energy? Interviews with optimal cognitive agers found that well over half rarely worked up a sweat in sports or in the gym but were otherwise unusually vigorous. Here are three examples from student interviews:

Mel (age 78) is very involved in his church in Springfield. He devotes much of his free time to church-related activities, such as the church bowling team, choir, and the after school youth program. He is a mentor in the teenagers' confirmation program also. After church on

Sunday, he goes to Wendy's for lunch with his church friends. During the afternoons, he spends time with younger children doing activities at the church. On Tuesday evenings, he bowls against other teams from churches in Springfield.

Gary (75), who is a widower, mows the lawn, tars his garage roof, hangs ceiling fans, and does his own shopping, cooking, and cleaning. In his spare time, he loves to build things like a rocking horse or a crib for his grandchildren.

Jane (73) said she is "busy all day long," and that there are "not enough hours in the day." She belongs to a book club and a weekly dancing group. She feels best in the morning, as well as right after her midday nap. "I need a little nap," she said, "if I'm going to be dancing until one in the morning!"

It stands to reason that any activity that burns calories contributes to our overall health. Barbara Ainsworth[12] and her colleagues at the University of South Carolina in Columbia rated a range of activities—leisure, household, and occupational as well as athletic—on the basis of how many METs (metabolic equivalents) are expended during the action.[13] A MET is defined as the number of kilocalories used per minute by an average person during an activity relative to that individual's basic metabolic rate. The MET scale goes like this: 1 MET would be lying in bed watching TV; 2–3 METs are used in cooking and light house cleaning; scrubbing floors or sweeping the garage expend 4–5 METs; moving furniture, lugging groceries upstairs account for 6–7 METs; cross-country skiing (4–5 mph) and shoveling snow burn 8–9 METs; running a 10-minute mile uses 10 METs. Modern exercise machines now rate the degree of exertion in METs as well as calories.

Table 4.1 compares leisure activities and exercise/sports on the basis of METs burned per hour of activity. The first of the three types of activities (e.g., walking the dog and golfing with a cart) are considered lightly vigorous, consuming 3–4 METs per minute. The second cluster (e.g., active yard work/gardening and doubles tennis) are rated moderately vigorous and burn 5–6 METs. The third type of activity (e.g., carrying groceries upstairs and backpacking/mountain climbing) is vigorous because these actions use 7–8 METs.

Scientific publications around the world have agreed that high levels of ordinary leisure activity provide nearly the same health benefits as vigorous exercise.[14] But, what about cognitive functions? Is there any evidence that ordinary daily activities have the same benefits on the mind as the body?

Table 4.1 Light, Moderate, and Vigorous Activities Equivalent to Exercise/Sports

Activities	Exercise/Sports
Light	
Putting groceries away	Canoeing for pleasure
Home care (sweeping, vacuuming)	Bowling
Walking the dog	Golf with a cart
Moderate	
Energetic dancing or clogging	Golf, carrying clubs or pulling cart
Active yard work/gardening	Doubles tennis
Mowing lawn with power mower	Aerobics, low impact
Heavy	
Shoveling at 10–15 pounds per minute	Cycling 12–14 mph
Cutting, hauling wood	Singles racquet sports
Carrying groceries upstairs	Backpacking/mountain climbing

Cross-sectional studies have found that the amount of time older people engage in everyday activities that do not involve going to the gym correlates with higher scores on mental tests.

At the Georgia Institute of Technology neuroscientists surveyed the activity levels of several hundred volunteers and then gave them a battery of aptitude tests. The more active individuals had higher mental ability scores. Even more interesting was that 3rd Agers who spent much of their time watching TV or listening to the radio did not perform as well on the tests. Reports from other parts of the world verified these findings.[15]

Icelandic women and men in their mid-70s who were highly active had significantly higher scores on tests of processing speed, memory, and executive functions than the less-active group.[16] The Iceland study showed that high levels of leisure activities had a beneficial effect on the brain. Greater activity benefitted even those older Icelanders whose brains were shown on the MRIs to have greater vulnerability to atrophy of the white matter.[17] Compared to less active 3rd Agers at risk for brain atrophy, those women and men who were more engaged in community activities were mentally quicker than their sedentary age-mates.

A problem with this type of research is that you test people at only one moment in time. Would longitudinal research that followed the same people over time, comparing activity level with mental ability, produce the same results? An answer to this question came from investigators who studied nearly 6,000 older women in four communities for 6 to 8 years.[18] They had a hunch that the more active women would retain their mental abilities better than those who were more sedentary. At the beginning and end of the study, the investigators gave each volunteer a brief mental exam. Then, they looked at whether there was a link between how much these women walked and the rate at which their mental ability declined.

The participants were asked questions about their physical activities in addition to exercise. The investigators scored each activity on the basis of kilocalories expended and added them together. Then, they divided the weekly sum by the kilocalories required to walk a city block.

The women were divided into four groups, with activity levels from low to high. The magnitude of the differences between the women in the most active top quarter and those in the other groups was striking. The energy expended by the lowest 25% of the subjects was enough to walk only 7 blocks per week, while the 50% in the middle would have covered an average of 53 blocks. By contrast, the energy output by the top quarter was enough to walk 175 blocks weekly, more than three times those in the middle of the pack.

Did those women who expended the most energy weekly have a lower incidence of significant cognitive decline and maintain their mental acuity compared to those who were the least active? The answer is both "Yes" and "No." Fewer of the active women showed significant cognitive decline as they moved from their early to late 70s—one in six women in the most active top quarter compared to about one in five for the other less-active females. Their scores on the brief mental test, however, were slightly lower than they had been 6–8 years earlier.[19] Reviews of other longitudinal investigations by investigators on four continents largely confirmed these results.[20]

Fight Obesity

Fighting obesity is an important lifestyle habit for 3rd Agers. The reason for using the term *fight obesity* rather than *avoid obesity* is that three of four older Americans are obese or are in danger of becoming obese. So, most of us in the 3rd Age are fighting obesity rather than trying to avoid it. Survey data in 2003–2006 found that 78% of men and 70.5% of women aged 65–74 met the criteria for being overweight or obese.[21] Carrying excess weight increases the risk in all adults of medical conditions such as heart disease, hypertension, and type 2 diabetes. Each has negative consequences for the intellect. Obesity has about the same negative effect on our health as smoking.

When experts use the terms *overweight* or *obese*, they are referring to the body mass index (BMI). The BMI is calculated by dividing your weight in kilograms by your height in meters squared. Thus, a man who is 6 feet 6 inches tall (about 2 meters) and weighs 220 pounds (100 kilograms) has a BMI of about 25. You also can enter BMI on your Internet search engine, and a calculator will pop up that will do the math for you. BMIs under 25 are considered ideal, while people in the 25–29 range are judged to be overweight. Slightly over one in three adults aged 65–74 is obese (BMIs of 30–34) or very obese (a BMI exceeding 35). In the 65–74 age group, 35.8% of females and 33% of males surveyed were obese.[22]

Medical researchers agree that adults with BMIs under 25 have a lower health risk than their heavier contemporaries, and that obese younger and middle-aged adults are much more vulnerable to weight-related diseases and earlier death. Medical scientists disagree about how much health risk is associated with being overweight in the 3rd Age and beyond. Some believe that older people with BMIs of more than 25 share many of the same risks of hypertension, type 2 diabetes, and heart disease as midlifers. Others point to a growing consensus in the United States that mortality risks are directly related to BMI in younger and middle-aged adults but not in older people. A follow-up of participants in the Baltimore Longitudinal Study of Aging found that overweight subjects aged 65–80 had less chance of contracting heart disease than the younger overweight men and women.[23]

There is no doubt that older obese adults have a greater risk of developing cognitive impairment than their thinner contemporaries. A series of prospective studies from Europe, Asia, and the United States reported a link between obesity and dementia. In each research project, the subjects were screened for BMI and then followed for 5 to 36 years. During the follow-up period, the subjects were tested for dementia. They found that adults with a BMI of 30 and above had three times the risk of becoming demented as those with BMIs in the normal range.[24] California investigators also discovered that those septuagenarians who were both obese and carried their adiposity in their belly were 3.6 times more likely to develop dementia than those women and men with normal weight and belly size.[25]

Long term studies in the United States and Europe reported worrisome cognitive consequences of obesity on the intellect among 3rd Agers who did not develop dementia.[26] In Boston, obese men in their mid-60s scored lower on tests of memory than those with BMIs under 30. A 4-year follow-up of middle-aged French adults found a similar link between adiposity and lower memory scores.

Heavy 3rd Agers who lose weight are likely to find their efforts rewarded by improved quality of life. Six different studies found weight loss had highly positive effects on osteoarthritis. Shedding pounds also was linked to far greater mobility, less pain, and reduced functional impairment. Weight loss resulted in lower blood pressure, cholesterol, and fasting glucose readings. And, when asked, the subjects who lost weight said they felt better about themselves. They liked the way they looked.[27]

As a group, the people who benefited most from weight loss were those who were the most unhealthy and obese when they began their efforts.

For older adults wanting to lose weight, what types of programs are more and less beneficial? A Minnesota group of experts in weight management evaluated a number of different programs that provided data on the effectiveness of the intervention at a minimum of 1 year. Eight types of weight loss programs were examined.[28]

The most effective programs were diet, diet and exercise, meal replacements, and medications. All of the successful interventions followed the same pattern. The most progress was made in the first 6 months, followed by a gradual decline toward baseline.[29] The most dramatic initial effects occurred with medications, while the meal replacements had the least impact. At 6 months, the weight loss ranged from 5 to 9% of the starting weight. Afterward, the subjects slowly regained some of the lost poundage whether they remained in the program or dropped out. When follow-up was available at 3 to 4 years, the average weight loss was still 3–6%, with no groups returning to baseline weight.

Eat Healthily

When I began my research on cognitive aging a quarter century ago, I did not pay much attention to the effect of diet. The reason was that the field of nutrition has been plagued by generations of false claims that this food or that supplement will keep us young and vigorous while our peers grow elderly and infirm on their ordinary diets. Typically, these claims were disproven by later research.

Then, as the 21st century dawned, books and articles written by experienced clinicians began to appear, followed by the publication of the first longitudinal studies reporting scientific evidence linking specific foods to better health as well as higher scores on the mental ability tests of older adults.[30] These publications caused me to rethink my views about nutrition and optimal aging. What influenced me most, however, were the observations of the students, who were way ahead of me in their vision about the role of diet in the optimal agers they interviewed. Here are four of their observations:

Lee (age 72) keeps a very healthy lifestyle. He does not take any prescription medications or vitamins. He eats three meals per day regularly, which he feels is the key to his health. In his diet, there is no butter, no sausage, no bacon, no fatty meat, and no alcohol, no coffee, and no cigarettes. Lee usually eats vegetables and fish—steamed, baked, or grilled rather than fried—which he sees as a healthy habit.

Sheilah (80) makes sure that she drinks plenty of water, milk, and orange juice each day. Occasionally, she "splurges" with a beverage such as pink lemonade, but she tries to stay away from empty-calorie beverages. She also makes sure to eat plenty of whole grains, fruits, and vegetables.

The medical condition that has had the most impact on her life was when Marilyn (62) was diagnosed with type 2 diabetes last year. Before that, she consumed any food she wanted, with no obvious concern about her increasing waist size. But, when the doctor said she had Type 2 diabetes, Marilyn completely turned her life around. For starters, she took classes on nutrition and spoke to a nutritionist about how she could lose weight and keep it off. Marilyn now goes to the gym five times a week. She also eats fruits and vegetables that have the most health benefits. In fact, during the interview she was drinking cranberry juice with a pinch of lemon. It was pretty good.

Carol (65) eats healthily most of the time since she found out she has high cholesterol and states that she "has to keep her body looking fine." She drinks a lot of water and milk to have healthy bones and beautiful skin. She believes that proper nutrition, with an emphasis on fruits and vegetables, oatmeal, and salmon, will have long-term health benefits.

What these students discovered from these optimally aging women and men was the conviction that eating "right" was a key to good health. As it turns out, their beliefs are supported by at least a dozen longitudinal investigations that focused on the value of a healthy general diet[31] to the body and mind.

Eating healthily is variously defined. At the minimum, a good diet includes at least five servings of high-fiber, whole-grain breads and cereals containing relatively few calories, fruits, and vegetables daily.[32] Several longitudinal studies examined the association between eating habits and other healthy lifestyle habits and the risk of serious disease. Men from the Physicians Health Study who scored above average on a food survey had a 16% lower likelihood of developing heart failure compared to those who scored below average. Women from the second Nurses' Health Study who consumed the healthiest diets had 18% less risk of hypertension than those with the poorest eating habits. The contribution of a good diet had nearly the same impact on health status as exercise.[33]

The effect of diet on the intellect has been studied as well. An example is the 11-year longitudinal study of the association between diet quality and cognitive decline among 3,634 older men and women in Utah.[34]

At baseline, subjects with the healthiest diets differed only slightly from the bottom quarter group who were not eating healthily. Eleven years later, those who had continued to follow the recommended guidelines showed over 30% less cognitive decline on a brief mental test than the bottom quarter of subjects.

What people eat also affects their mental health. Older women and men who reported that they experienced 14 or more mentally unhealthy days in the past 30 days were classified as having severe psychological distress.[35] A national survey of individuals aged 65 and older with and without severe psychological distress found three modifiable risk factors that made a difference in the subjects' mental health. Those in the best mental health were more likely to be nonsmokers and to engage in moderate-to-vigorous exercise each week. They also consumed at least five fruits or vegetables daily.[36]

Consume Alcohol Moderately

None of the other healthy lifestyle habits behaves quite like light alcohol consumption for older adults. For the other factors, the graph showing the relationship with health and cognition is a straight line angling up or down: No exercise is bad for you, while more exercise is good; people who do not smoke are healthier than people who do. For alcohol use among 3rd Age women and men, however, the curve looks like a check mark or J-shaped figure. Abstainers in the 3rd Age are a little less healthy than those who are moderate drinkers. But, as older people consume more than that amount, the danger to health and the intellect grows rapidly. It is interesting that this J curve does not apply to the young and middle aged. For them, the more they drink, the worse it is for their minds and bodies.

In the two Harvard long-term follow-up studies of older doctors and nurses, the moderate drinkers were less likely to die of heart failure or develop hypertension.[37] Those who abstained had a slightly higher risk of these medical conditions than the light imbibers, while those who drank heavily put themselves at far greater risk of ill health. Other studies of nonmedical subjects found that moderate alcohol use (up to two drinks per day) correlated with better health, including a lower incidence of heart disease, ischemic stroke, and hypertension when compared with heavy alcohol users and abstainers. A 9-year follow-up study of the effects of alcohol consumption on mortality, encompassing nearly a half million volunteers in the their mid-50s, noted the J-shaped curve, with the least mortality among moderately drinking men (two drinks per day) and women (one drink per day).[38]

Four European investigations agreed that the risk of developing dementia was reduced by moderate alcohol intake in the 3rd Age.[39] For instance, Danish women in their 70s who averaged one to two drinks a day were half as likely to have cognitive impairment compared to those who drank less; the moderate drinkers also were less vulnerable to dementia than the heavy drinkers.

Interestingly, wine consumers seemed to benefit more than those who favored beer or spirits. Opinions vary regarding why drinking wine is better for our minds and body than other forms of alcohol.[40]

In the past decade, MRI studies of the brains of midlife adults have found that alcohol consumption increases the normal shrinkage of the brain. In the 3rd Age of life, however, it appears that lighter alcohol consumption is linked in two reports to less brain shrinkage and higher performance on a variety of mental tests, including psychomotor speed, attention, memory, and verbal fluency.[41]

Why is a small amount of alcohol good for us and twice as much bad for our health? Casual observation of adults of any age tells us that low levels of alcohol consumption promote relaxation and facilitate socialization among older adults, suggesting that alcohol plays an important role in community life for older adults. It may be also that moderate alcohol consumption has a protective effect on vascular systems, including blood flow to the brain.[42]

Nationwide surveys reported that between 50 and 60% of 3rd Agers regularly consume some amount of alcohol. Of the remainder, about 50% are former drinkers. Slightly over half of older men imbibe, compared to just under 40% of the women.[43] Americans are drinking less than in the past. At the end of the 1990s, 63% of all adults said they drank. Ten years later, the proportion was 61%. This may not seem like much, but it means that over 4.5 million Americans who would have consumed alcohol if the 1997 percentage of adult drinkers remained constant are now abstainers. The increase in teetotalers occurred across the board—from all ages, both sexes, all income levels, and most racial and ethnic groups.[44]

The biggest change is that more 3rd Agers who drink are drinking heavily. This is especially true for older women. Some studies indicated that the number of female heavy drinkers has increased fractionally from 1997 to 2007 while the percentage of heavy drinkers has declined slightly for men.[45] A University of Chicago team asked more than 3,000 older adults questions about heavy alcohol consumption, including the number of days in the past 3 months in which they had at least four drinks. About 16% of the men and 6% of the women said they consumed four or more drinks between once a month and once a week. More women aged 65–74 said that they were heavy drinkers compared to those a decade younger, while 3rd Age men drank heavily far less often than males 10 years their junior.[46]

Frequent heavy drinking can damage all organ systems and increase the likelihood of liver disease, hypertension, diabetes, and stroke. It is implicated in gastrointestinal problems, osteoporosis, and suppression of the immune system. Heavy drinking also raises the risk of dangerous alcohol-drug interactions. Nine of ten adults 65 and older have taken at least one prescription medication in the past month.[47] Because the aging body is more susceptible to negative effects of multiple drugs, older persons experience about half of the total adverse drug interactions that lead to hospitalization.

Heavy alcohol intake is just as bad for the brain. A review of MRI studies of the brains of heavy drinkers found that normal age-associated brain shrinkage was accelerated 10–15% compared to that in normal imbibers. Heavy drinking contributes to the diagnosis of dementia in one of five older adults. Mental test performance of older alcoholics found them to be clinically impaired in processing speed, attention, memory, and reasoning.[48]

While the vast majority of 3rd Agers drink responsibly, over 3.5 million develop alcohol abuse or dependence.[49] When heavier-than-average drinking becomes alcohol abuse, it leads to problems in one or more of these areas: inability to fulfill obligations at work or at home; health or relationships; injuries or accidents; or legal problems. Heavy drinking becomes alcohol dependence when it involves significant impairment and results in the inability to control alcohol consumption. Other symptoms of alcohol dependence are increased tolerance—a growing need for larger amounts to achieve the same effect—and withdrawal symptoms. Also common are repeated physical, social, and psychological problems caused by continued drinking. Activities that were previously enjoyed are abandoned.[50]

What is the likelihood of those heavy-drinking or even alcohol-dependent 3rd Agers being able to reverse the pattern? The chances are only fair. Part of the problem in estimating the effectiveness of alcohol treatment programs is that follow-up research evaluating the success of large programs such as Alcoholics Anonymous (AA) has been largely missing. What reliable information there is tells us that people with drinking problems who stay in AA and other 12-step programs are twice as likely to be abstinent after a year compared to those in other forms of treatment.[51] Other efforts employing a mixture of brief efforts by doctors and other health care providers, ranging from exhortation to semistructured programs, helped a small fraction of older adults overcome their drinking problems. For instance, Spanish researchers found that brief interventions of many kinds—including brief discussions with medical caregivers—resulted in a 21% improvement in the drinking habits of the treated group compared to untreated alcohol abusers.[52]

Efforts to help older people stop drinking, or even learn to consume alcohol sensibly, have been just as successful as with younger individuals.

A University of California research team in San Francisco compared the outcome of treatment for older, middle-aged, and young adult alcohol abusers. After 6 months, more than half of all groups had been abstinent for at least a month. About the same proportion of 3rd Agers had stopped drinking as those in the younger age brackets.[53]

Maintain Satisfying Social Relationships

Satisfying social relationships have the same positive effect on our life expectancy as other well-established health lifestyle habits, such as not smoking, physical activity, and avoiding obesity. An analysis of 148 research studies found that people who feel cared about by others and are integrated into a social network have a 50% greater probability of survival than those who feel unsupported and isolated.[54]

Satisfaction with our circle of family and friends is strongly related to our resistance to disease, recovery from heart attacks, and life expectancy,[55] as well as how well our mental abilities are retained as we grow older.

Intuitively, we might imagine that the best kinds of social ties are ones in which we feel loved, supported, and listened to. In fact, there is much research evidence that older people live longer when warmed by the positive sentiments of loved ones.[56] Other findings about the quality of relations with others, however, may seem surprising at first glance. First, very positive social contacts can be bad for our health, and negative interaction actually can be beneficial.[57] It is not hard to imagine conditions in which highly positive connections are not good for our health: reinforcing sickly behavior with extreme solicitousness or rewarding dependency and helplessness by being overly "helpful."

The other side of the coin is that negative social contacts are sometimes good for 3rd Agers, even though they may feel temporarily unloved.[58] A man recovering from a heart attack may feel he is being treated insensitively by his daughter, who lets him know that it is time to stop feeling sorry for himself, begin taking his medication, and start those exercises the doctor prescribed. Though often helpful, these tough love interactions can be experienced negatively at first by older adults.

Eventually the man may come to understand that his daughter cares enough about him to be critical. Or, perhaps because of his shrunken social networks, the best he can manage is a relationship that is not entirely positive. Yet, a negative relationship is still a relationship.

Does satisfaction with our social relationships affect the intellect? It has always seemed to me that contact with a wider network of friends and acquaintances, especially those who have had life experiences different from our own, should stimulate the mind. We tested this theory by asking

3rd Age subjects from the Florida Geriatric Research Program about the decline in their cognitive functions and health over the past 5 years. Then, we compared their responses with four different aspects of social relationships.[59] Present social satisfaction and overall social satisfaction had the highest correlations with less decline in mental ability and health.

Findings by investigators studying 3rd Age subjects in the United States and Europe, agreed that people with more social ties exhibited less cognitive decline.[60] Over a 12-year period, neuroscientists in Baltimore, Maryland, examined the relationship between the social networks of 354 older adult volunteers and global cognitive status. They found that larger networks and feelings of emotional support were correlated with less cognitive decline. A Spanish research team examined the impact of social networks on cognitive test scores of nearly 1,000 subjects 65+ living outside Madrid. After 4 years, 31.6% had major or minor declines in test scores. Poor social connections, infrequent participation in social activities, and social disengagement predicted greater risk of cognitive decline.

Face-to-face interactions were more often associated with less decline than telephone contact. Neuroscientists from Sweden's Karolinska Institute in Stockholm published a number of articles supporting the theory that rich social networks are associated with a lower risk of dementia.[61] They followed over 700 older subjects for 3 years, comparing the social networks of subjects who developed dementia with those who did not. Those engaging in daily social contact had only 60% of the risk of dementia as those reporting no such activity. And, in the longest study of human intelligence on record, almost 70 years, researchers at the University of Edinburgh investigated the link between happiness with social relationships and cognitive change and life satisfaction among 1,000 Scottish women and men.[62] After adjustment for gender, education, social class, and IQ at age 11, at age 79 loneliness remained a significant predictor of IQ.[63]

Because these longitudinal investigations with different designs produced the same results in four different parts of the world and used different means of assessing social networks and cognition and used subjects ranging widely in age, education, and mental ability, we can be more certain that their findings are valid. Larger social networks do in fact reduce the risk of substantial deterioration of intellectual skills and dementia.

The most sobering information in these studies of social relationships is about the highly adverse effects of isolation and loneliness. While not everyone who lives alone feels lonely because they have the feeling of being connected to others,[64] it is clear that having no one we can count on in our life greatly increases our chances of serious illness, cognitive impairment, dementia, and death. As we might anticipate, those who feel cut off from family and lacking even one caring connection are usually the sickest and poorest among us.[65]

Manage Stress

Managing the stresses in day-to-day living remains a challenge to the end of our lives. Optimally aging individuals in our study were no strangers to stress. Many had to cope with remarkable challenges:

Lee

Lee (age 72) says his mental health is excellent, which is remarkable when you consider what he has been through. As a young dissident in China, Lee suffered years of government persecution. This included being taken away from his family and spending time in a labor camp for "re-education" when, as a middle-aged professor, he demonstrated with his students in the late 1980s. What happened after he was released, and how he got from China to the United States, he did not say, merely commenting, "It was quite an experience."

When his feet touched the ground in America, this land of immigrants, the feeling of freedom overwhelmed him. As he put it, "Just to be able to say what you think was incredible." Since he has been in the United States, his life has not been stress free. Ten years ago, he had a heart attack that he barely survived. Then 8 years ago, the company he was working for went out of business, so he got a part-time job at a computer repair shop. Four years later, his oldest daughter contracted leukemia and died, leaving his wife and himself to help raise two grandchildren. Then last year, his doctor found some small nodules on his prostate gland and suspected that he might have prostate cancer. He is now being treated with watchful waiting.

When Lee asked how he got through all of this, he said that he had always tried to get ready for the bad things in life. When the real thing came, he still felt angry, upset, and in a panic at first. When that happens, he said that you have to fight against your self-pity. One of the things that helps him is looking at pictures of African children suffering with AIDS. They have always shocked and touched him and made him feel fortunate compared to them. And then, he thinks of all that he has been through and how it has steeled him. Lee says his heart is filled with gratitude for his good fortune. To him, the biggest holiday is not Christmas or Chinese New Year, but Thanksgiving. On that holiday, Lee likes to say, "How lucky I am to live my twilight years on this free land."

Although less dramatic than Lee's story, a number of optimal cognitive agers told equally moving stories of confronting stresses in their lives: chronic abuse and injury at the hands of drunken, neglectful parents; the traumatic death of parents, leaving a boy to be raised in an orphanage; a woman having to drop out of college to support her mother and then spending the rest of her working life as a seamstress rather than the teacher she once dreamed of being; a 75-year-old with her own medical problems caring for a husband with mild Alzheimer's disease and 40-year-old daughter with Down syndrome.

What was most instructive about these case histories was the degree to which being an optimal ager depended on how they coped with the stresses in their lives rather than the traumatic events themselves. Certain patterns were repeated, some of which are illustrated in Lee's story. Experts in anxiety management describe two ways of lowering tensions associated with stress: problem-focused coping and emotion-focused coping.[66] Problem-focused coping actions reduce emotional distress by confronting a problem directly. When Lee had problems urinating, he went to the doctor to find out why. Prior to going to the doctor, he anticipated the possibility that he might have prostate cancer and planned how he was going to deal with it. Emotion-focused coping behaviors cause him to feel a little bit better, although they do little to relieve the source of the upset. Lee thinks about the people in Darfur who have it far worse than he does and how lucky he is to have access to first-rate medical care.

Although most of us have a sense of what is meant by the term *stress*, a precise definition is elusive.[67] The definition I have in mind is an event that disrupts normal physical and mental homeostatic balance and causes automatic physiological and psychological reactions. Canadian physician Hans Selye devoted much of his 60-year career to studying the nature of stress. He pointed to four different sources of stressors: overstress, having too much to deal with; understress, being bored because no interesting challenges await; bad stress, confronting negative, threatening events; and good stress, enjoying positive, exciting events.[68]

When does the stress in our lives change from being good to bad or from enough to too much? Two factors that influence the negative impact of stress on our body and mind are the amount of stress we confront and the length of time we must deal with it.

A number of people who are burdened with a great deal of stress also begin to have physical problems. They seem to be sick more often or may feel exhausted and function below par at work or at home. Pittsburgh scientists wondered whether the amount of stress people had to deal with affected their vulnerability to catching the flu.[69] When the researchers divided the volunteers into high and low scorers on a stress scale, they found that those with more stress developed the flu 50% more often than those whose stress scores were below average.

How long we have to endure the strain is another important factor in our reaction to unpleasant events. An example comes from the studies of bomber crews during World War II.[70] In June of 1944, those 8th Air Force crews who had flown between 6 and 15 missions had a sick call rate of 20%. But, half of the young men who had flown more than 30 combat missions reported to the medical clinic with a wide array of physical disorders and emotional maladjustments.

Why does stress make us more vulnerable to illness? The main reason is that stress activates the "fight-or-flight" response—an instinctive physical reaction to stress, probably inherited from our ancient ancestors, who needed all of their energies to engage or flee from a threat. When facing a stressful event, we secrete several chemicals into the blood, including two hormones called adrenalin and cortisol. Their functions are to mobilize those physiological systems essential for our immediate survival by enabling the release of fatty acids and the utilization of glucose for energy production to cope with the stresses. In addition, these mechanisms suppress functions unnecessary for immediate survival. Thus, cortisol and adrenalin combine to increase blood pressure, heart rate, and glucose levels while inhibiting digestion, reproduction, formation of antibodies and white blood cells, and any other systems that are not needed in the struggle to survive.[71]

This system works well when we are confronting a threat or running for our life. But, continued elevation of stress hormones can result in chronically high blood pressure and lower insulin levels, increasing the risk for developing hypertension, cardiovascular disease, and type 2 diabetes as well as promoting slower healing rates and neuronal loss.

The majority of studies performed in human populations reported negative effects of stress hormones on the memory functions of older adults.[72] Long-term exposure to high levels of stress-activated hormones is associated with both memory impairment and decreased volume in the hippocampus.[73]

Here is an example from another war. Figure 4.2 graphs the relation between the severity of exposure to combat and the brain's hippocampal volume.[74]

We can see that hippocampal volume decreased most among those veterans with the greatest combat exposure. The stress hormones that adversely affect the hippocampus also damage cortical and subcortical brain structures.[75] Though they're not being shot at, other individuals suffering from chronic stress, such as people who are chronically depressed, also exhibit significant cerebral atrophy.

While quite a bit is known about the adverse effects on younger brains, far less is known about how stress has an impact on cognitive performance in older age. We do know that older adults have higher baseline cortisol levels than younger adults when not under stress. This may be why the mere anticipation of being given a mental test increases already elevated cortisol levels sufficiently to impair memory in 3rd Agers, while younger subjects remain unaffected.[76] When the older subjects were able to lower their stress levels prior to the cognitive testing, their performance improved.

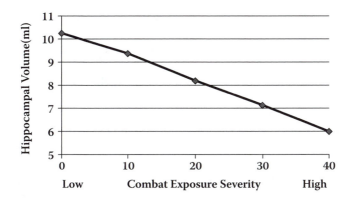

Figure 4.2 Severity of Viet Nam combat exposure and neuronal count in the hippocampus. (Adapted from Gurvits, T. V., Shenton, M. E., Hokama, H., Ohta, H., Lasko, N. B., Gilbertson, M. W., Orr, S. P., Kikinis, R., Jolesz, F. A., McCarley, R. W., & Pitman, R. H. (1996). Magnetic resonance imaging study of hippocampal volume in chronic combat-related posttraumatic stress disorder. *Biological Psychiatry, 40*, 1091-1099.)

Most older adults enjoy high levels of emotional well-being and emotional stability into their 70s and 80s. This has resulted in significantly lower worldwide percentages of anxiety, depression, and other mental disorders among 3rd Agers compared to those at midlife. Individuals 65+ living in four different communities were interviewed to determine whether they met the criteria for depression, anxiety disorders, or other mental conditions. Among the 45–64 midlifers, 16.4% were diagnosed with one of these disorders, compared to 10.2% of the 65+ group.[77]

My colleagues and I partially verified this last point by looking at the responses of the 3rd Age subjects from the Florida Geriatric Research Program. They had taken a personality test that scored them on the stress emotions of anxiety, depression, and anger.[78] The results showed that those 3rd Age subjects who were not anxious, depressed, or angry were in better health and exhibited less cognitive decline than those reporting more severe distress.

What changes occur in older adults that enable them to be better at controlling their emotions? A major factor contributing to an increased desire to keep their emotions under control is that elders have learned that when their stress response is switched on there is a sluggish return to a normal condition. Once the stress hormones begin circulating in the bloodstream, 3rd Agers quickly feel the heart racing, blood pressure rising, and respiration speeding up. However, instead of the hour or less it took in midlife for the adrenalin rush to shut down after the stress has passed, the older body takes 2–3 times as long to return to normal.[79] So, older adults tend to avoid disagreeable people and situations that are likely to trigger an adrenalin rush.

A second factor contributing to 3rd Agers being better at controlling their emotions is the "positivity effect."[80] This is a developmental pattern in which the attention gradually shifts from gathering knowledge, often novel and challenging, to expand their horizons in youth and midlife to a stronger focus on positive information that is less stimulating but more comforting emotionally in the 3rd Age. Many elders systematically regulate their emotional state by accentuating the positive and ignoring the negative. In laboratory settings, they pay more attention to pleasant than unpleasant material. When asked to remember the pictures or words they viewed earlier, older adults will recall many more of the pleasant ones than young and middle-aged adults. MRI studies found that they have less memory for negative material because they pay less attention to it in the first place, so the information is never encoded.[81]

Although 3rd Agers periodically push out the boundaries of their comfort zone by travel to foreign lands or auditing college classes, the relative importance of new knowledge acquisition diminishes with age. For instance, older and younger adults were shown two different ads for a cruise with exactly the same pictures. The only difference was in the slogans. The first said, "Capture those special moments," while the second read, "Capture the unexplored world." Guess which one the older adults favored? It was the first option because it focused on emotional satisfaction, while the younger group was drawn to the new experiences to be had in the unexplored world.[82]

Reflections and Applications

Few people would be surprised to read that these healthy lifestyle habits are linked to better overall health. For those caring for other people, however, it is useful to have this common wisdom buttressed by empirical evidence and clinical studies. These 21st century investigations also give us a clearer idea of how much each of these lifestyle habits contributes individually and collectively to better health and a keener intellect.

For practitioners, these healthy lifestyle habits are useful points to keep in mind when working with 3rd Agers. This information can be reassuring to our patients and clients who feel there is nothing they can do to slow the pace of their decline. Consider exercise. The long-term study of older doctors found that those who did not exercise or practice any of the other healthy lifestyle habits had a 21% greater chance of dying of a heart condition prior to age 75. Just exercising by itself reduced the risk by nearly half.[83]

Other healthy habits make a difference as well. We have already learned that nutrition has about the same positive effect as exercise on cardiovascular health and blood pressure. In combination, they are more potent. Any three of these modifiable lifestyle habits lower the threat of mortality due to heart disease or developing hypertension by 35–50%.[84]

The same healthy habits benefit the intellect. We learned that regular exercise for only 1 to 3 months brings cognitive benefits. Optimal agers do not have to work out to be mentally sharp. Nonathletic leisure activities provide much of the same value to the mind as regular exercise, including slowing atrophy of brain tissue.

In an article "Smoking Kills, Obesity Disables," Dutch researchers analyzing U.S. data made the point that, unlike most other medical conditions, obesity increases the likelihood of disability in older adults without substantially shortening life span.[85] While this conclusion requires verification,[86] growing agreement is also accumulating in the United States that obesity among people aged 65 and older raises the odds of their becoming disabled because of arthritis, the complications of type 2 diabetes, or heart disease without much reducing life expectancy. It also triples the likelihood of developing dementia.

Also worrisome is that the historically high percentage of obese 3rd Age women and men is likely to grow even larger as record numbers of corpulent baby boomers move into their retirement years. A health survey found that just over 40% of women and men aged 55–64 exceed the threshold for obesity compared to about 35% for those a decade older. And, the younger end of the baby boomer generation, those aged 45–54, also have a record high percentage of obese members.[87] While we await confirmation of these findings from other longer-term studies, these facts argue that unless medical science and technology can find a reliable means of helping older people control their adiposity, we can look forward to rising disability rates and greater obesity-related cognitive impairment in the visible future, along with greatly increased health care costs.

Elder care workers can contribute to reversing this trend. Begin by bringing up the hazards of excess weight with clients for whom this is an obvious problem. It is a rare overweight or obese older person who has not at some point tried or thought about trying to lose weight. And, just as with attempting to stop smoking or drinking, the failure rate is high. However, once started in a program such as those described (diet, diet and exercise, meal replacements, and medications), the success odds for older people are much better than chance.[88] Studies on the effect of voluntary weight loss in the 3rd Age are scarce, but they indicated that even small amounts of weight loss (between 5 and 10% of initial body weight) are beneficial. While these efforts with older women and men need to be cleared with health care providers before going ahead, the reality is that thousands of older people are helped every year to decrease their weight.

The momentum may already be shifting in a positive direction. One sign is the popularity of reality television programs such as *The Biggest Loser*, which showcases very obese people making concerted efforts to shed excess poundage. Each of these programs has a sympathetic view of the challenges of losing weight and demonstrates on a weekly basis that progress is possible. Another positive sign is that the U.S. first lady Michelle Obama has taken on the mission of combating childhood obesity. If that initiative is successful, the benefits should filter upward to the children's parents. Also, fast-food restaurants are beginning to offer healthier low-fat meals. Finally, it may be my imagination, but in the two gyms where I work out, an increasing number of overweight and obese people are keeping me company.

Experts in the field of alcohol misuse distinguish among people who are drinking normally, those who are at risk (also known as heavy drinkers), and problem drinkers (alcohol abuse and dependency).[89] For those who care for the elderly, defining "normal" drinking may be a major challenge. The reason is that specialists who advocate no more than one drink a day are often at odds with recent research evidence in community-based studies that show no significant risk to health of two to three daily drinks for men and two for women.[90] These standards also may be scoffed at by older women and men who have been drinking more than the recommended amount all their lives and have had no ill effects.

It is also true, however, that our elder clients need to be made aware that the data showing no substantial adverse health effects of heavier drinking were based on younger adults, and that these same patterns of alcohol use may be much riskier in the 3rd Age. This is because there are decreasing amounts of water in older bodies (less water to dilute the alcohol intake) and slower metabolism, as well as the increasing likelihood of being on medications that have the potential for dangerous interactions with alcohol. All evidence considered, it seems reasonable for 3rd Agers to have a lower threshold for alcohol intake.

Spotting older alcohol misusers can be difficult. One reason they are hard to identify is because about one in three did not develop drinking problems until late in life, which is contrary to the usual pattern of people drinking less as they grow older. Because they are late-onset problem drinkers and have a lengthy stable work and family history with no obvious health, psychosocial, or legal problems, and because they have a relatively briefer history of problem drinking, hurried providers may skip right over questions about alcohol use. These at-risk or problems drinkers appear too healthy, too "normal" to be misusing alcohol.

Another reason is that older patients who drink more than they should sometimes present health care providers with a diagnostic quandary. Are their symptoms of fatigue, irritability, insomnia, tremors, memory problems, or driving accidents produced by diagnosed medical conditions, or could they be related to another factor, such as alcohol abuse or dependence? Another barrier to diagnosing alcohol problems in older adults is stereotyping. Females are much less likely to be asked about their drinking patterns than males.[91]

Older adults who worry that they may be drinking too much may be ashamed to admit it, so they are relieved when the doctor does not bring it up. Often, the relatives and children of older imbibers collaborate in minimizing the seriousness of a loved one's condition. "Dad's cocktails are the only thing that make him happy now after Grandma died," or "What difference does it make if my sister gets a little high in the afternoon? She worked hard all her life, and she deserves a little fun."

When we are concerned about drinking habits of our clients, a useful instrument is the CAGE, a brief alcohol abuse screening instrument that has been used effectively with older adults. The CAGE (acronym for cut back, annoyed, guilt, and eye opener) asks these four questions:[92]

1. Have you ever felt that you should cut down on your drinking?
2. Have people ever annoyed you by criticizing your drinking?
3. Have you ever felt badly or guilty about drinking?
4. Have you ever had a drink the first thing in the morning to steady your nerves or get rid of a hangover?

Two or more positive responses are believed by some clinicians to indicate alcohol abuse and dependence. The National Institute on Alcohol Abuse and Alcoholism (NIAAA) recommends that one positive response is suitable for identifying problem drinkers among the elderly.[93]

The importance of social relationships for both physical and intellectual well-being has always been apparent to most caregivers. But, only recently has it become apparent that health care professionals and others looking after older adults should put social well-being high up on the list of healthy lifestyle habits to monitor. Older people with more friends are healthier and mentally keener than those with fewer friends. Adding to our understanding are the recent findings about the dangers of isolation. Recent evidence suggests that the difference in health benefits between more and fewer social connections is relatively small. The large negative impact on health and cognition occurs with people who are isolated, with no one to turn to in times of difficulty.[94]

Those in the 3rd Age are better at regulating their emotions when stressed than middle-aged men and women. One contributing factor is the positivity bias, which causes elders to more often ignore negative information and pay attention to more soothing positive material. While keeping stress-related emotions under control has a definite upside, the positivity bias can be a doubled-edged sword when complex decisions need to be made. When older adults were asked to choose among several models of cars, using a chart with six pieces of information (e.g., riding comfort, gas mileage, resale value, etc.), they spent more time thinking about the attractive qualities of each option and less time considering the less-appealing trade-offs such as better gas mileage coming at the cost of riding comfort.[95]

Now, suppose a woman in your care wants to talk to you about moving into a continuing care retirement community. Before she brings the matter up with her children who live half a continent away, she wants to have made the decision about where she is moving. She knows she wants to live independently in a one-bedroom apartment. In her town, there are three choices. All have attractive brochures heralding an active lifestyle in a country club atmosphere, with concierge and maid service and skilled chefs preparing the meals. On the spacious grounds are a fitness center, heated pool, and tennis courts. Medical care and beauty/barber shops are on site. Buses will take her shopping and to cultural and sporting events. Plus, there are opportunities for volunteer work, lifelong learning, and travel.

That is the appealing part. But, what about the comparative costs? Here are just five financial factors that she will need to weigh: (a) the initial cost of the apartment; (b) whether to pay more for the unit up front for her estate to recover 50% or 90% of the initial cost of the apartment; (c) monthly charges; (d) the choice of how comprehensive the coverage will be (does she want to live out her years there, moving from independent living to nursing care, or remain only through her independent-living years and move elsewhere when she needs more help?); and (e) the financial penalty if she moves in but decides she does not like it and wants to move out.

She can feel the stress hormones kick in as she confronts the chore of acquainting herself with the primary costs for each retirement community, writing down the comparative charges of each of the options, then thinking through the necessary compromises that work best for her. Does she decide to buy a less expensive apartment but then pay more per month or vice-versa? Is paying more monthly to ensure end-of-life nursing care worth it? What if she has a heart attack and dies playing tennis and never uses the nursing care?

Since you are not an attorney, how can you help this woman make a well-reasoned decision? You might begin by remembering that the positivity effect may predispose her to be drawn more to the appealing features of the brochures than gritty financial details. You will want to be sure that she does not make the same mistakes as the subjects who focused on the positive features of the cars and could recall much less about their negative qualities.

Research also showed that when older adults are encouraged to concentrate on the unpleasant as well as the pleasant aspects of information presented to them, they can let go of their positivity bias and balance the pluses and minuses, just as younger adults do.[96] Part of your job will be to make sure that she is focusing on the negatives as well as the positives of each option and to support her in the hard work of thinking carefully about the choices that she will have to make.

Another instance in which the positivity bias works against elders is telemarketing fraud, which robs Americans of an estimated $40 *billion* a year. A large proportion of those swindled are 3rd Agers. Findings from an Elder Fraud Project sponsored by AARP discovered that there are an estimated 14,000 illegal telemarketing operations bilking thousands of victims every day.[97] Older people are special targets because some may want to give the caller the benefit of the doubt, instinctively suspend disbelief, and embrace the telemarketer's good news that they have struck it rich.

For the clinical researchers among us, several cross-sectional studies might be interesting to consider. For instance, (a) what is the relation between diet and cognitive functions on tests other than dementia screening scales? (b) How much do 3rd Agers really drink compared to how much they say they consume? (c) How do older adults go about filling the gaps in their social circles? (d) When elders have difficult choices to make, what do they think helps them make good decisions? (e) Does the positivity effect, which sometimes causes elders not to pay attention to information that might be upsetting to them, affect their willingness to listen to opinions that differ from their own? (f) How frequently are elders in your care approached by probable swindlers?

Though we may not engage in these activities with the idea that they will directly benefit the mind, healthy lifestyle habits have a strong positive impact on the intellect. The next chapter looks at activities that do directly influence our intellectual capabilities.

5

Direct Actions That Benefit the Intellect

This chapter summarizes five actions older people can take that directly benefit the aging intellect. These are different from the healthy lifestyle habits—such as exercise or diet—discussed in Chapter 4, which enhance intellect at the same time that they contribute to physical well-being. When 3rd Agers practice these direct actions, they aim to maximize intellectual powers. The five actions that directly boost mental vigor are working smarter; applying selection, optimization, and compensation; recognizing that active experience matters; giving consideration to cognitive training; and engaging in attention restoration activities.

Working Smarter: Anticipate Cognitive Decline and Minimize Negative Effects

Even though considerable individual variation occurs in the rate at which mental abilities fall away, reports from even the best functioning 3rd Age women and men have confirmed that certain of their cognitive skills are weaker than in midlife. Impressive to my students and me were the number of older people who anticipated some of these mental challenges and developed ways of coping. This contributed to their aging optimally.

For instance, in Chapter 3 we looked at evidence showing an age-related slowing in processing speed and a shrinking of working memory. So, when an optimally aging couple begins to plan their son's surprise 50th birthday, they allocate plenty of time to think about the guests to invite, write out the shopping list, and decide on the house decorations. Accepting the fact that that their attention span was not what it once was, they work in a quiet space away from distractions. And, they avoid multitasking by stopping work on the party arrangements when they have to take a phone call.

Others found ways to cope with different reduced aptitudes. Several disciplined themselves to plan their route in advance for long driving trips and to check their progress frequently while en route. Others wrote down or memorized where they parked their car at the mall. One inspired man painted a smiley face on a yellow helium balloon that he kept in his trunk and tied to his antenna when he went grocery shopping.

Working smarter is to know when we are at our best. Consider our diurnal cycle, which is our biological 24-hour clock. During some portions of the day, we normally work, relax, and sleep. During some periods of our daily cycle, we are considerably sharper and more mentally vigorous than other parts of the day.

On the whole, 3rd Agers are livelier in the morning than later in the day, while the opposite applies to younger adults. The evidence comes from psychologists at Duke University.[1] Of the older women and men they studied, 96% said they were most alert during the morning. This tendency was even more striking because all the older volunteers were retired and could set their own schedules. Among the younger volunteers, a mere 12% said they were morning people.

The memory of older and younger subjects was tested when they were at the peak of their diurnal cycles and when they were at the low point. The subjects were asked to read 10 short stories. Later, they were shown a series of sentences, half of which were contained in the stories they had just read ("hits") and half that were not ("misses"). The subjects were asked if the sentences had appeared in any of the stories they had read.

The Duke investigators found that the older subjects outperformed the younger ones in the morning if we judge by hits, or how accurately a sentence was recognized as having been read. In the afternoon, the picture was very different. Young adults greatly improved their hits and also committed fewer errors. Among the older adults, the error rate (believing incorrectly that a sentence had been included in the stories read earlier) increased by nearly 50%. The investigators speculated that this was because older adults have more difficulty inhibiting incorrect answers in the afternoon.[2]

Because considerable variation exists among 3rd Agers, not everyone is at their best in the morning. But, each will have a time when his or her own intellectual skills are at their peak and at a low point. Appreciating this reality enables those who want to be the best they can be mentally to schedule their most demanding work when they are at their diurnal peak. One of the best strategies for maximizing intellectual function is the SOC technique.

Applying Selection, Optimization, and Compensation

If we anticipate that we are likely to experience an age-related decline in our mental abilities, we can apply some of the homemade tactics described above. We also can apply the strategy of selection, optimization, and compensation (SOC).[3] Developed by Paul Baltes and his coworkers at the Max Planck Institute in Germany, this strategy has three components.

The first component is selection. This involves giving up some activities to concentrate available mental energies on those remaining. Researchers distinguish between loss-based selection and elective selection. Loss-based selection occurs when someone can no longer engage in those activities that previously gave them pleasure. Examples are an executive's involuntary retirement or macular degeneration that closes the door on playing golf. Coping with these losses entails choosing alternative activities that provide a measure of gratification. The executive joins the community hospital board, which welcomes her management skills. The man with visual problems finds that swimming in the senior center pool provides him with a more vigorous workout than golf.

In elective selection, those activities that continue to have priority are usually chosen because of skills, motivations, and opportunities. An aging physician wishes to remain active. In midlife, he had a busy practice, taught medical students, and most years had a small clinical research project in progress. In his "spare time," he served on professional committees and boards. By his mid-60s, he chooses to focus his energies on those patients and types of activities he likes best, cutting back on other professional responsibilities he once enjoyed but are less central to patient care. He lets go of the committee work, the research, and the consulting and decides to take no new patients. While there are moments when he misses these "selected-out" activities, this decision enables him to keep working at what he most enjoys about medicine, which is practicing it.

The next ingredient of the SOC strategy is optimization. Continuing with the aging doctor, this means doing everything he can to maximize his performance by anticipating the potential negative effects of cognitive aging. Although he dislikes the idea of having to wear a hearing aid because he thinks it makes him look elderly, he recognizes that he is starting to miss some of the things his patients and coworkers are saying, so he is fitted with a device that optimizes his listening ability. Keeping up with the recent developments in medicine and taking short courses to maintain and upgrade his medical skills become priority items in his yearly schedule.

Optimization requires more time for preparation. For this older doctor, this entails carefully reviewing the charts of patients in advance of their appointments rather than counting on the ability to get a picture of the medical history with a quick scan while talking to the patient. The aging physician also begins to dictate notes right after seeing the patient instead of waiting until the end of the day. Cognitive optimization includes doing one task at a time. Aware of the hazards of multitasking, the still-working older physician avoids making notes in a patient's chart while talking to someone else on the telephone.

Compensation is the final component. If the aging physician is the sort of person whose mental functions are keener in the morning than later in the day, he tries to schedule his most difficult patients in the morning and slate other, less-challenging professional activities in the afternoon. He stops memorizing phone numbers and enters them in his smart phone. He now leans more heavily on computerized expert analyses of lab tests rather than relying on his once keen diagnostic skills to detect significant patterns.

Compensation also means doing everything that can be done to replenish the physician's energy during the workday. If he cannot avoid having to deal with late-day mental challenges, he may compensate for fading mental acuity in the late afternoon with a brief nap or a cup of tea and a sugar cookie. Research showed that older adults taking brief naps (20–50 minutes in length) felt less sleepy afterward and reported an increased sense of efficacy.[4] Whether feeling more awake actually translates into higher-quality mental operations has yet to be demonstrated. Certainly, the 3rd Age nappers believe this to be the case.

There have been decades of empirical support for the idea that something sweet helps maintain cognitive acuity. Nondiabetic adults of all ages exhibited improved memory when given glucose as opposed to a placebo. The evidence for this recommendation came from the work done by researchers at the universities of Illinois and Virginia.[5] In one study, the investigators wondered whether nondiabetic senior adults would exhibit better memory following the intake of glucose. To answer this question, they gave volunteers who had fasted the night before a beverage containing either glucose or saccharin. Then, the volunteers took memory tests. The next day, investigators repeated the process but switched drinks: Those participants who had been given glucose the day before received saccharin drinks; those who had saccharin previously were now given glucose. Then, the researchers repeated the testing.

When they compared the memory test scores of each volunteer on sugar and on saccharin, they found that both short- and long-term verbal memory were stronger on glucose. After ingesting sugar, volunteers recalled 38% more words correctly than when they had drunk saccharin. Longer-term memory also increased. Since short- and long-term verbal memory usually decline with age, we may find that a cup a tea with sugar in the later afternoon will help us maintain our mental vigor.

SOC has been one of the most actively researched strategies for maximizing intellectual powers in older adulthood. Investigators in many parts of the world, in disciplines ranging from medicine to business, have found significant correlations between the SOC strategy and optimal aging. They include maintaining job competence, enjoying leisure activities, moderating financial strain, and coping with physical disability.[6]

The SOC strategy can also be helpful for poorer, older, sicker people. Berlin investigators compared how often the technique was used by older subjects with fewer resources (lower income levels and cognitive test scores, poorer health, and smaller social networks) compared to their age mates with greater advantages. They discovered that, over a period of 1 year, less-advantaged 3rd Agers who applied the SOC strategy more often were happier with the quality of their lives than less-frequent users.[7]

The usefulness of the SOC strategy is not limited to older adults. Prime-of-lifers may also find it advantageous.[8] Imagine being a married, career-oriented female broker who has a baby. Following the birth of the child, she goes back to work. Here is how SOC can help her: Because of having less time, she focuses on her work with clients rather than networking within the organization. She optimizes by staying abreast of new developments in her field and studying for the Series 7 examination, which will qualify her to sell all types of financial products. She compensates for not being in the office as often by carrying a smart phone so that her clients can call or e-mail her at any time.

Recognizing That Experience Matters: Captain Chesley Sullenberger of Flight 1549

It was 90 seconds after takeoff from New York City's LaGuardia airport when U.S. Airways Flight 1549 hit the flock of geese. The pilots flinched as large birds filled the windscreen and heard loud thumps as the geese struck the airplane. When geese were sucked into the two jet engines of the Airbus 320, the turbines shut down. The smell of burning fowl filled the cabin as the powerless aircraft, carrying 155 passengers and crew, dropped silently from the sky over Manhattan.

When the two engines lost thrust, Captain Chesley Sullenberger's initial reaction was a very human one of disbelief. "I can't believe this is happening," he remembered thinking. "It was the worst, sickening, pit-of-your-stomach, falling-through-the-floor feeling I've ever felt in my life. I knew immediately it was very bad."[9] It was bad indeed. Imagine sitting in Captain Sullenberger's left cockpit seat. Warning lights suddenly flash all over the instrument panel, alarms ring, familiar gauges do not work, and video screens flash bad news about inoperative aircraft systems and scroll check-lists of emergency procedures.

If we were to hear the tapes of his conversations with the air traffic control center during this emergency, we would find that Captain Sullenberger's initial reactions were not apparent. He took control of the emergency, delegated responsibility, communicated clearly with the air traffic controller, rapidly assessed his options for landing the aircraft, made a decision, and demonstrated remarkable flying skill in the 3 minutes between the bird strike and when he executed what was called the "miracle on the Hudson" (Figure 5.1).

Here are just a few of the things that Captain Sullenberger had to do mentally while piloting the aircraft. His first action would have been to quickly control his own emotions, which he described as "an adrenalin rush," channeling this energy to meet the challenge of landing an airliner without working engines. Split seconds after the engines quit, he took control of the aircraft, saying, "My airplane." This freed the copilot to hurry through the checklists, including engine-restart procedures and instructions for emergency landings.

This left Captain Sullenberger with the decision of where to land the plane. It had to be somewhere close since he was descending at about 1,000 feet per minute. In less than 60 seconds, Captain Sullenberger considered and rejected three options offered by the air traffic controller, including returning to LaGuardia, which required a steep turn that could lead to a fatal stall over the Bronx. Then, he decided that the best choice was to set the Airbus 320 down in the Hudson River.

Captain Sullenberger made as gentle a crash landing as possible on the Hudson, if the word *gentle* can be used to describe what it must feel like to be inside an 80-ton aircraft slamming onto the water tail first at 130 mph. His skillful piloting enabled the aircraft to float long enough for the flight attendants to evacuate all the passengers before the plane flooded. They

Figure 5.1 The miracle on the Hudson: Flight 1549, Captain Chesley B. Sullenberger III, January 15, 2009. [Photo reprinted with permission of Thomson Reuters (Markets) LLC.]

were quickly surrounded by boats on the Hudson and rescued. The last person to leave the plane was Captain Sullenberger, who walked through the passenger cabin twice to verify that no one was left behind.

When he crash landed Flight 1549 into the Hudson River, saving all aboard, Captain Sullenberger was old in pilot years. At 57½, he was just a few years short of mandatory retirement.[10]

Active Experience Matters to All of Us

One of the reasons the remarkable saga of Captain Sullenberger captured my attention is that he demonstrated the value of active experience in maintaining those mental skills most vulnerable to aging. Processing speed slows with age, so most people nearing 60 need nearly twice as long to problem solve than 40-year-olds. On average, visuospatial aptitudes at 60 are 20% lower than at 40 years of age.[11] Yet, Captain Sullenberger reacted swiftly to the emergency and quickly visualized the possible scenarios—whether the powerless aircraft could glide back safely to LaGuardia, could make it to another airport, or should crash land in the Hudson River.

Captain Sullenberger also showed prime-of-life executive functions: attention, inhibition of distractions, planning, working memory, and mental flexibility. When the engines shut down as roasting geese jammed the turbines, the cockpit instrument panel came alive with warning lights, alarms, and scrolling videos. Captain Sullenberger had to block out all but the most important of this information to decide where to land the airplane.

To land safely, he needed a workable plan, which he created and modified twice in less than 60 seconds. Then, he exhibited an efficient working memory and a young person's ability to multitask as the Airbus 320 dropped out of the sky at 230 mph. While controlling the aircraft, Captain Sullenberger had to keep track of the airspeed, wind direction, and descent rate; stay in radio contact with air traffic control; mentally rehearse the ditching procedure checklist; and finally slow the plane to its minimal flying speed without stalling before setting it down tail first in the river.

The remarkable saga of Captain Sullenberger demonstrates the value of active experience to aging optimally. His story is particularly refreshing because for more than a half century experts have downplayed the value of experience in the mental functioning of older adults.[12] Beyond midlife, there is a normal tendency for people to accumulate new knowledge at a slower rate, relying more instead on familiar ways of thinking and doing things.[13]

Suppose that instead of coasting toward retirement after their 40s, individuals continue to be active learners—challenging themselves to think about new ways of doing things, keeping up with the latest technology, and subjecting themselves to continual upgrading of their occupational skills.

What happens then is that we have optimal cognitive agers like Captain Sullenberger.

The day after he landed in the Hudson River, he was asked if he had "ice water" running through his veins because of his cool demeanor throughout the emergency and afterward. Captain Sullenberger's reply, "No. This was business, doing what we were trained to do." Certainly, training had a lot to do with it. Airline pilots must pass yearly check rides by Federal Aviation Administration inspectors so they need to keep their skills current. Crews regularly practice working together in simulated emergencies—although probably loss of power because the engines were clogged with frying geese has not yet been included among the scenarios.

Captain Sullenberger's *active* professional experience was likely a major factor in his remarkable feat. Highlights from his résumé include these active experiences: When he landed in the Hudson River, he had logged over 19,000 flying hours while flying fighter jets for the U.S. Air Force and as a commercial airline pilot. Captain Sullenberger trained to be a flight instructor for conventional aircraft, as well as—believe it or not—gliders. He volunteered to become a check pilot, overseeing the upgrading of first officers to captain. Captain Sullenberger found the time to work on dozens of committees to promote flight safety and improve passenger comfort. He spearheaded the first effort to bring flight emergency training to airline crews. NASA used Captain Sullenberger's expertise in crew training, and he investigated airplane accidents with the National Transportation and Safety Board.

Captain Sullenberger spoke of the role of experience in his amazing feat this way: "For 42 years, I've been making small regular deposits in this bank of experience, education and training. And on January 15, the balance was sufficient so that I could make a very large withdrawal."

"Now wait a minute, how does this apply to me?" you might think. "I'm not a pilot, just an ordinary person living an ordinary life. I have nowhere near the same opportunities for learning new things or for being regularly checked out to see if I can still cut it." True, but all of us in the 3rd Age have had a life full of potential learning experiences: from those roads taken and not; from successes and failures; from those times we struggled to resolve unavoidable and difficult problems while being pulled this way and that by conflicting viewpoints; when every solution we could think of had something wrong with it—all the while struggling to control feelings of anxiety, uncertainty, and despair so that we could do our job and raise a family.

The special value of experience is that it can help us solve complex problems that require a judgment about important matters in our life for which the outcome is uncertain. Where are we going to live when we move from the big house? How do we best preserve our financial assets in this economy? Should we sign up for long-term health care insurance? Is it time to give up our driver's license?

Imagine being Hank, a 78-year-old widower, who for 40-some years has lived comfortably in a small, affordable house in Lincoln, Nebraska. He likes living independently, even mowing his own lawn and shoveling the snow in the winter. Then, one February Hank falls hard on the icy driveway and breaks his hip.

As Hank is recovering, his son, who lives in San Diego, calls and insists that dad come to live with them or at least rent an apartment nearby. His New York City daughter recommends that Hank move to that gated community in Florida where Hank has a time-share. Hank always enjoys those 4 weeks there in the winter, so wouldn't it be nice to be there most of the year? Then, his doctor reminds Hank that in addition to the broken hip he has a bad back and type 2 diabetes. She gently points out that in the future things are probably not going to get better physically for Hank and recommends that he consider moving into the new continuing care residential community in Lincoln. Some of his friends are already living there, plus he would not have to worry anymore about shoveling snow.

Hank's active experience makes several contributions to helping him reach important decisions about complicated matters. Hank knows he has faced tough choices before and has resolved most of them successfully. He remembers that time in his 40s when he was offered a promotion, but with regret turned the opportunity down because it involved moving away from a community he loved. In his early 60s, Hank was offered early retirement and, after giving it lots of thought, took it. Then, 5 years ago, following his wife's death, Hank thought about moving south but decided to stay put. While his current situation requires selecting among alternatives he has not confronted in the past, he is familiar with the challenge of sorting through the different options and making a decision. And, with one or two exceptions, the past results have been pretty good.

His experience also has taught Hank something about himself. While he does not dwell on it, Hank realizes that he is the sort of person who dislikes change. When he suddenly has to deal with a new problem, he is aware that initially he may feel overwhelmed by surges of anxiety and helplessness. These feelings pass, but once or twice in the past the initial anxiety made it difficult to make a choice, and Hank was late in pulling the trigger. As a result, Hank has learned to take his time solving a dilemma and to set a deadline for making a decision. Hank also knows that he likes having more, rather than less, information, so he reads the local California and Florida newspapers online to accumulate information about the differences in cost of living, tax advantages, lifestyle, social groups, volunteer opportunities, and access to health care. Looking at census tables, he calculates his active life expectancy at 78.

From his experience, Hank has an idea about how to proceed when the task is complicated. He has learned that every major decision, no matter how daunting it seems at first, consists of smaller and solvable components. In addition, Hank knows how to prioritize: First, he must face the fact that he will have to move; second, he needs to set out a preliminary list of the options; third, he should identify family and confidantes to consult; fourth, Hank has to make an approximate time schedule; and sixth, he will "field test" the alternatives by spending several weeks in California and Florida.

Over the years of problem solving, Hank has also discovered that he is not alone. Around him are friends, family, and experts who may not always agree with him but whose judgment he has come to respect. When every option seems to contain some good and bad and he is searching for the compromise that best suits him, Hank knows from past experience that the best resolution emerges when all stakeholders in the decision (son, daughter, doctor, self) feel that they have been heard and their opinions taken seriously.

Finally, a gift of experience is humility. A life fully lived has provided most of us with plenty of reasons to be humble. We are no strangers to opportunities whose knock we did not hear, to bad choices, to striving and failing. Then, there have been those random acts of misfortune that made a shambles of our best-laid plans. These humbling setbacks have been described by psychologists at the Max Planck Institute in Germany[14] as "wisdom-prone circumstances." That is, failure can lead to wisdom if we can bear the pain of looking at what we did to contribute to an unsuccessful outcome and reflect on what we might do differently the next time. Over our lifetime, we also have learned that we do not have to "win" every argument.[15] When we have a difficult choice to make and others we trust have opinions that differ from our instincts, humility teaches to rein in our competitive juices to prevail in the discussion and recognize objectively that someone else might have the better idea.

Giving Consideration to Cognitive Training

Interest in cognitive training has skyrocketed in the third millennium. Ten years earlier, there might have been three dozen books in our town library about improving the mind. These volumes were largely about tricks to develop a better memory, cure absent-mindedness, and upgrade the recall of names, numbers, and faces. A 2010 Google search[16] for "cognitive training" and "aging" returned 332,000 possibilities, including hundreds of books. The majority of the Web sites were for commercial publications and self-help products, programs, or books on the topic of "brain fitness." It is fair to say that most of these commercial enterprises believe their approaches will restore the aging intellect to the keenness of midlife. Here are three examples of what they say their programs can accomplish:[17]

At any stage of our life we can stimulate our memory and maintain our mental sharpness. This Program combines the essential elements of neurogenesis, neuroplasticity, and cognitive enhancement for a training tool that increases intelligence, visual and aural working memory, processing speed, multitasking and left–right brain interaction.

Our team of scientists has succeeded in scientifically validating the benefits of mental training in improving cognitive function. [This program] uses scientifically designed and validated brain fitness solutions created to improve the elasticity of all five main cognitive functions of the brain: memory, attention, language, executive functions, and visual/spatial skills.

Among the research findings from a famous longitudinal study are: (1) Through cognitive training older people can improve their abilities; (2) Certain abilities are more likely to decline with age than others—e.g., processing speed, reasoning, verbal memory, and visuospatial; (3) With training those who have had a decline in these abilities can get back to where they were 14 years earlier.

Currently, these statements are little more than faith-based assertions. While they have a veneer of science to them, none has been supported by rigorous longitudinal studies with humans.[18] A Johns Hopkins University group conducted an extensive review group of commercial memory training programs—including video and audiotapes, CDs, and online and computer-based approaches—and reached this conclusion:

> There were no greater gains in actual memory test performance in the treatment condition than in the no-treatment control condition. Despite the promises of rapid memory improvement with such programs, the effectiveness of commercial training programs for older adults remains to be demonstrated.[19]

It is premature to count on these brain fitness products to restore the 3rd Age intellect to what it was in the prime of life. Other approaches, however, do work and have demonstrated their effectiveness. These cognitive training techniques do not promise to increase the size and number of brain cells, but they have reversed the age-related downward slope of specific mental skills. A quarter century of research has generated evidence that a wide variety of these interventions improve scores on cognitive tests. Moreover, they have shown that they can improve those particular cognitive functions that are most likely to decline with age, such as visuospatial or reasoning skills.[20]

An example is the ACTIVE (Advanced Cognitive Training for Independent and Vital Elderly) project. The aim of this longitudinal investigation was to evaluate whether instruction improved mental abilities and the daily functioning of older, independently living adults.[21] Ten training sessions taught an eclectic mix of the theory and application of evidence-based techniques to improve performance in a specific aptitude. For example, participants were taught to apply these techniques to recall grocery lists or details from prescription labels. They were provided with many opportunities for practice, then given feedback from the instructor and the other participants. The program also included booster sessions at 11 and 35 months.

At the end of the cognitive training, the effectiveness of the experience was assessed by giving the subjects aptitude tests and checking their performance on everyday activities. The aptitude test scores of the trained subjects were compared to their baseline scores and to a control group who had no training. The scores were uniformly higher for the aptitudes in which the subjects were trained. The improvement extended to those abilities most vulnerable to age-based decline. Processing speed training improved the test scores in well over 80% of the subjects, compared to 32% of the control group. Reasoning test scores increased for about two thirds of those trained, compared to about one third of those receiving no instruction. Memory improvement was less dramatic but still significant: 24% of those trained improved their test scores, compared to 15% of the controls. These gains were also durable. Two years later, the trained subjects maintained their edge.[22]

While it is encouraging to see improvement in test scores following cognitive training, there is always the question of whether answering a few more questions correctly on a test generalizes to the everyday functions of real life. Thus, the ACTIVE investigators constructed a test of real-life cognitive challenges. They included activities like correctly identifying critical information on medication labels or medical forms, looking up a specific telephone number, or quickly locating food items on a crowded shelf of packaged goods. In these real life situations no differences were found between the trained and control volunteers.

Findings from this study summarize much of the current state of knowledge about the power of cognitive training to improve mental abilities. There are five points on which most experts agree. First, no doubt lingers that most interventions will improve the mental test scores of healthy older adults. Findings that instruction raises test scores for both crystallized and fluid abilities have been reproduced many times.[23] Second, the greatest gains are in those abilities for which the age-related decline in test scores is the greatest. The strong improvements in processing speed and reasoning by the ACTIVE subjects are examples.

The third point of agreement is that improvement occurs only in those skills targeted for training.[24] If the subjects learned to improve processing speed, posttesting found gains only in that aptitude, not in attendant memory and calculation skills. I believe the importance of this finding is that it indicates that cognitive training is not merely a placebo effect. That is, the gains in cognitive performance do not occur merely as a result of paying attention to older people and telling them that training may improve their intellectual functions.[25]

The fourth point is that the improvement has proven durable. Verifying existing knowledge about the effects of cognitive training extending well beyond the period of intervention, subjects in this research still evidenced improvement in their trained aptitudes 2 years later.[26]

The final result of the ACTIVE research is that improved mental test scores have little effect on everyday intellectual functions. In other words, higher mental ability test scores at the end of training are not generalizable to the real world.[27] So far, no one has proved that a woman who has just completed a course on memory improvement will be able to better recall a list of errands she has to run tomorrow morning or that a man will be able to more easily locate his car in the airport parking garage when he returns from a week-long vacation.

What might improve the transfer of cognitive training to real life? Two new ideas have been suggested. When clients or patients are able to add some of their own ideas to the cognitive training, the generalization to everyday activities may be more impressive than when they are simply following someone else's directions. Michigan 3rd Agers who were encouraged by researchers to devise their own strategies for a variety of memory tests outperformed subjects required to master a particular mnemonic strategy. Moreover, this greater skill transferred to real life in the form of fewer everyday memory errors.[28]

Second, single-modality training programs may not be as effective as those that employ multiple forms of intervention. For instance, we know that exercise benefits mental abilities, and that combining cognitive training with exercise improves memory more than aerobic activity or instruction alone. Might a combination of physical and cognitive training generalize to everyday life?

In an ambitious longitudinal project, German psychologists[29] integrated cognitive and physical training in older adults (90% of whom were between 75 and 84) to see whether there would be improved transfer to everyday quality of life 5 years after the end of training. Cognitive interventions worked on improving processing speed, attention, and memory, while the physical training focused on increasing balance, coordination, and flexibility. The project also included efforts to increase the participants' overall involvement in gymnastic exercises and games. At the

5-year follow-up, those subjects who received the combination physical and cognitive training felt generally more competent, rated themselves in better health, and had fewer signs of cognitive impairment compared to the controls.

Before closing this section on cognitive training, one more observation is in order based on my own clinical experience. The majority of subjects participating in these training programs, even those with mild cognitive impairment and dementia, benefited in some ways from the experience. Perhaps the best example comes from programs aimed at boosting the mental skills of older adults with mild cognitive impairment. To my knowledge, none of these programs reported higher test scores that improved everyday mental ability. But, they had other positive effects. The authors of one such study reported that "qualitative trends of improvement consisted of increased awareness of environment, increased socialization and initiation, increased alertness and improved affect." This was a surprise to the authors because none of these areas had been targeted for training.[30]

Engaging in Attention Restoration Activities

Attention is the cornerstone of most cognitive functions. Because attentional skills are worn down by the fatigue and boredom caused by the need to concentrate on tasks that must be accomplished in day-to-day life, actions that individuals can take to refresh their concentration will improve the likelihood of using their intellectual powers fully. These attention restorative activities are especially important to 3rd Agers because their ability to pay attention to necessary tasks is undermined by increasing age-related difficulty in suppressing distractions. Called attention restoration activities,[31] these actions soothe the mind and renew attention, memory, and other mental abilities. Here are three examples:

> Continuing to teach part time since her official retirement 3 years ago and still giving lectures around the country about attention deficit/ hyperactivity disorders in children, Carolyn (age 76) is in the process of editing the fourth edition of her textbook on that topic. She finds that these days she gets worn out from working on her manuscript after just 2 or 3 hours and stops. However, Carolyn has found that walking her dog around a little pond off a nearby country road the following morning and thinking about nothing special refreshes her ability to mobilize the concentration she needs to start on the manuscript again.

Although she still tends to her house and her husband—and some-times her children and grandchildren as well—Bernice (73) has taken up painting with watercolors and loves it. Bernice is a retired nurse and never studied art before taking lessons at the community art cen-ter. But now, she finds herself absorbed by it and can be found on part of most days in her studio painting or taking art classes.

Will (64) loves to read, something he rarely has a chance to do in his job as the head librarian of a large university near Miami, Florida. What he most enjoys is reading a book near the place where the book was written. Last summer, Will traveled to Concord, Massachusetts, to read Emerson and Thoreau at their graves in Sleepy Hollow Cemetery. During spring break, he drove up to Cross Creek, Florida, to read Marjorie Kennan Rawlings. Next summer, Will is thinking about read-ing Dylan Thomas in Dublin.

More than 100 years ago Harvard psychologist William James noted that there are two kinds of attention. The first is active or voluntary atten-tion, a directed and effortful concentration on a task, frequently associated with work. Since directed attention often requires maintaining focus while working for long periods, carrying out taxing, sometimes monotonous and unpleasant, tasks, it can be highly stressful. Part of the stress is created by the effort necessary to block out distracting thoughts, feelings, and physical sensations. Yet, keeping distracting thoughts out of our minds is essential to directed attention, a key ingredient in an effective and purposeful life.[32]

William James's contribution to our understanding of attention also included the recognition of a second type of attention, passive attention, which is an undirected, reflexive, effortless focus on something that attracts our interest. Carolyn's morning stroll with her dog is an example of what William James may have had in mind by passive attention. Without thinking about it, the ripples on the water draw Carolyn's spontaneous focus as she walks around the pond, reducing her stress level, evoking positive feelings, and refreshing her intellect. For Carolyn this walk around the pond is an attention restoration activity.

Research studies confirm Carolyn's experience. Psychologists at the University of Michigan demonstrated the restorative power of a walk in the woods on attention and memory.[33] Here is how they did it. Student volun-teers were given mentally fatiguing tasks, then randomly assigned to take a 2.8-mile walk in either the Ann Arbor Arboretum or downtown Ann Arbor. The path through the arboretum was tree lined and secluded from traffic. The downtown walk was on a crowded sidewalk sandwiched between a line of office buildings and a street heavy with vehicular traffic. Before and after the walks, participants were given a test of attention and memory (repeating digits backward). Those who strolled through the arboretum had a 19% improvement in their test scores, while those who walked down a busy street showed a smaller 6% change. Similar cognitive benefits to students following their actual or virtual exposure to nature have been reported at universities in the United States and Italy.[34]

The Michigan investigators added another twist to their research. A group of volunteers was asked to view 50 pictures of urban scenes or 50 pictures of natural scenery. Then, they were given 10 minutes to rate the pictures regarding how much they liked them. Both groups improved; students who viewed photos of natural scenery increased their cognitive test scores 18%; surprisingly, the test scores of those who looked at urban scenes rose 13%.

If looking at photographs of pastoral scenes and urban areas improves attention, might studying other forms of art enhance the intellect? No research I am aware of has directly addressed this question, but indirect support comes from reports on the positive effects of exposure to the arts on the observational skills of medical students.

Medical school faculty members in the United States and England have been interested in whether looking at art and learning a little bit about it would have a positive effect on the diagnostic skills of their students. First- and second-year students at Harvard Medical School volunteered to take an elective art class at the Boston Museum of Fine Arts. Classes consisted of eight weekly 2.5-hour sessions divided into an observation exercise, followed by a lecture linking visual arts concepts with physical diagnosis. The first half of the classes included observations about topics such as color and shadows, contour and line, and symmetry; the second half focused on possible diagnoses based on pallor and jaundice, pursed lips, or imbalance portrayed in the paintings. Before and after the classes, these medical students were given a visual skills exam that showed pictures of patients with various diseases. Their results, both before and after the art course, were compared with classmates who did not volunteer for the art classes.[35]

The medical students who took the classes increased their attentional skills test scores by 41%, while the test performance of their contemporaries who did not take the classes improved 3%. In addition, the art class students made more observations about the patients and wrote fuller descriptions of them. These findings have been supported empirically with medical students at Yale University and the University of London and clinically at other universities.[36]

Exposure to art did more than improve the attention of the medical students to their patients. The medical students also were aware of the benefits to them personally of attention restoration through exposure to art, which could help them lead better balanced lives as well as being more perceptive physicians. Here are two excerpts from their comments:[37]

In medical school there is little time allowed for observation and self-reflection in any sort of structured format. The Art of Observation did that for us.

Quite simply, it reminded me that I need to get out of the hospital and do something besides health and science whenever possible, which was wonderful for my mental health. I was a much better student during my second year.

Much of the research documenting the benefits of attention restoration activities have come from investigations demonstrating the positive impact of exposure to natural settings. But, as the examples opening this section indicate, getting close to nature is not the only avenue to mental restoration. People visiting churches, monasteries, and museums; exercising and pursuing hobbies; or visiting cafes and other favorite places in cities report feeling restored by these experiences.[38] While these surveys did not demonstrate that cognition was also enhanced, the results remind us that many forms of recreation may have the same potential for stress reduction, relaxation, and improved mood as well as intellectual renewal.

These attention restoration activities have in common several overlapping elements essential to cognitive renewal.[39] The primary component is fascination, such as when Carolyn allows her focus to be drawn to the tall grass waving in the gentle breeze or the shadows the sun makes as it shimmers through the birches around the pond. These complex, constantly shifting, scenes hold her attention effortlessly and provide her with opportunities for uninterrupted reflection. Carolyn finds that sometimes she is awash in pleasant musings from a lifetime of memories during these walks. And sometimes, thoughts useful to her work or writing materialize spontaneously.

Although fascination is the linchpin of the attention restoration experience, five additional properties distinguish these activities.[40] Attention restoration experiences are freely chosen, are compatible, create the feeling of being away, are enjoyed in the present moment, and do not require doing well. That is, when Bernice heads for the community center to begin a morning of painting or Will takes a break from his chores at the library to find a quiet spot on the campus to read, they do so by choice not because they are fulfilling an obligation. They paint and read for mental relaxation because these experiences are compatible with their own unique pattern of interests and pleasures. In addition, their attention-refreshing actions create the sense of being away, in a distant place in which they are disconnected from the responsibilities of work and family. The attention restoration activities are appreciated fully in the present. When Carolyn is walking around the pond, when Bernice is painting, or when Will is reading, they are fully immersed in that experience. Should thoughts about job or family occur, they pass quickly through their minds, receiving scant consideration.

Finally, there is no requirement for excellence. When they are engaged in their favorite attention restorative activities, they are appreciating the experience, and are little concerned with how well they are doing it.

The overwhelming majority of research thus far has been with students and other young adults. The small number of investigations that have included 3rd Age subjects has found that, like Carolyn, older adults also benefit from time spent in natural settings. A large cross section of Americans aged 65–84 was quizzed on walking habits and then given brief cognitive tests. Those with the highest scores walked on jogging trails or in parks; in contrast, those with lower scores more often spent their time walking in shopping malls or indoor athletic facilities.

At this point, the scientific evidence supporting value to the intellect of attention restoration activities is limited to exposure to natural scenes or the arts. Little is known about whether other relaxing activities might improve attention span—a short nap, listening to a symphony orchestra, or watching the constantly changing hues and structure of a campfire. It is also possible that hitting a bucket of golf balls or spending an afternoon riding a motorcycle is mentally refreshing for some of us.[41]

Furthermore, our current understanding of the intellectual benefit of attention restoration activities is limited to what changes occur in mental abilities rather than why these changes happen. Imagine a client of yours coming back from a 3-day hike through the mountains with her children and grandchildren. She tells you that she is tired and stiff but mentally refreshed because the long walk through the wooded mountains allowed her weary mind to rest and be restored. But, there are other possible explanations. Could it be that being with loved ones, lowering her stress level, or exercising by walking up and down mountains were the factors that sharpened her mental acuity? These discoveries lay ahead.[42]

What we do know for certain, however, is that attention restoration activities are beneficial without being taxing. Unlike exercising or eating healthily, a stroll through the woods does not require much willpower.

Reflections and Applications

As I write about these direct actions that maximize mental ability, I cannot resist thinking about how applying some of these activities has benefited my own aging intellect. For instance, I have taken to heart the Duke research finding that older people are largely morning people. Mornings are when I work on the most challenging tasks, such as preparing for classes, writing, or scheduling meetings about weighty matters. Also, the young-old differences in diurnal variation between my students and me are hard to miss. During the past decade, most of the e-mails that students send arrive well after the sun has set, while I send my messages to them in the early morning.

Also useful to keep in mind when findings from an investigation like this seem to fit us so well is that other studies may disagree. Moreover, much variation exists among 3rd Agers. Staying open to contrary evidence about times of day when older people are mentally keenest can be challenging. So, while recognizing my reflexive assumption that most 3rd Agers share my diurnal tendencies, when I talk to clients I usually try to ask, "Is there a part of the day that you feel the sharpest?"

Of all of the direct influences on the aging intellect, the strategy of selection, optimization, and compensation has been the most useful to me personally and one of the most valuable techniques for older persons in my care. In addition, it is among the most teachable tools. Most of my own selection has been loss based. Hardly a week goes by that I do not miss the active practice of clinical psychology. But, I have found it impossible to enjoy the spontaneity and freedom that retirement brings and still provide the care my patients need. Teaching, supervision, and writing partially fill that void.

The value of compensation has been apparent to me for some time. For several years, I worked with Carl, an older doctor with a busy practice, who always took time out in the late afternoon to have a cup of tea and a sugar cookie. That behavior always struck me as quaint, but it clearly worked for Carl because he continued to be a competent therapist well into his eighth decade. It was years later that I discovered that Carl was onto something important for the mental quality of older people: Intellectual functioning is influenced by the amount of glucose in the bloodstream. On my own, I discovered the invigorating power of the 20-minute nap during a busy working day.

We will never know precisely how much Captain Sullenberger's training and active experience contributed to his remarkable feat and to what extent other variables, such as his genetic makeup, played a role in his ability to react quickly and expertly to a dangerous situation. A reasonable theory is that his years of active experiences maximized his natural gifts. We do know that many optimal agers have taken the initiative to enrich their lives with exposure to the unfamiliar, to stimulating moments, and to horizon-expanding activities.[43] These ventures, along with making the effort to learn the lessons from the usual diet of stressful but "wisdom-prone" circumstances, enabled them to bring considerable active experience to complex problems typical of the 3rd Age.

For curious practitioner-researchers, Captain Sullenberger's story may stimulate an interest in thinking about how some of the older adults in your care used their experience when they had complicated problems to solve. Another question might be whether older and younger people confirm what some researchers say about when they are at their best intellectually. Finally, what types of attention restoration activities that benefit the intellect are reported by elders in your care?

In your caretaking of older women and men, you can count on being faced with 3rd Agers who are convinced that the reason their minds are as sharp as they ever were is because they play bridge regularly, are constantly engaged in mind-stretching games on the computer, or are still playing chess. As you listen to these passionate believers, it is sometimes hard to suppress all those tables and figures from scholarly publications that cross your mind showing how little effect these activities have on the rate at which mental abilities decline.

When you are faced with the challenge of wanting to be supportive but doubting the validity of a client's enthusiastic claims, it helps to remind yourself that your work is not neuroscience but the art and science of caring for the elderly. Moreover, all of the discoveries about the factors that benefit the mind and body have not yet been made. In these situations, you may find comfort and guidance in the words of University of Virginia professor Timothy Salthouse:[44]

> Although my professional opinion is that at the present time the mental-exercise hypothesis is more of an optimistic hope than an empirical reality, my personal recommendation is that people should behave as though it were true. ... The activities are often enjoyable and thus may contribute to a higher quality of life, and engagement in cognitively demanding activities serves as ... proof—if you can still do it, then you know that you have not yet lost it.

Among the most interesting material in this chapter is the research on attention restoration activities. It has long been known that merely having an opportunity to look out the window at patches of woods or a green-sward is good for health. Patients recovering from gall bladder surgery in rooms that overlooked a small stand of maple trees had shorter hospital stays and required less pain medication than patients whose view out the window was of a brown brick wall.[45] Only recently, however, has it been demonstrated that cognitive benefits also accrue to people of all ages from exposure to nature.

In our interviews with older volunteers, we confirmed the link between exposure to natural settings and optimal cognitive aging. We also discovered that these optimal agers found many other pathways to cognitive restoration, just as other surveys reported. For some, it was a good night's sleep, reading a mystery novel, or browsing a collection of paintings in a museum. Others, like Bernice, find that their mental renewal comes from the challenge of creating a work of art.

The caseload of adult caretakers is far more likely to consist of elders who will respond more positively to pastoral settings than challenges. But, there will be those occasional 3rd Agers who need stimulation to recharge their minds. What they all share is that each one has his or her special place for cognitive renewal. Health care providers might consider issuing "favorite place prescriptions" that advise seniors to regularly spend time at a favorite place away from their daily surroundings to refresh their attention and memory.[46]

The capacity of older adults to maintain concentration and suppress distractions grows increasingly fragile as the years pass. As a result, those periods of time shorten when we can direct our attention to a task without our mind wandering. This is important information for all of us in the 3rd Age. This enables each of us to choose those times of the day when we are mentally at our best to pay bills or read that interesting but challenging article in a favorite magazine. We also can take precautions not to overtax our ability to concentrate so that we can avoid making mental mistakes.

Because they are largely free of commitments to working and raising children, 3rd Agers have more leisure time to expose themselves to attention restorative activities. This may give them an advantage over time-starved midlifers when it comes to cognitive restoration from exposure to nature or other complex stimuli. Research in Boston involved adult volunteers with average and high-average mental ability, who were shown a series of slides containing mostly triangles, with occasional pictures of unusual figures. Among all age groups, the subjects with high-average ability looked longer at the novel figures than those with average ability. One of the most striking findings was that the elders with above-average mental ability looked at the unusual figures twice as long as equally bright young and middle-aged subjects. The higher-scoring older subjects also gazed at these novel stimuli four times longer than did the 3rd Agers with average intellectual ability.[47] This study showed that older people with higher mental ability may be disposed to be more attentive to novel experiences because they feel unhurried.

Being unhurried is essential to appreciate the unfamiliar. For many younger adults, not being rushed is an unnatural condition. Elizabeth Samet, a professor of English at West Point, writes about teaching poetry to cadets who are used to functioning at warp speed.[48] Anything slower seems abnormal. At the end of an hour-long class devoted to the first quatrain of an Elizabethan sonnet, one plebe looked up at the clock with chagrin and said, "We must be really stupid. We just spent an hour on one sentence."

"On the contrary," thought Professor Samet. "Finding an hour's worth of things to discuss about four lines shows pretty strong intelligence."

6

Optimal Cognitive Aging

Optimal aging is a popular topic these days. Articles, TV programs, and Internet postings about optimal, successful, or healthy aging are hard to miss.[1] Although interest in remaining physically vigorous for as long as possible is strong, much less is being said about optimal *cognitive* aging. Optimal cognitive aging is defined as avoiding risky lifestyle habits that endanger the intellect and practicing behaviors associated with maintaining or slowing the decline of mental skills. These individuals are mentally vigorous and regularly focus their intellectual powers on activities that interest them. As used in this book, the term *optimal cognitive aging* refers not only to those exceptional larger-than-life superagers whose contributions continue to be remarkable well into the 3rd Age of life and beyond[2] but also to ordinary older adults who are using their capabilities relatively fully and getting the most out of what is possible in their lives whether their IQs are average or exceptional.

Current thinking is that the factors that contribute to optimal cognitive aging are closely allied with those associated with optimal physical aging. A Mayo Clinic team published a comprehensive review of strategies that could make the difference in the quality of the aging intellect.[3] Their summary included four of the five healthy lifestyle factors that researchers have been emphasizing for two decades: exercise regularly, keep your weight down, eat healthily, maintain your social networks, and minimize stress. To this, they add controlling medical conditions, such as hypertension, that have adverse cognitive consequences.

Based on measures of health, activity level, functional capability, mental status, and intellectual functioning, the proportion of optimal cognitive agers in the United States and most developed countries is estimated to be 20–30%. This figure is derived from four large population-based studies of older adults, which defined an optimally aging group based on health-related or cognitive factors.[4]

This chapter, as well as the chapters on normal cognitive aging and high-risk cognitive aging that follow, grew out of the findings from two large research projects involving nearly 2,000 subjects and from face-to-face

interviews with 151 3rd Age volunteers. This chapter also contains two longer cases of people who illustrate the qualities of optimal cognitive aging.
Brief descriptions of health-related qualities exhibited by the majority of
optimal agers we interviewed as well as their attitudes and behaviors associated with maintaining their intellectual powers are presented.

Who Are the Optimal Cognitive Agers?

Our approach to classifying our subjects as optimal cognitive agers was
adapted from the method for diagnosing mental disorders in the *Diagnostic
and Statistical Manual of Mental Disorders, Fourth Edition, Text Revision
(DSM-IV-TR).*[5] We applied a combination of a global impression and the
presence of a specific number of behaviors and attitudes to classify the
subjects.

Using the Global Assessment of Functioning (GAF) scale of the *DSM-
IV-TR*, a clinician is able to rate on a scale from 1 to 100 someone's overall
level of functioning with respect to working, social relations, and coping
with life's problems. Optimal agers are at the top of the GAF scale, those
people rated 86–100. They function well across a range of activities, life's
problems are not out of hand, they have an active social network, they are
not limited by emotional problems, and they are satisfied with life.

The next step was to classify each person interviewed according to the
presence of specific health-related qualities as well as attitudes and behaviors that positively affect the intellect. *The DSM-IV-TR* approach makes a
psychiatric diagnosis based on the number of clinical symptoms present,
drawn from a larger number of possibilities. For instance, a major melan-
cholic/depressive episode is diagnosed if five of nine possible symptoms
have been present for 2 weeks (e.g., chronic depressed mood without apparent cause, anhedonia, psychomotor retardation, sleeping problems, loss of
appetite, feelings of worthlessness).

We applied this method to "diagnose" optimal cognitive aging among
our subjects. Knowing that many medical conditions affect the intellect,
we identified health-related characteristics—for example, taking medication as prescribed—that have cognitive consequences. These are shown in
Table 6.1. Table 6.2 summarizes attitudes and behaviors that are linked to
higher cognition, such as anticipating age-associated cognitive losses and
using selection, optimization, and compensation. We placed people in the
optimal cognitive aging category when they showed evidence of at least six
health-related qualities and five attitudes and behaviors typical of people
aging optimally.[6]

As expected, some of the optimally aging subjects were physically fit
and active, as well as bright and well educated, and had been successful

in school and on the job. But, we uncovered quite a few women and men whom we rated as optimal agers even though they were physically disabled, appeared to have unremarkable mental ability, a limited education, and average occupational accomplishments. Yet they were quite competent intellectually. Here are two examples:

Although she dropped out of high school to go to work because she says she was "not a student," Nancy at 78 is good at calculation and takes care of her bills and balancing her checkbook. She also pays the bills for her children and balances all their checkbooks. Every month, three older relatives give Nancy money to deposit in their respective checking accounts and rely on her to perform these tasks. This is not a burden for her because she likes doing it.

A 65-year-old correctional officer at a state prison, Ivan has been in this second career for almost 20 years. Before that, he was career Navy. Although he has never been much of a student and never had any exposure to music, Ivan found that he loved opera when he was stationed in Italy. Ivan and his wife treat themselves once a year to a week at the Sarasota Opera. At the prison, Ivan has to stay sharp because his job requires that he regularly conduct inmate counts and security checks and solve problems between the inmates. Attention to detail, and remembering these details exactly, has played a huge role in his life. Also, Ivan has to adapt to change. "Almost every month, there are new rules and procedures. I have to be up on these changes, or I wouldn't be doing my job." Ivan believes he is as mentally sharp now as he was in his 50s.

These behaviors are found among women and men at many levels of talent or accomplishment, in most strata of society and all educational levels, and among individuals across races and ethnic backgrounds. What differentiated these optimal cognitive agers from other older adults was a combination of high global functioning and positive health-related behaviors and attitudes. They also were remarkably vigorous.

Dominique's life story shows optimal cognitive aging in action.

Dominique

Dominique (73) was born in Haiti. Following the death of her husband from prostate cancer, she moved to Florida in her early 40s. She took training at a local community college to become a licensed practical nurse (LPN) and found employment in a suburban Tampa hospital. There Dominique worked until she was 65 and stayed on another 3 years part time. During that period, she often worked double shifts while raising two children, who both graduated from college and now live near her with their families. About her contact with her family, she says, "I talk to them on the phone or by e-mail all the time, see them at church on most Sundays, and we get together for birthdays, kids' events, and holidays. But, they are busy, and I have my own life. Besides, I don't want to be their built-in baby sitter."

Dominique has been busy since she retired. During the long Florida growing season, she and a neighbor raise vegetables in a community garden behind their apartment complex. She has been working out at a gym regularly and is currently taking a low-impact aerobics class. "I know I'm overweight (5 feet 3 inches, 160 pounds = body mass index [BMI] of 28.3)," laughs Dominique, "but at least I can be fit."

"I don't want to give the impression that all I do is get exercise," she adds. She loves to read mysteries. One night a week, she and her friends play bingo. Dominique has been active in her church in the Haitian community, hardly ever missing a service. She taught Sunday school until 3 years ago, although occasionally she still substitutes. She especially likes the fact that many of her former students, some of them now middle aged, are her friends.

About her health, Dominique says, "God has brought me this far, so I know he has been watching over my health, and I give thanks for that." However, Dominique does not leave her health care solely in the Lord's hands. Although she feels healthy and vigorous, she sees her doctor regularly for an annual physical and has been tested for breast and colon cancer, which run in her family. About 10 years ago, her doctor put her on high blood pressure medication, and recently she has started taking pills for elevated cholesterol readings. She is faithful about getting her flu shot every fall.

Overall, Dominique feels pretty well. She says that she is in much better health now than she was in her late 60s. Part of the reason is that she had a successful knee replacement and cataract surgery. She rates her energy level and overall health as much higher than most of the people she knows in her age group. She can do everything she wants to do.

Dominique worries more these days about mental decline. "So far," Dominique says, "progress in medicine has kept up with my ailments, but I'm not so sure doctors can do much about my mind." She told a story about being asked the last four digits of her Social Security number while she was questioning a bill from the phone company. For a moment, she blocked and could not remember it, but, after a minute or so, the number popped into her mind.

So, now she practices things that she thinks might strengthen her memory. At bingo, she plays two boards at a time. Before she goes shopping, Dominique tries to memorize the list of items she wants by associating them with different parts of the supermarket (e.g., "pro-duce"—lettuce tomatoes, plantains, and green peppers). But, she still puts the list in her purse just in case her memory is not quite up to it. She proudly reports that she has memorized the numbers and expiration date of her two credit cards. She hopes that someday there will be a memory pill.

Asked if there was anything that she has had to give up because of advancing age, Dominique replied, "Driving in heavy traffic at night or when the weather is bad and making left-hand turns." She does not see as well at night as she used to, so one of her friends drives when they go to their evening bingo games.

When asked what she was looking forward to in the future, Dominique replied, "Watching my grandchildren graduate from college." After a moment, she added, "Then maybe I'll go back."

Health-Related Qualities Associated With Optimal Cognitive Aging

Table 6.1 presents health-related qualities that were exhibited by those older adults whom we thought were aging optimally both mentally and physically. Each displayed six or more of the qualities.[7]

High Energy and Activity Level

Optimal agers are not just a little bit more active; they are three to four times more vigorous than their contemporaries.[8] For instance, as a

Table 6.1   Health-Related Qualities Associated With Optimal Cognitive Aging

1.	**High energy and activity level**
2.	**In good health compared to peers and to self 5 years ago**
3.	**Proactive about medical checkups and screenings when not symptomatic**
4.	**Compliance with medical recommendations**
5.	**Upbeat, forward-looking attitude**
6.	**Few "down" days; stress management adequate to maintain mental health**
7.	Awareness of benefits and adverse effects of certain health-related behaviors
8.	Activities benefit others
9.	Looks younger, cares about appearance

Characteristics in **bold print** found among at least 67% of optimal cognitive agers.

middle-aged woman, Dominique worked long and hard in a new country to support her family and put two children through college. She has remained unusually active after retirement, and at 73, she can keep up with friends two decades younger. Lest we think that Dominique is so unusual that she has no peers, here are short descriptions of two others we came to know.

Clara is quite a jock. She runs 2 miles a day and has recently incorporated weightlifting 3 days a week to prevent osteoporosis. She plays softball competitively, was on a team that won the national championship 3 years running, and played in the World Senior Games this year. Clara has always been good at any sport attempted. Last winter, she also entered a county ping-pong championship and won her age division. Clara is 72.

Besides his part-time volunteer job, Nick (age 74) keeps a beautiful garden blooming around his home. He mows four of his neighbor's lawns for them, and in the winter, he snow blows the same four driveways along with his own. Whether it is playing basketball or football or chopping his own firewood for the winter, Nick is just as active as his grandchildren are. He never needed to go to a gym to stay in shape.

In Good Health Compared to Peers and to Self Five Years Ago

Most older people who say they are in pretty good health are, in fact, usually in pretty good health.[9] Most optimal cognitive agers felt superior to their contemporaries and considered their health to be better or the same as 5 years ago. Optimally aging older adults were nearly three times as likely as normals to rate their functional health as good or better than that of their peers and twice as likely to see themselves as younger than their age.[10] Joanna is an example.

Joanna (70) rates her health as 10 out of 10. In her mind, she is healthier than most people over 60 she knows, and she feels as healthy today as 5 years ago. She still works part time for the town manager and does her daily workout in Gold's Gym before going to the office. Joanna loves to dance and move those hips.

Rob (77) has always been trim and fit. He still plays golf and tennis. When he goes to the gym, people usually think he is in his early 60s. When asked about his health compared to people his age, Rob replied, "It must be pretty good." Rob just returned from a weekend at a roller coaster amusement park in Sandusky, Ohio. With his son and grandson, he rode 10 of the 17 roller coasters, several more than once. Rob's favorite was the Extreme Dragster, which accelerates from 0 to 124 mph in 2 seconds.

Proactive About Medical Checkups and Screenings When Not Symptomatic

In the medical community, there has been a debate about the value of the annual physical checkup for older adults. Those in favor emphasize its value in detecting treatable medical conditions as well as discussing modifiable lifestyle factors. Those opposed argue that an annual checkup with otherwise healthy elders is wasteful and should be replaced by an age-specific, selective approach.[11]

This would be a hard sell for Dominique, who, like most aging optimally, appreciates the value of early diagnosis and intervention. It was at one of her annual physicals that Dominique discovered that she had hypertension and elevated cholesterol. As soon as the diagnosis was made at her checkup, Dominique began taking medication to control her blood pressure and lipid levels. She is not alone.

Kurt (75) is a citrus farmer and maintains that his annual checkup is responsible for his current good health. At his doctor's advice, he quit smoking at 55, which he believes improved his health immediately. Later, elevated high blood pressure and cholesterol were diagnosed and are now under control. Recently, he started to follow his children's suggestions about eating healthier. Overall, Kurt thinks that keeping healthy through regular doctor checkups and following the doctor's advice has enabled him to keep up with the younger generation and continue to work his farm.

Geisa (71) believes that beating breast cancer would not have been possible had the doctor not found a tiny lump during her annual physical. She now has been in remission for 6 months, and even though she still feels a little weak after the chemotherapy, Geisa believes she is healthier now than she has been in several years.

Compliance With Medical Recommendations

Unlike about half of the U.S. population who are not compliant, most optimal cognitive agers follow the advice that comes from regular medical checkups.[12] Dominique filled her prescriptions. Others follow suit.

> George (60) thought he was in great health until the doctor told him he had hypertension and type 2 diabetes. At first, he was upset, but then with a nurse's encouragement he began to check his weight and blood pressure daily and has been faithful about taking his medications. Monitoring his glucose levels and adjusting his diet is "a work in progress," as George puts it. Recently, he developed a spreadsheet system that helps him stay motivated. Also, George is eating healthier— the five food groups every day—and biking 3 days a week.

> Emma (70) loves being able to continue to work part time as an optometrist at Costco. She takes seven pills a day conscientiously for her medical conditions, which include atrial fibrillation, high blood pressure, asthma, and arthritis. Emma is certain that she is able to still work at the job she loves because medical science has been keeping pace with her physical problems.

Upbeat, Forward-Looking Attitude

A positive attitude and a zest for life in which they have found meaning characterizes optimal agers.[13] A positive attitude about the aging process also predicts higher functional levels later in life.[14] Those aging optimally pay special attention to what remains possible rather than what has been lost. After her husband died, Dominique responded by setting her sights on immigrating to the United States with her two small children and then training to be an LPN. Dominique's future-oriented attitude remains. She was not kidding when she talked about returning to college after her grandchildren graduate. Here are other examples of this upbeat attitude:

> Retired for 9 years from a senior executive position, Sherman (83) has a positive attitude and rates himself well compared to others his age. When asked if retirement had brought him any surprises, Sherman responded that the biggest surprise was how many opportunities and choices would be available and how busy he would be.

Just after Linda turned 70, her husband of 44 years left her for another woman. She was devastated. She spent the summer following her divorce talking to her confidantes, praying for support, and working with a counselor. By the fall, Linda had recovered her positive outlook. She set several goals for herself, which included working out regularly. She consulted a nutritionist, started taking golf lessons, and lost 15 pounds. When she ran into her ex-husband at the supermarket just before Thanksgiving, he commented on how great Linda looked. He wondered if they could have coffee and talk things over.

Few "Down" Days; Stress Management Adequate to Maintain Mental Health

The typical older adult has 2 to 3 "down days" per month.[15] Optimal agers average less than 1 down day. Nearly all develop effective ways of avoiding or coping with stress. Dominique's history exemplifies this quality, as do others.

A retired high school principal, Jay (69) attributes the improvement in his physical and mental health to reduction in stress that followed retirement. Plus, he avoids disagreeable people. "I had enough of that when I was principal and had to deal with them," he commented. "No more." Since retirement, he is sleeping through the night most of the time, and because he has stopped grinding his teeth, he no longer needs a mouth guard.

Two years before her husband left her, Linda (70) began to have joint pain in the ankles and knees, could not exercise, and had trouble walking for more than a few blocks. Medication did not help much. Then, after the divorce and her change in lifestyle, the joint pain began to diminish so that she could play golf again. While no one knew for certain why her joint pain moderated, her doctor theorized that the pain was caused by stress-induced inflammation of the joints. When Linda's stress level diminished, the inflammation and pain disappeared with it.

Awareness of Benefits and Adverse Effects of Certain Health-Related Behaviors

Most aging optimally are not scholars of the scientific literature about the correlates of aging well, but they pay attention to information about what is good and bad for them.[16]

After he turned 55, Robert (now 79) decided that it was time for him to "clean up my act." He started with giving up alcohol, which was not hard, although there still is not any other beverage he likes as well with a nice dinner. And, he misses those wine-tasting vacations in Napa Valley. Then, he gave up artificial sweeteners, which was also not difficult. But, stopping smoking was next to impossible. "I must have tried a thousand times before I could kick that habit," Robert reported.

Stacey (74) says she has absorbed the lessons about staying healthy as she gets older from watching how her parents and aunts did it. Stacey also reads the newspapers, checks out the Internet, and watches TV programs that keep her up to date about what is good and bad for her to eat. Sometimes, she compares notes with her golfing buddies. Every morning, she eats oatmeal with berries. In addition to her daily multivitamin, Stacey also takes supplements for memory, arthritis, mood enhancement, and energy.

Activities Benefit Others

High-functioning older people more often engage in volunteer activities than normal and high-risk older adults.[17] Giving to others is good for our health. According to behavioral scientists, people who provide more social support to others also receive more support from their social networks in return, which is no surprise. But, this research also discovered that those giving to others had lower blood pressure, felt less stress, and experienced stronger feelings of efficacy and self-esteem.[18]

Lakshmi (80) volunteers once a week at the main Goodwill store, where she sorts and hangs clothing donations. Lakshmi also teaches adult Bible study lessons at her church. After the service on Sunday, she delivers altar flowers to members of the congregation who could not attend the service. And, she usually helps organize the church elders' monthly luncheon.

Peter (78) volunteers 20 hours a week tutoring and otherwise helping out at a Boys and Girls Club. Although most of the kids are Cambodian and Peter is not, he loves working there, and the kids adore him. The boys and girls, and sometimes their parents, come to him for advice on many matters, including college. Likewise, the children give Peter a feeling of being needed and useful. Although the age gap is large, Peter never thinks about his age when he works with these children.

Looks Younger, Cares About Appearance

Student interviewers spontaneously commented that many of their optimally aging subjects appeared relatively younger, well groomed, and appearance conscious. Paying attention to their appearance may be another example of how optimal agers care for their bodies and minds. The 3rd Agers still in the workforce are judged as more youthful than those who are retired.[19] One of the reasons may be that working 3rd Agers go out of their way to maintain their appearance to keep pace with their younger coworkers. Opinions about the importance of appearance have changed in the past decade, and both men and women are now more interested in cosmetic interventions to combat the effects of aging.[20]

Even though the company he started, which franchises nail salons, is now being run by his two sons, Van (82) continues to go to the office every day. He still handles some of the office work and talks to employees and franchise owners he still knows. Van appears to be at least 15 years younger than his age. He colors his hair, has Botox treatments for his wrinkles, and enjoys going to the spa and having a full-body massage weekly. Van insists on taking cold showers every morning, which has been a lifelong habit. He says that the key to a healthy body and mind is maintaining a fit and clean appearance.

During a lecture in Houston, I mentioned the finding that many women and men rated as optimal agers were well groomed, made an effort to dress well, and appeared a decade or more younger than their age. Afterward, an older couple told me that these comments fit them perfectly. The woman, who was 67, said that after her first husband died 15 years prior she returned to school to become a mental health counselor. During that period, she began exercising regularly, lost weight, and had a breast reduction. Her husband, 10 years older, said that when he was in his early 50s and a senior portfolio manager for an investment firm, he decided to have eyelid surgery to remove the excess skin and wrinkles. His reasoning was, "I knew I was still as sharp as the young analysts, and I wanted to look it."

Attitudes and Behaviors Associated With Optimal Cognitive Aging

Rich's story is another example of optimal cognitive aging.

Rich

Now 78, Rich spent 35 years with General Motors before he retired almost two decades ago. After high school and a hitch in the Air Force, Rich tried college for a semester, hoping to become an automotive engineer, but he had trouble with the reading and writing in a required English class and was told he had a learning disability. Discouraged, he dropped out of college, trained to be a tool-and-die maker, and married his high school sweetheart. A decade and three children later, Rich saw an opportunity to move into a management role, but he needed more education. He entered the General Motors Institute,[21] which had a co-op program that allowed him to go to college part time while keeping his job. It took another 9 years before Rich earned a bachelor's degree and a master's in business administration. The additional education paid off for Rich. He spent most of his last decade with GM as a plant manager.

The added years of education paid off in another way. While taking required courses in liberal arts for his undergraduate business major, Rich found that he no longer had problems reading, and spell-checking software minimized his anxiety about writing.

It was in college during his mid-30s that Rich found a lifelong appreciation of Shakespeare. While he was working, he and his family would spend a weekend in Stratford, Ontario, for the Shakespeare Festival, taking in several plays. Since retirement, Rich and his wife have been to "the real" Stratford, the home of the bard in England. They have also discovered three dozen Shakespeare festivals in the United States. Every 2 or 3 years, they rent an RV and take a leisurely drive to one of these festivals to see parts of the United States they have not visited and enjoy a few days of seeing Shakespeare's plays performed.

Rich says that retirement has been more active than they anticipated. With 3 kids and 13 grandchildren, they spend considerable time visiting or entertaining their immediate family. Rich has been on the school board in his hometown and on the library committee. Shortly after retiring, Rich learned how to play chess and now beats his children and grandchildren and most of his friends. When he is not with them, he stays in touch with the younger generation by computer and smart phone.

Rich and his spouse used to enjoy sailing on the Great Lakes and up into Canada. Shortly after his 70th birthday, Rich began to find that long sails were becoming taxing, mentally as well as physically, because of all of the factors he had to keep in mind—wind, tides, navigation, weather forecasts, and the state of guests they had on board. They decided to sell the sailboat and buy a condo in Florida, where they now spend the winter.

Rich still sails, only now with model sailboats. These boats are a meter long, and Rich controls the movement of the sails and rudder by a remote device. He looks forward to the regattas in the pond every Saturday afternoon during the winter sailing season. He also plays golf and tennis regularly with a group of men, most of whom are 10–15 years his junior.

Asked about any cognitive problems, Rich commented that he still feels pretty keen mentally, especially when he is not rushed. He does notice that sometimes in a long tennis match he loses concentration briefly. Sometimes, he has a short period of feeling unfocused and has trouble getting himself ready to hit the ball. But then, his attention returns, and he is back to normal. During these periods, Rich does not feel tired, just momentarily unfocused.

In addition to the six common health-related characteristics shared by optimal agers, five or more attitudes and behaviors are linked to optimal cognitive aging. Table 6.2 summarizes these qualities as discussed in the sections that follow.

Are Mentally Vigorous and Regularly Focus Their Intellectual Powers on Activities That Interest Them

Among the optimal cognitive agers, the most common quality was intellectual vigor.[22] Nearly all invested their mental skills in something they considered worthwhile—continuing to work part time, volunteering in the

Table 6.2 Attitudes and Behaviors Associated With Optimal Cognitive Aging

1.	**Are mentally vigorous and regularly focus their intellectual powers on activities that interest them**
2.	**Feel pretty sharp mentally compared to peers and to 5 years ago**
3.	**Minor decline or transient cognitive problems do not compromise overall intellectual functioning**
4.	**Have satisfying social relationships**
5.	**Are able to operate necessary communication technology**
6.	Engage in activities aimed at improving/maintaining the intellect
7.	Apply selection, optimization, and compensation
8.	Open to novel experiences
9.	Feel in control, competent, and useful

Characteristics in **bold print** found among 67% or more of optimal cognitive agers.

community, getting involved in politics. Many challenged themselves by starting something they dreamed of doing since midlife—buying a bed and breakfast in a small Vermont town, taking piano lessons again after a 50-year hiatus, or learning small engine repair. While the majority were physically energetic, a few were physically disabled. Here are two examples:

Paul (80) only had 9 years of school before he dropped out during World War II to join the Air Force. After the war, he stayed in the Air Force and eventually became a chief master sergeant. During his 25 years in the service, Paul took advantage of the educational opportunities and earned a college degree. The Air Force discovered that he had an aptitude for language, so he went to schools to learn Russian and Vietnamese. On his own, he picked up Spanish and Italian. After his discharge, Paul became a real estate broker in Ft. Myers, Florida. Being multilingual has helped him to do well, and he still works part time.

Jennifer (age 79) is a quiet, thin, gray-haired woman. She has been partially handicapped since being in a motor vehicle accident when she was in the sixth grade and gets around with a cane. She has to stretch every day to remain mobile. In spite of her physical limitations, she had a successful legal career before she retired. Now, she lends her legal knowledge to local organizations and charities. In addition to donating her time to community organizations, Jennifer teaches part time in a local law school. Her biggest problem, she says, is that "my body keeps falling apart, but my mind is 30 years younger."

Feel Pretty Sharp Mentally Compared to Peers and to Five Years Ago

Longitudinal studies have found that a substantial minority of older adults, optimal cognitive agers among them, show little loss of mental powers.[23] Rich, for instance, is confident that he is as strong a chess player as a half decade ago. In fact, he does not know anyone near his age who is as quick as he is at the game.

Joe (66), who lets you know that he is a Mensa (the international high IQ society) member, feels that he is much sharper than most people he meets, never mind just his own age group. He runs the pro shop on the golf course of a country club in Vero Beach, Florida. He does not feel that he has had any change mentally in the past 5 years. When there are new procedures for computerized billing or ordering, everyone turns to Joe.

Joan (73) believes that she is far keener than people her age and does not feel that her mental ability has changed in the past 5 years. Joan is fond of saying "you shouldn't confuse intelligence and judgment" because she feels that age has brought her greater wisdom. Joan thinks she is better able to reason now than when she was younger because she can see the reasons for different choices. "I'm a little less cocksure of what the right answer is these days, but that's not a bad thing."

Minor Decline or Transient Cognitive Problems Do Not Compromise Overall Intellectual Functioning

Optimal cognitive agers are not immune to periodic age-related difficulties with remaining focused; memory lapses for familiar names, numbers, or things; tip-of-the-tongue blockages; and getting more easily distracted, which increase with age.[24] Rich has noticed occasional lapses in his ability to maintain his concentration while playing tennis. While mildly bothersome, these problems are transient, so they do not significantly affect the quality of his daily living.

Melina (70) says she has problems sometimes with verbal memory and recalling names. When these memory problems get in the way, she concentrates harder. For example, sometimes she does not remember precisely where she parked her car in a large lot outside the supermarket. When this happens, she focuses her attention on the route she walked from the parking lot to get into the store and then mentally retraces those steps in reverse. It works for her.

Occasionally, Nick (74) has problems remembering phone numbers, names of things, or new people. He sometimes has to reread what he has just read to remember details because he was distracted by a thought or some other background noise. Lately, he has been making an effort to concentrate his attention on something he hears or reads when he wants to remember it later.

Have Satisfying Social Relationships

A major finding described in Chapter 4 was the strong link between grat-ifying social relationships and better health and less cognitive decline.[25] Researchers at the University of Edinburgh[26] found that satisfaction with social relationships played an important role in maintaining IQ and in the quality-of-life ratings at age 79. Not all beneficial relationships are with people.[27]

> Jorge (66) is satisfied with his social life and has seen no changes over the past 5 years. In addition to his wife, whom he considers his best friend, he has two confidantes with whom he can talk about per-sonal things and three people he considers close friends. Also, Jorge sees his children, grandchildren, in-laws, club members, neighbors, and coworkers at least once a month. To find people as vigorous as he is, Jorge spends most of his time with people who are at least 10 years younger.

> Widowed 12 years ago and not remarried, Gary (78) has plenty of friends. But, an essential element in his social life is his boxer dog, Sam. Sam goes everywhere with him, including for car rides, to fam-ily members' houses, on errands and vacations. This is not Gary's first Sam. Over the years, boxer dogs named Sam have come and gone, but Gary gets a new boxer puppy and names it Sam every time his "old Sam" dies. The Sams have given him a lot of pleasure. "Unlike some people in my life, they are always happy to see me, they are forgiving, and there is always something I can do to make them happy." After a moment of reflection, Gary added, "My Sams give me something to live for because I have to stay healthy to take care of them."

Are Able to Operate Necessary Communication Technology

A 75-year-old friend told me that among a group of 24 golfers he plays with regularly, only 8 have e-mail addresses. That is not a surprise since fewer than one third of older adults can operate a computer or use the Internet.[28] Among those aging optimally, however, well over three quarters are com-puter savvy and access the Internet regularly. Many e-mail their children and grandchildren as well as shopping and paying bills online. Some get all their news online, while others just love to surf. Like Rich, several carry a smart phone and Skype with their friends and family.

Sirinthornthip (75), or "Sara" to her American friends, immigrated to the United States from Thailand nearly 40 years ago. She is up to date with computer technology and devotes several hours a day to e-mailing family and friends. Sara even has a Facebook page so that she can stay in contact with some of her youngest grandchildren and great-grandchildren.

Quentin (62) uses the computer to manage the inventory of his furniture store and pays most of his own bills online. He also sends e-mails to friends and family. He loves to receive short videos of his new granddaughter on his smart phone.

Engage in Activities Aimed at Improving/Maintaining the Intellect

More than half of optimal cognitive agers make regular efforts to engage in activities that they believe might keep them mentally sharp. Some exercise, knowing that it enhances the intellect. Dominique memorizes her credit card numbers to keep mentally sharp. Rich plays chess. Others take courses, knit, solve Sudoku or crossword puzzles, or play bridge, chess, and Scrabble. Even though empirical support that such pursuits help us to age well is currently lacking,[29] engaging in these activities is enjoyable and stimulating, connects us with others, and is proof that we are still mentally active.

Every Tuesday and Thursday afternoon, Caroline (78) and her friends come together to knit and to share with each other their current projects. This usually results in Caroline being stimulated to think of something new to engage herself. Her favorite activity is cross-stitching, and she is a firm believer that the fine motor skills required in needlework keep her mentally fit.

Matt (64) has been in a wheelchair since an auto accident 9 years ago. After he sold his plumbing contracting business, he focused on doing everything he could to optimize his physical ability, which included eating healthily, fitness training, massage, and wheelchair yoga. This has resulted in his becoming fully independent again, including being able to drive. To keep his mind vigorous, he has returned to college part time; he is now in his third year and majoring in philosophy. Matt says those undergraduates really keep him on his toes.

Apply Selection, Optimization, and Compensation

Driving is one of the areas in which even a small amount of cognitive decline becomes noticeable. But, there are ways to overcome any problems. Dominique has changed her driving habits to avoid as much as possible driving at night, in heavy traffic, when the weather is bad, and trips that require making left-hand turns. Other optimal cognitive agers also find ways to select, optimize, and compensate.[30]

Nick (74) always loved woodworking. Over the years, he has made furniture for his children and friends. However, he is finding that making furniture is harder and less enjoyable than it used to be when his eyesight was better. Now, he makes fancy birdhouses, designed to look like the recipients' own houses, for special occasions like anniversaries or birthdays. They are very popular.

As she has grown older, Lauren (76) says that her driving habits have changed. She travels less at night, tries to avoid traffic, and no longer takes long trips without a friend or family member. Lauren also noticed that she has growing difficulty with parallel parking and was avoiding it. So, she forced herself to practice until she improved enough to park comfortably next to the curb.

Open to Novel Experiences

Optimal cognitive agers more often travel to new places to experience cultures not their own, learn new skills, experience new sensations, and try out new ideas. Rich loves traveling to various locations to see different productions of Shakespeare's plays. Recent evidence suggests that the older individuals with stronger mental ability show a greater interest in novel experiences than their contemporaries with average intelligence.[31]

"I had no idea I would like barbershop singing as much as I have," David (71) told me as we were walking our dogs one morning. A former high school teacher, David said that he had always wanted to sing in something besides the church choir but never had the time. He made it a point to attend the annual New England competitions of the Barbershop Harmony Society. When he retired, David began taking singing lessons to expand his range and then joined a senior barbershop quartet. He is hoping that they will qualify for the regional championships this year.

Marisol (72) and her husband love traveling to new countries as part of an archeological expedition; they hike and study the cultures of other civilizations. For the last 3 years, they have spent up to 3 weeks in Chile and on Easter Island. They also have excavated an ancient Mayan city in Central America and walked part of the Lambert Basin in Antarctica. Next summer, they are headed for a small island off the coast of Ireland.

Feel in Control, Competent, and Useful

Well over half of optimal cognitive agers have made the transition from basing their self-worth on their work and the care of others to being involved with other people, worthwhile undertakings, or self-development.[32] Rich's involvement with his family and with the school board and library committee is an example, as are those of the following 3rd Agers:

Most people do not know that Gabriela (69) suffers from hypertension, high cholesterol, and rheumatoid arthritis and lives with chronic pain in her right knee. This is because when there are social activities in the church, Gabriela is always in charge of the kitchen. Last week, she prepared food for 150 people after a wedding. Although there are people helping her, she likes to do most of the cooking herself. When there is dancing, she loves to show how well she can still do the salsa and merengue. Gabriela reflected that she hardly ever feels the arthritic pain when she is cooking or dancing.

In her former life, Jane (73) was an event planner in Minneapolis, Minnesota. Asked how she made the transition from the working world to retirement, she replied, "Well, I knew I needed to be busy. Playing golf all the time I knew wasn't going to work for me." Jane looked at volunteer opportunities and found that she loved helping build homes with Habitat for Humanity. Summing up why pounding nails for Habitat was so satisfying, she said, "There's nothing like that moment when you watch the keys being handed to the owners of the house you've helped build."

Reflections and Applications

One of the major challenges in the field of cognitive aging has been to identify the qualities that distinguish those who age optimally and those who do not.[33] The health-related characteristics and other behaviors linked to optimal cognitive aging in our sample of subjects add several promising variables to the accumulating list of the qualities associated with aging well.

What impressed me most about the optimal cognitive agers was the magnitude of differences in their behavior and those in the normal and high-risk groups. Consider activity level. San Francisco researchers followed almost 6,000 female septuagenarians on their activity level. They found that the top 25% were more than three times more physically active those in the middle of the group.[34]

These large differences between optimal cognitive agers and the others are not limited to exercise. High-functioning subjects between 70 and 79 years old who participated in the MacArthur studies of aging spent three to four times the number of hours in volunteer activities (22) as those in medium (6) and low (5) groups. A study by Daffner and his colleagues in Boston found that older adults with above average mental ability spent four times as long looking at novel stimuli as those with average scores.[35]

It is clear that the efforts are worth it. Consider the results of a lengthy research project aimed at identifying factors that contribute to continued optimal cognitive aging. Participants—9,704 women who were about 70 years old when the study began—were screened physically, psychosocially, and cognitively. Then, they were followed until the survivors were 85 years old.[36] When the researchers retested the remaining subjects, they discovered that 9% had no cognitive decline. The investigators then identified the factors that differentiated those in the optimal range from others whose mental skills had waned. We should not be surprised at their findings: absence of serious medical conditions; physical fitness; and the presence of healthy lifestyle behaviors that included not smoking, exercising, consuming alcohol in moderation, avoiding depression, and maintaining an enjoyable social network.

Why should caregivers concern themselves with optimal cognitive agers who are doing well and are currently problem free? After all, your time is likely to be needed by those who are not doing as well and those who are the most troubled or troublesome. Here are four reasons to pay attention to optimal cognitive agers: First, many are comfortable around people with expert knowledge, whose brains they might pick to be sure that they are doing all they can to keep themselves aging optimally.

Second, remember that the 3rd Age, like every other stage of the life span, has its unique set of developmental hurdles to be negotiated. In some respects, many 3rd Agers share with their adolescent grandchildren the feeling that big changes are occurring in their lives, that within the last few years there have been a lot of changes in their contemporaries, and that important decisions loom. And just as those things that made someone a star at 13 often do not matter much at 18, the satisfactions that came from child rearing and from working are largely a thing of the past when a person is retired and the kids are half a continent away.

Compared to midlife, the physical changes that occur in a short time span are dramatic in the 3rd Age, as are the differences in the rate at which the bodies of young-old adults grow older. Like 15-year-olds, there can be a great deal of physical and mental differences in a group of men and women at 72. Also, many 3rd Agers have serious decisions to make: when to retire from work or a major volunteer activity; whether to remain in the now-too-big home or downsize and, if so, where to go. Some of these older women and men will be eager to talk about these matters, while others will not.

Your appreciation that aging optimally is hard work is a third reason for you to be involved in their lives. Some seem to be more vigorous of body and mind to begin with, so it is not as hard for them to be active. However, the largest proportion of optimal cognitive agers have to push themselves every day to work out, do stimulating things, and remain active, involved, and useful. They struggle to maintain their self-discipline, saying "No" to that scrumptious-looking piece of pecan pie when they want to say "Yes" and forcing themselves to the gym on a rainy day when they would much rather stay snuggled up with a good book. They also will be challenged to apply the principles of selection, optimization, and compensation to remain engaged in those activities they most enjoy. Knowing that you notice and applaud their efforts will help some of your optimal agers sustain their motivation.

Finally, there will be those optimal agers who will benefit from your accompanying them through their 3rd Age years and beyond. Some may begin to show signs of cognitive and physical decline before they die, although they have done everything "right." Even if they remain vigorous, they are keenly aware that they may be one doctor's visit or lab report away from substantial medical challenges. A friend of mine calls this state "walking the knife's edge," named for the treacherous approach to the summit of Mt. Katahdin in Maine. Novelist Tom Wolfe[37] described it this way:

> At 55 you still think you're a young man. You still think your power and energy are boundless and eternal; in fact you're attached to your youth by only a thread, not a cord, not a cable, and that thread can snap at any moment.

Optimal cognitive agers have been through stressful circumstances—the loss of loved ones, financial hardship, debilitating medical conditions, and random misfortune. Most optimal cognitive agers are skilled at controlling their responses to adverse events and continuing to enjoy their lives. Even though they seemingly have everything under control, some will be grateful to a caregiver who is willing to keep them company on their journey through this portion of the life cycle.

7

Normal Cognitive Aging

Normal behavior has never been an especially popular topic for clinicians and academics, and the same is true for normal cognitive aging. Even in scientific journals, the interest is small. A search of the biomedical and life sciences database[1] in December 2010 found just 53 articles on "normal cognitive aging," whereas "optimal cognitive aging" yielded 1455 references, and "at risk for cognitive impairment" produced 4659.

While reading these publications, I noticed two missing elements. First is the absence of a positive definition of normal cognitive aging, except to say what it is not. If older adults do not meet the standards for aging optimally or being impaired, then they must be aging normally. *Normal* is said to be the lack of impairment—that is, "In normal aging there is nonpathological cognitive decline."[2] Other researchers have explained normal cognitive agers as the group that is left over when those aging successfully and those who are impaired were subtracted. One study described this middle group as "others."[3] This is a little like defining autumn as a season that falls between summer and winter rather than identifying those qualities unique to that time of the year.

The second missing element is the lack of other clinical observations about normal cognitive agers. Aside from declining health and unexceptional test scores as they grow into the 3rd Age, what else do we know about these normally aging individuals? Do they have modifiable risk factors that might be tied to mental ability scores that, if altered, might slow the downward trend of their mental ability?

As used here, *normal cognitive aging* is synonymous with "average" or "usual" cognitive aging. It refers to older adults who have experienced minor physical problems and who use their intellectual abilities in a manner typical of those in their age group with the same educational background. Most exhibit a small number of health conditions, risky lifestyle habits, and psychosocial qualities that set them apart from the optimal cognitive agers, but they are functioning at a noticeably higher level than those at high risk for cognitive impairment.

The estimated proportion of normal cognitive agers in the United States and most developed countries is 50 to 60%. This figure comes from four large population-based studies of 3rd Age subjects that included data on a normal group.[4]

Who Is Normal?

We classified normal cognitive agers using the same combination of global assessment and list of specific behavioral patterns unique to this group that was described in Chapter 6 about optimal cognitive aging.[5] This approach draws from the method for classifying overall mental health in the *Diagnostic and Statistical Manual of Mental Disorders, Fourth Edition, Text Revision*, and from its approach to diagnosing mental disorders by the number of clinical symptoms present.

Using the Global Assessment of Functioning scale, the description of those in the 71–85 age range corresponds best to the normal cognitive agers. They function well most of the time in their major work and activities and in interpersonal relations. When problems occur, they are transient and not disabling. Most in the normal range have one or two chronic medical conditions and the same number of risky lifestyle characteristics. More than half live with some residual dissatisfaction and bothersome symptoms, but these do not much diminish their overall quality of life.

When it came to distinguishing normal cognitive agers, the two lists of characteristics linked to normal cognitive aging were especially helpful in differentiating these 3rd Agers from those aging optimally or the group at high risk for cognitive impairment. Reading the reports of student interviews with older women and men rated in the normal range, I was struck by the number of descriptions of their health-related qualities, as well as attitudes and behaviors, which were unique to the group rather than being merely "not optimal." Frequently, the students described the normal agers as having "moderate energy," "seeing the doctor only when something hurts or is broken," and "accepting cognitive decline without doing anything about it."

Each of the health-related characteristics and attitudes and behaviors affecting the intellect was scored based on whether it was present or not. If six of the nine qualities shown in Table 7.1 and Table 7.2 were present, the subject was placed among the normal cognitive agers.[6] Illustrating the life of individuals classified in the normal range is Courtney.

Courtney

Now 61, Courtney has worked as a hairdresser for the past 30 years and is good at what she does. Even though she moved into the

Ashville, North Carolina, community from Pittsburgh, Pennsylvania, just 2 years ago, she is much in demand. One reason is that Courtney stays current with the always-changing cosmetology industry and radiates a lot of confidence in herself. Although slightly overweight (body mass index [BMI] of 27.6), she is physically fit and goes to Curves twice a week.

Courtney's in-control exterior belies the stresses that she has been coping with for the past decade—a divorce, a melanoma, and remarriage to an older man who now has kidney disease. Then, 6 months ago her daughter separated from her husband and moved to Asheville with her two young children. Both her husband and daughter are now partially dependent on Courtney. This could be one of the reasons that her trouble sleeping through the night has been gradually getting worse over the last year.

Overall, Courtney feels that her mind and body are declining at an average rate compared to her age group, but she feels that she is not much different from 5 years ago. Although she has good health coverage, she does not go to her doctor regularly because she does not like hearing bad news or being scolded. She says she already knows that smoking is bad for her, and she is aware that it puts her at greater risk for a recurrence of the cancer. She tried everything she could think of to stop—nicotine gum, hypnosis, and smoking cessation programs—for a short time but then loses momentum. "I wonder if any of these doctors or nurses ever smoked," Courtney remarked. "If so, they wouldn't yell at me so much."

Besides smoking, Courtney lives with another medically risky behavior—noncompliance with prescribed medication. At her last medical visit nearly 6 months ago, the doctor diagnosed Courtney with hypertension and elevated cholesterol and wrote prescriptions. She has not yet filled them because she knows "it's stress related" and that both will come down when she gets some time to relax. Unfortunately, she does not know when that will be.

Mentally, Courtney thinks that she is okay and may be just a little slower than 5 years ago. On the plus side, she always recognizes her customers and calls them by name, and she remembers how they like their hair done and the details of their families. "As soon as they start talking," says Courtney, "I can recall all sorts of things they have told me. But, I couldn't have told you anything about them before they started to talk."

Courtney has never been comfortable with the new communication technologies. She firmly believes that she is "computer illiterate," although she is slowly learning to use e-mail and to schedule appointments on the computer. Courtney does not like voice mail, she can barely work a cell phone, and texting is beyond her. "What's wrong with the ordinary telephone?" she asks.

"My biggest problem," Courtney says, "is when I have to think about two things at once." When she is working on somebody's hair, she cannot remember a phone number someone gives her to write down, so she asks them to repeat it, sometimes more than once. "It's like things just don't penetrate into my memory," Courtney reflects. Sometimes these problems bother her, but then she decides this is just part of the normal process of getting older, and there is nothing anyone can do. So, why get upset?

Considering the stresses Courtney is dealing with, it is not surprising that she rates herself at 5 on a scale of 1 to 10 as far as how happy she is with her life in general. Her stress level is 7 out of 10, which means that stress interferes with her life quite a bit. Courtney says that she feels lonely more now than a year ago. In the last year, her number of "down" days has increased from one or two to two or three a month.

What gets her down most of all is her lack of girlfriends. Being independent is something she used to view with pride. After her divorce, she lived alone for 11 years before remarrying and had all the friends she wanted. Now, she lives in a different part of the country, with her nonwork time consumed by caring for her husband and now her grandchildren. The loneliness is her own fault, Courtney concludes. She is so tired after working on the job and at home, she does not have the energy to do much else. "I think I'm just getting old," is her explanation.

Health-Related Qualities Associated With Normal Cognitive Aging

Normal cognitive agers show six or more of the nine health-related qualities listed in Table 7.1. Courtney exhibits at least seven of these qualities.

Moderate Energy and Activity Level

Like Courtney, most normal cognitive agers say their energy is moderate, and that their activity level has declined compared to 5 years earlier. Their activity level is 25–50% of their optimally aging contemporaries.[7] Here is what some other normal agers say about their energy levels:

"Before we get started here," said Frank, "I would like to point out that I'm an 83-year-old man who just goes with the flow. Nature will take its course, and time stops for no one." Overall, Frank characterizes his

Table 7.1 Health-Related Qualities Associated With Normal Cognitive Aging

1. **Moderate energy and activity level**
2. **Relative health no better than peers and may have declined in the past 5 years**
3. **Not proactive about medical checkups and screenings when not symptomatic**
4. **Lives with two or three medical conditions known to adversely affect the body and mind**
5. **Exhibits one to two risky lifestyle habits**
6. **Physical problems restrict satisfaction from previously enjoyed activities**
7. Stress adversely affects health-related quality of life
8. Two to three "down" days per month
9. Awareness of actions that benefit health does not lead to concerted corrective action

Characteristics in **bold print** found among 67% or more of normal cognitive agers.

general health as "fair" because he never feels full of energy; on the other hand, he never feels all that bad either.

Emily (age 65) says she had about the same energy level as people in her age group, but added that in the last 5 years her energy level has been lower. When asked to elaborate, she replied, "Well, 5 years ago I was more active, traveling more, and still exercising, and now that just seems like so much work." She sounded tired when she told me this.

Relative Health No Better Than Peers and May Have Declined in the Past Five Years

Courtney reports that her health is about the same as her age mates, who say that they are not as healthy as 5 years ago. Courtney has some new physical symptoms (insomnia) that are troubling. This self-perception of poorer health is not imaginary. Longitudinal investigations have found that nearly two thirds of normal older subjects say that their functional physical ability is no better, and possibly worse, than that of their peers.[8]

Ashley (57) is a fourth-grade teacher. Although she knows she is obese, Ashley rates her overall health similar to people her age but a little lower than 5 years ago. Because of her constant exposure to whatever diseases her students bring to school, Ashley thinks she gets sick easier than most people her age.

Based on her diagnoses of chronic obstructive pulmonary disease, congestive heart failure, and hypertension and her overall medical history, I expected that Sara (68) would be more impaired than she is. But, she still works full time. She credits her medications and her Buddhist spiritual practice, as well as her spouse and friends, for keeping her going. Sara reports that her energy level is lower than it was 5 years ago and no better than that of others her age. She rates her health as fair and says it is about on a par with her peers but worse than it was 5 years ago.

Not Proactive About Medical Checkups and Screenings When Not Symptomatic

Over half of 3rd Agers have not seen a primary care doctor or medical specialist in the past 12 months.[9] One reason the normal cognitive agers are less proactive about seeking medical care is that they do not appear to be as tuned in to their bodies as those aging optimally. And, some do not like the message they receive when they finally do see their health care provider. Courtney's avoidance of physicians illustrates that point. She has plenty of company.

Yenny (73) does not regularly appraise her physical status, which resulted in her having an increasingly painful ovarian cyst that grew to the size of a grapefruit before she went to see the doctor.

Joel (69) has joint pain and dizzy spells. He also reports periods of rapid heartbeat and blurred vision. When asked what medications he was on, Joel replied, "None." In the last year, he also acknowledged that the joint pain and dizziness made it hard to be with friends. But, he did not think that his problems were bad enough yet to see a doctor. Joel chalks it all up to just getting older and his body breaking down.

Lives with Two or Three Medical Conditions Known to Adversely Affect the Body and Mind

Like Courtney, who suffers from hypertension and excessive stress, over half of those older than 65 live with two or more chronic medical conditions that have negative consequences for health and cognition.[10] For instance, in longitudinal studies 3rd Agers in the normal range show a higher percentage of cardiovascular disease and diabetes compared to optimal agers.[11] These conditions can develop on the younger end of the 3rd Age, as the following examples illustrate:

A retired college music professor, Hillary (68) and her husband now run a bed and breakfast on a lake near Austin, Texas. They are connoisseurs of Texas wines and proudly serve the local vintages to their guests. They are regularly invited to wine tastings in the region and wine-related social and cultural events. Since retirement 3 years ago, Hillary says that her health has "gone to pot in more ways than one." Since starting the B&B, she has put on 10 pounds. And, her BMI (28.3) now makes her "officially overweight." She also has hypertension. Then, after knee surgery a year ago, her blood glucose levels became elevated, causing the doctor to worry about her developing type 2 diabetes. She cautioned Hillary to watch her diet, get more exercise, and drink no more than one glass of wine daily. "So far, I'm batting 0 for 3," Hillary says. Because of her occasionally painful knee, she does not exercise; she has not cut back on her calorie intake. And, she cannot imagine just having one glass of wine a day. At this point, Hillary feels fine, but periodically she worries about the next medical visit.

Kayla (58) feels that her emphysema has limited her activities quite a bit, and that her other conditions (periodic very rapid heartbeats) have also had a limiting effect. She cannot move around without becoming winded or exhausted, and since she stopped smoking 3 years ago, she has gained a lot of weight (BMI of 34.2). While Kayla realizes this, she still feels that food is one of only a few pleasures left to her. Also, she loves to cook for her friends.

Exhibits One to Two Risky Lifestyle Habits

Normal cognitive agers routinely showed evidence of one or more of the risky behaviors listed (e.g., smoking, heavy drinking, as well as being sedentary, obese, and noncompliant).[12] Consider Courtney's smoking and failure to fill the prescription to treat high cholesterol. One consequence of these lifestyle behaviors is premature death; another is an increased likelihood of disability.[13]

Since his second wife left him to move back to Texas, Charlie (62) says that he drinks more than he should. And, when he drinks, he also smokes. Charlie owns an electrical contracting business, and after work (since there is no one at home), he meets his buddies at a local bar for a couple of drinks and dinner two to three nights a week. He admits to occasionally reaching the point of intoxication but does not feel that he is in any danger because he takes a cab home. Charlie says he never really is hung over and has not missed a day of work in the past 15 years.

Jamal (64) works full time in a Home Depot and is on his feet all day. He mixes paint, which is all done by computers these days. Jamal says that he is the best in his department, and sometimes some of the younger guys call him at home for advice on how to mix a certain exotic color. His major problem now is that he is very obese (BMI of approximately 36) and has back problems and high blood pressure. Jamal says that he takes his antihypertension medication "when he thinks to do it" but admits that he does not take the pills regularly. He has given up his power walking, which he used to enjoy, "because it's more effort than it's worth."

Physical Problems Restrict Satisfaction From Previously Enjoyed Activities

Because of physical problems, nearly half of those in the normal range have given up major activities that they used to enjoy.[14] Some of the time, these restrictions were caused by medical conditions that might have been prevented or treated.

The biggest factor in the decision Homer (73) made to take early retirement a decade ago is that he began to have trouble with his hips in his mid-50s. Homer thoroughly enjoyed his work as a ceramics engineer, but by 60 the arthritis in both hips was so painful that he had trouble even sitting in a chair. In Homer's mind, his body parts were "giving up," so he felt he had no choice but to retire. Because of his hip problems, Homer said with a sad look, "I also had to give up my power boat and golf, and I miss them."

"Since I remarried and retired, I've put on about 5 pounds a year," Phyllis (68) said. During her career in the bank and as a single mother raising two children, Phyllis never had trouble keeping her weight under control. "Dinner after the kids left home was often a bowl of Cheerios while I was returning phone calls from home," she remembered. Plus, she played tennis twice a week at 6:30 in the morning before going to work. After remarrying and moving to St. Petersburg with her husband, who is older and not athletic, Phyllis has been "about as active as a mushroom." She has gone out a couple of times to play tennis, but it did not go well. She is convinced that she is now "too heavy, too old, and hitting the ball too poorly" to ever again be able to play.

Stress Adversely Affects Health-Related Quality of Life

Excessive stress can cause serious physical and cognitive problems, affecting overall quality of life. The chronic strain of caring for others, most often family members, worsens caregivers' self-reported health and increases frequency of illness, medical visits, and medication use.[15] Like Courtney, whose husband and daughter are now partially dependent on her, large numbers of 3rd Agers have had more than their share of stressful circumstances.[16] Here are two:

> Rose (75) is more upbeat when she is with others, but her social life has been closed down by her husband's ill health. He is in his early 80s and "needs a lot of maintenance." He does not want anyone else to do things for him. He also has severe arthritis and emphysema, so they cannot get out like in the past. Periodically, Rose gets depressed and aggravated but gets over it.

> The major stress Pia (64) feels in her life is the constant monitoring of her mother, who moved in with her 6 months ago. Her mother's mild dementia has worsened in the last year, to the point that she can no longer live alone and care for herself. Pia feels the physical and mental stress of balancing her work life with her mother's needs—bathing, dressing, and cooking for her. "This is something like having a child again," Pia laughs, "but I'm a lot older now and get tired a lot quicker than when I raised my daughter."

Two to Three "Down" Days per Month

Stress management among normal 3rd Age adults is average, meaning that their ways of coping are working pretty well most of the time. But, 2 to 3 days a month emotional problems erode the usual sense of well-being for those 65 or older.[17] The reasons vary. Some low periods are in response to feeling temporarily overwhelmed by unremitting physical problems, social isolation, financial worries, or care for others. Some stresses emanate from regrets about what might have been.[18] The mental distress passes after a short period.

Yvette (61) works in a busy mall shoe store. Divorced, she lives alone with a cat and has one son she seldom sees. She says that she is in the middle of a 1–10 scale as far as how happy she is with the quality of her life. Yvette rates her stress level at an 8, meaning that she feels a lot of pressure most of the time. While her anxiety is a 5, she grades her anger as an 8. The stress builds up during her work week, and it takes a lot out of her. Every Friday, she and friends go out after work for drinks and dinner. "Friday is get-high night," a time to socialize and unload. Yvette says that this is therapeutic for her but acknowledges that one to two times a month she "has too much medicine" and is hung over the next day. But, Yvette believes these get-togethers keep her going.

Helen (70) lives with several regrets, which get her down a couple of days every month or so. She gets down on herself periodically for not trying hard enough to find a husband and build a family. But, the decades passed, and she now lives with her niece instead of a spouse and children of her own. Helen regrets also not pursuing her dream of being a writer. These days, she writes letters to the editor and occasionally edits books for her friends, which partially make up for these lost dreams. Periodically, she cannot seem to let go of the thought that she did not try hard enough to realize those dreams that she had back in her 20s. But these moods pass, and she feels okay again.

Awareness of Actions That Benefit Quality of Life Does Not Lead to Concerted Corrective Action

Most normal agers know that they should be taking action to maintain better health, but this awareness does not lead to a consistent change in behavior.[19] In fact, recognizing they "should" lose weight or exercise creates feelings of shame and guilt in a subgroup of people, which cause them to withdraw rather than make an effort to diet or work out.[20] Courtney's sporadic efforts to stop smoking illustrate the point, as do the following examples:

Tianna (57) knows all about the health hazards of being overweight (which she is) and getting no exercise (which she does not). She signed up for Pilates at the "Y" but is too tired at the end of the workday to go. She cannot stay with a weight loss program for more than a couple of weeks. "I bet I've lost 100 pounds on all the diets I've been on, but then I put it all back." Because she is obese, Tianna does not like the way she looks and so does not go out to meet friends the way she used to do. Most nights she stays home, watches TV, and snacks.

Although diagnosed with weight-related type 2 diabetes almost 20 years ago, Frankie (64) has made no progress in controlling his obesity nor has he complied with his doctor's urging to eat and drink less and exercise more. As a result, Frankie has elevated blood pressure and cholesterol. He admits that is because he has overeaten and consumed too much bourbon. Otherwise, Frankie feels that he leads a full life—gardening, cooking, and being on call as the neighborhood handyman. He knows that someday he has got to get back in shape and lose some weight, but not right now.

Attitudes and Behaviors Associated With Normal Cognitive Aging

In addition to the health-related qualities shown in Table 7.1, normal cognitive agers have their own set of typical attitudes and behaviors, many of which Keith illustrates.

Keith

At 67, Keith believes he gets sick a little easier than he used to and definitely is not as healthy or as energetic as he was 5 years ago. On the other hand, he feels as though his health is about the same as his peers. "Most of my friends about my age are going downhill at about the same speed—mentally and physically," is how he puts it. Overall, Keith thinks that his physical state limits him some of the time at work and in what he does for fun.

Keith is half owner of a heating and air conditioning business, which he and his older brother founded 35 years ago. Sadly, his brother died 2 years ago, so now Keith's son and nephew pretty much run the business. Although Keith still comes into the office regularly, he comments that the business "is for young men," and he cannot work the way he did in the past. He spends most of his time in the office handling the finances. At the end of the year, he plans to turn the books over to the younger generation.

Everything Keith does these days takes more effort than it used to take. This may be because he misses his brother. Working side by side in the office or on jobs, they were a great team. And, his brother was Keith's best friend. While Keith does not appear to be depressed, he has several days a month when he definitely feels a little sad and is not quite himself. When comparing his happiness level now to that of 5 years ago, Keith rates himself as a "tiny bit" less happy.

Also hard for Keith was giving up his place in Colorado, where he used to ski and hike. But, he tires more easily now, has put on some weight, and cannot stand on his feet that long anymore. In fact, climbing more than one flight of stairs and walking more than a mile are a challenge for Keith.

Keith believes his mind has been hit harder by aging than his body. The biggest problem he has noticed is remembering names and numbers. And, sometimes he has a tip-of-the-tongue lapse—for instance, when he could not come up with the word for that game you play with phony money and little houses. He understands that it is all a part of the aging process; therefore, he tries not to let it bother him.

On the other hand, Keith enjoys reading biographies, and averages about two books a month. "Not too bad for a guy who dropped out of college after a semester," Keith said. "I can't imagine what my teachers would think if they could see me now."

His biggest worry, Keith admits, is that he gets disoriented or lost more these days than formerly. Last fall, he drove down to visit his son in Miami, Florida. While there, Keith went out on unfamiliar roads nearby to buy gas. He became lost and disoriented and could not find his way back. He finally had to call his son to get directions. Last Christmas, he received a smart phone from his son that has a global positioning system (GPS) application. Keith was so embarrassed that he did not take it out of the box for almost three months. Now, he uses it all the time.

He sees the doctor as needed. A two-pack-a-day man, Keith gave up smoking 17 years ago after he had a mild heart attack and had three cardiac stents put in to open the blockages in his coronary arteries. He also has been diagnosed with sleep apnea, for which he has been prescribed a continuous positive air pressure (CPAP) breathing mask. He has yet to buy the device. He has not discussed his concerns about his memory or disorientation problems with his doctor.

Keith and his wife, who is 3 years younger, have realized that when Keith stops working they will need something to give their lives a boost. Because they like to travel and love going to Tallahassee to watch football games, Keith and his wife are thinking about buying a recreational vehicle (RV) and driving around North America to visit places they have talked about seeing and catch up with old friends. "Thinking about it" is as far as they have gotten.

Table 7.2 Attitudes and Behaviors Associated With Normal Cognitive Aging

1.	**Feel cognitive abilities are holding up or declining normally, are equal to or less than they were 5 years earlier, and are in line with their peers**
2.	**Rarely appraise cognitive status or make small adjustments as needed**
3.	**Accepts cognitive decline, lets nature take its course**
4.	**Reduced number of and satisfaction with social relationships**
5.	**Limited use of communication technology**
6.	**Some use of elements of selection, optimization, and compensation**
7.	Mild executive dysfunction
8.	Does not actively seek new experiences
9.	Avoids some former intellectual activities

Characteristics in **bold print** found among 67% or more of normal cognitive agers.

As is the case with Keith, normal cognitive agers have at least six of the nine attitudes and behaviors delineated in Table 7.2.

Feel Cognitive Abilities Are Holding Up or Declining Normally, Are Equal to or Less Than They Were Five Years Earlier, and Are in Line With Their Peers

Although many normal agers in our study were bright, well educated, and accomplished, the majority were more modest than the optimal agers in their beliefs about their mental ability. In their minds, their intellectual powers were not what they once were, whether compared to their peers or themselves 5 years earlier.[21] Both Keith and Courtney reported that their cognitive skills are waning at an average rate, and that they are functioning below the level of 5 years ago. Here are two other examples:

Sharon (age 77) feels that her overall mental abilities have declined since she was 72, but that she is about on par with those she knows who are about her age. She notices a lot more tip-of-the-tongue problems these days, and sometimes she loses her way when she is telling a story. She thinks this happens more when she is talking with the women in her knitting group. Sharon wonders if she should stop knitting when she is telling a story.

Stan (83) offered an example of how his memory has declined with age. Recently, he and his wife met their college student granddaughter for lunch at a restaurant. It was chilly, and his wife asked him to retrieve a sweater she had left in the car. Their granddaughter asked if he would also get hers; it was pink, she told him, and he would find it inside the backpack in the trunk of her car. Stan was gone a long time, and when he finally returned, he had the granddaughter's down jacket, which was in a duffle bag, and had forgotten the sweater for his wife. As soon as he returned to the restaurant, he realized his mistake and went back for the sweaters. No one said a word because Stan was so obviously embarrassed.

Rarely Appraise Cognitive Status or Make Small Adjustments as Needed

A common pattern among the normal cognitive agers is little apparent effort to evaluate how they are functioning mentally and make the necessary accommodations. This problem appears among some who continue to drive in spite of diminished mental skills. About one in five older adults show impairment of visuospatial skills sufficient to compromise driving proficiency.[22] This deficit may occur singly or in combination with other diminished mental skills. A frequent problem is being unaware that visuospatial abilities are among the first aptitudes to decline and thus continuing to have navigational problems while driving rather than developing strategies for not getting lost. The spatial problems also may affect judgment about maintaining the proper speed and intervals between other vehicles.

Probably because Axel (82) is a retired professor and thinks of himself as having strongly crystallized intelligence as well as a superpositive attitude, he views himself as aging optimally. Although Axel is still "with it" mentally, his wife recognizes his declining mental ability, especially his memory for the names of people he meets for the first time at their retirement community and his increasing problems remembering what people say to him. He has always been a little "absent minded," but she thinks it is getting much worse. He does not recognize the decline in his mental abilities, so he does not think he needs to do anything to fix the problem.

For more than 20 years, Janis (78) and her good friend Brenda have enjoyed driving from Boston to Ft. Lauderdale, Florida, where Janis has an apartment right on the beach. After Brenda died 3 years ago, Janis insisted on driving down alone. When her son and daughter both objected, Janis became indignant. "All I have to do is follow 95 straight south, which I have been doing for over two decades." Two days later, the son was called by the police in Florence, South Carolina. His mother was in their custody. There had been a construction detour, and she had become lost and was found stuck in a farmer's field.

Accepts Cognitive Decline, Lets Nature Take Its Course

Many normal agers choose to accept cognitive decline and let nature take its course to deal with the realities of growing older, which includes the gradual decline of physical and mental abilities.[23] For them, it seems easier to accept these age-related cognitive limitations than to struggle to reduce their impact. Keith's and Courtney's attributing their cognitive problems to aging and accepting this decline rather than considering strategies to minimize the problem are prime examples, as are the following two brief sketches:

> On occasion, Lonzetta (69) notices that she is having trouble recalling people's names and the zip codes of addresses. She still reads a lot but it is mostly magazines now. She says that the novels she reads are shorter because she does not have the patience she used to have for elaborate plots and descriptions. She just wants the story. Lonzetta acknowledged that this fading of her mental ability bothers her occasionally. But, she understands that it is all a part of the aging process, so she does not let it interfere with her enjoyment of life.

> Sara (68) believes that health problems have taken a toll on her mental status. She finds that she has slowed noticeably, and it takes longer to do most things. Sara has learned not to trust her reasoning or instincts any more, unless she has plenty of time to think things out and then recheck her thinking. She used to be able to multitask, but one task or one conversation at a time is all that she can handle now. Distractibility is also increasing. Sara finds noises outside, like a lawnmower or someone working in the street bother her. Even worse are people talking and laughing in the office next to hers.

Reduced Number of and Satisfaction With Social Relationships

One of the consistent findings is that the number of social relationships and satisfaction with these contacts are associated with a higher quality of life,[24] and that it minimizes cognitive decline. We found small differences between the normal and optimal agers in the satisfaction that they felt with their circle of friends.[25] Many, like Keith, allowed their social networks to contract following a loss or a change in circumstances.

> After moving to Florida 5 years ago following her retirement from Delta Airlines, Grace (65) lost touch with many of her close friends back in Dayton, Ohio. Neither a golfer nor a tennis player, Grace became a docent at the community art museum and trained to be a hospice volunteer. She and her husband have made some friends in their condo community, but they have not really connected with anyone. "It's not the same making friends at 60 or 70 as it was back when you were 30 or 40." While she loves the weather and life outdoors in the winter, Grace really misses her old friends back home in Dayton.

> When his wife died from cancer 3 years ago, it was a huge loss for Ryan (78). They shared just about everything, and his wife usually took care of their social life. Now, Ryan rarely reaches out to others, so his circle of friends has shriveled. Both his children and their families live up north, and Ryan does not see much of them. He does not go to church and belongs to no social groups. Right now he is down to one friend, Ted, who encourages Ryan to get out of the house, accompanies him on trips to IKEA, and has an early-bird dinner with him once in a while. Sometimes, they catch a hockey game together. Ryan's children worry about what would become of their father should Ted move away.

Limited Use of Communication Technology

A minority of normal cognitive agers are competent with modern communication technology and have mastered the use of the computer and the Internet. A larger fraction of 3rd Agers find computers difficult because of the complexity, the constantly changing technology, and their declining physical and mental powers.[26] Courtney's description of herself as computer illiterate is one example. Here are two others:

> Axel (82) cheerfully admits he is a "technophobe," unable and unwilling to grasp new computer technologies. He proudly states that before he retired, he was the only professor in the history department who did not use e-mail. Unable to do anything with his cell phone beyond make an occasional call and barely able to work the computer beyond sending and receiving e-mails, he feels frustrated by and alienated from the new technology. Fortunately, his wife loves technology and

troubleshoots any problems Axel has with the computer. Recently, she has had a new satellite TV system installed, which still baffles him. "As long as she is around to handle the clickers, I'm okay," says Axel.

Tara (61) knows she has to keep up with current technology in her job as a pharmacy technician. She went back to work after her husband had a stroke and died 2 years ago. He took care of communicating with family and friends using the computer. Since starting her job, Tara has learned how to operate a computer, fax doctors for prescriptions or refills for their patients, and use the complex phone-messaging system at the pharmacy. It frustrates Tara when she cannot remember what she learned the day before. She is hoping that the company will be patient with her.

Some Use of Elements of Selection, Optimization, and Compensation

The use of selection, optimization, and compensation (SOC) techniques typically declines with age.[27] Because using these techniques requires good health, energy, and social support, normal cognitive agers typically use just some of the components of SOC, depending on their circumstances.[28] People with more resources tend to use more SOC elements. For example, Courtney stays up to date with new developments in cosmetology because she has a job that requires optimizing her skills. Here is what a couple of other normal agers do:

In her job as a vascular access nurse, Pia (64) explains that her primary task is inserting intravenous lines in patients with serious diseases, such as cancer, that require regular infusions. Pia has always had "the touch" with patients, who commend her for her relatively pain-free insertion of these intravenous catheters. She works in a fast-paced hospital environment with no room for mistakes. She likes her work, but Pia is beginning to notice that she has more trouble remembering her patients' names when she checks their catheters and occasionally has forgotten additional tasks that her supervisors ask her to do. She is compensating by writing down everything she has to do every day, including the names of her patients, and has resigned from a hospital IRB committee that she has enjoyed because she no longer has the energy for it.

"There's always tomorrow," Frankie (64) says about being retired. "This means I don't have to jam those things I try to do every day into a particular time slot. So, I don't get all worked up if a project in our flower garden takes 3 hours instead of the 2 hours I planned, or if it is hot and I want to stop and have a glass of cold water. And if I decide to watch an inning of the Red Sox game on TV, I do it. There's always tomorrow."

Mild Executive Dysfunction

Among the cognitive skills included among the executive functions are being able to focus attention without being distracted, processing speed, planning, working memory, judgment, and mental flexibility.[29] Although empirical evidence about the effect of aging on executive functions as a group is scant, considerable research has accumulated about the individual components. For instance, mental flexibility was much reduced among normally functioning 3rd Agers.[30] We observed a small number of normal cognitive agers with mildly impaired executive functions.

Henry (77) waited to pick up his wife in the airport cell phone lot. They had arranged for her to call him when she retrieved her bags in the terminal. Before leaving home, he had checked the arrival time of her flight and found that it would be on time. But, no call came. The other cars in the lot departed, leaving Henry waiting. He thought that his wife's flight must be late. After an hour of waiting, he decided to drive to the terminal and ask when his wife's flight would arrive and was shocked to see his wife waiting for him. Her cell phone battery was dead, so she could not call. She asked him why he did not guess what had happened and drive over to see if she had arrived. Henry had no answer.

Ben (75) was pleased when he was asked to talk at the History Department's monthly brown bag lunch about the student protests of the late 1960s. Few of the current members of the department were around then when Ben had been the chair. Ben did not think that he needed to prepare. He would talk off the cuff as he always had, which turned out to be a mistake. In his prime, Ben was known for his crisp, well-organized, get-right-to-the-point remarks. But, on this occasion his remarks were disjointed and rambling. He lost his place halfway through two anecdotes and had to be reminded of what he was discussing. He also found himself becoming uncharacteristically angry, using epithets when talking about the protesters who shut down his beloved university. Ben also lost track of time. When the current chair stopped his talk, Ben had been speaking for an hour and 15 minutes to a room now nearly empty.

Does Not Actively Seek New Experiences

Most normal cognitive agers let novel experiences come to them.[31] They know that exposure to new ideas benefits their minds, and they have not given up on being open to them. When encouraged by others, normal agers make an effort to occasionally do new things, such as traveling across the state to see the King Tut exhibit or taking a Caribbean cruise. But, as soon as the external motivation disappears, their interest in new experiences fades, and they return to their high-definition TV set. Often, they dream without it leading to action, just as Keith frequently thinks of traveling around the country in retirement, but so far he has not gotten around even to window shop for an RV.

It has been almost 15 years since Bob (73) left Wall Street and retired to a golf course condo in the Florida panhandle. These days, he spends most of his time playing golf or watching golf and other sports on TV. Because of all the tournaments at their country club, and with the nonstop social life surrounding these activities, most people he and his wife meet are golfers. For a change of scene, they go to their summer place on Hilton Head, South Carolina, where some of their golfing buddies also have places. He has been invited to join a cruise along the Turquoise Coast of Turkey organized by his Northwestern Business School class next fall, but he declined because the trip conflicts with the opening golf weekend in Florida.

Roger (66) is a retired state trooper. He is happy to be off the road and taking care of their small house on 20 acres south of Atlanta. Roger likes caring for the grounds and tending to their beehives, which produce high-quality honey that he bottles himself and sells in stores in the area. His wife, 3 years younger, still works part time as a physical therapist. When she is not working, there is nothing she would rather do than travel around the world seeing new places. Once a year, Roger joins his wife on a trip, but he could not tell you much about it afterward. Roger's idea of an exciting trip is to the Atlanta speedway to watch the NASCAR races.

Avoids Some Former Intellectual Activities

Most people become more cautious with age. Older adults show a growing tendency to avoid particular cognitive tasks if there is a risk of poor performance or uncertain outcome.[32] This includes cognitive tasks that in midlife were wholeheartedly undertaken. The reasons for avoiding this cognitive activity include a perceived reduction in competence, for example, Keith's belief that his heating and air conditioning business was a young man's game after his brother died.

Christine (58) turned down the invitation from the superintendent to apply for promotion to assistant principal of an elementary school. The reason is that the position requires that she complete a master's degree. It was not long ago that Christine was working on her master's but gradually lost momentum. Now, she does not feel up to taking the two more courses to finish her master's in education. "It's not that I can't do it," Christine rationalizes, "It's just that I have better things to do in the summer than to learn and regurgitate more educational theory."

Ashley (73) rates her mental ability as a little slower than 5 years ago and occasionally has problems with attention and memory. Ashley says that she avoids certain things regularly. Increasingly, she prefers the afternoon TV dramas, movies, and the reality shows because it was sometimes "stressful " to watch fast-paced news shows. Watching CNN is challenging because there are so many things going on at once—the host talking, several people being interviewed, and the strip of other news running along the bottom of the screen. Now, Ashley prefers a more leisurely pace and one thing at a time.

Reflections and Applications

We did not have to interview a lot of normal cognitive agers before we realized that many of them were bright, ambitious, and capable. Quite a few, however, had been dealt bad hands. They faced limited opportunities, had to shoulder heavy burdens at a young age, confronted devastating losses, and endured serious injury and chronic illness. A few made bad choices and lived with the consequences. Stories of remarkable grit, courage, and tenacity were common. Most of these normally aging women and men have kept on going no matter what the weather or terrain, putting one foot in front of the other, finding ways to cope with enormous stresses, raising their families, working their jobs, fighting our wars, and fighting against our wars. They are the backbone of their communities.

Like Courtney, several of the 3rd Agers we interviewed were caring for elderly loved ones, and a few were also helping out their children and grandchildren. This caretaking can be highly stressful and harmful to the aging mind and body. How caregivers reacted to stress greatly influenced the health consequences of being responsible for others. Experts tell us that caregivers who use problem-based solutions fared better than those who employed emotion-based coping strategies.[33]

No doubt that is true, but sometimes the best those in stressful situations can do is to comfort themselves. So, they have that second helping or the third drink, knowing the relief is temporary. Why? Because temporary and ineffective as these maneuvers are, they enable these caregivers to dissipate some of their tension so that they can get up tomorrow and continue taking care of those they love. Perhaps later they can work out more adaptive ways of handling these problems.

The men and women described in this chapter were selected because elements of their story illustrate the health-related characteristics and the behaviors and attitudes typical of normal cognitive agers. It was only after I began writing their stories that several features of these 3rd Agers in the normal range became apparent to me. A large proportion were on the younger side of the 3rd Age, in their late 50s and early 60s—in contrast to the majority of those aging optimally, who were well into their eighth decade and beyond. This observation makes me think that caregivers to the elderly should try to spend some time sending the message to their middle-aged children and others in this age group that the road to optimal aging begins in the 30s and 40s.

For instance, a large number of the younger normal agers—including Christine, Kayla, and Jamal—had been obese or overweight since midlife. Individuals struggling with excess adiposity remind us that the baby boomers entering the 3rd Age in the next decade include a higher percentage of obese individuals than in previous generations.[34] This extra weight brings with it an increased vulnerability to hypertension, elevated cholesterol, and type 2 diabetes, chronic medical conditions that can lead to more rapid cognitive decline. Current media attention on the successful efforts of adults with severe adiposity to lose weight and the interest of the First Lady in combating childhood obesity may slow or even reverse this trend in the next decade. Definitely, keep your eye on this.

Obesity is not the only bad habit that if modified could make a difference in the quality of life enjoyed by these normal cognitive agers. Two other frequently mentioned bad habits were excessive alcohol consumption and social isolation. What strikes the clinical psychologist in me is the potential that so many normal agers have to become optimal agers. Quite a few were just one improved habit or attitude change away from aging optimally. By the same token, it is fair to say that some of these presently functioning normally were on the brink of becoming at high risk for cognitive impairment. Might the knowledge that their continued heavy drinking is likely to lower their intellectual voltage help Charlie and Hillary find the motivation to cut back on their alcohol intake? Could Janis find someone else to accompany her on her drives to Florida and Ryan expand his social network beyond one person?

Of all of the bad habits normal agers accumulate, it would seem that non-compliance should be one of the easiest to improve. It is not an addiction and does not require going hungry or working up a sweat. Yet, as many as half of all 3rd Agers with prescriptions have not filled them or do not take them as directed. If this topic does not emerge spontaneously in a clinical contact, it is reasonable to ask older adults in your care about their adherence to medical advice and prescriptions.

Suppose you were to find that Courtney has not been taking her hypertension medication. The first task is to find out the reason for her noncompliance. The answer may be as simple as that she does not understand why she has been given the prescription.[35] Or, she may not believe in the effectiveness of the medication or may worry about the side effects.[36] Once she is able to express her reservations, she is likely to be open to hearing the reasons for adherence. Courtney might not know that untreated high blood pressure has a strong likelihood of lowering her IQ, along with adversely affecting her health, whereas taking medication may well protect her from this decline.

Attitudes about growing older matter. Several normal cognitive agers we met suffer from self-inflicted ageism. Ageism initially referred to discrimination against people because they believed too old to function normally.[37] Not long ago, physically and mentally able individuals were forced to retire at 65. This was because of the negative stereotype, based on no evidence, that older individuals were for the most part frail, sickly, and mentally compromised, with their productive years behind them.[38]

This negative stereotype has been internalized by some in the 3rd Age, causing them to believe that they are helpless to change the trajectory of their personal physical and mental decline.[39] Homer views his hip and other body parts as "giving up," being part of an irreversible decline, instead of consulting a surgeon to see if his hip could be replaced and normal function restored. Because Helen is certain that she is "too old" to imagine writing something that could be published, she sees no reason to consider signing up for a writing course to see if she could bring her skills up a notch and find encouragement to try writing again.

Experienced clinicians have no illusions about how easy it is to help people make even small changes in their behavior patterns or begin to view their attitudes in a different light. But, my experience has been that sometimes listening, empathizing, offering information, even giving a bit of advice now and then can make a difference. And, on occasion a well-timed piece of information casually shared with someone rings an alarm that sets off remarkable behavioral change.

At a November meeting in San Antonio, Texas, I presented a paper on this book's topic. Preston, a former student whom I had not seen since he moved to Texas, waited for me outside the door afterward. As we talked, he picked up a handout describing the findings from this research. He smiled when he told me that he had just turned 55, which according to the handout put him in the 3rd Age. Then, Preston commented that he had most of the qualities of optimal agers except that he still smoked. He had tried several smoking cessation programs without success and asked if I had any new ideas. I did not, but I remember saying that there was an old idea that helped me personally. This was visualizing myself as a nonsmoker, as someone who did not smoke rather than as a smoker trying to quit. He said nothing, and I was not certain he even heard me. Then, he left to go to another meeting. After that, I had no contact with Preston until I received his e-mail the following summer. In it, he thanked me for "motivating" him to stop smoking. Preston said he has taken up bicycling and just completed a 150-mile weekend charity ride up to Austin and back. He added that he could not have done it without me.

I wish I knew more about what it was that stimulated Preston to stop smoking. Maybe it was as simple as thinking of himself as a nonsmoker, but I doubt it. What triggered the impetus for Preston could just as easily have come from another casual one-to-one contact, a handout, a lecture, a newspaper piece, or a random event. While I will never know what caused the light to go on for Preston, this experience reminds me that nearly everyone has periods when they are ready to make healthy changes in their lives. A little nudge at that moment is all it takes.

8

High-Risk Cognitive Aging

Among the 3rd Agers interviewed were a small number whose multiple medical conditions and poor lifestyle habits put them at higher risk for cognitive impairment. We labeled them high-risk cognitive agers. Other research that classified groups of older adults into "major decliner" or "low" groups used one or more criteria similar to those we applied to differentiate those at high risk for cognitive impairment from the higher-functioning subjects.[1]

The criterion most often applied to the high risk groups was a major decline in health status. This deterioration of health frequently stemmed from cardiovascular disease, hypertension, diabetes, and other medical conditions that accelerate the rate of cognitive decline and increase the risk for dementia.[2]

More than two-thirds of older adults in the high risk groups in our research and the studies of others functioned below normal intellectually.[3] The apparent reasons for their subpar intellectual acuity differed slightly. These older adults at high risk shared one or more of the following characteristics: (1) They were burdened by five or more severe medical conditions or risky behaviors that are linked to a more rapid decline in intellectual powers. (2) They evidenced periodic diminished intellectual functions because of depressed mood, anxiety, or anger related to psychosocial, behavioral, or situational causes but could recover and function normally. (3) They exhibited chronic memory and other persistent cognitive problems that seemed independent of psychological or situational factors and more characteristic of what was described in Chapter 3 as aging-associated cognitive decline (AACD) or mild cognitive impairment (MCI).[4]

Estimates are that 15–20% of 3rd Agers exhibit behaviors that put them at high risk for cognitive impairment.[5]

Assessing Individuals at High Risk for Cognitive Impairment

To assess women and men in the high-risk group, we applied the same approach that was used to identify those aging optimally and normally. This included rating a person's overall functioning, along with identifying particular characteristics linked to high-risk cognitive agings.[6] On the Global Assessment of Functioning scale, the psychological adjustment range from about 56 to 70 describes this group. Although many were still functioning above the threshold for a psychiatric diagnosis, their activity level and their relationships were problematic or unsatisfying. Psychological symptoms, most often anxiety and depression, lurked and threatened to undermine their mental health. As a result, they had far more "down" days per month than the normal agers.

The model also enables the clinician to assess a person's level of intellectual functioning based on a number of observable characteristics. Tables 8.1 and 8.2 set out health-related qualities and specific attitudes and behaviors associated with being at high risk for cognitive impairment.

Although their overall functioning was below average, those at the high-risk level were not severely disabled. This may have been because all of the high-risk agers we interviewed had other people in their lives who looked after them (spouses, children) and took over some of their responsibilities (paying bills, shopping, cooking, maintaining a small social life), enabling them to live on their own. While many were noticeably slower than average intellectually, a few still functioned well. Regardless of their intelligence level, however, a common denominator among those in this group was that they had accumulated a number of medical conditions, risky lifestyle behaviors, and other qualities that put them at serious risk for cognitive impairment. They were an accident waiting to happen.[7] Meet Lenny.

Lenny

At 6 feet 4 inches and well over 300 pounds for most of his adult life, 62-year-old Lenny has always been the "big guy" in the room. He lives with his wife on a small farm south of Gainesville, Florida. Until 2 years ago, Lenny was energetic and happy and ran several successful car dealerships. In those days, Lenny remembered himself as a "little wild" but always the life of the party, always having fun. Adventuresome by nature, he collected Harley-Davidson motorcycles and especially enjoyed riding with his friends over to Daytona or up to Laconia for bike week. His friends nicknamed him the "biking bear."

A former college football player, Lenny always had been physically active. He bowled and played on the softball team for the dealership. In season, he hunted and fished, and he had season tickets to the Gators football games. He traveled the world in luxury with alumni members of the Young Presidents' Organization. He once thought of running for mayor but decided against it because he did not want to be tied down.

Lenny loved eating, knew he ate too much, and always said, "I enjoy every bite." In fact, he had tried "every diet there ever was," but nothing worked. In his 40s, he went on medication for elevated blood pressure and cholesterol. Carrying all that weight caused chronic pain in his knees, which eventually resulted in a double-knee replacement when he was in his mid-50s. Right after the surgery, Lenny developed type 2 diabetes. Then, the week before his 60th birthday, Lenny had a heart attack. Although he was treated successfully, the doctor said that he was lucky this time. Unless he took a lot of weight off, the odds of his avoiding and surviving another heart attack were unfavorable. That scared him so much that Lenny made a decision to sell his car dealerships and retire.

Shortly afterward, he decided, along with his family and physicians, that having bariatric surgery was his best chance of getting healthier and living longer. The procedure chosen for Lenny reduced the size of his stomach surgically, which causes the recipients to feel full more quickly. It also allows food to bypass part of the small intestine, resulting in absorption of fewer calories.

This decision would change his life for the better and for the worse. The "better" was that 2 years after his surgery Lenny was no longer obese. The surgery transformed the once big guy into a good-size 206-pound male with a normal body mass index (BMI). His doctors told Lenny that he was in better health than ever. For Lenny, however, the "worse" was that he felt he had lost his old self. He missed being the biggest man in the room, being the biking bear. Even though he could do a lot more physically, when Lenny looked in the mirror he hated what he saw. All that excess skin on his face and body was unattractive, and Lenny thought it made him look like just an average old geezer.

He confessed that his embarrassment over the way he looked was one of the reasons he had withdrawn from most of his old friends. He does not travel with the Young Presidents' alumni group anymore. Gone are his days of motorcycle riding and hunting, softball, and bowling and the parties. He said he does not have the energy for them these days. Mostly now, he can be found on his tractor in the large field behind his house, mowing the fields and caring for several acres of vegetables and flowers.

Now, Lenny's immediate family is his primary social network. Fortunately, he and his wife live close to their daughter, her husband, and two granddaughters. Lenny drops by their house daily. There his mood lifts, and he is talkative and interacts with everyone. He still likes to play cards or board games and often wins. That cheers him up for a few hours.

Lenny sometimes wished he had never opted to have the stomach surgery. He did not realize how much he liked being large. Also, he becomes frustrated because "the surgery took away one of my favorite things to do in life." He sometimes feels jealous of others who can eat whatever they want while he consumes only tiny amounts. His wife says he sometimes eats too much and throws up—and she suspects these episodes have increased. She has also noticed that Lenny is erratic about taking his blood pressure medication. What she does not know is that he still has an occasional cigarette.

Lenny admitted that he now "gets down" a lot more than previously. The thoughts of what he cannot do anymore have made him angry, and the anger, he confesses, "sometimes gets taken out on the wrong people, like my family." His wife says that Lenny has changed for the worse. He is not much fun to be with now, and several people who have known him for a long time think he is depressed. When a well-meaning friend suggested that he see a therapist, Lenny rejected the idea, saying he thought his wife was the one who needed therapy. Maybe he was right, his wife thought to herself. She loves him, but these efforts have worn her out. Recently, she has noticed more wrinkles and is thinking of calling a counselor for herself.

Health-Related Qualities Associated With High-Risk Cognitive Aging

Why is Lenny, whose family considers his mental ability to be as strong as ever, classified among the high-risk group? This is because his physical, social, and psychological state put him at risk for serious health problems that are likely to compromise his intellect. Table 8.1 lists the health-related qualities found among the high-risk group. High risk cognitive agers typically exhibit five or more of these qualities.[7] Lenny shows evidence of at least six of them.

Low/Moderate Energy and Activity Level, Less Than Peers and Than Five Years Earlier

A feeling of being less energetic than in the recent past and less vigorous than peers characterizes those at high risk.[8] The magnitude of their difference from the normal cognitive agers is striking.[9] You feel their energy deficit when you are around them. Lenny's story captures this quality. Here are other illustrations:

Table 8.1 Health-Related Qualities Associated With High-Risk Cognitive Aging

1. **Low/moderate energy and activity level, less than peers and than 5 years earlier**
2. **Five or more medical conditions or risky lifestyle behaviors known to adversely affect health and cognition**
3. **Physical/psychosocial problems greatly reduce enjoyment from two or more activities that previously provided pleasure**
4. **Failure to confront major risk factors to health and cognition**
5. **A week or more of "down" days per month**
6. Failure to recover from a stressful event
7. One to two instrumental activities of daily living compromised

Characteristics in **bold print** found among 67% or more of the high-risk group.

At 74, Delores looks her age, maybe even a little older. She has numerous wrinkles around her mouth, which appear to be caused by years of smoking, a habit she continues. She hunches over when she walks, moves slowly, and has a hard time getting around. Delores rates her energy level as a little lower compared to others her age, feels she has less pep, and feels that her health is much worse than 5 years ago.

A thin and frail-looking man with a sweet and courtly disposition, Robert (age 70) says that he is far below where he was 5 years ago physically and also does not have the same energy level. Robert remains interested in the outside world, but has stopped reading two newspapers daily. Now he stays current by watching the TV news channels. He does not think much about how he compares to people his own age, but he guesses he is below average. Robert thinks the reasons have to do with his poor health, which he says is "self-inflicted." He smoked for over 50 years, only giving it up 2 years ago when he had surgery for lung cancer. He is currently in remission but has type 2 diabetes "because of all those fast food meals when I was working." He has poor circulation in his legs that he says makes exercise impossible.

Five or More Medical Conditions or Risky Lifestyle Behaviors Known to Adversely Affect Health and Cognition

An impressive number of medical conditions and risky lifestyle behaviors were found among the high-risk agers. Take Lenny. He is living with two medical conditions that put his intellect at risk: hypertension and type 2 diabetes. He also has at least three unhealthy lifestyle habits: smoking, not taking his hypertension medication, and little exercise. His overeating to the point of nausea also qualifies as risky behavior. Studies of adults who had three persistent medical conditions at midlife showed them to be at considerably higher risk for dementia in later life.[10] Here are two more examples:

Aging has taken a heavy toll on Ernst (76), who gave up teaching law part time 2 years ago. "I loved it, but it was taking too much out of me," he explains. Although he has always been overweight, Ernst remembers being a vigorous younger man. However, a heart attack at age 49 and coronary problems afterward slowed him down. Several stents have been put in because of blockages, and a year ago, he had a pacemaker installed. In addition, he is dealing with high blood pressure and elevated triglyceride readings. Then, there is the chronic pain in his left hip, so the treadmill in the basement goes unused.

Louisa (78) has to have oxygen at night. This is because of her chronic obstructive pulmonary disease, which means she does not get enough oxygen into her blood from just room air. "It's not fair," she says with a wry smile. "I gave up smoking almost 10 years ago because I was afraid of getting something like this," Louisa says. She is also on medications for atrial fibrillation and high blood pressure. She admits that she sometimes has trouble remembering "to take all my pills." In addition to her physical problems, Louisa has no family around and has lost several friends in the last couple of years, including her best friend, who died 6 months ago. She is feeling pretty isolated and lonely right now.

Physical/Psychosocial Problems Greatly Reduce Enjoyment From Two or More Major Activities That Previously Provided Pleasure

Compared to normal individuals, more than twice as many of those in the high-risk range feel that their life is far less enjoyable than in the recent past. Pleasure is reduced from at least two types of activities that used to provide pleasure, such as working, loving relationships, sports/exercise, and spiritual activities.[11] Even though he is physically healthier than he used to be, Lenny does not like the way he looks; he no longer enjoys working, he is not involved in the community anymore, his social life has dried up, and those recreational activities that provided much pleasure—riding his motorcycle, hunting and fishing, bowling and softball, and world travel—are distant memories. Here are two others whose satisfaction from living has been greatly reduced:

Hannah (75) says she is tired of her life. It is obvious to her why she feels this way. Her husband—the light of her life, her best friend, and the only man she ever loved—was killed in a car accident 2 years ago. They used to do everything together, and now she finds she cannot enjoy anything without him. She also has noticed that friends she and her husband had as a couple no longer include her, and she does not have the energy to reach out to them. Since his death, Hannah says she has let herself go, has stopped working out, is not watching what she eats, and feels unfit. Last week, when Hannah went for a walk she had to stop after 10 minutes because her chest started to hurt. She knows that she should see a doctor but has not yet. When Hannah told her daughter about the chest pain, she remarked, "You know, I'm not holding on to life with both hands anymore."

Retirement has not gone well for Richard (75). An accountant, he worked for a small firm for most of his career. A year after a larger organization absorbed the company, Richard was told that he was no longer needed. That was 4 years ago. Some of his friends suggested that he work part time for someone else or set up his own practice, but Richard does not want to return to accounting because he knows that he could never find the same pleasure from this work as before. Those days are long gone, he tells himself. Richard also has health issues. Just after retirement, he developed a balance problem that has been diagnosed as Ménière's disease, along with a hearing loss in his left ear. Because of this, he stopped playing golf, and most of his friends have stopped coming by his house.

Failure to Confront Major Risk Factors to Health and Cognition

Compared to normal agers, women in their early 70s who were similar to those in the high-risk group had almost twice the frequency of strokes as well as a greater incidence of diabetes and hypertension during a 15-year follow-up study.[12] Whether because of being too busy, being unwilling to confront the seriousness of a problem, or being unaware of the potential grave consequences of their harmful health practices to the body and mind, many high-risk older adults make little apparent effort to alter their actions to improve their physical and mental outlook.

Because of his hearing loss, Richard (75) has difficulty picking up what other people are saying. This makes conversations a challenge because he misses a good many words and has to guess from the context what the person is saying. Still, Richard will not wear a hearing aid because he thinks it makes him look ancient. And, even though his wife and at least two of his friends have wondered if he might be depressed and would benefit from seeing a therapist, Richard has refused. "What can they do to help?" he muttered. "There's no pill for someone with old-age disease."

Dan (61) is aware that his obesity, hypertension, high triglycerides, and type 2 diabetes are four of the ingredients in what medical professionals call the "metabolic syndrome."[13] And, he does not need to be reminded of that. "I can read and don't need another doctor to give me a lecture about taking off 30 pounds," he says. Then, he adds, "I don't have the courage to tell him that I still occasionally drink more than I should." Dan is a successful senior vice-president of a large national health care organization that own hospitals throughout the South. He works hard and travels constantly. Dan's former wife divorced him because she said that he was more "in love with his job than me." Dan has read the statistics showing that metabolic syndrome raises his risk of cardiovascular disease about 20 times. He has tried to lose weight off and on, but he is so busy he cannot sustain his motivation for more than a week or two. His excess weight embarrasses him, but he feels helpless to reverse the trend right now. So, he tries not to think about it.

A Week or More of "Down" Days per Month

On average, 3rd Agers have two to three down days a month. As a group, the high-risk agers have at least a week every 30 days when they feel morose, negative, anxious, frustrated, or obsessed with their own problems.[14] Some can be unpleasant to be with, yet are dependent on others to lift their spirits. Not only is chronic psychological distress hard on the individual and their loved ones, but also it reduces the likelihood of seeking needed medical care or being compliant.[15] Here are other examples of people who suffer from down days for more than a week each month:

Sometimes, the rabbi has moments of thinking that 79-year-old Irving is a bottomless pit of self-pity. A long-time member of the synagogue, Irving does nothing but talk about how sick he feels, how he has no friends anymore, how the fun has gone out of his life, and how unhappy he is. Yet, he is in good health, his kids are doing well, and he is financially comfortable. But, then the rabbi reminds herself that Irving's wife died 2 years ago, his two children live on the West Coast, and his social life is barren these days. The rabbi remembers when Irving ran a successful business and was a member of the city council. How things have changed. When the rabbi suggested some ideas to help—a spiritual enrichment group, grief counseling, a therapist—Irving rejected them. Sometimes, she has the impulse to tell Irving that many people in the congregation are coping with far greater tragedies than his. The rabbi knows this will not work, but she is about out of ideas on how to help this man.

"For the past 15 years, my husband's health has been declining. He has a heart condition, severe osteoporosis, gastrointestinal problems, and now prostate cancer." This was how Nina (77) introduced the topic of how stressful her life has been. Five years previously, they moved to another part of the state to a retirement community with assisted living so that she could have relief in caring for him. But she does not like living "in a home," has made no friends, is lonely, and feels depressed. Nina does not want to see a professional about her depressed feelings because "no doctor can change what I'm dealing with." Meanwhile, Nina has given up quite a few of things she used to enjoy. She used to exercise, but now feels it is pointless; she used to read but has stopped; she used to do needlepoint but has given it up. Now, she mostly watches TV and periodically wonders if her mind is turning to mush.

Failure to Recover From a Stressful Event

One of the qualities that differentiate some high-risk agers from other older adults is their inability to recover from the effects of highly stressful but not unusual experiences associated with growing older. Examples are serious health problems, death of loved ones, retirement, relocation, or other losses. Their reactions to these events resemble the lengthy melancholic grieving so well described by Freud.[16] Lenny's great difficulty in dealing with the changes in his body is an example. Here are others:

His health started to deteriorate at age 60. That is when JB, now 73, began to have severe arthritis in his back and knees, which prompted him to retire from his successful real estate business. Previously, he had been an avid hiker and mountain climber and skied the double black diamond trails. Now, JB has given up all these activities. Part of the reason is that he cannot do them as well as he he had. "I'm not skiing those blue squares," is how he dismissed the suggestion that he ski the intermediate slopes. "If I can't ski the way I used to, it's not worth doing." He applies the same reasoning to hiking and climbing.

What Hannah (75) says she's looking forward to most is seeing her husband again in heaven. Even though it has been 2 years, there are still days when she does not think she can bear the pain of missing him. She reminisces about the wonderful times they had together—raising their children, working side by side when he was establishing his chiropractic practice, walking the beach together on Sanibel Island, taking cruises to the Caribbean. Since her husband's death, several men have shown an interest in her, but Hannah cannot imagine being with anyone else.

One or More Instrumental Activities of Daily Living Compromised

Between 10 and 15% of older adults have problems carrying out one or more instrumental activities of daily living, which are crucial to being able to live independently.[17] These include the ability to use the phone or other communication devices, shop, prepare food, keep house, do laundry, travel independently, manage medications, and handle finances. These problems often are masked by the presence of a spouse, child, or other caregiver. Without someone to assume these responsibilities, many high-risk cognitive agers could not live on their own. The following are examples of the kind of thing that might have happened to Lenny without his wife or family members living next door.

After her husband's death a year ago, Laura (73) continued to live in the house in a small seacoast community in Maine. Part of the reason was that her youngest sister lived in the next town. Although her husband always handled the money, Laura thought she knew how to pay bills. After all, she had done it the first 10 years of their marriage. Six months after her husband's death, Laura found that her electricity was shut off. When she called the power company to complain, the phone menus were so complicated that she gave up and called her sister for help. Her sister contacted the power company and learned that Laura's bill was 6 months overdue. Furthermore, she had not responded to several warnings, so they turned off her electricity. Then, Laura's sister asked to see how she had been paying her bills. She discovered that they were scattered haphazardly on the big dining room table, and Laura had not indicated whether they had been paid or not. The checkbook log of payments was blank. The sister discovered hefty penalties on several of the bills for late or no payment. Looking around the house, she also found rotten food in the refrigerator and a basement full of unwashed clothes. When she confronted her sister, Laura began to weep.

When his son made his semiannual visit to see Ralph (81), who lived alone in a mobile home park, he noticed that the trailer was dirtier than he remembered it. When he looked in the pantry, he found it stocked with cans of beef stew and a case of 1.75-liter bottles of Pinot Grigio. Then, his son discovered a half dozen pills of different kinds littering the floor near the nightstand in his father's bedroom. When asked about these, Ralph said that he takes 11 different medications a day, and sometimes he drops some of them. "But I make up for the missing dose by taking two pills in the next round," Ralph explained. Not reassured, his son observed his father during the next 2 days and found that sometimes Ralph forgot to take some of his medications entirely. His son also found an unfilled prescription for hypertension drugs. When asked, his father responded irritably, "I'm already taking almost a dozen pills a day now. Don't you think that's enough?"

Attitudes and Behaviors Associated With High-Risk Cognitive Aging

In addition to the health-related qualities shown in Table 8.1, the high-risk cognitive agers also share many attitudes and behaviors described in Table 8.2 below. Here is Valerie's saga:

Valerie

After their two children left home, Valerie (74) started working part time in the office of her husband's insurance agency in Green Bay, Wisconsin, and then passed the exams to become a broker. Over the next two decades, Valerie was successful, and the office did well. Then, in her early 70s Valerie's life began unraveling. Her husband had a stroke and died within a week. Six months later, Valerie was diagnosed with breast cancer and had surgery and a breast reconstruction. This was followed by a lengthy period of debilitating radiation and chemotherapy.

The only good thing to come from the cancer, Valerie thought to herself while recuperating, was that she stopped smoking cold turkey. What she did not like was the 20-pound weight gain that occurred over the next year. Valerie was not surprised when she was diagnosed with elevated blood pressure and cholesterol at her next physical.

Because the cancer made her future uncertain, Valerie decided to sell the business to a younger associate. Then, she sold her house in Wisconsin and bought a golf course condo in Sarasota, Florida. And, she loved it. "Never liked snowshoeing or ice fishing," Valerie joked. "Here, I am outdoors almost every day in the winter, playing golf or tennis. Plus there is something to do every day and people to do it with. It's like going to the playground when you were a kid."

Valerie especially liked going out with her friends to the early bird dinners that featured two-for-one drinks. Valerie had been a moderate social drinker when she worked, but now that she did not have to get up early the next morning, Valerie began to drink more heavily. Although she never appeared drunk, Valerie's drinking increased to the point that a friend began to notice that she was mildly intoxicated after dinner more than once a week.

When Valerie's daughter called late one evening and found Valerie slightly incoherent again, she expressed concern over Valerie's drinking. She gently suggested that Valerie discuss this with her doctor. Valerie brushed her daughter's worries aside, saying the doctor was not concerned. What Valerie did not say was the doctor never asked about her alcohol intake, so she saw no reason to bring it up.

Shortly afterwards Valerie's drinking brought everything to a head. Driving home alone after dinner and several rounds of two-for-one drinks, Valerie ran a stoplight and was pulled over by the police. She failed the field sobriety test and was arrested, handcuffed, and taken to the station. When a breath analyzer found her blood alcohol level was twice the legal limit, Valerie spent the night in jail. Afterward, she was fined, her driver's license was suspended, and she was required to complete a drug and alcohol counseling program.[18]

The details of her arrest appeared in the police blotter of the local paper. An acquaintance on vacation from back home happened to read the report. She called Valerie's daughter in Green Bay to share the news.

Shocked, Valerie's daughter flew to Sarasota immediately. Although Valerie was well dressed when she met her at the airport, her daughter was surprised by the change in Valerie's appearance. In the 6 months since she had seen her, Valerie seemed to have gained weight and looked unfit and puffy.

The first inkling of cognitive trouble was when they walked into the airport parking garage and Valerie pushed the panic button on the car key to locate her automobile. Then, she made several wrong turns before she located the exit. When they arrived at the condo, there were unwashed dishes in the sink and an unmade bed. This was in sharp contrast to her mother's usually neat housekeeping. They talked about Valerie's drinking, which she acknowledged was "on the heavy side," although she thought it was the interaction with her medications that made her appear to be drunk on the tests. But, her daughter should not worry, said Valerie, promising to cut back to no more than two drinks a night.

The next day, a phone call set off another alarm bell for her daughter. While Valerie was taking a shower, she picked up a call from a financial advisor, who mistakenly thought he was talking to Valerie. He was calling to confirm that he had made a $100,000 investment on her behalf. When she identified herself and asked what the investment was for, he abruptly hung up. When asked about this investment, Valerie told her daughter that this was none of her business. Because her mother had been financially responsible and prudent for as long as she could remember, she called her brother in Atlanta to tell him about the worrisome changes in their mother. He agreed to come to Sarasota the following day.

The next day, they both sat down with Valerie and expressed their concerns about her well-being, her drinking, and how she was managing her finances. They told Valerie that they wanted her to have a complete physical examination, along with cognitive testing, at a nearby university medical center. They also asked for permission to go through her financial records and checkbook to see if she were living within her means and to get an idea of how she was spending her money.

Valerie agreed. The news was mixed. On the plus side, Valerie was continuing to live within her income. The negative finding was that for the past year the new broker she hired had been investing heavily in the subprime market. Valerie had been doing well and was planning to send another $100,000 this month. Her children objected, saying that they had consulted the man who had taken over her business, and he said that these were dangerous investments, to which Valerie huffed, "Well, there are other ways to make money besides annuities and CDs. Those people in Green Bay have probably never heard of senior tranches or mezzanine CDOs."

Table 8.2 shows the specific attitudes and behaviors we found linked to the group at high risk for cognitive aging. Individuals classified in this group had at least six of the qualities detailed in addition to exhibiting five or more of the health-related characteristics in Table 8.1. Valerie exhibited at least seven of the attitudes and behaviors contained in Table 8.2.

Table 8.2   Attitudes and Behaviors Associated With High-Risk Cognitive Aging

1. **Feels mental ability is diminished, has declined considerably in the past 5 years, and is weaker than their peers**
2. **Persistent, frustrating memory problems**
3. **Other chronic cognitive problems**
4. **Certain mental activities avoided**
5. **Not satisfied with social relationships**
6. Continuing to drive in spite of dangerously poor performance
7. Exhibits dysexecutive cognitive symptoms
8. Vulnerable to financial misjudgment and swindles

Characteristics in **bold print** found among 67% or more of the high-risk group.

Feels Mental Ability Is Diminished, Has Declined Considerably in the Past Five Years, and Is Weaker Than Their Peers

Like Lenny, the majority of high-risk cognitive agers say that their mental capacity is much less than it used to be, and that they are definitely less intellectually able than they were a few years ago. Most believe that their mental abilities have fallen off more rapidly than their contemporaries.[19]

> In the last year or so, Andrea's family and friends have noticed that she is not as quick as she once was. This was especially noticeable in discussions during the last presidential campaign. A staunch conservative and well informed, Andrea (76) enjoyed nothing more than friendly debates with her liberal friends. Watching the presidential debates 4 years ago with Andrea was entertaining as she skewered the Democratic candidate with a razor-sharp commentary on the inconsistencies between what he was saying and how he had voted. But, during this election season, Andrea seemed far less interested in the presidential campaign, and when she watched a debate, she no longer articulated her ideas with the usual verve. In fact, Andrea seemed almost apathetic. When Andrea could not remember Rush Limbaugh's name, her husband became concerned and called the doctor.

> Graham (81) is sure that he is on the road to Alzheimer's disease. He says that he is having trouble paying attention and cannot remember what he has just seen on TV. He is also starting to have trouble matching faces with names. The problem is that his wife, his children, or those who know him are worried about his intelligence. They think he is depressed and should see a therapist. "I'd better see a neurologist before I talk to a shrink," responds Graham. "But I'm not sure that I'm ready to hear that I've got Alzheimer's."

Persistent, Frustrating Memory Problems

No longer intermittent and benign, chronic and frustrating memory problems interfere with important daily activities, which can result in the inability to carry out responsibilities at work or at home. These problems come in several guises: difficulty recalling information just learned (a name, phone number, address); visuospatial problems (constantly being unable to recall on which side of a big, oft-frequented supermarket the vegetables and fruits are displayed); and working memory (following directions).[20] Here are two real life examples.

Compared to other people, Nanette (71) rates her mental ability lower than most. But, she needed a job after her pension was cut and went back to work half time for a busy dry cleaner. She worked at the counter, receiving soiled garments and retrieving clothes that had been cleaned. Things were fine when business was slow, but Nanette noticed that when the customers were lined up at the counter, her short-term memory was erratic. Her inability to remember is in sharp contrast to that of her coworkers, who not only remember the customers' names but also what they brought in to be cleaned. Twice in one week, she forgot a customer's name that was just given to her. Then, Nanette tried to cover another memory lapse by asking the customer to spell her name. "Jones," the customer replied testily. "That's J-O-N-E-S." This morning, the owner told Nanette that she was no longer needed.

Recently, Harry (77) was out for dinner with his son and family at a large restaurant that was divided into several small dining rooms. During dinner, Harry had to visit the men's room, which was off one of the other dining rooms. When he failed to return 15 minutes later, his son went to look for him and found Harry wandering around another dining room. Harry had been too embarrassed to ask a waiter for help. This is the third time this sort of thing has happened in the past year.

Other Chronic Cognitive Problems

Common among those in the high-risk category are continuing problems with non-memory-related mental tasks such as being able sustain attention and reasoning.[21] Often, this characteristic presents in the form of a noticeable change from the recent past. One example is Valerie's messy condo, which stands in contrast to her previous neat housekeeping. Here are two more:

Anna (84) has been having problems with her attention span since last year. When she watches a movie or reads a book for more than a short time, her mind begins to wander, and she forgets what she has just watched or read. Now, she is starting to have trouble maintaining her attention when phone conversations go beyond a few minutes. Sometimes, she has to make up a reason to hang up, then refocus, and call the person back.

JB (73) considers himself much slower across the board than he was five years ago. Especially he can't concentrate. "I have trouble paying attention, so I don't remember things," he says, "and it's too much work to write things down." JB thinks he should "get out of his chair" and do more things, but he is stiff and his joints ache so he doesn't do much.

Certain Mental Activities Poorly Executed or Consistently Avoided

Among normally aging adults, there is an increasing tendency to avoid those mental tasks if the risk of difficulty or failure is thought to be likely.[22] Prior to cognitive decline, these intellectual tasks were engaged in readily and carried out competently. Valerie's giving up on trying to recall where her car was parked and push the panic button on her car key to locate it illustrates this characteristic.

Loretta (81) takes medication for her high blood pressure and cholesterol, as well as for back pain, and wonders if the medications interfere with her ability to concentrate. She says that she has had to stop working at Goodwill because she had trouble learning to work the new computerized cash register. She explained that she also gave up on the daily crossword puzzle because, "I can't keep two or three options in my head for '5 across' anymore." Loretta can still play checkers with her grandchildren but no longer plays chess because it takes her too long to make a move.

His daughter remembers when Irving (79) could add a column of four-figure numbers in his head faster than the adding machines of that era. She was surprised, then, to receive the call from the president of the bank in the small midwestern town where her widowed father lived. Because they held this account jointly, the banker told the daughter that Irving had been having problems with the account in the past 6 months, and they should talk face to face. Was she planning a visit soon? The following week, she flew in to visit her father and meet with the banker. Her father seemed about the same to her, but the bank president said that in the last 6 months Irving had begun to call the bank to see if checks had cleared because he could not recall whether he had paid a bill or not. When the bank tellers checked the records, they found that some bills had been paid twice. What prompted the call to the daughter was when Irving approached one of the tellers and asked if she could help him balance his checking account.

Not Satisfied With Social Relationships

Dissatisfaction with social relationships is common among the high-risk agers.[23] Think about Lenny, who went from being the unofficial mayor of his community to being dependent on his wife and his daughter's family next door for his entire social life. Research studies found isolated and lonely older individuals are at considerably greater risk for cognitive decline than those with satisfying social relationships.[24]

Margaret (78), widowed in her 50s and living happily alone with her two cats, remembers that it was just 10 years ago when her life was perfect. She loved running the nursery school, enjoyed her four grand-children who lived close by, and had a pleasant and active social life organized around playing bridge and golf. But, after she retired, her two daughters and their families moved out of the area, and both cats died. Her osteoporosis worsened, making it hard for her to get around, so she stopped playing golf. Then, her bridge group slowly dissolved. Margaret now has no one she can really talk with anymore face to face; in fact, she has had virtually no social life for the past 2 years. Margaret can feel her mind shriveling up because she lacks outside stimulation. She does not want to bother her daughters by admitting how lonely and depressed she sometimes feels.

When his wife died suddenly of a stroke a year and half ago, Jerry (78) was devastated. She was his only real friend and orchestrated their social life. Both of his children and their families live up north, so Jerry does not see much of them. Since he does not reach out to others and does not belong to any social groups, he spends a lot of time alone. This year, a bright spot appeared in his social life when his grandson began attending college nearby. When he visited, his grandson could see that Jerry was lonely. All he did was watch TV and shoot an occasional game of pool. The grandson remembered that it was not so long ago that his grandpa enjoyed collecting and repairing lamps and chandeliers he bought at yard sales. After he restored them in his garage, Jerry sold them at a flea market. He made a profit and met interesting people, some of whom became flea market friends. But, when the grandson walked into the garage, it was filled with half-repaired chandeliers and lamps. When Jerry came out to work on them, his grandson noticed that his grandpa would start working on one lamp, then shift his attention to another one. Nothing ever was finished. When he asked why his grandfather did not finish some of the pieces so he could sell them at the flea market, Jerry just shook his head.

Continuing to Drive in Spite of Dangerously Poor Performance

Driving is a complicated, multitasking activity, involving the simultaneous use of several mental abilities. Among them are attention, psychomotor skills, memory, and visuospatial aptitude—all of which decline with age.[25] Recognizing these realities, the largest number of older drivers restrict their driving to daylight hours, familiar areas, shorter distances, times of low traffic, and good weather conditions to compensate for the loss of some cognitive functions.[26] A small fraction continue risky driving habits that endanger themselves and others, like those mentioned next:

It was twilight when Karl (76) took a shortcut home and drove straight up, over, and almost through a boulder-strewn traffic rotary before his ruined car came to a smoking stop. Karl was returning home from the Veterans Affairs hospital where he worked part time. Karl is a widowed psychiatrist, specializing in the treatment of veterans suffering from posttraumatic stress disorder. Fortunately, no one was hurt. "The only damage was to my pride," he said to his three children. They were not so sure. While vacationing in Florida last winter, Karl missed the exit off a highway and was saved only by a passenger's scream from turning onto an access ramp and into a line of traffic coming right at them. The passenger called Karl's daughter to say that she thought her father should not be driving. Karl has ignored these worries. He cannot explain why he drove over the rotary instead of around it because he has taken this shortcut dozens of times. Maybe it was the new hypertension medication he has been prescribed, he thought to himself. He will know the answer soon because the court suspended his license until he has a complete medical checkup.

Kathy (74) thinks everyone—especially her husband and children—who says she drives too fast and takes too many chances is a "nervous Nelly." Kathy maintains her opinion even after being flagged down by a state trooper for driving 20 mph over the speed limit in a construction area. This was her second speeding ticket in a year. A month ago, she was T-boned by the driver of a pickup truck who did not expect her to suddenly turn left in front of him. She is worried now that the state will take away her license. Her husband worries that it will not.

Exhibits Dysexecutive Cognitive Symptoms

A pattern in a minority of the high-risk group was evidence of more than one potentially dangerous mental lapse in the past year—sometimes called "dysexecutive mild cognitive impairment." These lapses include persistent distractibility, difficulty multitasking, poor reasoning, and an inability to adjust to changing circumstances.[27] Some dysexecutive behaviors are potentially harmful, such as setting fire to the kitchen while cooking dinner, leaving the stove or oven on overnight, or forgetting to turn off a water faucet.

It was her son-in-law, a third-year resident, who began to suspect that Ester (76) was starting to lose it mentally. Her husband had died 2 years earlier, and Ester now lived by herself. She kept her new off-white carpet spotless by vacuuming it several times a day. But, should the phone or doorbell ring while she was vacuuming, Ester often left the machine turned on while she answered the phone or door—which happened multiple times during a weekend visit by her daughter and son-in-law. When she returned, Ester seemed surprised to find the vacuum cleaner still running. Her son-in-law's worries about her mental condition intensified when he noticed water dripping down from the ceiling. She had left the water running in the second floor bathroom tub. When he talked to his wife about Ester, she said that her mother had always been "a little flaky," although this was worse than usual.

Since he had business nearby, Allan's nephew drove to Burlington, Vermont, to visit his favorite uncle. A retired college professor, Allan

(82) had always been charming, witty, and bright, and in his prime wore expensive three-piece suits. Since his spouse's death, Allan lived alone. His son was in Montana. When they met for lunch, the nephew was shocked to see how much his uncle had changed in the year and half since his last visit. Allan seemed slower mentally, and his usual verve was absent. He had shaved but had missed several spots. Allan wore a nice suit, but it was full of small holes. Initially, the nephew thought that they were the work of moths. That evening he discovered the moths were innocent. After dinner, Allan put the newspapers and other trash into a barrel in the backyard and set it alight. "Saves money on trash pickups," Allan explained. While the fire blazed, Allan's nephew could see the flying embers landing on his uncle's suit. Before leaving the next morning, the nephew met Allan for breakfast. Allan was dressed in another elegant suit, but there were also holes in this one. The nephew called Alan's son in Montana as soon as he reached the highway to let him know how concerned he was about his dad.

Vulnerable to Financial Misjudgment and Swindles

Consumer fraud targets older adults like Valerie worldwide. In the United States alone, sweepstakes scams, home repair fraud, money transfer cons, and refinancing swindles are just a few examples of a growing industry that zeroes in on the elderly. Especially vulnerable are the high-risk cognitive agers.[28] Because complex financial decisions, many of which are stressful, are often made in the 3rd Age, and because the executive skills necessary to make these decisions may not be as strong among those at high risk, they are vulnerable to making money management mistakes. This is especially true in the case of those who live alone. Swindlers know this and prey on them.

Because Irving (79) could not do it anymore, his daughter took over his financial affairs. Going through the checkbook, she was appalled to find checks totaling nearly $50,000 written in the past 3 months to an organization called YOU WON!! When she asked him to explain the checks, Irving said that he had been called by someone from a company in Las Vegas. Because Irving had enjoyed betting small amounts of money in online Texas hold 'em, the man told Irving that he had been randomly selected to receive $3.4 million from a pool of unclaimed Internet gambling prize money. Irving had to pay a few hundred dollars in processing fees up front. After a few days, he received another call saying that state taxes, totaling $36,814.82, had to be withheld before they could wire the money. When the prize money failed to arrive after he sent the tax money, Irving called the company. A man answered the phone saying that he was a sheriff. He told Irving that, as he had probably guessed, the YOU WON!! company was fraudulent. The good news, however, was that Irving in fact had won the $3.4 million. If Irving would send another certified check for $8,976.27 to cover fees and shipping costs, the sheriff would place the cash in an armored truck and escort it personally to Irving. When the armored truck did not arrive, Irving knew he had been duped but was too embarrassed to discuss it with anyone.

Until 2 years ago, Heather (60) and her husband had lived a frugal life. After paying back loans for three college tuitions and two weddings. they planned to begin saving for retirement. Then, her husband died of colon cancer in a six-week period. Prior to his death, Heather's husband had handled the finances. After the funeral, she had a frank talk with their banker and discovered how little money she had. So, when the call came right after the funeral offering her a reverse mortgage on her house, it was an answer to her prayers. As Heather understood it, she would receive a loan for up to half the value of the equity in her house. Presuming that her house continued to appreciate in value as it had over the past decade, when she sold the house Heather could repay the loan and pocket most of the increased value. Even though she had an instinct to call her daughters before committing herself, Heather felt that it was time to make a decision on her own. It was not long after she signed the papers that the housing market nosedived. Heather was notified that the terms of the loan had changed. The interest nearly doubled, and her monthly check was 50% less because her home was now worth about half of its original value. Now Heather did not have the money to make her house payments. As nearly as Heather could comprehend, she was about to lose her house and most of its cash value.

Reflections and Applications

The magnitude of the differences between high-risk cognitive agers and those functioning normally was significant.[29] The high-risk group were two to three times less active than normal cognitive agers. Not only were they engaged in a much smaller number of activities, but also they exhibited a relative lack of energy compared to normal older adults.

Reading the histories of those in the high-risk group, it was easy to be impressed by the potential damage to the intellect associated with several chronic medical conditions as well as risky lifestyle habits. The majority of those at high risk had elevated blood pressure and cholesterol readings that accompanied obesity. A significant number had type 2 diabetes as well. Also common among the high-risk cognitive agers were dangerous habits that predict reduced intellectual powers. A high percentage smoked, drank heavily, ate poorly, failed to exercise, and were uninvolved in community activities. Quite a few took their medications erratically or not at all and ignored other advice, such as to get a hearing aid.

It is fair to say, however, that the treatment of some chronic conditions requires considerable management by the patient. An example are people with atrial fibrillation, who must take an anticoagulant daily, watch their diets carefully, have their blood drawn regularly to monitor clotting levels, and frequently readjust their medication. Type 2 diabetics taking insulin have an even more complicated regimen to follow. Many who take medications have difficulty being compliant all of the time. It is important to remember, however, that being compliant 80% of the time compared to 20% of the time is linked to substantially less cognitive as well as less physical decline.[30]

Also impressive was how frequently the high-risk cognitive agers could be distinguished by the absence of the attitudes and behaviors typical of normal and optimally aging women and men. Most did not believe that they were functioning well intellectually, which for the most part was an accurate assessment. Even those, like Lenny, whose intelligence seemed well above average, were convinced that they were cognitively inferior to themselves a few years earlier. Compared to those aging optimally or normally, those in the high-risk group seem to have largely given up hope of being able to reverse the steepening angle of their cognitive decline.

Within this population of high-risk agers are a number for whom the glass is half empty. Some have not recovered from a loss of a loved one or other traumatic event. There is Lenny, who fell into a decline because he is no longer the biggest man in the room. Hannah and Richard feel that nothing will ever bring them the same pleasure as her husband and his accounting career, respectively, and both have sunk into melancholia.

Another response to the losses that come with age is to become resentful and passive, forsaking the pleasures that are still available. For example, JB is angry that his arthritis prevents him from skiing the black diamonds and reacts by refusing to ski the lesser trails or finding another enjoyable outdoor activity within his capabilities. Because Nina dislikes the continuing care community she and her husband are living in, she expresses frustration by isolating herself from others and giving up activities she enjoys, such as needlepoint. Many of these high-risk cognitive agers cause their children and caregivers to feel as though they have given up living and are waiting to die.

When working with people like this, it can be tempting to try to pull them out of their despondent state by recounting inspirational stories of others overcoming losses far greater than theirs. I have found that most will not be moved by these tales. However, what I have found useful is to explore the anger associated with the losses.[31]

The vignettes in this chapter underscore how quickly things can change with 3rd Age adults. Within a year or two, their intellectual functioning can fall from being well above average to at high risk for becoming impaired. Sometimes, these relatively sudden cognitive declines follow a traumatic event such as the loss of a spouse. The events do not even have to be traumatic. Diminished mental ability in older adults can appear after a minor surgical intervention or even a bad case of the flu. Just as often as not, there is no obvious precipitating event.

Because the rate of decline can steepen so rapidly, caregivers and family members need to know that regular monitoring of older adults should be a priority, even with those who appear to be aging well. The case of Irving illustrates the point. He had been healthy most of his life. Although unhappy following the death of his wife, he recovered with the help of his rabbi. But, then things began to unravel for him cognitively. There were the problems managing his checking account and being conned out of nearly $50,000. Fortunately, the problem was discovered by his daughter. Convinced that he had rapidly progressing Alzheimer's disease, she consulted the family doctor. He suggested a comprehensive evaluation at the Mayo Clinic, a few hundred miles away. The results showed that Irving did not have Alzheimer's disease. However, he did have pancreatic cancer that had metastasized to the brain, which is why he was cognitively impaired. Irving died 6 weeks later. His case reminds us that a good place to start when someone is suspected of being at risk for cognitive impairment is with a complete physical examination.

For the clinicians among us, it may be hard to read these case vignettes without summoning ideas about how to intervene. Before beginning a discussion of potentially useful interventions, it is helpful to remind ourselves that not everyone who might benefit from our help wants it. Some see no point because in their minds their situation is hopeless. They consider their problems to be a normal part of growing older, so why fight it? Or, they are in denial, frightened of the potential consequences of looking objectively at what is happening to them. Some hear our concerns about them and do not appreciate how much at risk they are intellectually and physically. They know that they have to make some major changes, but they first want to try to improve things on their own.

In several decades of working as a clinician, I have witnessed the considerable benefit that comes to high-risk agers from being able to sit down and talk with professionals—practicing physicians, social workers, nurses, and psychologists. Frequently, they make short work of situations that baffle competent and interested laypeople. They know the importance of a history and the significance of particular symptoms, know when to tread heavily and when to tiptoe, and have an array of ideas about how to treat the problem.

Should you become engaged with a client, there are times that working with high-risk cognitive agers demands all of the understanding and skill you possess. After being confronted by the worries of his wife and daughter about him, Lenny reluctantly agreed to an evaluation at the university medical center. The intake interview was done by a young social worker. Lenny could not have been nastier. In the first 5 minutes, he let her know that there was nothing wrong with him. He had been dragged in here by these "hysterical women, who are the ones that need therapy," not him. True, he has had a few adjustment problems, but who would not when they take away three fourths of your stomach. Plus, he is a medical success story. Since the surgery, he has lost 150 pounds, and his doctor says he's "doing great." Yes, he still smokes a little and overeats, but he can stop any time he wants. He has no idea why his wife and daughter think he is depressed. "If they want to see depression, they should look in the mirror. And by the way, how long you been out of high school?"

The social worker did not write in her notes what she really thought of Lenny—which was that he was "the patient from Hell."

Hard as it is to believe, Lenny began to improve after the examination at the university hospital. This was in large part due to the senior psychiatrist in charge of his case. She appreciated the impact of dramatic medical procedures on the psyche. Also, she knew from long experience that Lenny's denial of problems, his trivializing of the mental health professions, and his obnoxious attitude could in fact be a plea for help. Sometimes, the most provocative patients are subconsciously testing the professionals to see if they have the skill and commitment to help them.

The psychiatrist convinced Lenny to see her for "a few sessions," which turned out to be bimonthly visits for the better part of a year. She hung in there with him, ignoring Lenny's nasty attitude and keeping her own annoyance in check. Soon, they developed a plan for his rehabilitation, which initially involved a fitness program and another attempt to stop smoking. Both were successful. Lenny proudly told people he weighed the same now as when he played for the Gators. His social life reignited. At the final meeting with the psychiatrist, Lenny told her that he and his buddies were planning a hunting trip to Wyoming in the fall. But first, the biking bear was going to Daytona Beach for bike week.

Stories like Lenny's are not isolated events. Although less frequently reported in the professional literature, excellent counseling results have also been achieved by clergy, health care administrators, volunteers at senior citizen centers, and personal trainers. On occasion, those at high risk for impairment or their families seek out these people precisely because they are *not* professional health care providers. They want help but refuse a referral to a professional because they are not "that bad off." Under these circumstances, the best results I have seen come from an agreement made in advance to spend two to three sessions talking and then to re-evaluate whether a referral to a professional is appropriate.

Surely not everyone has the potential to improve, and only a small number may actually be willing to make the required effort. But, for those few your involvement with them may alter the trajectory of their lives in the 3rd Age. Remember, those with the furthest to go often make the most progress.

9

Writing and Learning About the Aging Intellect

At the beginning of a new class, I usually tell my students that I expect to learn at least as much as they will during the course because teaching and learning travel in both directions in the classroom. The same learning process occurred for me while writing this book. Even though I thought I knew quite a bit about cognitive aging when I began to think seriously about this project, my understanding of the topic has been refreshed, broadened, and added to during the research and the writing of this book. The following is a distillation of what I now know about maximizing intellectual potential in the 3rd Age of life. I start with an unexpected finding.

Older Americans Are in Better Health Now Than at Any Time in History

That is right: Older Americans are in better health now than at any time in history. Had I read this sentence 5 years ago, I might have thought to myself, "What? Doesn't whoever wrote these words ever read the newspapers or watch TV?" Nearly every month, there is another report of increasing rates of heart disease, hypertension, type 2 diabetes, obesity, increased stress, and growing isolation.[1] All of those facts are correct, but they tell only part of the story. During the first decade of this millennium, a steady stream of scientific findings has appeared about the improving health and healthy lifestyle habits of older women and men in the United States.[2] These rarely make the news.

Here are just four examples of underreported good news about the improving health of older Americans. First, more 3rd Age women and men say that they are in good-to-excellent health. Between 1991 and 2007, the percentage of people 65–74 reporting themselves to be in good-to-excellent health increased from 74 to 76.6%. Although this may seem to be only a small percentage increase, these differences add up. Over a half million more women and men aged 65–74 were in better health in 2007 than they would have been had the health of older adults not improved since 1991.[3] Better health in this age group is not strictly a U.S. event. In Goteborg, Sweden, a retrospective study of three successive cohorts of 70-year-olds found that those born most recently were in better health, had fewer symptoms, and were more physically active than those born 10 years earlier.[4]

The second piece of good news is that older Americans are taking better care of themselves today. Consider these examples: During the short period from the mid-1990s to 2007, the percentage of older nonsmokers decreased by more than a third. The number of alcohol abstainers rose 4%, while those 3rd Agers who work out regularly grew by over 8%.[5]

Increasing numbers of older adults have gotten the message about prevention and are taking action. The largest proportion of 3rd Agers in history are getting flu shots and having Pap smears and mammograms. Recent surveys also have found double-digit decreases in the percentage of 3rd Agers with high serum cholesterol readings. By the way, this 65+ age group has made more progress in lowering their average cholesterol readings than the young and middle aged.[6]

The third piece of good news is that disability rates for those 65 and older have declined dramatically. In 1984, one American in four over the age of 65 suffered from a chronic disability. By 2004, the percentage fell to under 20%. Expressed differently, this means that close to 3 million Americans 60–79 who would have been projected to have a disability 20 years earlier were able to avoid it.[7]

Finally, because more 3rd Agers are taking better care of themselves, many believe that this will result in longer life expectancy free of disabilities and a shorter period of being frail and dependent at the end of life. This is called the "compression of morbidity."[8] The centerpiece of this idea is that our years of disability will be squeezed into a shorter time span at the end of life because of healthier lifestyle habits and advances in medicine. In 2007, empirical evidence for the compression of morbidity thesis was reported.[9] Examining changes in life expectancy and active (disability-free) life span from 1992 to 2002, demographers found that total life expectancy grew 6 months during this decade, whereas active life span increased by more than 9 months. Elements of the compression of morbidity theory have been supported by researchers in several other countries.[10]

Encouraging as these results are, the majority of older women and men who could make positive changes in their health-related behaviors have not done so. Most of the gains have been made by those with more education and higher income levels.[11] Also tempering the good news are worrisome increases in the numbers of 3rd Age adults with chronic diseases such as hypertension and type 2 diabetes, as well as risky lifestyle behaviors such as obesity.

While we have reason to be disappointed, let's not fall into the trap of paying attention exclusively to what is wrong with the health of aging adults and overlooking the accumulating evidence that so many trends are going in the right direction. Moreover, these gains are not random statistical variations. They are broadly based improvements in health-related quality of life and likely have come as a result of putting into practice lessons learned from scientific investigations carried out in the last half of the 20th century. Examples are lifestyle habits within our control—stopping smoking, getting more exercise, drinking moderately, paying attention to the value of social networks, and lowering stress levels. As the second decade of the current millennium opens, we can anticipate new discoveries by neuroscientists worldwide that will continue to extend our years of remaining mentally and physically vigorous.

Healthy Lifestyle Habits That Benefit the Intellect

Another surprise was that so many medical conditions, so widespread among us older adults, have such power to reduce our mental powers. At the beginning of this project, I was aware of the dangers of cardiovascular disease and hypertension to the mind as well as the body but had little knowledge that most of the other medical conditions common to the 3rd Age would have an adverse impact on the intellect. I hope that sharing this awareness will give each of us additional motivation to do all we can to avoid as many chronic medical conditions as possible for as long as possible. Toward that end, the most important strategy is to practice healthy lifestyle habits.

The list of healthy lifestyle habits might not surprise our grandparents or experienced clinicians, but the recent empirical support of their intuition is comforting. The seven evidence-based lifestyle habits that benefit the aging body and intellect have been mentioned throughout this book.

> *Be a nonsmoker:* A history of smoking is highly correlated with adverse changes in the brain, accelerated cognitive decline, and increased risk for dementia. This is because smoking is associated with an increased incidence of diseases linked to cognitive impairment. These include cardiovascular disease, hypertension, and stroke. Smoking is the primary cause of chronic obstructive pulmonary disease (COPD) and a significant risk factor for type 2 diabetes.[12] Most smokers know this, which is why 7 of 10 would like to quit.

Although difficult, willpower and smoking cessation programs have proved successful.[13] By 2007, there were an estimated 47.3 million former smokers in the United States.

Exercise regularly: The cognitive benefits of exercise are well established.[14] Some debate exists about how vigorous the physical activity must be to provide benefit, and this may depend on the person's fitness level when beginning an exercise program. Special note should be made of active optimal agers who rarely went to a gym. They derived the same benefit from regularly engaging in active leisure or community activities.[15]

Fight obesity: In addition to the well-documented health risks that obese people face, studies in France and the United States have reported that memory impairment is associated with long-term obesity.[16] At present, older adults are becoming obese in record numbers. A U.S. survey found that 35% of those 65–74 are obese. Younger adults are at greater risk. Two of five baby boomers are currently obese. Unless this trend reverses, the proportion of obese older adults will increase as the baby boomers move into their retirement years.[17]

Eat healthily: The contribution of a good diet had almost the same relationship to health status as exercise.[18] Eating healthily has been variously defined, but usually includes at least five daily servings of high-fiber, whole-grain breads and cereals containing relatively few calories, along with fruits and vegetables. Research that tracked the eating habits of adults in Utah for 11 years found that those following the healthiest diets had 30% less cognitive decline than those with the poorest eating habits.[19] Eating healthily is also associated with a lower risk for cardiovascular disease, hypertension, diabetes, and other medical conditions that are associated with lower mental ability scores.

Take medication as prescribed: Of the possible modifications in lifestyle habits that benefit the aging mind and body, one of the easiest ones to change is compliance with the recommendations of a health care provider. Whether it is taking those hypertension pills or medication prescribed for type 2 diabetes, consistently monitoring your blood levels for sugar or clotting time, or wearing a continuous positive airway pressure (CPAP) mask or hearing aid if you need it, there is no doubt that complying with medical advice is good for the aging intellect.[20]

While it is hard for older people to have perfect records of compliance when they may be taking a half dozen or more pills per day, taking our medication as prescribed four days out of five instead of less than half of the time makes a great difference to the intellect as well as to physical health.[21]

Repopulate social networks: Losing people important to us is a reality of growing older. A continuing challenge is to fill the gaps in social networks as they occur. The common wisdom is that larger social networks are more beneficial physically than smaller networks of friends and acquaintances.[22] While there is some truth in this assumption, many 3rd Agers get along just fine with one or two confidantes. Danger comes when those few loved ones depart. Repopulating social networks is essential because those among us who feel isolated and alone are at greatest risk for ill health and more rapid cognitive decline.[23]

Manage stress: Numerous optimal agers we interviewed were well acquainted with stress—some of it severe and lengthy—in the present or recent past. Those 3rd Agers who managed their emotions competently to avoid high levels of anxiety, depression, or anger were in better health and exhibited less cognitive decline than those reporting more severe distress. One of the reasons the optimal agers were able to manage their stress level was that many became skilled at avoiding stressful circumstances and disagreeable people. They often reflexively apply a positivity bias, resulting in their being less attentive to negative information and thoughts.[24] When stress was unavoidable, some focused on trying to reduce the source of the stress. When that was impossible, they found other ways to soothe their distress. They turned to friends, food and drink, religion, exercise, and hobbies or thought of people less fortunate. A few sought psychological help or found comfort from yoga or other alternative interventions.

Evidence is that those healthier lifestyle habits older adults practice, lower the risk of an adverse medical event. Consider risk of heart failure: Practicing four healthy lifestyle habits (e.g., not smoking, having a body mass index [BMI] < 25, exercising five times weekly, eating fruits/vegetables more than four times a day) reduces the chance of a coronary event by more than half.[25]

Those in the 3rd Age do not have to bat a thousand to benefit. Changing a single habit makes a difference. Follow-up studies of 3rd Age doctors found that having just one healthy habit made a difference. Exercising by itself reduced the risk of dying of a heart condition 15–20%. There are no guarantees that practicing these healthy lifestyle habits will lead to aging optimally, but we can be pretty certain that not following these directions makes optimal aging unlikely.

Three Levels of Cognitive Aging

The primary purpose of this book has been to identify empirically based behaviors linked to optimal, normal, and high-risk cognitive aging. Optimal agers avoid risky lifestyle habits that endanger the intellect and practice behaviors associated with maintaining or slowing the decline of mental skills. They show unusually high mental vigor. They get most of what is possible for them whether their IQs are exceptional or ordinary.

Drawing from our discussions on the research of others,[26] my students and I developed lists of healthy lifestyle habits as well as attitudes and behaviors associated with optimal, normal, and high-risk cognitive aging. Following pilot testing, we refined the lists of characteristics that we thought would be found among older adults functioning optimally or normally or who were at high risk for cognitive impairment. Then, 151 volunteers were classified into one of the three levels of cognitive aging that are used in this book.

It bears repeating that what was most impressive about the optimal cognitive agers was the magnitude of the differences between them and the other older women and men. As a group, those aging optimally were three to four times more active than the normal group and six to ten times more vigorous than the high-risk agers. The large differences also played out in other areas. Optimal cognitive agers volunteered more often, had larger and more diverse social networks and were more open to new or challenging experiences.

Here, it should be noted that there were few paragons among the optimal aging group. There were occasional smokers, individuals who drank more than moderately, people who were not winning the battle with obesity, and those who did not believe that they were healthier and mentally keener than their age mates. Nor were these optimal agers strangers to serious illness, traumatic circumstances, or financial hardship. In their ranks is a man in his mid-60s with hypertension, heart disease, and sleep apnea. Wounded in Viet Nam, he goes to work every day in a wheelchair and counsels disabled veterans. While coping with a move to Florida and a recent diagnosis of COPD, an optimally aging woman lost her spouse, mother, and beloved golden retriever in an 11-month period. Few optimal agers we met were affluent. A 79-year-old woman has been living solely on Social Security for almost 15 years. She described herself as someone who is frugal, eats simply, and buys her clothes at a thrift shop. She does not complain about her financial limitations because she has "the freedom to think and do as I choose."

Aside from its potential value to caregivers in sizing up how well, or not so well, people they are looking after are aging, the characteristics that distinguish among those aging optimally, normally, or who are at high risk can be a useful tool for those interested in objective self-assessment. It also is a guide for those who seem one or two healthy lifestyle habits or attitude changes away from joining those aging optimally. Suppose Courtney, mentioned in Chapter 7, were to begin to take her hypertension medicine regularly and then try to overcome her anxiety about the new communication technology by hiring a high school student to tutor her. Or, consider Keith, also discussed in Chapter 7. While he does not have the classic signs of clinical depression, it is a good bet that he is still grieving over the death of his brother, and that his dysphoric mental state is weighing on the rest of his life. Talking to a professional about this loss might help him recover and begin to imagine a life full of the potential pleasures within his reach.

Suppose you gauge some people in your care to be among those at high risk for cognitive impairment. They have an energy deficit and have a half dozen medical conditions and risky habits that correlate with diminished mental acuity. They know that they are not functioning well mentally, even if they seem well above average. Keep in mind that it is not always hopeless.

Hard as it is to believe, those with the furthest to go often make the most progress. Poor minority older women in Baltimore, Maryland, were recruited to work with elementary school children for a year. Those 3rd Age women who were in the lowest group on tests measuring attention and memory at the beginning of their work with the children improved their mental skills more than those with higher mental ability at the beginning. The same findings have occurred with exercise: Groups who are the least fit at the beginning progress faster than those in better physical condition.[27]

Moreover, there was more than one story like Lenny's, recounted in Chapter 8. A common denominator is that these individuals were reached by a person or by a program that targeted one of their central problems. In Lenny's case, it was a therapist who helped him come to terms with the loss of his former identity and encouraged him to use what remained to create a new one. Valerie's drinking problem in Chapter 8 was addressed through an alcohol education program that she was required to take following her arrest. It was not successful, but it led to the recognition that Valerie's reasoning abilities had declined. When a neuropsychological evaluation showed her to have dysexecutive mild cognitive aging, her daughter assumed control of her finances.

The qualities described in this book that distinguish among optimal, normal, and high-risk cognitive aging are based on the research of many others and one clinical study. It is hoped that this list of variables will be useful to other investigators working in this arena. For the clinician or caregiver, these characteristics may also provide useful criteria for assessment as well as a guide for intervention.

Clinical Notes for Caregivers

Busy health care providers among the readers will have their own ideas about how some of the material in this book might be useful in their work. The following is a potpourri of observations and thoughts that have accumulated during the preparation of this book that may be useful to some in your care. I shall start with a finding that broadened my view about why older people have trouble remembering.

Attention Is the Cornerstone of Memory and Requires the Inhibition of Distracting Thoughts

For some years, psychologists have known that memory depends on attention, the ability to focus on the knowledge to be encoded such as the names of new neighbors or to concentrate on scanning memory banks for stored information like your Social Security number. Research reported in Chapter 3 made a strong case for the importance of cognitive inhibition in enhancing attention. Inhibition is the capacity to block out distractions that disrupt concentration and interfere with recall.

For attention to function effectively, three components of cognitive inhibition must suppress other preoccupations that compete for attention.[28] The first component of inhibition is the *access* function, denying admission of nonrelevant knowledge during new learning (during a discussion with your daughter about her son's 16th birthday party remembering that his name is Jim, and blocking out the name Mike, your son's 16-year-old). Next is applying the *restraint* function, which operates to hold back an automatic response triggered by a familiar cue that does not apply to the current circumstances (remembering that the drawer in which to put the knives, forks, and spoons in the rented cottage is to the left of the sink, not on the right like at home). The final component of inhibition is the *delete* function, which works to suppress information that is no longer relevant (blocking out the distracting names of the former residents of the house next door when being introduced to the new owners).

The capacity to inhibit distracting thoughts that disrupt attention and memory is highly vulnerable to the aging process. People who come to you because of "memory problems" might benefit from understanding that their problems may be caused by decreased ability to suppress unwanted distracting thoughts and feelings, which impede the retrieval of information. If I were running a memory training program, I would include a discussion of the adverse effects of distractions on attention, along with a discussion of strategies to minimize their impact. In that discussion, I would be sure to point out the benefits of attention restoration activities.

The Power of Attention Restoration Activities

The finding that a walk in the woods restores attention, which has been fatigued by the necessity of focusing on obligatory activities, is not a surprise. Indeed, it might be said that the surprise is that it has taken psychology so long to validate this piece of common experience. But, few of us would have guessed that an hour-long walk through an arboretum in Ann Arbor, Michigan could improve attention and memory by nearly 20%.[29]

Psychologists have wondered what other kinds of external experience have the same potential to refresh the intellect. Exposure to several forms of art has been good for the minds of young people. Students who studied photos of natural scenes or urban areas improved their scores on attentional tasks. Following a brief course in art appreciation, Harvard Medical School students greatly improved their patient observational skills.[30] Similarly, students at other medical schools have improved their attention when given exposure to other forms of art.

So far, the most convincing empirical research has been mostly with young adults. However, because the ability to maintain our concentration on tasks while suppressing distracting thoughts is degraded by age, older people—and those caring for them—have a large stake in thinking about how attention-restoration activities could work for them. Surveys of adults have reported the restorative psychological benefits of walking in parks, exercising, or visiting monasteries, cafes, or museums.[31] Although the cognitive benefits have not been documented with older people, these results are promising.

While the research continues, elder caregivers can apply some of the knowledge from attention restoration research right now with their clients. For example, with 3rd Agers who are having trouble maintaining their focus, you might try a "favorite place" prescription.[32] Each person is likely to have a special place or activity that is particularly beneficial to his or her mental health. It might be a nap, a good book, working out, going window shopping, or putting the paddle down and gazing at the sky while letting the river current take the kayak where it pleases.

Odds are that spending time in these favorite places also refreshes individuals' attention and memory. And, it is a good bet that they bring pleasure, reduce tension, and promote positive feelings. And, unlike losing weight or working out, they require little self-discipline or hard work.

Diminished Executive Functions Become More Apparent

Executive functions include the capacity to block out distractions as well as planning, working memory, reasoning, and flexibility. Like most other abilities, executive functions decline with age. Sometimes, the deterioration appears episodically, as in the experiences of Henry and Ben mentioned in Chapter 7. In other cases, the onset is more rapid and global, resulting in dysexecutive mild cognitive impairment (MCI).

As many as one of four 3rd Agers may exhibit one or more signs of diminishing executive functions.[33] Recognizing that weakened executive functions are a potential problem and planning in advance to compensate for these diminished skills has much to recommend it. Failing that, much can be learned from painful experience. When Henry replayed his mistake of waiting for his wife to call him well beyond the time her plane was scheduled to arrive rather than driving to the terminal to see if she was there, he had no trouble recognizing his error and will not make that mistake in the future. Ben, the former department chair, painfully relived his garrulous remarks and pledged to himself not to speak again in a similar setting unless he knew what he was going to say and outlined his remarks in advance.

Diminished Driving Skills May Require Attention

The more 3rd Agers we interviewed, the more we became convinced that making adjustments to drive safely was one of the hallmarks of optimal cognitive aging. A few 3rd Agers decided to stop driving altogether. The majority cut back on the type of driving they were finding increasingly difficult. They avoid night driving, take the back roads when possible, and have a companion on long trips. More rigorous trip planning and the use of the GPS (global positioning system) have become common among those seeking to compensate for memories that no longer are as quick as they once were.

At the other end of the spectrum were those who tenaciously clung to their usual driving habits in spite of repeated episodes of demonstrated incompetence, dangerous driving, and accidents. Hard as it may be to imagine, many of these dangerous but not cognitively impaired older drivers can improve with practice. Several of our subjects strengthened what they recognized as diminished skills in backing up or parallel parking by practicing early on Sunday mornings in the supermarket parking lot. It did not take them long to refresh these skills. One woman hired the driver's education teacher at the high school to work with her.

In the decades ahead, much larger numbers of older adults will want to continue to drive. Among them will be a growing population of cognitively impaired elders who should not be behind the wheel. In just over half of the states, the decision of when to give up the operator's license is left in the hands of the elderly drivers themselves. In other states, only a vision test is required.[34] Discussions are under way in many states and in Washington, DC, about screening criteria to clear unsafe drivers from the road.

The toughest cases are those people who are no longer cognitively fit to operate a vehicle but refuse to stop driving. For them, operating a car is a symbol of their competence, independence, and being in control. Consider Maurice, who was helped with his navigational weaknesses 5 years ago when his kids gave him a GPS. But, he has stopped using the device, perhaps because he has forgotten how to work it. He gets lost regularly now, has had small fender benders, and people are afraid to ride with him. His children constantly worry about him hurting himself or someone else.

It is a good bet that those involved in elder care are going to be on the front lines of this complicated decision-making process for quite a while. Imagine talking to Maurice about giving up his driver's license. How would you approach him? Experienced elder care workers have made several suggestions.[35] They include recognizing how important driving is to Maurice, then helping him realize his responsibility to drive safely. The financial advantages of giving up driving might be pointed out, along with the fact that other forms of transportation are available through community services for the elderly. There also may be an opportunity to help him grieve the loss of driving independence.

The Positivity Effect Has a Downside

In contrast to the decline in cognitive skills, emotional regulation improves with age. One of the reasons is that elders have been found to put a positive spin on their experiences—this has been called the "positivity effect." In a nutshell, the positivity effect is a tendency to pay more attention to positive information than negative facts and to have a better recall for that material that stimulates positive feelings rather than negative ones.[36] This is because 3rd Agers are drawn more to information that soothes rather than excites emotions.

The benefits of this downward regulation of negative emotions include better emotional control and fewer instances of getting upset or saying things that one later regrets. The downside of the positivity effect comes when choices must be made, and 3rd Agers reflexively focus on the pleasant positive features and ignore the negative information because these important facts disturb their emotional balance.[37] I have known personally three optimal agers who signed the preliminary papers to enter a continuing care residential community and then decided against it. In each case, the reason was that too little attention was paid to the unpleasant aspects of the choice prior to making the decision.

If the positivity effect is appreciated in advance when difficult decisions loom, the potential negative consequences can be minimized by encouraging 3rd Agers to take the time to weigh the importance of contrary information prior to a choice being made.

Anxiety: An Underappreciated Symptom in Normal Older Adults

Anxiety symptoms are as troubling to community-dwelling older adults as depression or other emotions. My clinical and research experience has been that anxiety takes a heavy toll on the intellect at any age, but especially older age. This statement runs counter to the prevailing sentiment among many mental health practitioners who have focused on depression as the primary symptom of concern among the elderly. But, in fact generalized anxiety disorders, phobias, and panic attacks are found slightly more often among 3rd Agers than depression.

Among community-dwelling volunteers in the United States, 7% reported signs of anxiety compared with 2% for depression. Comparable percentages were found in the Netherlands.[38] Clinicians know this is not a matter of either/or. Approximately one in four patients with an anxiety disorder also suffers from depression. Of those diagnosed with a major depressive episode, about half also have symptoms of an anxiety disorder. The lesson for practitioners is to remain as sensitive to signs of anxiety as they are to depression. Should anxiety symptoms appear (e.g., phobias or panic attacks), there is a rich array of cognitive and behavioral therapeutics that have proved effective with these disorders.[39] These therapies, which range from relaxation training to systematic desensitization, are especially helpful when anxiety regularly impairs cognitive performance.

Respect the "Doctor Within"

I find the "doctor within"—Dr. Albert Schweitzer's concept described in Chapter 1—a useful metaphor to characterize people's efforts to understand their own problems and take action to help themselves. During my years in clinical practice, my colleagues and I were sometimes curious about those clients who called in considerable distress, set up an appointment, and then either cancelled or were no-shows. On two occasions, we sent letters to these individuals wishing them well and inviting them to tell us how things were going. Of the number who responded, between 10 and 20% said that things had improved after scheduling an appointment.

Sometimes, as Dr. Schweitzer noted, this happens with the help of loved ones, but just as often people meet these challenges alone. In Chapter 1, the first example of the doctor within was Evan's story of how his ability to forgive played a major role in lowering his blood pressure. In the pages that followed, there were stories of other older adults who found the resources within themselves to adapt and make positive changes in the face of extraordinarily stressful events.

Appreciating that many of your clients have an active doctor within already on duty gives you an ally. Take, for example, an 80-year-old woman who consults you about her weakening ability to concentrate. She describes all the problems she has with attention. If you ask her what she has tried on her own, you might find that she has a list of homemade remedies that often work for her. She tells you that when she gets lost midway through a story, it is usually because she has gotten distracted by another thought that suddenly popped up. Now, she knows to avoid interesting detours and to get right to the point. If you ask her about other ways that she has found to cope with attentional problems, she may add that when she has tip-of-the-tongue problems, she puts the word to be remembered in the back of her mind and moves on. The word comes back within a few minutes nearly every time. It would not take long to accumulate a list of self-help remedies for attention and memory problems that may be useful to others who have these difficulties but do not want to ask for help.

Those "Little Differences" in Mind and Body Achieved by Optimal Cognitive Agers Require Hard Work

What William James did not mention (as discussed in Chapter 1) was that the little differences between those older adults who are aging optimally and the others come as a result of considerable effort. For most, optimal aging is not a state that most 3rd Agers ascended to effortlessly because they had the right ancestors or enjoyed a stress-free life. Rather, they worked hard to gain that small margin of difference between themselves and their contemporaries. The example that has been cited several times is that optimally aging women were three times more physically active than those in the middle of the pack.[40]

For 3rd Agers, this hard work results in improved overall fitness and a lower likelihood of developing serious medical conditions compared to those who do not push themselves, being content to go with the flow. When contrasted with those in the high-risk group, those with a greater abundance of healthy lifestyle habits also reduce their risk of mental impairment. A question that is rarely asked, however, is whether mental ability actually improves during the 3rd Age, holds its own, or declines less steeply as a result of putting into practice these behaviors associated with aging optimally.

The answer seems to be that optimally aging older adults continue to decline intellectually with age, but the downward trend is slightly shallower than for the normals, and falls away far less dramatically than the high-risk cognitive agers. No longitudinal study of which I am aware found that the top group of subjects (equivalent to our optimal cognitive agers) actually improved their test scores over the years of the research.[41]

In other words, we use it and still lose it as we grow older. This is not news to most 3rd Agers. They know that following these recommendations for aging optimally is unlikely to restore them to the way they functioned at midlife. Rather, the benefit of these ideas is to extend their years of active healthy aging, including optimal cognitive aging, and compress the period of poor health and inactivity into the shortest possible time period.

Still More to Learn

How far we have come in my professional lifetime in improving our knowledge about the factors influencing optimal aging. Consider exercise. In the past half century, our view of exercise has changed from worrying about "athlete's heart" to viewing workouts as a necessary component of optimal aging.[42] Equally impressive is the rate at which knowledge about optimal cognitive aging has been increasing. Most of the publications cited in this book about the effect of chronic diseases, healthy lifestyle habits, and other behaviors on the intellect have appeared since 2000.

There is little question that the most interesting research area in the field of cognitive aging is neuroplasticity. Brain-scanning technology such as functional MRIs has made it possible to observe the brain in action and study changes in brain function, structure, and connectivity that occur as a result of aging. More important, those working in this field are beginning to understand how certain activities, such as exercise or developing new skills such as I did learning to juggle, affect the brain. How exciting it is to imagine the discoveries that will be made in cognitive neuroscience in the decades ahead.

Most elder caregivers will be too busy with their own responsibilities to involve themselves much in research. But, in the process of working with older people, some practitioners may have detected patterns that they believe are associated with aging optimally. I encourage you to find a way to study these hunches systematically because so much remains to be understood about factors that influence the quality of life in older age. In earlier chapters, several research topics were mentioned that might interest those caring for older adults. Here are two additional topics that clinicians with research interests might study that would enhance our knowledge about optimal cognitive aging.

Which Other Healthy Lifestyle Habits, Attitudes, and Behaviors Are Associated With Optimal Cognitive Aging?

The short lists of qualities linked to optimal cognitive aging in this book are based on our interviews with a sample of 3rd Agers and the research of others. They merely open the door to what I hope will be an exploration of dozens of other factors that may explain why some older adults age optimally and others do not.

Much remains to be understood. For instance, investigators at the Karolinska Institute in Stockholm, Sweden, were interested in the relative contributions of factors known to be associated with age-related cognitive decline. Variables of interest were age, health, years of education, and gender. They analyzed medical, neuroimaging and psychological test data on healthy volunteers.[43] Not unexpectedly, they found that mental ability scores fell off with chronological age. But, other factors—medical conditions and years of education—had more effect than age on the decline of intellectual abilities. Figure 9.1 shows that health status accounts for about 11% and education a little over 8.3% of factors affecting cognitive performance, while age alone contributes roughly 7%.[44]

As we can see from Figure 9.1, more than 70% of the factors that contribute to optimal cognitive aging are not yet understood. Perhaps some of you will fill this void with your discoveries.

Among MCI Patients, Which Factors Link to Nonprogression to Dementia?

Among adults diagnosed with MCI who were followed for a minimum of 3 years, about 15% progressed to dementia each year. That was anticipated. What was not expected was that just over 14% of the patients originally diagnosed with cognitive impairment were no longer impaired at the end of the study. Add to that number approximately one third of the group who did not progress to dementia, and there is a sizable group of people whose

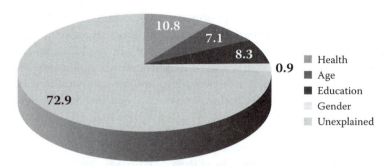

Figure 9.1   Percentage contributions of health, age, and demographics to cognitive decline. Copyright ©Wiley (2007). Reprinted from Bergman, I., Blomberg, M., & Almkvist, O. (2007). The importance of impaired physical health and age in normal cognitive aging. *Scandinavian Journal of Psychology, 48,* 115–125. With permission.

cognitive impairment did not worsen as expected during the period of the study.[45]

So far, explanations about the differences between those who do and do not progress to dementia have centered on the age of the patients, other demographics, the type of cognitive impairment, or the possibility of misdiagnosis. As far as I know, no one has yet studied whether healthy lifestyle habits, being open to new experiences, engaging in attention restoration activities, or other psychosocial factors might make a difference. On the basis of their demonstrated power to reduce the likelihood of chronic diseases and slow their advance, some of these factors should improve the odds of not progressing to dementia.

Appreciating the Richness of the 3rd Age

When beginning this book, I thought of the 3rd Age as the autumn of our years, following the first age of preparation and maturation and the second age of raising a family and working but prior to the years of old age. This still holds true. It is a time of reasonably good health when we have an opportunity to live life as we choose. As our research progressed, however, I began to appreciate a richer array of challenges and opportunities the 3rd Age presents.

Several of these have been described by investigators working with different groups of subjects. For example, Rowe and Kahn[46] identified three characteristics of successful aging that represent three challenges for those aspiring to age successfully: avoiding disease, maintaining high levels of cognitive and physical functions, and remaining actively engaged with life.[47] Others have added specific challenges typical of the 3rd Age, such as the need to redefine an identity when one is no longer working and the kids leave home or accepting the reality that we become more dependent on others, meaning certain aspects of daily living will no longer be within our personal control.

Another contributor to my understanding the challenges and opportunities of this life stage is not a behavioral scientist but a former business executive, Eugene O'Kelly. In his book, *Chasing Daylight,* he describes what he learned first hand about the challenges and opportunities of the 3rd Age when the doctors diagnosed him with inoperable brain cancer and told him that he had 3 months to live.[48] At the time he was diagnosed, O'Kelly was 53, the chief executive officer of one of the world's largest accounting firms, and at the top of his game. When he received the bad news, O'Kelly made a decision to live his life as fully as possible in the time he had left. The remarkable plan he put together illustrates some of the development issues unique to the 3rd Age. Although O'Kelly had to compress these into 3 months rather than 3 decades, his list of challenges and opportunities is a useful addition to what is already known.

For instance, he had to disengage from activities that had been the center of his life. But if he were going to live as fully as possible in the short time he had left, O'Kelly realized that he had to resign completely from his position as CEO and board chair of the company. For someone at the peak of his powers, who loved his work and his position, this was disengagement wrenching. He could not, however, take advantage of the opportunities that were possible for him to enjoy unless he could let go of his job.[49]

O'Kelly's recognition of the importance of disengagement from a position that was once the core of his identity to live as fully as possible underscores its significance for all 3rd Agers.[50] On a less dramatic level, there comes a time for most in the 3rd Age to orchestrate your disengagement—your retirement, resignation, or withdrawal from those organizations and activities to which you once felt connected, which contributed to your feelings of belonging and being competent and useful when you are younger, but no longer play a role in your life. Not especially difficult is deciding when to terminate your membership in that club you have not used in several years and those organizations whose meetings you no longer attend. It is far more difficult to separate yourself from those jobs you once performed well and were central to your feeling of competence and self-worth. For example, you might have been the chair of the board of the local hospital and helped raise the money for the new children's wing; however, your term as chair is now over, and there is no longer a key role for you.

A second challenge in the 3rd Age is to learn to accept the reality that fewer of life's activities will be under your direct control. For O'Kelly, who was used to micromanaging every aspect of his life, this was not easy. He wisely selected those tasks that he could still control—getting medical treatment to extend his active life expectancy, putting his legal and financial affairs in order, and planning his funeral. Then, he let go of trying to manage those activities that were no longer central to his goal of making every day left to him the best day possible.

O'Kelly's decision to give up control of some activities while continuing to manage those aspects of his life he could still control is a lesson for older adults who may have three decades to make decisions about which aspect of their lives they can actively control and which should be given to others. Research on this topic has found that older people who are the most comfortable making realistic decisions about what is and is not within their control as they grow older are those with a positive attitude, who have people in their lives encouraging them to do all they can do to remain independent, and who can appreciate the pleasures that remain available to them.[51]

The 3rd Age is not just about challenges and losses. It is about enhanced powers and opportunities unique to this season. I wonder if this might have been what Henry Wadsworth Longfellow had in mind more than a century ago when he wrote the following:

> For age is an opportunity no less
> Than youth itself, though in another dress.
> And as the evening twilight fades away
> The sky is filled with stars, invisible by day.[52]

One interpretation of those "stars" that are invisible during the daylight of midlife, is that they represent those opportunities that are far more available in the 3rd Age than earlier in life. Examples are touching base with important people and moments, reveling in the abundance of unhurried time, having greater ability to regulate emotions, and being more open to new experiences.

One of these "stars" that O'Kelly discovered is the pleasure of "touching base," reconnecting with those people and experiences that evoked pleasant memories when he thought of them. He wrote of meeting once more with cherished golfing friends, intimates with whom he had shared an excellent dinner and bottle of wine, and those who had accompanied him skiing the white powder. When O'Kelly recalled those unique times with old friends, he felt a surge of the same emotions he experienced those many years ago. Other older people feel that same surge of powerful emotions when visiting their hometown, their old high school, summer camp, or the place where they were married; when attending a reunion of classmates, team members, or fellow pilots with whom they graduated from primary training decades ago; or when walking a particular beach that was a favorite haunt, looking at mountains where they used to hike every fall, or standing on the dock of the community boathouse and watching the young people sail as they did once upon a time.

Not only do such occasions sometimes enable us to reexperience these moments, but also we can reconnect with ourselves at that much younger age, perhaps for a few moments feeling that surge of energy and excitement, possibly even that arrogance, unique to our 20s and 30s.

A second of these opportunities is a relative abundance of unhurried time. Instead of a life filled with meeting the needs of others and generating the necessary income to support our lifestyle, we have a greater opportunity to design our lives to work at things we choose, to take time for playful activities, and to devote quality time to loved ones. A number of 3rd Agers commented that time seems to pass so rapidly for them, and they do not know why. One woman told me that "all" she had done that day so far was Skype with her grandchildren and begin to clean up her small garden, and suddenly it was time to prepare dinner. I wonder if the reason is that 3rd Agers are able to savor the moment more fully because they no longer feel as hurried.

A third positive feature is that 3rd Agers are likely to be better at regulating their emotions as senior citizens than they were as younger adults. This is partly the case because seniors are wiser about avoiding disagreeable people and circumstances. They also may be more attentive to positive than negative information, as well as more disposed to recall the best and not the worst about situations and people in their lives. This disposition to view people and situations in a more positive light may be one of the reasons that several of our research subjects commented that their children paid more attention to their advice now that they were in the 3rd Age than when they were in midlife.

A final star is that optimally aging 3rd Agers can be more curious and more open to the unfamiliar than those a quarter to a half century younger.[53] My own research discovered that measures of curiosity were positively correlated with less cognitive and physical decline in 3rd Agers. Also there was the study in Chapter 5 showing that bright older adults looked longer at novel stimuli than those younger and at midlife. These findings are contrary to the stereotype of older adults being inflexible and stuck in their ways.

This is only a tiny sample of the challenges and opportunities inherent in the 3rd Age. With a record number of adults already among this group and even larger numbers of baby boomers at the threshold of the 3rd Age, we can anticipate that research on subjects that have an impact on these individuals will increase. Perhaps this short list may stimulate clinicians and researchers to identify other challenges and opportunities unique to this stage of life.

Optimal Agers as Exemplars

Like many teachers, I found that giving the students an opportunity to understand more about the aging process by interviewing older adults was a powerful learning experience for them. What I had not anticipated was how much these older volunteers would serve as role models for the students. Here is a sample of what the students learned from their elders about how to age optimally.

> Optimal aging is not a chance phenomenon. I truly learned from these interviews, mainly what I want and don't want my life to be like when I'm older. A nonchalant attitude toward health, which I see all around me in my friends and in my family, is not something I want to inherit. I want to make the most of my life and take precautions so that I am aging optimally.

> Optimal agers often feel passionate about something—loved ones, arts, working out, a cause, some activity in the community, travel—and live to be involved with these things.

> I believe that optimal aging is a gift, as well as a proactive choice. Some people seem to be optimal agers with almost no obvious effort. They have always done the right things to stay healthy and mentally sharp compared to people their age. It comes naturally. Others, though, have had to deal with some really bad situations, and they've had a lot of work to do to become optimal agers and stay that way.

> I was left with many questions after the interviews, one of the most important being, "Do we feel as though we are living the rest of our lives, or putting off dying the rest of our lives?"

> Every year on October 29th, my birthday, I secretly think about how I feel I am growing up too fast. Before I know it, I'll be 25. I can imagine that this sort of feeling will persist 'til I am 30; then I'll worry about becoming 40. I can't even imagine being 50. But then I think about getting to be 60, and nothing soothes my mind more than thinking that I might have a chance to turn out to be an optimal ager like the people I interviewed.

Glossary of Frequently Used Terms

This glossary is intended to provide the reader with a general idea of what I have in mind when using specific terms about cognitive aging. References to these frequently used terms are contained in the chapter endnotes.

Activities of daily living (ADLs): Professionals who care for elders use six categories of ADLs to describe a person's ability to perform everyday self-care actions that enable them to live without outside assistance: hygiene (bathing, grooming, shaving, and oral care); continence; dressing; feeding oneself; toileting; and transferring (moving from a seated to standing position and getting in and out of bed).

Age-related cognitive decline (ARCD): A mental condition at the extreme lower end of normal intellectual functioning and more likely to remain stable, the major identifying characteristics are memory impairment or other weakened mental skills in otherwise healthy normal older adults. Lower mental ability should be verified by test scores in the lower ranges of normal IQ but above the threshold for dementia. Conditions resembling ARCD are "age-associated cognitive decline," "age-associated memory impairment," and "age-consistent memory decline."

Alzheimer's disease: Experts distinguish between Alzheimer's disease and dementia of the Alzheimer type (DAT). The former can only be confirmed by autopsy. DAT refers to those conditions for which the presence of dementia is inferred by clinical symptoms. Symptoms include memory impairment that gradually increases in severity over at least a 6-month period; loss of at least one other mental ability, such as attention, orientation, or judgment; and greatly impaired capacity to function normally in self-care and day-to-day activities. Other causes for cognitive impairment are ruled out, such as disease, other systemic conditions, psychiatric disorders, or alcohol or drug abuse. The diagnosis of DAT is often supported by neuropsychological testing, laboratory findings, and brain-imaging studies.

Attention: The ability to concentrate on a portion of experience while blocking out other potentially distracting stimuli.

Attention restoration activities: Actions that individuals can take to refresh their concentration and improve the likelihood of using their intellectual powers fully. Examples are a walk in the woods, other exposure to nature, and appreciating art.

Calculation: Simple arithmetic such as checking the arithmetic on a bill. This mental skill is relatively age resistant.

Cognition: Also called "intellectual functioning"; refers to global mental operations in which information is perceived, stored, and recovered and used to understand, problem solve, and reason. Cognition is involved in nearly every human activity.

Cognitive reserve: A theory that an increase in connections occurs between neurons in response to environmental influences. It is characterized by a long-term change in the strength and efficacy of the contact between the pre- and postsynaptic membranes. More numerous connections between the neurons may mean that as some become inoperative due to disease, injury, or aging, the remaining connections can reroute communication between neurons that support continued high-level cognition.

Compensation: Making up for age-related losses by changing habits or using technology to be able to function effectively. An example is taking a brief nap to counteract diminished energy.

Cross-sectional studies: Research investigations that study age-associated changes in different subjects who are grouped by age. For example, the decline in memory might be measured over the life span by comparing the recall of short story content of different subjects in age groups 50, 60, and 70.

Crystallized abilities: Also called "verbal" aptitudes, tests of these abilities do not usually involve time pressure. Vocabulary is an example. These skills decline gradually with age.

Dementia: Refers to severe cognitive impairment, featuring a progressive decline in memory over a 6-month period or more. In addition to memory loss, other mental skills are diminished, including orientation, motor skills, and the ability to use language. Alzheimer's disease is the most common form of dementia. Other frequent causes are vascular and Lewy body dementia.

Digit–symbol substitution test: A frequently used test of working memory and processing speed. It requires subjects to learn a digit–symbol code and substitute the correct symbol for a series of single-digit random numbers under time pressure. Like most fluid abilities, this skill declines with age.

Executive functions: A multiple-aptitude cluster that encompasses several of these skills: attention, inhibition of distractions, planning, verbal fluency, working memory, mental flexibility, visuospatial abilities, and processing speed.

Favorable attrition: In longitudinal studies, the tendency to lose subjects who at the beginning of the project were less healthy, lower in mental ability, and had fewer years of education.

Fluid abilities: Also called "performance" aptitudes, tests of these skills often involve time pressure. Block design and digit–symbol substitution are examples. On average, they decline more rapidly than crystallized abilities with age.

Gray matter: Also spelled "grey matter," this is the primary operating component of the central nervous system (CNS). It contains neural cell bodies and is distributed on the cerebral cortex as well as deeper within the brain. Gray matter structures process sensory information and route this and other stimuli through the central nervous system to create a response via synaptic activity.

High risk for cognitive impairment: A heterogeneous group of 3rd Agers whose several medical conditions, poor lifestyle habits, or psychological problems put them at a higher risk for cognitive impairment. Some already exhibit chronic memory and other persistent cognitive problems. Those at high risk for cognitive impairment make up 10–20% of the 3rd Age population.

Hippocampus: The hippocampus is a major component of the human brain. Located in the lower middle of the brain, it plays an important role in memory and spatial navigation.

Inhibition: The capacity to block out distractions while working at a task. An illustration is suppressing the sound of someone talking while trying to concentrate on a newspaper editorial. The ability to inhibit distractions declines with age.

Instrumental activities of daily living (IADLs): Older adults who can live independently are regularly able to carry out these IADLs: finding and utilizing resources (looking up phone numbers, using a telephone, making and keeping doctor's appointments); driving or arranging travel; preparing meals; shopping; doing housework; managing medication; and managing finances.

Intelligence: The ability to solve everyday problems. It is often measured by IQ and other mental tests.

Longitudinal studies: Research projects that study age-related changes in the same subjects who are re-examined several times over the life of the study. For example, the decline in memory might be measured over the life span by comparing the recall of short-story content when the subjects are 50, 60, and 70. Longitudinal studies may continue for many decades.

Memory, after delay: Recall after a time lapse. Trying to remember that phone number your friend gave you a half hour ago that you did not write down. Mild-to-moderate age effects.

Memory, immediate: Recall of material recently presented, such as remembering and writing down a phone number a friend has just given you. Little affected by age.

Memory, name-number-things: Episodic inability to remember the name of a person, number, or thing (e.g., umbrella or stapler). Moderately age related.

Memory, tip of the tongue: Occasional blocked recall of name of a person or thing while feeling on the verge of remembering. Moderately affected by age.

Memory, working: Capacity to hold information in the mind while carrying out related mental operations using that information (e.g., repeating numbers backward). Strongly affected by age.

MicroCog: A computerized test of intellectual functioning consisting of 13 subtests measuring both crystallized and fluid abilities. Administered to 1,002 physicians ages 25–92 and 561 nonphysician (normal) subjects.

Mild cognitive impairment (MCI): Is viewed as a transitional phase leading to dementia. Primary identifying characteristics are symptoms of memory impairment or other weakened mental skills in otherwise healthy normal older adults. Mental ability tests are needed to verify that the person with MCI has mental ability scores below the normal range but higher than the cutoff scores for Alzheimer's disease.

Mini-Mental State Exam (MMSE): A commonly used brief screening test in longitudinal studies to assess cognitive decline or impairment. It measures orientation, immediate and delayed recall, naming, following directions, attention, working memory, and spatial memory. While the MMSE is sensitive to moderate and severe degrees of dementia, it is less accurate in assessing mild cognitive impairment and the lower end of normal intellectual functioning.

Multitasking: Engaging in two mental tasks simultaneously. One example is divided attention, in which individuals must focus on two different sources of information at the same time. An example is closely following an interesting political debate on TV and at the same time taking a call from your accountant, who asks questions about your tax return. Another example is dual-task attention, which requires the subjects to carry out two mental activities simultaneously—having a face-to-face conversation with a friend while texting another person. All forms of multitasking find untrained older adults achieving lower scores than younger subjects.

Neuroimaging: Imaging technology that enables investigators to observe how the brain functions when carrying out specific intellectual tasks. PET (positron emission tomography) and fMRI (functional magnetic resonance imaging) are examples.

Neuroplasticity: The capacity of the human brain to change in response to environmental stimulation. The effects of the external experience may be on the structure, connectivity, or the functioning of the brain.

Normal cognitive aging: Refers to older adults who may have experienced minor physical problems and whose intellectual abilities are typical of their age group and educational background. Normal cognitive agers comprise about 50–60% of those in the 3rd Age of life.

Optimal cognitive aging: Characterized by avoiding risky lifestyle habits that endanger the intellect and practicing behaviors associated with maintaining or slowing the decline of mental skills. Optimally aging individuals are mentally vigorous and regularly focus their intellectual powers on activities that interest them. Estimates are that between 20 and 30% of 3rd Age adults fall in this range.

Optimization: Doing what is possible to maximize performance by minimizing the negative cognitive effects of aging. For example, a teacher begins wearing a hearing aid when growing deafness begins to impair communication with students.

Positivity effect: A developmental pattern in which the attention gradually shifts from gathering new knowledge to expand horizons during young and middle adulthood to a stronger focus in the 3rd Age on positive information that is less stimulating but more comforting emotionally. Most 3rd Agers regulate their emotional state by accentuating the positive and ignoring the negative. The positivity effect can adversely affect complex decision making because of the failure to consider the downside aspects of the choices.

Processing speed: Refers to how rapidly a problem is solved. Most standardized cognitive tests base their scores on how quickly a test is completed along with the number of correct answers. Processing speed declines with age and is more noticeable on measures of fluid ability such as visuospatial or reasoning tasks.

Reasoning: Problem solving when the task is new, arriving at a conclusion or understanding using induction, deduction, or a combination. Tests measuring reasoning are analogies or the interpretation of proverbs. Reasoning skills decline moderately with age.

Selection: Involves giving up some activities to concentrate available mental energies on those remaining. An aging doctor stops teaching to focus on caring for the patients in his practice.

Shifting set: Also called mental flexibility; being able to adjust to a new set of circumstances to problem solve. An example is becoming momentarily confused when trying to remember which kitchen drawer the flatware goes in when we move from our home to the summer cottage. Eventually, we adjust and get it right.

Subjects: Unless otherwise noted, independently living and community-dwelling women and men who volunteered to participate in a research project. Research subjects typically differ from nonvolunteers in several ways; for example, they have more years of education, higher socioeconomic class, are more sociable, and have a more positive view of self.

3rd Age: That period of the life span beyond the first age of preparation and maturation and the second age of necessary concentration on work and child rearing, but prior to the final stage of old age and death. Spanning roughly the years from 60 to 80, the 3rd Age is based not only on chronological age but also on health, freedom from significant disability, activity level, and social engagement. Hence, the 3rd Ager may be 55 or 85.

Variance: Also called "standard deviation" or "variability," refers to how widely dispersed from top to bottom the individual scores within an age group may be. Variance within age groups usually increases with age.

Visuospatial: Includes the understanding of, memory for, and the manipulation of spatial information. Everyday examples are knowing in which direction home is, map reading in unfamiliar territory, locating the car in a crowded mall parking lot, and following directions when "some assembly is required." Tests of visuospatial ability typically involve time pressure—putting together puzzles as quickly as possible. Visuospatial abilities decline with age more rapidly than most other mental skills.

Wechsler Adult Intelligence Scale (WAIS): A family of individually administered global tests of IQ, such as the Wechsler-Bellevue, WAIS, and WAIS-IV. It contains measures of crystallized and fluid abilities and has norms for older adults.

White matter: One of the two components of the central nervous system, consisting largely of myelinated axons. So called because of the color of the fatty tissue insulating the nerve fibers, white matter tissue forms the communication system that enables messages to pass between different areas of gray matter within the nervous system.

White matter hyperintensities (WMHs): Because they are seen on MRIs as ultrawhite patches, WMHs indicate damage to the axons. WMHs increase with age. A greater incidence of WMHs is correlated with greater brain atrophy and lower cognitive test scores.

Notes

Introduction

Powell, D. H. (in collaboration with D. K. Whitla). (1994). *Profiles in cognitive aging*. Cambridge, MA: Harvard University Press.

Chapter 1

To avoid confusion regarding the many different labels used in studies cited, when reference is made to research projects that classified subjects into high/medium/low groups such as "minimal/minor/major decliners," "positive/negative/other," and so on, the terms *optimal*, *normal*, and *high risk* are used to identify these clusters, respectively, when they reflect the criteria similar to those used by the referenced research.

50th Reunion

1. Cambridge professor Peter Laslett is credited with introducing the term *3rd Age* into the social sciences [Laslett, P. (1989). *A fresh map of life: The emergence of the Third Age*. Cambridge, MA: Harvard University Press]. As used in this book, the 3rd Age encompasses what also has been called the "young-old" and the "middle-old" years. University of Chicago sociologist Bernice Neugarten introduced the concept of the young-old years [Neugarten, B. L. (1974). Age groups in American society and the rise of the young-old. *The Annals of the American Academy of Political and Social Science, 415,* 187–198]. The young-old years are based not only on chronological age but also on health, freedom from significant disability, activity level, and social engagement. Hence, the young-old person may be 55 or 85 [Neugarten, B. L., & Neugarten, D. A. (1986). Changing meanings of age in the aging society. In A. Pifer & L. Bronte (Eds.), *Our aging society: Paradox and promise* (pp. 33–51). New York: Norton]. Later researchers differentiated the middle-old years, which most often refer to the age span of 75–85 [e.g., Reed, R. J., Lowrey, C. R., & Vallis, L. A. (2006). Middle-old and old-old retirement dwelling adults respond differently to locomotor challenges in cluttered environments. *Gait and Posture, 23,* 486–491].

2. In 2010, the U.S. population is projected to be 310,223,000. The 3rd Age population (age 60–79) is expected to be about 45,503,000, or 14.7%. In 2020, the 3rd Agers are forecast to number about 62,978,000, or 18.5% of the anticipated total population of 341,387,000 [U.S. Census Bureau (2008). 2008 National population projections. *Statistical Abstracts of the United States*. Retrieved August 11, 2010, from http://www.census.gov/population/www/projections/2008projections.html].

The Growing Importance of the Intellect

3. This definition is taken from the Preamble to the Constitution of the World Health Organization. This constitution was presented at the International Health Conference in New York on July 22, 1946. The original version of the document can be seen at http://www.who.int/suggestions/faq/en/ (accessed August 11, 2010).

4. One survey was the National Long Term Care Survey (NLTCS) (http://www.nltcs.aas.duke.edu/data.htm, retrieved August 11, 2010). The NLTCS included a national sample of approximately 35,789 adults 65+ interviewed in five waves from 1982 to 2005. The closest the survey came to a question about cognition was when it asked participants if they or any family members needed help in handling routine daily activities because of physical, mental, or emotional problems. One might argue that some of the instrumental activities of daily living (IADLs), such as handling finances, are an indirect measure of intellectual functioning. Another survey was the Third National Health and Nutrition Examination Survey (NHANES III; http://www.cdc.gov/search.do?q=Third+National+Health+and+Nutrition+Examination+Survey&btnG.x=38&btnG.y=7&sort=date:D:L:d1&oe=UTF-8&ie=UTF-8&ud=1&site=default_collection, accessed August 11, 2010). It was designed to obtain nationally representative information on the health and nutritional status of the U.S. population through interviews and direct physical examinations conducted from 1988 to 1994. NHANES III included a computerized neuropsychological test that assessed reaction time, short-term memory, and working memory, which are components of the Neurobehavioral Evaluation System 2 [Baker, E. L., Letz, R., & Fiddler, A. (1985). A computer-administered neurobehavioral evaluation system for occupational and environmental epidemiology. *Journal of Occupational Medicine, 27*, 206–212]. The third survey was the National Health Interview Survey (NHIS; http://www.cdc.gov/nchs/nhis.htm, accessed August 11, 2010). Versions of this survey were carried out initially in 1957 and every 10–15 years thereafter. In 2007, NHIS interviewed 75,764 persons in 29,915 families. None of the surveys directly asked subjects about cognitive problems. There was, however, interest by the survey investigators in assessing cognitive functions. Three waves of subjects in the NLTCS were given a version of the Mini-Mental State Exam and the Short Portable Mental Status Questionnaire.

5. Twenty-eight data-based studies of successful aging were reviewed with the intention of identifying the essential components of the concept. Following absence of disability, the next most frequent component was cognitive functioning. Depp, C. A., & Jeste, D. V. (2006). Definitions and predictors of successful aging: A comprehensive review of larger quantitative studies. *American Journal of Geriatric Psychiatry, 14*, 6–20.

6. Ditto, P. H., Druley, J. A., Moore, K. A., Danks, J. H., & Smucker, W. D. (1996). Fates worse than death: The role of valued life activities in health-state evaluations. *Health Psychology, 15*, 332–343. Scientists at the University of Minnesota asked normal subjects 65+ to imagine that they were suffering from moderate or severe dementia and required a lifesaving intervention such as use of a respirator or a feeding tube. Would they want it? Three quarters of the subjects asked to imagine that they had moderate dementia said "No." Of those asked to imagine severe dementia, 85% said they would not want these procedures. In the absence of cognitive impairment, three of four subjects opted for lifesaving interventions if needed [Gjerdingen, D. K., Neff, J. A., Wang, M., & Chaloner, K.

(1999). Older persons' opinions about life-sustaining procedures in the face of dementia. *Archives of Family Medicine, 8,* 421–425].

7. We do well to recognize, however, that the preferences of older adults regarding which chronic medical conditions and disabilities they can live with as an alternative to death may change with time [Lockhart, L. K., Ditto, P. H., Danks, J. H., Coppola, K. M., & Smucker, W. D. (2001). The stability of older adults' judgments of fates better and worse than death. *Death Studies, 25,* 299–317; also Mold, J. W., Looney, S. W., Viviane, N. J., & Quiggins, P. A. (1994). Predicting the health-related values and preferences of geriatric patients. *Journal of Family Practice, 39,* 461–467].

8. Ditto et al., 1996.

9. Albus, J. S., Bekey, G. A., Holland, J. H., Kanwisher, N. G., Krichmar, J. L., Mishkin, M., et al. (2007). A proposal for a decade of the mind initiative. *Science, 317,* 1321.

Three Levels of Intellectual Functioning in the 3rd Age

10. Although they use slightly different terms to describe the categories, several groups of investigators have used a tripartite model to portray the differences along the continuum of functioning among older adults [Yaffe, S. K., Fiocco, A. J., Lindquist, K., Vittinghoff, E., Simonsick, E. M., Newman A. B., et al. (2009). Predictors of maintaining cognitive function in older adults: The Health ABC Study. *Neurology, 72,* 2029–2035; Barnes, D. E., Cauley, J. A., Lui, L.-Y., Fink, H. A., McCulloch, C., Stone, K. L., et al. (2007). Women who maintain optimal cognitive function into old age. *Journal of the American Geriatrics Society, 55,* 259–264; Uotinen, V., Suutama, Y., & Ruoppila, I. (2003). Age identification in the framework of successful aging: A study of older Finnish people. *International Journal of Aging and Human Development, 56,* 173–195; and Ylikoski, R., Ylikoski, A., Keskivaara, P., Tilvis, T., Sulkava, R., & Erkinjuntti, T. (1999). Heterogeneity of cognitive profiles in aging: Successful aging, normal aging, and individuals at-risk for cognitive decline. *European Journal of Neurology, 6,* 645–652]. Most longitudinal studies classify older subjects on the basis of minimal physical and cognitive decline, minor decline, or major decline during the period of investigation. The estimated proportions of 3rd Agers in the optimal, normal, and high-risk categories are based on median percentages from these studies.

Healthy Lifestyle Habits That Minimize Decline and Maximize Intellectual Capability

11. Data on smoking cessation and numbers of adults with smoking-related illnesses from U.S. Public Health Service. (1964). *Smoking and health* (Report of the Advisory Committee to the Surgeon General of the Public Health Service. U.S. Department of Health, Education, and Welfare, Public Health Service, Center for Disease Control. PHS Publication No. 1103). Washington, DC: U.S. Department of Health and Human Services.

12. Data on decrease in percentage of older adults with elevated cholesterol levels from [Schober, S. E., Carroll, M. D., Lacher, D. A., & Hirsch, R. (2007). *High serum total cholesterol—an indicator for monitoring cholesterol lowering efforts: U.S. adults, 2005–2006*

(NCHS Data Brief No. 2). Hyattsville, MD: National Center for Health Statistics]. Unless otherwise noted, all data on health status and health practices in this section are from the National Center for Health Statistics. (2010). *Health, United States, 2009: With special feature on medical technology.* Hyattsville, MD. During the years 1991–2007, all age groups from 55 to 84 reported higher percentages of subjects rating themselves in good, very good, or excellent health.

13. See Djoussé, L., Driver, J. A., & Gaziano, J. M. (2009). Relation between modifiable life-style factors and lifetime risk of heart failure. *Journal of the American Medical Association, 302,* 394–400. Subjects were 20,900 men from the Physicians' Health Study I, followed for an average of 22.4 years. Their mean age was 76 at this follow-up. Six modifiable lifestyle factors were studied: body weight, smoking, exercise, alcohol intake, eating breakfast cereals, and consuming fruits and vegetables. A body mass index (BMI) of 25 or less, not smoking, regular exercise, moderate alcohol intake, and consumption of cereals and fruits/vegetables were individually and jointly associated with substantially lower lifetime risk of heart failure. The risk of heart failure for those subjects adhering to four or more healthy lifestyle factors was 10.1%, compared with 21.2% for those who practiced none. See also Forman, J. P., Stampfer, M. J., & Curhan, G. C. (2009). Diet and lifestyle risk factors associated with incident hypertension in women. *Journal of the American Medical Association, 302,* 401–411. This research demonstrated the independent value of these modifiable risk factors in reducing the rate of hypertension of 12,319 older women. Also see Chiuve, S. E., McCullough, M. L., Sacks, F. M., & Rimm, E. B. (2006). Healthy lifestyle factors in the primary prevention of coronary heart disease among men: Benefits among users and nonusers of lipid-lowering and antihypertensive medications. *Circulation, 114,* 160–167. Subjects were 42,847 men who were part of the Health Professionals Follow-up Study. Between 40 and 75 years of age when the study began, they were followed for 16 years. Lifestyle factors investigated were similar to those in the 2009 study of Djoussé et al. Those adhering to four healthy lifestyle factors had 22% the risk of heart disease of those who adhered to none.

14. For instance, Colcombe, S., & Kramer, A. F. (2003). Fitness effects on the cognitive function of older adults: A meta-analytic study. *Psychological Sciences, 14,* 125–130.

15. Two relevant articles are as follows: Ferini-Strambi, L., Baietto, C., Di Gioia, M. R., Castaldi, P., Castronovo, C., Zucconi, M., et al. (2003). Cognitive dysfunction in patients with obstructive sleep apnea (OSA): Partial reversibility after continuous positive airway pressure (CPAP). *Brain Research Bulletin, 61,* 87–92. Also, Valencia-Flores, M., Bliwise, D., Guilleminault, C., Cilveti, R., & Clerk, A. (1996). Cognitive function in patients with sleep apnea after acute nocturnal nasal continuous positive airway pressure (CPAP) treatment: Sleepiness and hypoxemia effects. *Journal of Clinical and Experimental Neuropsychology, 18,* 197–210.

16. For a review article, see MacLaughlin, E. J., Raehl, C. L., Treadway, A. S. K., Sterling, T. L., Zoller, D. P., & Bond, C. A. (2005). Assessing medication adherence in the elderly: Which tools to use in clinical practice? *Drugs and Aging, 22,* 231–255.

17. Meta-analyses and longitudinal investigations have demonstrated the benefit of larger social networks to intellect and physical vigor [Holt-Lunstad, J., Smith, T. B., & Layton, J. B. (2010). Social relationships and mortality risk: A meta-analytic review. *PLoS Medicine, 7,* e1000316]. Those at particular risk are those with the fewest confidantes [Holtzman, R. E., Rebok, G. W., Saczynski, J. S., Kouzis, A. C., Doyle, K. W., & Eaton, W. W. (2004).

Social network characteristics and cognition in middle-aged and older adults. *The Journal of Gerontology: Psychological Sciences, 59B,* 278-284.

18. Although the evidence is largely clinical and the measured correlations are small, there are demonstrable relationships between stress and loss of hippocampal volume [Sapolsky, R. M. (1996). Why stress is bad for your brain. *Science, 273,* 749–750]. An increased state of anxiety also links to lower scores on a cognitive test battery. See Powell, D. H., 1994.

19. Sometimes called "selective optimization with compensation," this technique works effectively with older adults who recognize their declining cognitive skills and put into place techniques to augment them. See Baltes, P. B. (1997). On the incomplete architecture of human ontogeny: Selection, optimization, and compensation as foundations of developmental theory. *American Psychologist, 52,* 366–380.

Reflections, Assessment, and Applications

20. See Barnes et al., 2007.

21. James, W. (1896). *The will to believe: And other essays in popular philosophy.* New York: Longmans Green, pp. 257–258.

22. The lifetime risk of heart failure among 3rd Age physicians was 12.9% for those eating one or more servings of whole grain breakfast cereal per week compared to 15% among those eating less than one serving weekly (Djousse et al., 2009).

23. Subjects volunteering at least once a week had an odds ration of 1.24 of being a cognitive maintainer compared to 1.0 for those not volunteering (Yaffee et al, 2009). French subjects studied longitudinally who ate one serving of fish weekly had an odds ratio of .81 of developing dementia or Alzheimer's disease compared to those who eat fish less than weekly (Barberger-Gateau, P., Raffaitin, C., Letenneur, L., et al., 2007. Dietary patterns and risk of dementia: The Three-City cohort study. *Neurology, 69,* 1921-1930).

24. Cousins, N. (1979). *Anatomy of an illness as perceived by the patient: Reflections on healing and regeneration.* New York: Norton, p. 69.

25. From the client's perspective, frequently mentioned qualities of a beneficial therapeutic alliance are a feeling of therapist warmth and agreement on the purpose of the treatment and the methods of therapy. A useful review of this literature is contained in Elvins, R., & Green, J. (2008). The conceptualization and measurement of therapeutic alliance: An empirical review. *Clinical Psychology Review, 28,* 1167–1187.

Chapter 2

1. In their excellent book about successful aging, Rowe and Kahn identify three primary components: avoiding disease, maintaining a high level of physical and cognitive functioning, and being actively engaged in social and community activities. The first element includes activities aimed at preventing or postponing disease, as well as healthy lifestyle habits [Rowe, J. W., & Kahn, R. L. (1998). *Successful aging.* New York: Pantheon]. Vaillant's research about aging well agreed with that of Rowe and Kahn, finding that the men studied reported no disability at 75 and reported themselves to be in good health [Vaillant, G. E. (2002). *Aging well: Surprising guidepost to a happier life.* Boston: Little, Brown].

Chronic Medical Conditions and the Intellect

2. The chronic disease categories are those used by the National Health Interview Survey, which serves as the main source of data on health for the U.S. civilian noninstitutionalized population. Not all of the chronic diseases found among older adults were included in this review. Excluded were conditions that are well known to be associated with cognitive impairment, such as heart attacks, cardiac insufficiency, stroke, alcohol abuse, and high levels of stress, anxiety, and depression. Added to the list were three afflictions frequently first diagnosed in the 3rd Age that adversely affect cognition: atrial fibrillation, sleep apnea, and hearing loss.

3. The databases were PubMed and PsychINFO, occasionally supplemented by the Web of Science and Google Scholar. For each chronic disease, the literature for at least 10 years was reviewed, focusing on those studies that included independently living 3rd Age subjects.

4. Because of its brevity and worldwide clinical use as a dementia screening test, the MMSE score was often the only measure of cognitive change [Folstein, M. F., Folstein, S. E., & McHugh, P. R. (1975). Mini-Mental State—A practical method for grading the cognitive state of patients for the clinician. *Journal of Psychiatric Research, 12,* 189–198]. It has spawned several offspring, among them the 3MS [Teng, E. L. & Chui, H. C. (1987). The modified Mini-Mental-State (3MS) examination. *Journal of Clinical Psychiatry, 48,* 314–318].

Hypertension

5. For research purposes, hypertension has been defined as having blood pressure of 140/90 and above or taking antihypertensive medication. Of those 65–74, the percentage reporting hypertension in 2003–2006 was 70.8% for females and 64.1% for males. Of subjects surveyed, 81% had their blood pressure taken three times. Data from National Health and Nutrition Examination Survey (NHANES) and National Center for Health Statistics. (2010). *Health, United States, 2009. With special feature on medical technology.* Hyattsville, MD.

6. The characteristics of hypertension are drawn from three sources: Sutters, M. (2008). Systemic hypertension. In S. J. McPhee, M. A. Papadakis, & L. M. Tierney, Jr. (Eds.), *Current medical diagnosis and treatment 2008,* 47th Edition, pp. 370–397. New York: McGraw-Hill; Chobanian, A. V., Bakris, G. L., Black, H. R., Cushman, W. C., Green, L. E., Izzo, J. L., Jr., et al. & the National High Blood Pressure Education Program Coordinating Committee. (2003). The Seventh Report of the Joint National Committee on Prevention, Detection, Evaluation, and Treatment of High Blood Pressure. Bethesda, MD: U.S. Department of Health and Human Services, National Institutes of Health, National Heart, Lung and Blood Institute; Mayo Clinic Web site. Retrieved August 11, 2010, from http://mayoclinic.com.

7. *Japanese Americans:* In this study, every 10-mmHg increase in systolic blood pressure was associated with a 9% increased risk for poor cognitive function [Launer, L. J., Masaki, K., Petrovich, H., Foley, D., & Havlik, R. J. (1995). The association between midlife blood pressure levels and late-life cognitive function. The Honolulu-Asia Aging Study. *Journal*

of the American Medical Association, 274, 1846–1851]. *Whites:* Elias, M. F., D'Agostino, R. B., Elias, P. K., & Wolf, P. A. (1995). Neuropsychological test performance, cognitive functioning, blood pressure, and age: The Framingham Heart Study. *Experimental Aging Research, 21,* 369–391. *Blacks:* Murray, M. D., Lane, K. A., Gao, S., Evans, R. M., Unverzagt, F. W., Hall, K. S., et al. (2002). Preservation of cognitive function with antihypertensive medications: A longitudinal analysis of a community-based sample of African Americans. *Archives of Internal Medicine, 162,* 2090–2096.

8. The international interest in this topic is illustrated by the following publications: *Argentina:* Vicario, A., Martinez, C. D., Baretto, D., Diaz-Casale, A., & Nicolosi, L. (2005). Hypertension and cognitive decline: Impact on executive function. *Journal of Clinical Hypertension, 7,* 598–604. *Great Britain:* Cervilla, J. A., Prince, M., Lovestone, S., & Mann, A. (2000). Long-term predictors of cognitive outcome in a cohort of older people with hypertension. *The British Journal of Psychiatry, 177,* 66–71. *France:* Hanon, O., Pequignot, R., Seux, M. L., Lenoir, H., Bune, A., Rigaud, A. S., et al. (2006). Relationship between antihypertensive drug therapy and cognitive function in elderly hypertensive patients with memory complaints. *Journal of Hypertension, 24,* 2101–2117. *Germany:* Knecht, S., Wersching, H., Lohmann, H., Bruchmann, M., Duning, T., Dziewas, R., et al. (2008). High-normal blood pressure is associated with poor cognitive performance. *Hypertension, 51,* 663–668. *Sweden:* Kilander, L., Nyman, H., Boberg, M., Hansson, L., & Lithell, H. (1998). Hypertension is related to cognitive impairment: A 20-year follow-up of 999 men. *Hypertension, 31,* 780–786. *United States:* Elias, P. K., Elias, M. F., Robbins, M. A., & Budge, M. M. (2004). Blood pressure-related cognitive decline: Does age make a difference? *Hypertension, 44,* 631–636; Elias, M. F., Robbins, M. A., Schultz, N. R., Jr., & Pierce, T. W. (1990). Is blood pressure an important variable in research on aging and neuropsychological test performance? *Journals of Gerontology: Psychological Sciences, 45B,* 128–135.

9. From an analysis of data drawn from a 6-year longitudinal study of over 15,000 multiracial subjects aged 47–70 from four sites: Forsyth County, North Carolina; Jackson, Mississippi; Minneapolis, Minnesota; and Washington County, Maryland [Knopman, D., Boland, L. L., Mosley, T., Howard, G., Liao, D., Szklo, M., et al. & the ARIC Study Investigators. (2001). Cardiovascular risk factors and cognitive decline in middle-aged adults. *Neurology, 56,* 42–48].

10. The differences in attention, inhibition, and working memory were small but statistically significant. One potential confounding variable was higher trait anxiety among the young hypertensives that could have contributed to their lower test scores [Waldstein, S. R., Jennings, J. R., Ryan, C. M., Muldoon, M. F., Shapiro, A. P., Polefrone, J. M., et al. (1996). Hypertension and neuropsychological performance in men. Interactive effects of age. *Health Psychology, 15,* 102–109].

11. de Leeuw, F.-E., de Groot, J. C., Oudkerk, M., Witteman, J. C. M., Hofman, A., van Gijn, J., et al. (2002). Hypertension and cerebral white matter lesions in a prospective cohort study. *Brain, 125,* 765–772; and van Gijn. J. (2000). White matters: Small vessels and slow thinking in old age. *Lancet, 356,* 612–613.

12. Koga, H., Yuzuriha, T., Yao, H., Endo, K., Hiejima, S., Takashima, Y., et al. (2002). Quantitative MRI findings and cognitive impairment among community dwelling elderly subjects. *Journal of Neurology, Neurosurgery and Psychiatry, 72,* 737–741; also Raz, N., Lindenberger, U., Rodrigue, K. M., Kennedy, K. M., Head, D., Williamson, A., et

al. (2005). Regional brain changes in aging healthy adults: General trends, individual differences and modifiers. *Cerebral Cortex, 15,* 1676–1689.

13. Two studies demonstrating the benefit to the intellect of taking antihypertensive medication are Hajjar, I., Catoe, H., Sixta, S., Boland, R., Johnson, D., Hirth, V., et al. (2005). Cross-sectional and longitudinal association between antihypertensive medications and cognitive impairment in an elderly population. *Journals of Gerontology, Series A: Biological Sciences Medical Sciences, 60,* 67–73; and Murray et al., 2002.

14. de Leeuw et al., 2002.

Atrial Fibrillation

15. Atrial fibrillation (AFib; sometimes also called afib, A-Fib, or AF) occurs when the natural pacemaker of the heart, called the sinus node, is compromised by disease or damage. The results are irregular electrical impulses to the atria, causing them to quiver or flutter erratically, out of coordination with the ventricles. AFib divides into two types, *paroxysmal* and *persistent*, depending on heart rate and whether the arrhythmia terminates spontaneously. When the heart beats erratically 200 or more times a minute for 1–7 days but returns to normal sinus rhythm without treatment, the AFib is said to be paroxysmal. The rapid and erratic heartbeat of persistent AFib sufferers may be in the 80–150 range and typically does not normalize without pharmacological or other medical intervention. Persistent AFib sufferers may feel the same cardiac and pulmonary symptoms as those with paroxysmal AFib, although they may be less disabling. Description and characteristics of AFib were taken from the Web site of the American Heart Association (http://www.americanheart.org/presenter.jhtml?identifier=4451) and the Mayo Clinic (http://www.mayoclinic.com/health/atrial-fibrillation/DS00291) (accessed August 11, 2010).

16. The odds of developing dementia were 2.83 times greater for 2,837 subjects with AFib followed by Mayo Clinic investigators for 5 years [Miyasaka, Y., Barnes, M. E., Petersen, R. C., Cha, S. S., Bailey, K. R., et al. (2007). Risk of dementia in stroke-free patients diagnosed with atrial fibrillation: Data from a community-based cohort. *European Heart Journal, 28,* 1962–1967]. In Brescia, Italy, a medical research team found a 3.3 times greater dementia risk for their patients with AFib in a cross-sectional study [Rozzini, R., Sabatini, T., & Trabucchi, M. (1999). Chronic atrial fibrillation and low cognitive function. *Stroke, 30,* 190–191]. Framingham investigators estimated the risk of stroke among their patients with AFib to be five times that of older subjects with normal sinus rhythm. See, for example, Wolf, P. A., Dawber, T. R., Thomas, H. E., & Kannel, W. B. (1978). Epidemiologic assessment of chronic atrial fibrillation and risk of stroke: The Framingham Study. *Neurology, 28,* 973–977.

17. *Italy:* Forti, P., Maioli, F., Pisacane, N., Rietti, E., Montesi, F., & Ravaglia, G. (2007). Atrial fibrillation and risk of dementia in non-demented elderly subjects with and without mild cognitive impairment (MCI). *Archives of Gerontology and Geriatrics, 44,* 155–165; Rozzini et al. *Netherlands:* Ott, A., Breteler, M. M. B., de Bruyne, M. C., van Harskamp, F., Grobbee, D. E., & Hofman, A. (1997). Atrial fibrillation and dementia in a population-based study. The Rotterdam Study. *Stroke, 28,* 316–321.

Sweden: Kilander, L., Andrén, B., Nyman, H., Lind, L., Boberg, M., & Lithell, H. (1998). Atrial fibrillation is an independent determinant of low cognitive function. A cross-sectional study in elderly men. *Stroke, 29,* 1816–1820. *United Kingdom:* O'Connell, J. E., Gray, C. S., French, J. M., & Robertson, I. H. (1998). Atrial fibrillation and cognitive function: A case-control study. *Neurology, Neurosurgery and Psychiatry, 65,* 386–389. *United States:* Miyasaka et al., 2007; Elias, M. F., Sullivan, L. M., Elias, P. K., Vasan, R. S., D'Agostino, R. B. Sr., Seshadri, S., et al. (2006). Atrial fibrillation is associated with lower cognitive performance in the Framingham offspring men. *Journal of Stroke, 15,* 214–222.

18. For example, Richards, M., Meade, T. W., Peart, S., Brennan, P. J., & Mann, A. H. (1997). Is there any evidence for a protective effect of antithrombotic medication on cognitive function in men at risk of cardiovascular disease? Some preliminary findings. *Journal of Neurology, Neurosurgery, and Psychiatry, 62,* 269–272; also Kilander et al., 1998; and Elias et al., 2006.

19. For example, Ott et al., 1997.

20. The primary theories are thromboembolic and hemodynamic [Knecht, S., Oelschlager, C., Duning, T., Lohmann, H., Albers, J., Stehling, C., et al. (2008). Atrial fibrillation in stroke-free patients is associated with memory impairment and hippocampal atrophy. *European Heart Journal, 29,* 2125–2132].

21. Estimates are from two research summaries with similar findings conducted 15 years apart: Ali, S., Hong, M., Antezano, E. S., & Mangat, I. (2006). Evaluation and management of atrial fibrillation. *Cardiovascular and Haematological Disorders—Drug Targets, 6,* 233–244; also Wolf, P. A., Abbott, R. D., & Kannel, W. B. (1991). Atrial fibrillation as an independent risk factor for stroke: The Framingham Study. *Stroke, 22,* 983–988.

22. Study by Richards et al., 1997.

23. Ali et al., 2006. A later multicenter observational study was conducted in Germany to evaluate the current anticoagulation treatment pattern in patients with AFib. INR levels were within the therapeutic range 56% of the time [McBride, D., Brüggenjürgen, B., Roll, S., & Willich, S. N. (2007). Anticoagulation treatment for the reduction of stroke in atrial fibrillation: A cohort study to examine the gap between guidelines and routine medical practice. *Journal of Thrombosis and Thrombolysis, 24,* 65–72].

24. Cognitive impairment was defined as a score of 23 or less on the MMSE, which only proves an association between the two variables. We do not know whether subjects with cognitive impairment at the beginning had more difficulty remembering to take their medications and therefore had higher INR levels or whether a chronic pattern of irregular INR maintenance led to greater cognitive impairment [van Deelen, B. A., van den Bemt, P. M., Egberts, T. C., van't Hoff, A., & Maas, H. A. (2005). Cognitive impairment as determinant for sub-optimal control of oral anticoagulation treatment in elderly patients with atrial fibrillation. *Drugs and Aging, 22,* 353–360].

Chronic Pulmonary Disease

25. Data and descriptions about pulmonary diseases and their physical effects were drawn from the Web site of the American Lung Association. (http://www.lungusa.org//lung-disease, accessed August 11, 2010).

26. In contrast to the large number of publications on hypertension, and to a lesser extent on AFib, that were based on longitudinal studies, the majority of relevant articles about the effects of pulmonary conditions on the intellect were cross sectional.

Chronic Obstructive Pulmonary Disease

27. Grant, I., Heaton, R. K., McSweeny, A. J., Adams, K. M., & Timms, R. M. (1982). Neuropsychological findings in hypoxemic chronic obstructive pulmonary disease. *Archives of Internal Medicine, 142*, 1470–1476; Grant, I., Prigatano, G. P., Heaton, R. K., McSweeny, A. J., Wright, E. C., & Adams, K. M. (1987). Progressive neuropsychologic impairment and hypoxemia. *Archives of General Psychiatry, 44*, 999–1006.

28. Two examples are Incalzi, R. A., Chiappini, F., Fuso, L., Torrice, M. P., Gemma, A., & Pistelli, R. (1998). Predicting cognitive decline in patients with hypoxaemic COPD. *Respiratory Medicine, 92*, 527–533; and Stuss, D. T., Peterkin, I., Guzman, D. A., Guzman, C., & Troyer, A. K. (1997). Chronic obstructive pulmonary disease: Effects of hypoxia on neurological and neuropsychological measures. *Journal of Clinical and Experimental Neuropsychology, 19*, 515–524.

29. Although the number of subjects was small in each study, the fact that the same findings occurred in two different research settings is encouraging. The findings await confirmation from larger-scale prospective investigations. *Turkey:* Ortapamuk, H., & Naldoken, S. (2006). Brain perfusion abnormalities in chronic obstructive pulmonary disease: Comparison with cognitive impairment. *Annals of Nuclear Medicine, 20*, 99–106. *Italy:* Antonelli Incalzi, R. A., Marra, C., Giordano, A., Calcagni, M. L., Cappa, A., Basso, S., et al. (2003). Cognitive impairment in chronic obstructive pulmonary disease: A neuropsychological and SPECT study. *Journal of Neurology, 250*, 325–332.

30. Medications prescribed include bronchodilators, anti-inflammatories, corticosteroids, mucokinetics, and antibiotics. A positive view of various treatments to relieve the symptoms of COPD is in Celli, B. R. (2006). Chronic obstructive pulmonary disease: From unjustified nihilism to evidence-based optimism. *Proceedings of the American Thoracic Society, 3*, 58–65.

31. Also included in this study were a subgroup of subjects with mild Alzheimer's disease. The treated patients with COPD were stronger on all of the mental tests than those with mild Alzheimer's [Kozora, E., Filley, C. M., Julian, L. J., & Collum, C. M. (1999). Cognitive functioning in patients with chronic obstructive pulmonary disease and mild hypoxemia compared with patients with mild Alzheimer disease and normal controls. *Neuropsychiatry, Neuropsychology and Behavioral Neurology, 12*, 178–183].

32. Because of the small number of patients (10) and the method of analysis, none of the gains was statistically significant, although every subtest score tended in a positive direction [Hjalmarsen, A., Waterloo, K., Dahl, A., Jorde, R., & Viitanen, M. (1999). Effect of long-term oxygen therapy on cognitive and neurological dysfunction in chronic obstructive pulmonary disease. *European Neurology, 42*, 27–35].

33. *Wake Forest:* Etnier, J., Johnston, R., Dagenbach, D., Pollard, R. J., Rejeski, W. J., & Berry, M. (1999). The relationships among pulmonary function, aerobic fitness, and cognitive functioning in older COPD patients. *Chest, 116*, 953–960; and Etnier, J. L., & Berry, M. (2001). Fluid intelligence in an older COPD sample after short- or long-term exercise.

Medicine and Science in Sports and Exercise, 33, 1620–1628. *Ohio State:* Emery, C. F., Schein, R. L., Hauck, E. R., & MacIntyre, N. R. (1998). Psychological and cognitive outcomes of a randomized trial of exercise among patients with chronic obstructive pulmonary disease. *Health Psychology, 17,* 232–240. There was no further improvement in cognitive functions among subjects who continued to exercise for a year or more. Most of the improvement in intellectual functioning came within the first 10–12 weeks.

34. Example from Emery, C. F., Shermer, R. L., Hauck, E. R., Hsiao, E. T., & MacIntyre, N. R. (2003). Cognitive and psychological outcomes in a 1-year follow-up study of patients with chronic obstructive pulmonary disease. *Health Psychology, 22,* 598–604.

Obstructive Sleep Apnea

35. OSA has been given different labels, most frequently "sleep apnea," "obstructive sleep apnea syndrome," "sleep apnea syndrome," "sleep apnea/hypopnea syndrome," "obstructive sleep apnea hypopnea," and sleep-disordered breathing." They have slightly different meanings but share the characteristics. Prevalence rates for older adults are from Young, T., Shahar, E., Nieto, F. J., Redline, S., Newman, A. B., Gottlieb, D. J., et al., Sleep Heart Health Study Research Group. (2002). Predictors of sleep-disordered breathing in community-dwelling adults: The Sleep Heart Health Study. *Archives of Internal Medicine, 162,* 893–900.

36. Elements of the description and diagnosis were taken from the Web site of the American Sleep Apnea Association (http://www.sleepapnea.org/info/index.html, accessed August 11, 2010).

37. *Finland:* Saunamaki, T., & Jehkonen, M. (2007). A review of executive functions in obstructive sleep apnea syndrome. *Acta Neurologica Scandinavica, 115,* 1–11. *Ohio:* Beebe, D. W., Groesz, L., Wells, C., Nichols, A., & McGee, K. (2003). The neuropsychological effects of obstructive sleep apnea: A meta-analysis of norm-referenced and case-controlled data. *Sleep, 26,* 298–307.

38. At least half of the reported findings searching for a link between sleep apnea and lower test performance were statistically insignificant. Research that produced data in support of the theory was with middle-aged patients [e.g., Young, T., Palta, M., Dempsy, J., Skatrud, J. B., Weber S., & Badr, S. (1993). The occurrence of sleep-disordered breathing among middle-aged adults. *New England Journal of Medicine, 328,* 1230–1235] and those with more severe OSA [e.g., Naegele, B., Thouvard, V., Pepin, J-L., Levy, P., Bonnet, C., Perret, J. E., et al. (1995). Deficits of cognitive executive functions in patients with sleep apnea syndrome. *Sleep, 18,* 43–52]. There was general agreement about the aptitudes impaired. In Beebe's meta-analysis, effect size differences between subjects with OSA and controls on normative standards were substantial—above −.50 for executive functions and −1.0 for vigilance and psychomotor speed.

39. *France:* Naegele, B. (1995). *Germany:* Verstraeten, E., Cluydts, R., Pevernagie, D., & Hoffmann, G. (2004). Executive function in sleep apnea: Controlling for attentional capacity in assessing executive attention. *Sleep, 27,* 685–693.

40. Subjects with hypoxemia had poorer memories—both long term and working—than those with normal blood oxygen levels. Adams, N., Strauss, M., Schluchter, M., & Redline,

S. (2001). Relation of measures of sleep-disordered breathing to neuropsychological functioning. *American Journal of Respiratory Critical Care Medicine, 163,* 1626–1631.

41. *Grenoble:* Naegele, B., Launois, S. H., Mazza, S., Feuerstein, C., Pepin, J-L., & Levy, P. (2006). Which memory processes are affected in patients with obstructive sleep apnea? An evaluation of 3 types of memory. *Sleep, 29,* 533–544. *Montreal:* Montplaisir, J., Bédard, M. A., Richer, F., & Rouleau, I. (1992). Neurobehavioral manifestations in obstructive sleep apnea syndrome before and after treatment with continuous positive airway pressure. *Sleep, 15,* S17–S19.

42. After adjusting for gender, age, smoking habits, and baseline BMI, weight change was positively related to an Apnea-Hypopnea Index (AHI) per hour of sleep. The AHI adds the number of apneas lasting 10 or more seconds per hour and the number of times a reduction of 4% or more occurs in oxyhemoglobin saturation. Research found that for every 1% loss in weight there is a 3% reduction in the number of AHI events [Peppard, P. E., Young, T., Palta, M., Dempsey, J., & Skatrud, J. (2000). Longitudinal study of moderate weight change and sleep-disordered breathing. *Journal of the American Medical Association, 284,* 3015–3021].

43. When the subjects who initially received the placebo were given the real CPAP, they made similar improvements compared with their baseline scores [Montserrat, J. M., Ferrer, M., Hernandez, L., Farré, R., Vilagut, G., Navajas, D., et al. (2001). Effectiveness of CPAP treatment in daytime function in sleep apnea syndrome: A randomized controlled study with an optimized placebo. *American Journal of Respiratory Critical Care Medicine, 164,* 608–613].

44. *Canada:* Bédard, M. A., Montplaisir, J., Malo, J., Richer, F., & Rouleau, I. (1993). Persistent neuropsychological deficits and vigilance impairment in sleep apnea syndrome after treatment with continuous positive airways pressure (CPAP). *Journal of Clinical and Experimental Neuropsychology, 15,* 330–341. *Italy:* Ferini-Strambi, L., Baietto, C., Di Gioia, M. R., Castaldi, P., Castronovo, C., Zucconi, M., et al. (2003). Cognitive dysfunction in patients with obstructive sleep apnea (OSA): Partial reversibility after continuous positive airway pressure (CPAP). *Brain Research Bulletin, 61,* 87–92. *Mexico:* Valencia-Flores, M., Bliwise, D., Guilleminault, C., Cilveti, R., & Clerk, A. (1996). Cognitive function in patients with sleep apnea after acute nocturnal nasal continuous positive airway pressure (CPAP) treatment: Sleepiness and hypoxemia effects. *Journal of Clinical and Experimental Neuropsychology, 18,* 197–210. Not every deficit was reversed. Lower performance persisted in distractibility, manual dexterity, working memory, visuospatial skills, and verbal fluency.

Diabetes

45. Although the number of diagnosed cases of diabetes has increased, it is unclear whether the incidence of the disease is growing or whether more people recognize the symptoms and are seeking medical help. Statistics about and descriptions of diabetes were drawn from the Web sites of the Centers for Disease Control and Prevention (http://www.cdc.gov/diabetes/statistics/prev/national/figbyage.htm) and the American Diabetes Association (http://www.diabetes.org/type-2-diabetes.jsp) (accessed August 11, 2010). Also, a probability sample of more than 14,000 individuals—the 2003–2006 NHANES

survey—estimated that of the 21.1% of adults age 60–74 who suffered from diabetes, 3.5% had positive findings on the A1C test but had not been diagnosed by a health care provider [Cowie, C. C., Rust, K. F., Byrd-Holt, D. D., Gregg, E. W., Ford, E. S., Geiss, L. S., et al. (2010). Prevalence of diabetes and high risk for diabetes using A1C criteria in the U.S. population in 1988–2006. *Diabetes Care, 33,* 562–568].

46. Affected memory skills included working memory and recall of word lists, faces, pictures, and numbers, with lower scores on measures of reasoning and processing speed. The first studies were cross sectional, which produced substantial differences in the non-insulin-dependent diabetics and normal subjects. Examples are Mogi, N., Umegaki, H., Hattori, A., Maeda, N., Miura, H., Kuzuya, M., et al. (2004). Cognitive function in Japanese elderly with type 2 diabetes mellitus. *Journal of Diabetes and Its Complications, 18,* 42–46; Vanhanen, M., Koivisto, K., Kuusisto, J., Mykkanen, L., Helkala, E-L., Hänninen, T., et al. (1998). Cognitive function in an elderly population with persistent impaired glucose. *Diabetes Care, 21,* 398–403. Later longitudinal investigations found similar, although smaller, differences [e.g., Ryan, C. M., & Geckle, M. O. (2000). Circumscribed cognitive dysfunction in middle-aged adults with type 2 diabetes. *Diabetes Care, 23,* 1486–1493; also Fontbonne, A., Berr, C., Ducimetiere, P., & Alperovich, A. (2001). Changes in cognitive abilities are unfavorably affected in elderly diabetic patients: Results of the epidemiology of vascular aging study. *Diabetes Care, 24,* 366–371]. Significant findings occurred less than half the time, but when differences were found in mental ability scores between the patient and healthy populations, they ranged from 2.5 to 13.5%.

47. Examples of investigations finding greater white matter hyperintensities among individuals with type 2 diabetes are Last, D., Alsop, D. C. Abduljalil, A. M., Marquis, R. P., de Bazelaire, C., Hu, K., et al. (2007). Global and regional effects of type 2 diabetes on brain tissue volumes and cerebral vasoreactivity. *Diabetes Care, 30,* 1193–1199; Manschot, S. M., Brands, A. M. A., van der Grond, J., Kessels, R. P. C., Algra, A., Kappelle, L. J., et al. on behalf of the Utrecht Diabetic Encephalopathy Study Group. (2006). Brain magnetic resonance imaging correlates of impaired cognition in patients with type 2 diabetes. *Diabetes, 55,* 1106–1113; also Akisaki, T., Sakurai, T., Takata, T., Umegaki, H., Araki, A., Mizuno, S., et al. (2006). Cognitive dysfunction associated with white matter hyperintensities and subcortical atrophy on magnetic resonance imaging of the elderly diabetes mellitus Japanese Elderly Diabetes Intervention Trial (J-EDIT). *Diabetes/Metabolism Research and Reviews, 22,* 376–384.

48. The multicenter study was of both type 1 and type 2 middle-aged diabetics. Subjects were required to take glucose readings and complete a short cognitive battery two to three times a day for 4 weeks. Of the subjects, 55% showed mild decline in working memory [Cox, D. J., Kovatchev, B. P., Gonder-Frederick, L. A., Summers, K. H., McCall, A., Grimm, K. J., et al. (2005). Relationships between hyperglycemia and cognitive performance among adults with type 1 and type 2 diabetes. *Diabetes Care, 28,* 71–77].

49. In brief follow-up studies in the Netherlands, 73% responded positively to outreach visits and keeping flowcharts [Goudswaard, A. N., Stolk, R. P., de Valk, H. W., & Rutten, G. E. H. M. (2003). Improving glycaemic control in patients with type 2 diabetes mellitus without insulin therapy. *Diabetic Medicine, 20,* 540–544]; in two towns in southern India, 68% of the subjects followed dietary restrictions after consulting a dietician. [Kapur, K., Kapur, A., Ramachandran, S., Mohan, V., Aravind, S. R., Badgandi, M., et al. (2008). Barriers to changing dietary behavior. *Journal of the Association of Physicians of India, 56,* 27–32]; and 70% of HMO patients in Seattle who had relationships with

doctors that were not negative were more faithful in monitoring their glucose levels [Ciechanowski, P. S., Katon, W. J., Russo, J. E., & Walker, E. A. (2001). The patient-provider relationship: Attachment theory and adherence to treatment in diabetes. *American Journal of Psychiatry, 158,* 29–35].

Hearing Loss

50. In the 2008 National Health Interview Survey, subjects were asked "WITHOUT the use of hearing aids or other listening devices. Is your hearing excellent, good, [do you have] a little trouble hearing, moderate trouble, a lot of trouble, or are you deaf?'" When those without excellent or good hearing were combined into one category, 27.8% of those 65–74 reported some hearing loss. Among those 45–64, the percentage was 18.4%. Men (11.3%) were more than three times as likely to have more severe hearing loss as women (Pleis, J. R., Lucas, J. W., & Ward, B. W. (2009). Summary health statistics for U.S. adults: National Health Interview Survey, 2008. *National Center for Health Statistics, 10,* 242.

51. Material about causes of hearing loss adapted from the Web site of the American Speech-Language-Hearing Association (http://www.asha.org/public/hearing/disorders/types.htm, accessed August 11, 2010.

52. Of the 2,442 subjects, 48% of those age 50 to 80+ reported some hearing loss in the 1-year Alameda County Study. Based on odds ratios, subjects with even mild hearing loss were 25–52% more likely to feel left out and lonely and experience difficulty paying attention [Wallhagen, M. I., Strawbridge, W. J., Shema, S. J., Kurata, J., & Kaplan, G. A. (2001). Comparative impact of hearing and vision impairment on subsequent functioning. *Journal of the American Geriatrics Society, 49,* 1086–1092]. Similar results were found in large-scale Australian and Dutch surveys [Hogan, A., O'Loughlin, K., Miller, P., & Kendig, H. (2009). The health impact of a hearing disability on older people in Australia. *Journal of Aging and Health, 21,* 1098–1111; also Ormel, J., Kempen, G. I. J. M., Penninx, B. W. I. H., Brilman, E. J., Beekman, A. T. F., & van Sonderen, E. (1997). Chronic medical conditions and mental health in older people: Disability and psychosocial resources mediate specific mental health effects. *Psychological Medicine, 27,* 1065–1077].

53. The subjects were from the Berlin Aging Study. Correlations between unaided hearing acuity and scores on five aptitudes (speed, reasoning, memory, knowledge, and verbal fluency) and a composite score were typically above −.40 for the specific aptitudes and −.53 with the composite measure of IQ. [Lindenberger, U., & Baltes, P. B. (1994). Sensory functioning and intelligence in old age: A strong connection. *Psychology and Aging, 9,* 339–355].

54. The correlations between hearing acuity and aptitude scores were more than two times higher for the older subjects (average age 84.9) compared to younger subjects (48.2). The correlations for hearing level and five aptitudes averaged .492 for the older group and .176 for the younger group [Baltes, P. B., & Lindenberger, U. (1997). Emergence of a powerful connection between sensory and cognitive functions across the adult life span: A new window to the study of cognitive aging? *Psychology and Aging, 12,* 12–21].

55. See Pichora-Fuller, M. K. (2003). Processing speed and timing in aging adults: Psychoacoustics, speech perception, and comprehension. *International Journal of Audiology, 42*, S59–S67.

56. Observations about the misattribution of cognitive decline to central changes that may be the result of remediable sensory changes such as hearing loss were made by Rabbitt but have yet to be verified by longitudinal research [Rabbitt, P. (1990). Mild hearing loss can cause apparent memory failures, which increase with age and reduce with IQ. *Acta-Laryngologica, 176*(Supplement 476), 167–176] and supported later by many others [Cervera, T. C., Soler, M. J., Dasi, C., & Ruiz, J. C. (2009). Speech recognition and working memory capacity in young-elderly listeners: Effects of hearing sensitivity. *Canadian Journal of Experimental Psychology, 63*, 216–226; also Baltes & Lindenberger, 1997; and Pichora-Fuller, M. K., Schneider, B. A., & Daneman, M. (1995). How young and old adults listen to and remember speech in noise. *Journal of the Acoustical Society of America, 97*, 593–608].

57. This estimate among independently living subjects 65+ with auditory impairment who use hearing aids is in keeping with other findings [Popelka, M. M., Cruickshanks, K. J., & Wiley, T. L., Tweed, T. S., Klein, B. E., & Klein, R. (1998). Low prevalence of hearing aid use among older adults with hearing loss: The Epidemiology of Hearing Loss Study. *Journal of the American Geriatrics Society, 46*, 1075–1078]. Other estimates varied from 10% among the Framingham Heart Study subjects [Gates, G. A., Cooper, J. C. Jr., Kannel, W. B., & Miller, N. J. (1990). Hearing in the elderly: The Framingham cohort, 1983–1985. Part I. Basic audiometric test results. *Ear and Hearing, 11*, 247–256] to 25% in the United Kingdom [Davis, A., Smith, P., Ferguson, M., Stephens, D., & Gianopoulos, I. (2007). Acceptability, benefit and costs of early screening for hearing disability: A study of potential screening tests and models. *Health Technology Assessment, 11*, 1–294]. Even these low estimates may be optimistic since hearing loss remains undiagnosed among large numbers of elders, especially those with limited access to health care.

58. Examples of digital hearing aids include single-microphone noise reduction systems and wide dynamic range compression, both of which enhance the volume of the target speech while turning down the background noise [Sprinzl, G. M., & Riechelmann, H. (2010). Current trends in treating hearing loss in elderly people: A review of the technology and treatment options—A mini-review. *Gerontology, 56*, 351–358]; Lunner, T., Rudner, M., & Ronnberg, J. (2009). Cognition and hearing aids. *Scandinavian Journal of Psychology, 50*, 395–403].

59. Of individuals fitted with hearing aids, 25–40% do not use them regularly (Sprinzl & Riechelmann, 2010).

60. Global ability was less affected than specific mental skills such as working memory [Akeroyd, M. A. (2008). Are individual differences in speech reception related to individual differences in cognitive ability? A survey of twenty experimental studies with normal and hearing-impaired adults. *International Journal of Audiology, 47*(Supplement 2), S53–S71].

61. From Pichora-Fuller, 2003.

Declining Disability: An Unanticipated Event

62. For example, Gruenberg, E. M. (1997). The failure of success. *Milbank Quarterly, 55,* 3–34.

63. To my knowledge, disability rates for older adults were not available until 1982. However, analogous data are available in the form of Social Security Disability Insurance payments made to disabled workers over the age of 50. The proportion of the workforce receiving such payments was 7% in 1962, 10.5% in 1968, 11% in 1973, and 10.7% in 1980 [Wolfe, B. L., & Haveman, R. (1990). Trends in the prevalence of work disability from 1962 to 1984, and their correlates. *The Milbank Quarterly, 68,* 53–80].

64. One of the most informative of these was the National Long Term Care Survey (NLTCS), designed to study changes in the health and functional status of older Americans. The survey sample of 35,000 people drawn from national Medicare enrollment files in 1982 has been augmented with approximately 20,000 Medicare enrollees, obtained by adding 5,000 people passing age 65 between successive surveys done approximately every 5 years. Both the elderly in the community and those residing in institutions are represented in the samples. The analysis was carried out by researchers at Duke University's Center for Demographic Studies [Manton, K. G., Gu, X., & Lamb, V. L. (2006). Change in chronic disability from 1982 to 2004/2005 as measured by long-term changes in function and health in the U.S. elderly population. *Proceedings of the National Academy of Sciences of the United States of America, 103,* 18374–18379; also Manton, K. G,. & Gu, X. (2001). Changes in the prevalence of chronic disability in the United States black and nonblack population above age 65 from 1982 to 1999. *Proceedings of the National Academy of Sciences of the United States of America, 98,* 6354–6359]. Declining trends from the analysis of the 1999 survey were confirmed from a review of eight cross-sectional and cohort studies [Freedman, V. A., Martin, L. G., & Schoeni, R. F. (2002). Recent trends in disability and functioning among older adults in the United States: A systematic review. *Journal of the American Medical Association, 288,* 3137–3146].

65. The NLTCS survey also obtained information on disability based on (a) self-care at home or activities of daily living (ADLs), such as bathing, dressing, eating, getting in or out of bed or chairs, walking, and using the toilet; (b) instrumental activities of daily living (IADLs) necessary to live independently, such as shopping, using the telephone, doing housework, preparing meals, and managing money. *ADLs:* Katz, S., Ford, A. B., Moskowitz, R. W., Jackson, B. A., & Jaffe, M. W. (1963). Studies of illness in the aged. The index of ADL: A standardized measure of biological and psychosocial function. *The Journal of the American Medical Association,185,* 914–919; *IADLs:* Lawton, M. P., & Brody, E. M. (1969). Assessment of older people: Self-maintaining and instrumental activities of daily living. *The Gerontologist, 9,* 179–186. Total disability estimates are the sum of four classifications: mild disability (some IADLs); moderate disability (one to four ADLs); severe disability (five or more ADLs); being in an institution such as a nursing home.

66. In the interval between 1984 and 2004, the disability rate declined from 26.2 to 19%. In 2004, the population of women and men aged 60–79 was approximately 39,659,276. Had these older Americans suffered the 1984 disability rate of 26.2% rather than 19%, another 2,855,458 would have become disabled. Estimates from the U.S. Census Bureau: Annual estimates of the resident population by sex and five-year age groups for the

United States: April 1, 2000 to July 1, 2008. Retrieved August 11, 2010, from http://www.census.gov/popest/national/asrh/NC-EST2008-sa.html.

67. From Freedman, V. A., Schoeni, R. F., Martin, L. G., & Cornman, J. C. (2007). Chronic conditions and the decline in late-life disability. *Demography, 44,* 459–477. From 1997 to 2004, significant declines occurred only for mental distress (3.4 to 2.1%) and vision limitations (18 to 16.3%).

68. In an annual survey of a random sample of Swedish citizens, investigators analyzed data on 29,786 women and men aged 65–84 who were in poor health and had great difficulty carrying out normal activities. They then compared the percentages of those who reported difficulties with daily self-care with the frequencies of diabetes, hypertension, and heart disease and tabulated the data for three periods: 1980–1987, 1988–1994, 1995–2002. In nearly every period-to-period comparison, the rate of poor health and restricted activity declined while the proportion of chronic disease increased [Rosen, M., & Haglund, B. (2005). From healthy survivors to sick survivors—implications for the twenty-first century. *Scandinavian Journal of Public Health, 33,* 151–155]. The Spanish study did not find an increasing rate of poor health except for those aged 90 and above [Zunzunegui, M. V., Nunez, O., Durban, M., García de Yébenes, M. J., & Otero, A. (2006). Decreasing prevalence of disability in activities of daily living, functional limitations and poor self-rated health: A 6-year follow-up study in Spain. *Aging Clinical and Experimental Research, 18,* 352–358].

69. Among Fries many publications on this topic is Fries, J. F. (2005). The compression of morbidity. *Milbank Quarterly, 83,* 801–823.

How Is Your Health Compared With Five Years Ago?
Some Unexpected Findings

70. The Florida Geriatric Research Program is a longitudinal study of aging that began in 1978 [Hale, W. E., Marks, R. G., & Stewart, R. B. (1980). The Dunedin program, a Florida geriatric screening process; Design and initial data. *Journal of the American Geriatrics Society, 28,* 377–380]. Compared with 2001 data from the CDC—based on the national Behavioral Risk Factor Surveillance System (BRFSS) survey of adults aged 55–74—similar proportions of the 3rd Age Study subjects (22.7%) and the BRFSS subjects (23.7%) rated their health as poor or fair. In addition, both groups had about the same percentage of self-rated health (SRH) ratings in the good/very good/excellent categories (77.3 vs. 76.3%) (information from Health-related quality of life surveillance—United States, 1993–2002. *Morbidity and Mortality Weekly Report, 54*(SS-4). Retrieved August 11, 2010, from http://www.cdc.gov/mmwr/PDF/ss/ss5404.pdf).

71. A study of the relationship between SRH and medical and functional ratings of health in six developed European countries found a strong correlation between SRH and ADLs, chronic illness, and home care [Bardage, C., Puijm, S. M. E., Pedersen, N. L., Deeg, D. G. H., Jylha, M., Noale, M., et al. (2005) Self-rated health among older adults: A cross-national comparison. *European Journal of Ageing, 2,* 149–158]. French and English investigators interested in the question of what SRH scales actually measure analyzed cross-sectional data on 27,988 subjects from two longitudinal studies (Whitehall II and Gazel cohort study). Stepwise multiple regressions identified five determinants (symptom

score, sickness absence, long-standing illness, minor psychiatric morbidity, number of recurring health problems) in Whitehall II, explaining 34.7% of the variance in SRH. In Gazel, four measures (physical tiredness, number of health problems in the past year, physical mobility, and number of prescription drugs used) explained 41.4% of the variance in SRH [Singh-Manoux, A., Martikainen, P., Ferrie, J., Zins, M., Marmot, M., & Goldberg, M. (2006). What does self rated health measure? Results from the British Whitehall II and French Gazel cohort studies. *Journal of Epidemiology and Community Health, 60,* 364–372]. Others have argued that the power of SRH to forecast future medical events is stronger than other measures [Winter, L., Lawton, M. P., Langston, C. A., Ruckdeschel, K., & Sando, R. (2007). Symptoms, affects, and self-rated health: Evidence for a subjective trajectory of health. *Journal of Aging and Health, 19,* 453–469].

Reflections and Applications

72. For U.S. data on the relative frequency of chronic disease and disability by race, education, and socioeconomic status, see National Center for Health Statistics, 2010.

73. At age 30, life expectancy is 47.9 years for white males and 45.0 years for black males. There is a small difference for white (52.1 years) and black (53.1 years) females. At age 65, the healthy life expectancy for female and male blacks with some college (22.3 years and 18.1 years) slightly exceeds that of whites (20.2 years for females and 17.6 years for males). See Crimmins, E. M., & Saito, Y. (2001). Trends in healthy life expectancy in the United States, 1970–1990: Gender, racial, and educational differences. *Social Science and Medicine, 52,* 1629–1641.

74. Demographers at the National Center for Health Statistics analyzed data on 43,000+ subjects interviewed in person and followed for 10 years as part of the Medicare Current Beneficiary Survey. Using a statistical model, they calculated the changes in total life expectancy from 1992 to 2002, and they computed the number of remaining years that a 65-year-old would likely be free of disability [Cai, L., & Lubitz, J. (2007). Was there compression of disability for older Americans from 1992 to 2003? *Demography, 44,* 479–495].

75. National Center for Health Statistics, 2010. Based on 2003–2006/2007 surveys, the percentages listed are for all female and male adults ages 65–74, except for COPD (55–74) and smoking and diabetes (65+). Migraine and neck and back pain were reported more frequently among females 65–74 as well. Other sources were as follows: Cowie et al., 2010; Naccarelli, G. V., Varker, H., Lin, J., & Schulman, K. L. (2009). Increasing prevalence of atrial fibrillation and flutter in the United States. *The American Journal of Cardiology, 104,* 1534–1539; Chapman, K. R. (2004). Chronic obstructive pulmonary disease: Are women more susceptible than men? *Clinics in Chest Medicine, 25,* 331–341; and Jordan, A. S., & McEvoy, R. D. (2003). Gender differences in sleep apnea: Epidemiology, clinical presentation and pathogenic mechanisms. *Sleep Medicine Reviews, 7,* 377–389.

76. The compliance rate for all prescribed medications in older adults is influenced by many variables, including criteria for compliance [Ruppar, T. M., Conn, V. S., & Russell, C. L. (2008). Medication adherence interventions for older adults: Literature review. *Research and Theory for Nursing Practice: An International Journal, 22,* 114–147]. A frequently used definition of compliance is the mean medication possession ratio (MPR; defined as

the number of treatment days divided by the number of days between prescription refills. For example, a patient who is prescribed 90 days of medication but does not refill the prescription until 10 days later has an MPR of 90/100 or 90%. Another commonly used criterion of compliance is the percentage of patients with an MPR of more than 80% over a certain period of time [Cramer, J. A., Benedict, A., Muszbek, N., Keskinaslan, A., & Khan, Z. M. (2008). The significance of compliance and persistence in the treatment of diabetes, hypertension and dyslipidaemia: A review. *International Journal of Clinical Practice, 62*, 76–87].

77. For example, the cognitive effects of two medical conditions—hypertension and atrial fibrillation—were small. The actual degree of difference in test scores between older subjects with normal blood pressure and the hypertensives reviewed varied from 1 to 17% in the longitudinal studies. Also, not every study found a connection between hypertension and lower cognition. Australian medical researcher Kaarin Anstey reviewed 10 longitudinal studies, and 3 of them found no measurable negative effects [Anstey, K., & Christensen, H. (2000). Education, activity, health, blood pressure and apolipoprotein E as predictors of cognitive change in old age: A review. *Gerontology, 46*, 163–177]. The differences in both the raw global and specific cognitive test scores were 3 to 8% between AFib sufferers and control subjects; also, a review of the research on AFib and cognition found that 30% of the publications failed to find a significant association [Mead, G. E., & Keir, S. (2001). Association between cognitive impairment and atrial fibrillation: A systematic review. *Journal of Stroke and Cerebrovascular Disorders, 10*, 35–43].

Chapter 3

1. Data for Figure 3.1 from Kaufman, A. S., & Lichtenberger, E. O. (2006). *Assessing adolescent and adult intelligence* (3rd ed.). Hoboken, NJ: Wiley. The curve is derived by comparing the average of WAIS III scaled scores of each older age group decade with the norms for age 25–34. The samples of subjects for each age group were matched for educational attainment with the U.S. Census proportions. The downward slope of the age-associated cognitive decline is slightly more optimistic than other cross-sectional and longitudinal studies that found a more rapid rate of decline after 70 in education-matched subjects. See Powell, D. H. (in collaboration with D. K. Whitla). (1994). *Profiles in cognitive aging*. Cambridge, MA: Harvard University Press; and Schaie, K. W. (1994). The course of adult intellectual development. *American Psychologist, 49*, 304–313.

2. Virtues of cross-sectional studies are that they enable investigators to examine the effect of specific independent variables such as age on dependent variables (e.g., IQ) for a large number of subjects in a brief period. Potential limitations of cross-sectional studies are cohort differences (those born in the 1920s and 1940s will have had different life experiences that could affect cognition) and the failure to match subjects on factors besides age (e.g., medical condition, income, educational level), which influence scores on intelligence tests. A virtue of longitudinal studies is that they follow the same subjects over time, so that whatever changes occur can be assumed to be age related. Among their limitations has been favorable attrition, which is the loss of subjects during the course of the study who were poorer, had poorer health, and had fewer years of education at baseline. This limits the generalizability of the findings to the sort of subjects that remained in the study

at the time of data analysis. Debates about the virtues and limitations of cross-sectional and longitudinal studies have attracted many participants [Salthouse, T. A., Schroeder, D. H., & Ferrer, E. (2004). Estimating retest effects in longitudinal assessments of cognitive functioning in adults between 18 and 60 years of age. *Developmental Psychology, 40,* 813–822; and Hofer, S. M., & Sliwinski, M. J. (2002). Understanding ageing. An evaluation of research designs for assessing the interdependence of ageing-related changes. *Gerontology, 47,* 341–352; also Williams, J. D., & Klug, M. G. (1996). Aging and cognition: Methodological differences in outcome. *Experimental Aging Research, 22,* 219–244].

3. Nearly all longitudinal studies of cognitive aging worldwide find a greater decline in test scores among subjects living near the poverty level, who have less education, are in poorer health, and have less access to adequate medical care. See, for example, National Center for Health Statistics. (2010). *Health, United States, 2009: With special feature on medical technology.* Hyattsville, MD.

4. The normal subjects were a convenience sample with an average of 14.13 years of education compared to 20+ years for the physicians. Average age of medical doctors, all older than 75, was 78.38. Their profiles of their cognitive decline were similar to the physicians'. The data on MicroCog were drawn from Powell (1994).

5. For example, the number of correct answers on MicroCog for 60-year-old physicians was 156.41, compared to 145.88 for normals; at age 70, the physicians averaged 146.04 and the normals 133.94; beyond 75, the differences narrowed: The means were125.24 for the medical doctors and 119.03 for the normals.

Mental Abilities That Decline Least and Most With Age: Research Findings

6. Based on 13 different studies summarized in Salthouse, T. A. (1996). The processing-speed theory of adult age differences in cognition. *Psychological Review, 103,* 403–428. Processing speed is a leading indicator of age changes in memory and spatial ability but not verbal skills [Finkel, D., Reynolds, C. A., McArdle, J. J., & Pederson, N. L. (2007). Age changes in processing speed as a leading indicator of cognitive aging. *Psychology and Aging, 22,* 558–568]. An overview of the role of speed and aging is contained in Birren, J. E., & Fisher, L. M. (1995). Aging and speed of behavior: Possible consequences for psychological functioning. *Annual Review of Psychology, 46,* 329–353.

7. From Salthouse, T. A. (1992). *Mechanisms of age-cognition relations in adulthood.* Hillsdale, NJ: Erlbaum.

8. Salthouse, 1992.

9. Studies in the United States and China agreed that reaction time and processing speed play as large a role as age in the decline in all aptitudes. See Salthouse, T. A. (1992). Why do adult age differences increase with task complexity? *Developmental Psychology, 28,* 905-918; also Dahua, W., Jiliang, S., Huamao, P., Dan, T., & Liang, Z. (2005). The model of educational effect on old adult's cognition. *Acta Psychologica Sinica, 37,* 511–516.

10. See Kaufman & Lichtenberger, 2006.

11. Powell, 1994. The age group studied was 65–74.

12. Research by Kaufman & Lichtenberger, 2006. The age group used for comparison with age 30 was 70–74.

Effects of Aging on Working Memory and Multitasking

13. An extensive literature exists on working memory. A classic article is Baddeley, A. (1992). Working memory. *Science, 255,* 556–559.

14. Hale, S., Myerson, J., Emery, L. J., Lawrence, B. M., & DuFault, C. Variation in working memory across the life span. (2007). In A. R. A. Conway, C. Jarrold, M. J. Kane, A. Miyake, & J. N. Towse. (Eds.), *Variations in working memory* (pp. 194–224). New York: Oxford University Press.

15. Although some elders perform as well as those in midlife, studies of complex decision-making competence typically find that older adults work more slowly, make more errors in comprehending the factors involved, and make nonoptimal decisions more frequently than younger people about matters of health, finance, and nutrition. At present, little is known about these optimal decision makers, but speculation is that several factors contribute, including more education, emotional stability, openness to advice from others, and willingness to delegate. Health plan example from Finucane, M. L., Mertz, C. K., Slovic, P., & Schmidt, E. S. (2005). Task complexity and older adults' decision-making competence. *Psychology and Aging, 20,* 71–84.

16. Conservative estimates of the frequency of accidents while using a cell phone from McCartt, A. T., Hellinga, L. A., & Bratiman, K. A. (2006). Cell phones and driving: Review of research. *Traffic Injury Prevention, 7,* 89–106; and Redelmeier, D. A., & Tibshirani, R. J. (1997). Association between cellular telephone calls and motor vehicle collisions. *New England Journal of Medicine, 336,* 453–458.

17. Over the past three decades, scientific studies consistently reported that younger adults outperformed older adults on many different dual-task and divided-attention tasks. Examples are two meta-analyses by Verhaeghen and his colleagues [Verhaeghen, P., Steitz, D. W., Sliwinski, M. J., & Cerella, J. (2003). Aging and dual-task performance: A meta-analysis. *Psychology and Aging, 18,* 443–460; and Verhaeghen, P.,& Salthouse, T. A. (1997). Meta-analyses of age-cognition relations in adulthood: Estimates of linear and non-linear age effects and structural models. *Psychological Bulletin, 122,* 231–249].

18. Imagine being in a study of how dual tasking affects encoding (putting information into memory) and retrieval. While trying to memorize or recall a list of words, you are also instructed to listen to a string of numbers and push a button when hearing two odd numbers in a row. The results of such experiments find that multitasking older adults have far more difficulty with encoding than retrieval [Anderson, N. D., Craik, F. I. M., & Naveh-Benjamin, M. (1998). The attentional demands of encoding and retrieval in younger and older adults: Evidence from divided attention costs. *Psychology and Aging, 13,* 403–423]. When one of the activities is physical and the other mental (walking along a designated path while memorizing a list of words), dual taskers do a better job at staying on the path than memorizing the words [Lindenberger, U., Marsiske, M., & Baltes, P. B. (2000). Memorizing while walking: Increase in dual-task costs from young adulthood to old age. *Psychology and Aging, 15,* 417–430; and Li, K. Z., Lindenberger, U., Freund, A. M., & Baltes, P. B. (2001). Walking while memorizing: Age-related differences in compensatory behavior. *Psychological Science, 12,* 230–237].

19. In the Colorado study, the women were videotaped doing other single-task household chores as well, such as vacuuming or making the bed [Dickerson, A. E., & Fisher, A. E.

(1993). Age differences in functional performance. *American Journal of Occupational Therapy, 47,* 686–692].

20. A weakness in the Toronto study is that the simulated cooking task involved sophisticated use of the computer, which may have been far easier for younger subjects [Craik, F. I. M., & Bialystok, E. (2006). Planning and task management in older adults: Cooking breakfast. *Memory and Cognition, 34,* 1236–1249].

Mental Skills That Decline With Age: Interview Findings

21. James, W. (1950). *The principles of psychology, Volume I.* (Dover paperback edition). New York: Dover, p. 251. (Original work published 1890.) I am grateful to doctoral dissertation author Jasmeet K. Pannu for bringing this quotation to my attention [Pannu, J. K. (2006). Tip-of-the-tongue states in aging: Evidence from behavioral and neuroimaging studies. *Dissertation Abstracts International: Section B: The Sciences and Engineering, 67(5-B),* 2842].

22. There were 30 subjects in each group. Mean age was as follows: young, 20.8; young–old, 66.7; and older, 83.8. The raw TOT averages over the 4-week period and the percentage of eventual recall of the blocked memory for the three groups were as follows: young, 5.21 (91% recall); young–old, 6.62 (95% recall); older, 9.33 (98% recall). The time to spontaneous recall of blocked words was 16.3% slower in the subjects 80+ years old. In addition to the diary-based TOT events, the subjects were compared on experimentally produced TOT events. The same pattern occurred, with the oldest and youngest groups having the most and least TOT experiences, respectively [Heine, M. K., Ober, B. A., & Shenaut, G. K. (1999). Naturally occurring and experimentally induced tip-of-the-tongue experiences in three adult age groups *Psychology and Aging, 14,* 445–457]. The frequency differences in TOT events among younger and older subjects and greater spontaneous recovery of blocked memory by 3rd Agers were supported by the research of Burke, D. M., MacKay, D. G., Worthley, J. S., & Wade, E. (1991). On the tip of the tongue: What causes word finding failures in young and older adults? *Journal of Memory and Language, 30,* 542–579.

23. Research has found no consistent evidence that memory problems occur more frequently for one of the categories (names, numbers, or things) among older adults. Research to date on TOT and other brief memory lapses has been cross sectional. Therefore, we do not know how much of the differences between groups is a function of cohort effect [James, L. E. (2006). Specific effects of aging on proper name retrieval: Now you see them now you don't. *The Journals of Gerontology: Psychological Sciences and Social Sciences, 61B,* 180–183; and Schwartz, B. L., & Frazier, L. D. (2005). Tip-of-the-tongue states and aging: Contrasting psycholinguistic and metacognitive perspectives. *The Journal of General Psychology, 132,* 377–391].

24. Belgian and Swiss psychologists matched younger and older subjects on baseline memory skills and asked them to memorize a list of individually presented words. Half of the time subjects were instructed to forget the word immediately after it was presented. When asked to recall the words to be remembered, both older and younger subjects recalled more to-be-remembered than to-be-forgotten words. Investigators concluded that older adults have more difficulty with new learning because of a weakened

capacity to suppress previously learned distracting information rather than because of differences in overall memory competence [Collette, F., Germain, S., Hogge, M., & Van der Linden, M. (2009). Inhibitory control of memory in normal ageing: Dissociation between impaired intentional and preserved unintentional processes. *Memory, 17,* 104–122].

25. Material in this section draws from the nearly two decades of research by Lynn Hasher and her colleagues [e.g., Healey, M. K., Campbell, K. L., & Hasher, L. (2008). Cognitive aging and increased distractibility: Costs and potential benefits. *Progress in Brain Research, 169,* 353–363; Hasher, L., Zacks, R., & May, C. (1999). Inhibitory control, circadian arousal, and age. In D. Gopher & A. Koriat (Eds.), *Attention and performance XVII: Cognitive regulation of performance: Interaction of theory and application* (pp. 653–675). Cambridge, MA: MIT Press]. Not all research found evidence of impaired access, deletion, and restraint when comparing older and younger adults [Dumas, J. A., & Hartman, M. (2008). Adult age differences in the access and deletion functions of inhibition. *Neuropsychology, Development, and Cognition, Section B, Aging, Neuropsychology and Cognition, 15,* 330–357].

26. Research on age-related lessening of the access function from Lustig, C., Hasher, L., & Tonev, S. T. (2006). Distraction as a determinant of processing speed. *Psychonomic Bulletin and Review, 13,* 619–625.

Neuroplasticity

27. Summaries of age-related cognitive changes can be found in Cabeza, R., Anderson, N. D., Locantore, J. K., & McIntosh, A. R. (2002). Aging gracefully: Compensatory brain activity in high-performing older adults. *NeuroImage, 17,* 1394–1402; also Raz, N. (2000). Aging of the brain and its impact on cognitive performance: Integration of structural and functional findings. In F. I. M. Craik & T. A. Salthouse (Eds.), *Handbook of aging and cognition—II* (pp. 1–90). Mahwah, NJ: Erlbaum.

28. The brain-scanning technologies most often used in this research are fMRI and PET. They have been valuable tools in the diagnosis of brain pathology. These neuroimaging techniques allow neuroscientists to view the regions of the brain that are activated during cognitive tasks such as memorizing a list of words [Persson, J., & Nyberg, L. (2006). Altered brain activity in healthy seniors: What does it mean? *Progress in Brain Research, 157,* 45–56; Less activation in the hippocampal area is common among older adults. It is often accompanied by stronger bilateral prefrontal and parietal activity than younger adults. This is consistent with the theory that older people recruit other areas of their brain to solve cognitive problems to compensate for neural decline in other regions. Daselaar, S. M., Dolcos, F., Prince, S. E., Budde, M., & Nyberg, L. (2004). Task-independent and task-specific age effects on brain activity during working memory, visual attention and episodic retrieval. *Cerebral Cortex, 14,* 364–375]. These findings provide convincing support of widespread regional over-activation in the brains of older adults when they problem-solve. This reorganization may play a useful compensatory role when cognitive decline is not extensive. It may also be of neurocognitive inefficiency. See Persson, J., & Nyberg, L. (2006).

29. Neuroplasticity also has been called "functional plasticity," "neurocognitive scaffolding," "plastic reorganization," or just "plasticity" and is used to describe the effects of external experience on neural ensembles in the brain. Although cellular structures such as neurons or glial cells are usually stable and nonplastic, they are integrated into highly dynamic neural networks that influence the brain structure as they adapt to environmental changes [Jessberger, S., & Gage, F. H. (2008). Stem cell-associated structural and functional plasticity in the aging hippocampus. *Psychology and Aging, 23,* 684–691; and Mahncke, H. W., Connor, B. B., Appelman, J., Ahsanuddin, O. N., Hardy, J. L., Wood, R. A., et al. (2006). Memory enhancement in healthy older adults using a brain plasticity-based training program: A randomized, controlled study. *Proceedings of the National Academy of Sciences of the United States of America, 103,* 12523–12528].

30. These researchers predicted that cognitively well-functioning older adults would show more frequent bilateral activation in the prefrontal cortex while solving memory problems than elders with weaker recall skills or younger adults. During PET scans, elders with weaker recall and young adults both used the right hemisphere of the prefrontal cortex, while older subjects with strong memories showed bilateral activation (Cabeza et al., 2002).

31. Neuroscientists in other parts of North America confirmed these results. Texas researchers Denise Park and Patricia Reuter-Lorenz maintained that an adaptive brain responds to the challenges posed by declining neural structures and functions by developing alternative neural circuits to achieve a particular cognitive goal [Park, D. C., & Reuter-Lorenz, P. (2009). The adaptive brain: Aging and neurocognitive scaffolding. *Annual Review of Psychology, 60,* 173–196]. Not all age overrecruitment of the prefrontal cortex can be interpreted as compensatory. In some cases, it may indicate neural inefficiency [Grady, C. L. (2008). Cognitive neuroscience of aging. *Annals of the New York Academy of Sciences, 1124,* 127–144].

32. Examples of lifestyle habits believed to be associated with cognitive plasticity on the basis of clinical experience or cross-sectional research include *exercise*: Park & Reuter-Lorenz, 2009; *diet:* van Praag, H. (2009). Exercise and the brain: Something to chew on. *Trends in Neurosciences, 32,* 283–290; *stress reduction:* Monje, M. L., Toda, H., & Palmer, T. D. (2003). Inflammatory blockade restores adult hippocampal neurogenesis. *Science, 302,* 1760–1765; and Xiong, G. L., & Doraiswarmy, P. M. (2009). Does meditation enhance cognition and brain plasticity? *Annals of the New York Academy of Sciences, 1172,* 63–69; *treatment of depression and other mental disorders:* Jessberger & Gage, 2008; *cognitive stimulation:* Park & Reuter-Lorenz, 2009; *cognitive training:* Li, S. C., Schmiedek, F., Huxhold, O., Röcke, C., Smith, J., & Lindenberger, U. (2008). Working memory plasticity in old age: Practice gain, transfer, and maintenance, *Psychology and Aging, 23,* 731–742; and Vance, D. E., & Farr, K. F. (2007). Spaced retrieval for enhancing memory: Implications for nursing practice and research. *Journal of Gerontological Nursing, 33,* 46–52.

33. Erickson, K. I., & Kramer, A. F. (2009). Aerobic exercise effects on cognitive and neural plasticity in older adults. *British Journal of Sports Medicine, 43,* 22–24; and Colcombe, S. J., Erickson, K. I., Scalf, P. E., Kim, J. S., Prakash, R., McAuley, E., et al. (2006). Aerobic exercise training increases brain volume in aging humans. *Journals of Gerontology, Series A: Biological Sciences and Medical Sciences, 61,* 1166–1170.

34. Although 93 subjects began the study, only 25 could be included in the final analysis, which compared the jugglers who approximated the 60-second criterion (average of

56.7) with 25 controls. Those who learned to juggle demonstrated a significant increase in gray matter in the hippocampus, in the medial temporal region of the visual cortex, and in the nucleus accumbens. No changes in gray matter were found among the controls [Boyke, J., Driemeyer, J., Gaser, C., Buchel, C., & May, A. (2008). Training-induced brain structure changes in the elderly. *The Journal of Neuroscience, 28,* 7031–7035].

35. The same pattern of new-learning-activated increase in gray matter and disuse-associated shrinkage was found in the MRIs of young adults taught to juggle. Investigators were aware that larger amounts of gray matter could have many causes, including an increase in cell size, neural or glial cell genesis, spine density, or changes in blood flow [Driemeyer, J., Boyke, J., Gaser, C., Buchel, C., & May, A. (2008). Changes in gray matter induced by learning—Revisited. *PLoS ONE, 3,* e2669].

36. As with all new theories, neuroplasticity research has raised many questions. Several neuroscientists have pointed out aspects of the theory that will benefit from greater understanding [Grady, 2008; Raz, N. (2007). Comment on Greenwood (2007): Which side of plasticity? *Neuropsychology, 21,* 676–677; Salthouse, T. A. (2007). Comment on Greenwood (2007): Functional plasticity in cognitive aging. *Neuropsychology, 21,* 678–679].

The Lower End of the Bell Curve: Age-Related Cognitive Decline, Mild Cognitive Impairment, and Dementia

37. Age-related cognitive decline defined in American Psychiatric Association. (2000). *Diagnostic and statistical manual of mental disorders* (4th ed., text revision). Washington, DC: Author. As used here, this condition is based on clinical assessment, history, and/or the reports of others, usually unsupported by cognitive testing.

38. Other terms that have been used to describe this mental state, and which have approximately the same meaning, are "benign senescent forgetfulness," "age-consistent memory decline," and "age-associated memory impairment." Kral, V. A. (1962). Senescent forgetfulness: Benign and malignant. *Journal of the Canadian Medical Association, 86,* 257–260; American Psychological Association. (1998). *Guidelines for the evaluation of dementia and age-consistent memory decline.* Washington, DC: Author; Crook, T., & Larrabee, C. J. (1988). Age-associated memory impairment: Diagnostic criteria and treatment strategies. *Psychopharmacology Bulletin, 24,* 509–514.

39. A clear and informative summary article about dementia and Alzheimer's disease is Kidd, P. M. (2008). Alzheimer's disease, amnestic mild cognitive impairment, and age-associated memory impairment: Current understanding and progress toward integrative prevention. *Alternative Medicine Review, 13,* 85–115.

40. Criteria for AD from American Psychiatric Association, 2000. Although the term AD is commonly used by professionals and researchers alike to describe this condition, the disease cannot be confirmed until autopsy. One of the terms for suspected AD on the basis of clinical symptoms is "dementia of the Alzheimer's type" or DAT.

41. Data on frequency of AD among Americans age 65 and older from Alzheimer's Association. *Alzheimer's disease: Facts and figures.* Retrieved October 20, 2009, from http://www.alz.org.

42. Half-decade frequencies from Jorm, A. F., Korten, A. E., & Henderson, A. S. (1987). The prevalence of dementia: A quantitative integration of the literature. *Acta Psychiatrica Scandinavica, 76,* 465–479. While these older data may underestimate the frequencies based on more sophisticated diagnostic techniques, the proportions are similar to later estimates [O'Connor, D. W., Pollitt, P. A., Hyde, J. B., Fellows, J. L., Miller, N. D., & Roth, M. (1990). A follow-up study of dementia diagnosed in the community using the Cambridge Mental Disorders of the Elderly Examination. *Acta Psychiatrica Scandinavica, 81,* 78–82; also Hanninen, T., Hallikainen, M., Tuomainen, S., Vanhanen, M., & Soininen, H. (2002). Prevalence of mild cognitive impairment: A population-based study in elderly subjects. *Acta Neurologica Scandinavica, 106,* 148–154].

43. Of older individuals with dementia, 15–25% have dementia with Lewy bodies (DLB). The diagnosis of DLB is made if Parkinson's disease is diagnosed within a year following the onset of dementia. There is considerable overlap with AD [Hanson, J. C., & Lippa, C. F. (2009). Lewy body dementia. *International Review of Neurobiology, 84,* 215–228; and Oda, H., Yamamoto, Y., & Maeda, K. (2009). Neuropsychological profile of dementia with Lewy bodies. *Psychogeriatrics, 9,* 85–90].

44. Vascular dementia accounts for 8–15% of cognitively impaired patients in Western countries and 22–35% in Japan [Moorhouse, P., & Rockwood, K. (2008). Vascular cognitive impairment: Current concepts and clinical developments. *The Lancet Neurology, 7,* 246–255; and Jellinger, K. A. (2008). The pathology of vascular dementia: A critical update. *Journal of Alzheimer's Disease, 14,* 107–123; also Bowler, J. V. (2007). Modern concept of vascular cognitive impairment. *British Medical Bulletin, 83,* 291–305].

45. For characteristics of AACD, see Levy, R. (1994). Aging-associated cognitive decline. *International Psychogeriatrics, 6,* 63–68. Consensus diagnostic criteria for MCI were described by Petersen and Ritchie [Petersen, R. C. (2004). Mild cognitive impairment as a diagnostic entity. *Journal of Internal Medicine, 256,* 183–194; also Petersen, C. P., Doody, R., Kurz, A., Mohs, R. C., Morris, J. C., Rabins, P. V., et al. (2001). Current concepts in mild cognitive impairment. *Archives of Neurology, 58,* 1985–1992; and Ritchie, K., Artero, S., & Touchon, J. (2001). Classification criteria for mild cognitive impairment: A population-based validation study. *Neurology, 56,* 37–42].

46. The neuropsychological test score clusters of older normal, AACD, and MCI subjects were factor analyzed; over half had similar patterns of scores [Ylikoski, R., Ylikoski, A., Keskivaara, P., Tilvis, R., Sulkava, R., & Erkinjuntti, T. (1999). Heterogeneity of cognitive profiles in aging: Successful aging, normal aging, and individuals at-risk for cognitive decline. *European Journal of Neurology, 6,* 645–652].

47. Frequency of MCI increases with age: 4.8% of those 65–69; 8.4% of those 70–76. MCI decreases with education: incidence among Finnish elders with less than 5 years of education, 13.3%; 6–8 years, 6.8%; 9+ years, 3.0% [Hanninen et al., 2002].

48. The proportion of subjects diagnosed with AACD converting to dementia ranged from 24.7 to 47% in three studies [Busse, A., Bischkopf, J., Riedel-Heller, S. G., & Angermeyer, M. C. (2003). Mild cognitive impairment: Prevalence and incidence according to different diagnostic criteria: Results of the Leipzig Longitudinal Study of the Aged (LEILA75+). *British Journal of Psychiatry, 182,* 449–454; also Ritchie et al., 2001; and Schönknecht, P., Pantel, J., Kruse, A., & Schröder, J. (2005). Prevalence and natural course of aging-associated cognitive decline in a population-based sample of young-old subjects. *American Journal of Psychiatry, 162,* 2071–2077]. Subjects diagnosed with AAMI are included because the progression rate to dementia from AAMI has been found to be

as high as 42% [Goldman, W. P., & Morris, J. C. (2001). Evidence that age-associated memory impairment is not a normal variant of aging. *Alzheimer's Disease and Associated Disorders, 15*, 72–79].

49. Nine longitudinal studies at least 3 years in length, which divided MCI subjects at follow-up into three categories (progression to dementia, stable, and no longer impaired) were included. The median progression rate to dementia for all nine studies was 44.9% (range 53.9 to 19.2%); median percentage of patients remaining stable was 35.0% (75.8 to 11.2%); median for those no longer impaired was 16.7% (34.9 to 5.0%). The four studies selected for Table 3.1 were community based, 3 or more years duration, and retained at least two thirds of their subjects. The studies were as follows: *Italy*: Ravaglia, G., Forti, P., Montesi, F., Lucicesare, A., Pisacane, N., Rietti, E., et al. (2008). Mild cognitive impairment: Epidemiology and dementia risk in a large elderly Italian population. *Journal of the American Geriatrics Society, 56*, 51–58. *United States*: Lopez, O. L., Kuller, L. H., Becker, J. T., Dulberg, C., Sweet, R. A., Gach, H. M., et al. (2007). Incidence of dementia in mild cognitive impairment in the Cardiovascular Health Study Cognition Study. *Archives of Neurology, 64*, 416–420; and Tschanz, J. T., Welsh-Bohmer, K. A., Lyketsos, C. G., Corcoran, C., Green, R. C., Hayden, K., et al., & the Cache County Investigators. (2006). Conversion to dementia from mild cognitive disorder: The Cache County Study. *Neurology, 67*, 229–234. *China*: Huang, J., Meyer, J. S., Zhang, Z., Wei, J., Hong, X., Wang, J., et al. (2005). Progression of mild cognitive impairment to Alzheimer's or vascular dementia versus normative aging among elderly Chinese. *Current Alzheimer Research, 2*, 571–578.

50. For example, Palmer, K., Berger, A. K., Monastero, R., Winblad, B., Bäckman, L., & Fratiglioni, L., (2007). Predictors of progression from mild cognitive impairment to Alzheimer disease. *Neurology, 68*, 1596–1602; and Robert, P. H., Berr, C., Volteau, M., Bertogliati-Fileau, C., Benoit, M., Guerin, O., et al. (2008). Importance of lack of interest in patients with mild cognitive impairment. *American Journal of Geriatric Psychiatry, 16*, 770–776.

Cognitive Aging: How Much Is Hereditary?

51. Three examples are the OctoTwin Study, the Swedish Adoption Twin Study, and the Minnesota Twin Study [Petrill, S. A., Plomin, R., Berg, S., Johansson B., Pedersen, N. L., Ahern, F., et al. (1998). The genetic and environmental relationship between general and specific cognitive abilities in twins age 80 and older. *Psychological Science, 9*, 183–189; and McClearn, G. E., Johansson, B., Berg, S., Pedersen, N. L., Ahern, F., Petrill, S. A., et al. (1997). Substantial genetic influence on cognitive abilities in twins 80 or more years old. *Science, 276*, 1560–1563; also Devlin, B., Daniels, M., & Roeder, K. (1997). The heritability of IQ. *Nature, 388*, 468–471; and Finkel, D., Pedersen, N.L., & McGue, M. (1995). Genetic influences on memory performance in adulthood: Comparison of Minnesota and Swedish twin data. *Psychology and Aging, 10*, 437-446.

52. Bouchard, T. J., Jr., Liken, D. T., McGue, M., Segal, N. L., & Tillage, A. (1990). Sources of human psychological differences: The Minnesota study of twins reared apart. *Science, 250*, 223–228.

53. From Stiles, J. (2008). *The fundamentals of brain development: Integrating nature and nurture.* Cambridge, MA: Harvard University Press. This book was brought to my attention by a 2008 review by Mriganka Sur, "The emerging nature of nurture," in *Science, 322,* 1636.
54. Colcombe, et al., 2006.

Reflections and Applications

55. The same differences in decline rate in crystallized and fluid abilities occurred among the normal subjects. The cross-sectional data in Figure 3.4 cannot verify the theory that people's worst aptitudes worsen with age. However, evidence from the Seattle Longitudinal Study does support the theory. The fluid aptitude spatial orientation declines nearly twice as much, from 32 to 74, as the crystallized ability verbal meaning (Schaie, 1994).
56. A comprehensive review of the literature that remains relevant today is contained in Brown, A. S. (1991). A review of the tip-of-the-tongue experience. *Psychological Bulletin, 109,* 204–223.
57. For a review of the possibilities of neuroplasticity research to extend the years of optimal aging along with a series of questions that must be addressed by empirical research before this theory can be usefully applied to older adults, see Grady, 2008; also Jessberger & Gage, 2008; and Salthouse, 2007.
58. This was a 2-year substudy of the ACTIVE (Advanced Cognitive Training for Independent Vital Elderly) research project. ACTIVE is a multicenter, randomized, controlled clinical trial that has been examining the long-term effectiveness of cognitive training on enhancing mental ability and preserving instrumental activities of daily living in older adults [Unverzagt, F. W., Smith, D. M., Rebok, G. W., Marsiske, M., Morris, J. N., Jones, R., et al. (2009). The Indiana Alzheimer Disease Center's Symposium on Mild Cognitive Impairment. Cognitive training in older adults: Lessons from the ACTIVE Study. *Current Alzheimer Research, 6,* 375–383]. In keeping with previous studies, memory skills among the MCI subjects did not improve with training. Small cross-sectional studies have recently reported some improvement among MCI subjects in measures of memory (autobiographical and face-name recall) following training [Belleville, S. (2008). Cognitive training for persons with mild cognitive impairment. *International Psychogeriatrics, 20,* 57–66].
59. Story excerpted and used with permission of Arthur Rivin, MD.

Chapter 4

1. Avoiding smoking is not discussed among the healthy lifestyle habits because its hazards and benefits are well known.

Exercise Regularly

2. Dustman, R. E., Ruhling, R. O., Russell, E. M., Shearer, D. E., Bonekat, H. W., Shigoeka, J. W., et al. (1984). Aerobic exercise training and improved neuropsychological function of older individuals. *Neurobiology of Aging, 5,* 35–42.

3. The subjects, part of the MacArthur Studies of Successful Aging, were followed for just over 2 years [Albert, M. S., Jones, K., Savage, C. R., Berkman, L., Seeman, T., Boazer, D., et al. (1995). Predictors of cognitive change in older persons: MacArthur Studies of Successful Aging. *Psychology and Aging, 10,* 578–589].

4. Based on other research, I believe that the reason that some benefit from moderate exercise while others require a more vigorous workout to achieve the same gains has to do with how physically fit the exercisers are at the beginning. Those in the best shape may need more strenuous exercise to achieve the same gains that those less fit accomplish with only moderate exercise. In a study that looked at the effect of exercise on ventricular stroke volume, subjects who were in the best shape (as judged by BMI and heart rate) at the beginning of the investigation improved less than those less fit [Ogawa, T., Spina, R. J., Martin, W. H., Jr., Kohrt, W. M., Schectman, K. D., Holloszy, J. O., et al. (1992). Effects of age, sex, and physical training on cardiovascular response to exercise. *Circulation, 86,* 26–35].

5. Each of the studies included older subjects and compared exercisers with nonexercisers. All subjects were classified as "young-old" (55–65), "mid-old" (66–70), and "old-old" (71–80), then identified as engaging in aerobic exercise only or in a combination of aerobics and strength/flexibility [Colcombe, S., & Kramer, A. F. (2003). Fitness effects on the cognitive function of older adults: A meta-analytic study. *Psychological Sciences, 14,* 125–130]. The statistical analyses combined aerobic and strength and flexibility exercises, with results reported in terms of effect sizes, which assess the strength of a relationship between two variables. Like T-shirt sizes, they are classified as small (.2 to .3), medium (.4 to .6), or large (.8 and above). See Cohen, J. (1988). *Statistical power analysis for the behavioral sciences* (2nd ed.). Hillsdale, NJ: Erlbaum.

6. For example, Woo, E., & Sharps, M. J. (2003). Cognitive aging and physical exercise. *Educational Gerontology, 29,* 327–337.

7. Hein, P., Area, B. C., & Ottenbacher, K. J. (2004). The effects of exercise training on elderly persons with cognitive impairment and dementia: A meta-analysis. *Archives Physical Medicine Rehabilitation, 85,* 1694–1704. In this meta-analysis, the investigators located 30 published articles and nonpublished manuscripts from 1970 to 2003 that met their selection criteria, which included randomized trials of the effect of exercise on cognition in subjects 65+ with cognitive impairment. They compared the before and after mental aptitude scores of those who did or did not participate in the exercise training. The effect size for exercise and cognitive performance was .57, about the same benefit reported for the normal subjects by Colcombe and Kramer (2003).

8. Rogers, R. L., Meyer, J. S., & Mortel, K. F. (1990). After reaching retirement age, physical activity sustains cerebral perfusion and cognition. *Journal of the American Geriatric Society, 38,* 123–128. On average, the weekly activity level of active retirees was more than three times the level of their sedentary counterparts.

9. The sedentary group scored about 10% lower on cognitive tests at the end of the study. These findings should be viewed with caution since no pretest data were reported (Rogers et al., 1990).

10. Colcombe, S. J., Erickson, K. I., Scalf, P. E., Kim, J. S., Prakash, R., McAuley, E., et al. (2006). Aerobic exercise training increases brain volume in aging humans. *Journals of Gerontology: Biological Sciences and Medical Sciences, 61A,* 1166–1170.

11. Erickson, K. I., & Kramer, A. F. (2009). Aerobic exercise effects on cognitive and neural plasticity in older adults. *British Journal of Sports Medicine, 43,* 22–24.

Engage in Active Leisure Pursuits

12. Ainsworth, B. E., Haskell, W. L., Leon, A. S., Jacobs, D. R., Jr., Montoye, H. J., Sallis, J. F., et al. (1993). Compendium of physical activities: Classification of energy costs of human physical activities. *Medicine and Science in Sports and Exercise, 25,* 71–80; also Ainsworth, B. E., Haskell, W. L., Whitt, M. C., Irwin, M. L., Swartz, A. M., Strath, S. J., et al. (2000). Compendium of physical activities: An update of activity codes and MET intensities. *Medicine and Science in Sports and Exercise, 32,* S498–S516.

13. An "average" person is considered to weigh 154 pounds and is in the 30–50 age range for men and 20–40 range for women. METs expended in activity vary with age. A middle-aged woman will burn fewer kilocalories in a round of golf than a 70-year-old. Therefore, for the fit younger person, 18 holes of golf is moderate exercise, while the same round for a normal septuagenarian is considered vigorous (Ainsworth et al., 1993).

14. Studies of the link between health and activity levels of older adults, which did not include regular exercise and included long-term follow-up and adjustments for potentially confounding factors, were carried out in the United States, Spain, Canada, and the United Kingdom. *United States:* Kushi, L. H., Fee, R. M., Folsom, A. R., Mink, P. J., Anderson, K. E., & Sellers, T. A. (1997). Physical activity and mortality in postmenopausal women. *Journal of the American Medical Association, 277,* 1287–1292; Rakowski, W., & Mor, V. (1992). The association of physical activity with mortality among older adults in the Longitudinal Study of Aging 1984–1988. (1992). *Journal of Gerontology, 47,* M122–M129; LaCroix, A. Z., Leveille, S. G., Hecht, J. A., Grothaus, L. C., & Wagner, E. H. (1996). Does walking decrease the risk of cardiovascular disease hospitalizations and death in older adults? *Journal of the American Geriatric Society, 44,* 113–120. *Canada:* Villeneuve, P. J., Morrison, H. I., Craig, C. L., & Schnaubel, D. E. (1998). Physical activity, physical fitness, and risk of dying. *Epidemiology, 9,* 626–631. *Spain:* Ruigómez, A., Alonso, J., & Anto, J. M. (1995). Relationship of health behaviours to five-year mortality in an elderly cohort. *Age and Ageing, 24,* 113–119. *United Kingdom:* Bath, P. A., & Morgan, K. (1998). Customary physical activity and physical health outcomes in later life. *Age and Ageing, 27,* 29–34.

15. *Georgia Tech:* Jopp, D., & Hertzog, C. (2007). Activities, self-referent memory beliefs, and cognitive performance: Evidence for direct and mediated relations. *Psychology and Aging, 22,* 811–825. *Other parts of the world:* Borglin, G., Jakobsson, U., Edberg, A.-K., & Hallberg, I. R. (2006). Older people in Sweden with various degrees of present quality of life: Their health, social support, everyday activities and sense of coherence. *Health and Social Care in the Community, 14,* 136–146; Christensen, H., Korten, A. E., Jorm, A. F., Henderson, A. S., Scott, R., & Mackinnon, A. J. (1996). Activity levels and cognitive functioning in an elderly community sample. *Age and Ageing, 25,* 72–80.

16. This cross-sectional analysis studied 1,787 subjects from the Age Gene/Environment Susceptibility-Reykjavik (AGES) study begun in 1967. The focus was on the relationships among activity level, cognitive performance, and white matter load (WML). The white matter consists of myelinated axons that pass signals through portions of the grey matter. White matter load (WML) has approximately the same meaning as white matter lesions or hyperintensities. These are associated with white matter atrophy and loss of brain volume. Using MRI scans, subcortical WML load was calculated as a weighted sum based on size of lesions in the four lobes. Periventricular WML load was calculated as

the sum of lesion scores, based on size, for the frontal caps, occipitoparietal caps, and bands. Ten activities surveyed did not include exercise or sports and were scored on the basis of frequency per month. Processing speed was measured by digit-symbol substitution, figure comparison, and Parts I and II of the Stroop Test; memory tests included immediate and delayed recall; executive functions included Part III of the Stroop, digits backward, and the CANTAB Spatial Working Memory Test [Saczynski, J. S., Jonsdottir, M. K., Sigurdsson, S., Eiriksdottir, G., Jonsson, P. V., Garcia, M. F., et al. (2008). White matter lesions and cognitive performance: The role of cognitively complex leisure activity. *Journals of Gerontology: Biological Sciences and Medical Sciences, 63A,* 848–854].

17. Useful references about WML in an older normal population are Ikram, M. A., Vrooman, H. A., Vernooij, M. W., van der Lijn, F., Hofman, A., van der Lugt, A., et al. (2008). Brain tissue volumes in the general elderly population: The Rotterdam Scan Study. *Neurobiology of Aging 29,* 882–890; and Hentschel, F., Damian, M., Krumm, B., & Froelich, L. (2007). White matter lesions—Age-adjusted values for cognitively healthy and demented subjects. *Acta Neurologica Scandinavica, 115,* 174–180.

18. The 5,925 community dwelling, predominantly white female high school graduates, mean age about 71, examined as part of a longitudinal study of osteoporosis were from Baltimore, Pittsburgh, Minneapolis, and Portland, Oregon [Yaffe, K., Barnes, D., Nevitt, M., Lui, L.-Y., & Covinsky, K. (2001). A prospective study of physical activity and cognitive decline in elderly women: Women who walk. *Archives of Internal Medicine, 161,* 1703–1708]. A city block was defined as 160 meters, burning about 8 kilocalories. Among the 33 activities surveyed was exercise, including walking, walking up flights of stairs, gardening, and dancing.

19. The brief pre- and posttest given was the mMMSE [Folstein, M. F., Robins, L. N., & Helzer, J. E. (1983). The Mini-Mental State Examination. *Archives of General Psychiatry, 40,* 812], which is a shortened version of the Mini-Mental State Exam without the orientation questions [Folstein, M. F., Folstein, S. E., & McHugh, P. R. (1975). Mini-Mental State: A practical method for grading the cognitive state of patients for clinicians. *Journal of Psychiatric Research, 12,* 189–198]. It has inspired several similar instruments. At posttesting, 16% of subjects in the top quarter, compared with 24% in the bottom quartile, had less than a 3-point decline in mMMSE scores, thought to be a possible clinical indicator of dementia. The absolute differences in decline of average mMMSE scores from baseline for the most and least-active women were small—3.5 versus 4.5%.

20. Lautenschlager, N. T., & Almeida, O. P. (2006). Physical activity and cognition in old age. *Current Opinion in Psychiatry, 19,* 190–193; Hertzog, C., Kramer, A. F., Wilson, R. S., & Lindenberger, U. (2009). Enrichment effects on adult cognitive development: Can the functional capacity of older adults be preserved and enhanced? *Psychological Science in the Public Interest, 9,* 1–65; Leung, G. T. Y., & Lam, L. C. W. (2007). Leisure activities and cognitive impairment in late life—A selective literature review of longitudinal cohort studies. *Hong Kong Journal of Psychiatry, 17,* 91–100.

Fight Obesity

21. Among all adults, a higher percentage of black (78.9%) and Mexican (73.9%) women were overweight or obese compared to white females (57.4%). Small differences occurred

among the males. Statistics from National Center for Health Statistics. (2010). *Health, United States, 2009: With special feature on medical technology.* Hyattsville, MD.

22. In the 65–74 age group, 35.8% of females and 33% of males surveyed were obese (National Center for Health Statistics, 2010).

23. Opinions vary about the health risks of being overweight/obese, especially for older people. Several well-designed studies, mostly of men, have found that the mortality risk of obese individuals is similar in all adult age groups [Ajani, U. A., Lotufo, P. A., Gaziano, J. M., Lee, I.-M., Spelsberg, A., Buring, J. E., et al. (2004). Body mass index and mortality among U.S. male physicians. *Annals of Epidemiology, 14*, 731–739; and Freedman, D. M., Ron, E., Ballard-Barbash, R., Doody, M. M., & Linet, M. S. (2006). Body mass index and all-cause mortality in a nationwide U.S. cohort. *International Journal of Obesity, 30*, 822–829; also Grabowski, D. C., & Ellis, J. E. (2001). High body mass index does not predict mortality in older people: Analysis of the Longitudinal Study of Aging. *Journal of the American Geriatrics Society, 49*, 968–979].

24. Fourteen of these reports were analyzed by Deborah Gustafson, a senior researcher in Gothenburg, Sweden. Gustafson, D. (2008). A life course of adiposity and dementia. *European Journal of Pharmacology, 585*, 163–175.

25. Of 8,664 subjects first evaluated when they were 40–45, at follow-up 36 years later 1,048 were diagnosed with dementia using *ICD*-9 (*International Classification of Diseases, Ninth Revision*) criteria. Sagittal abdominal diameter alone was more strongly associated with dementia than BMI alone. Whitmer, R. A., Gunderson, E. P., Barrett-Connor, E., Queensberry, C. P., Jr., & Yaffe K. (2008). Central obesity and increased risk of dementia more than three decades later. *Neurology, 71*, 1057–1064.

26. Follow-up period for 1,423 subjects from the Framingham Heart Study was 4–6 years. After adjusting for confounds, both obesity and hypertension were significantly associated with a lower total cognitive score in men but not women. Among males, obesity had a slightly higher correlation with lower scores on memory tests than hypertension [Elias, M. F., Elias, P. K., Sullivan, L. M., Wolf, P. A., & D'Agostino, R. B. (2003). Lower cognitive function in the presence of obesity and hypertension: The Framingham Heart Study. *International Journal of Obesity, 27*, 260–268]. The French sample was 2,223 women and men aged 32–62 who were followed for 5 years. Baseline and follow-up BMIs were associated with lower scores on memory-related tests (digit symbol substitution and word list learning) after adjustment for age, sex, educational level, blood pressure, diabetes, and other psychosocial potential confounds [Cournot, M., Marquie, J. C., Ansiau, D., Martinaud, C., Fonds, H., Ferrières, J., et al. (2006). Relation between body mass index and cognitive function in healthy middle-aged men and women. *Neurology, 67*, 1208–1214].

27. The primary review of the osteoarthritis studies, as well as results of other physical variables, is Bales, C. W., & Buhr, G. (2008). Is obesity bad for older persons? A systematic review of the pros and cons of weight reduction in later life. *Journal of the American Medical Directors Association, 9*, 302–312; the findings about lower blood pressure, cholesterol, and glucose levels were confirmed in a review by McTigue, K. M., Hess, R., & Ziouras, J. (2006). Obesity in older adults: A systematic review of the evidence for diagnosis and treatment. *Obesity, 14*, 1485–1497. At present, no evidence of which I am aware supports the conclusion that losing weight in the 3rd Age will much extend the length of life. A review of 26 prospective studies through 2008 found that subjects who intentionally lost weight had the same life expectancy as those who continued to

carry excess weight [Harrington, M., Gibson, S., & Cottrell, R. C. (2009). A review and meta-analysis of the effect of weight loss on all-cause mortality risk. *Nutrition Research Reviews, 22,* 93–108].

28. There was no change in weight over a 4-year period among those who received advice alone. Subjects who engaged in exercise alone lost about 2 kilograms at 6 months but returned to baseline at 1 year (Franz, M. J., van Wormer, J. J., Crain, A. L., Boucher, J. L., Histon, T., Caplan, W., et al. (2007). Weight-loss outcomes: A systematic review and meta-analysis of weight-loss clinical trials with a minimum 1-year follow-up. *Journal of the American Dietetic Association, 107,* 1755–1767).

29. A total of 80 studies were analyzed, among them 6 that examined subjects 55+. In all but one case, their results placed them in the middle third of weight loss. Effect sizes comparing treatment program subjects using advice alone or exercise alone were medium to small. About 30% of the people entering the program dropped out (Franz et al., 2007).

Eat Healthily

30. Recent reports from longitudinal studies correlating diet and health are Djoussé, L., Driver, J. A., & Gaziano, J. M. (2009). Relation between modifiable lifestyle factors and lifetime risk of heart failure. *Journal of the American Medical Association, 302,* 394–400; also Forman, J. P., Stampfer, M. J., & Curhan, G. C. (2009). Diet and lifestyle risk factors associated with incident hypertension in women. *Journal of the American Medical Association, 302,* 401–411; and Chiuve, S. E., McCullough, M. L., Sacks, F. M., & Rimm, E. B. (2006). Healthy lifestyle factors in the primary prevention of coronary heart disease among men: Benefits among users and nonusers of lipid-lowering and antihypertensive medications. *Circulation, 114,* 160–167. A useful evidence-based book on the subject of diet and overall health is Michael F. Roizen's *Real age: Are you as young as you can be?* New York: Ballantine, 1999.

31. In response to the terms "diet and cognition and aging," PubMed produced 199 articles and book chapters. Including only publications with longitudinal design, with diet as the independent variable, reduced the number to 11. All have positive conclusions about the benefit of a healthy diet on the intellect. Here is a sample: Barberger-Gateau, P., Raffaitin, C., Letenneur, L., Berr, C., Tzourio, C., Dartigues, J. F., et al. (2007). Dietary patterns and risk of dementia: The Three-City cohort study. *Neurology, 69,* 1921–1930; Scarmeas, N., Stern, Y., Tang, M. X., Mayeux, R., & Luchsinger, J. A. (2006). Mediterranean diet and risk for Alzheimer's disease. *Annals of Neurology, 59,* 912–921; Morris, M. C., Evans, D. A., Tangney, C. C., Bienias, J. L., & Wilson, R. S. (2006). Associations of vegetable and fruit consumption with age-related cognitive change. *Neurology, 67,* 1370–1376; and Kang, J. H., Ascherio, A. L., & Grodstein, F. (2005). Fruit and vegetable consumption and cognitive decline in aging women. *Annals of Neurology, 57,* 713–720.

32. One reference for healthy eating habits is the 2005 *Dietary Guidelines for Americans* published by the Department of Health and Human Services and the Department of agriculture can be accessed via http://www.health.gov/DietaryGuidelines/ (retrieved December 14, 2010).

33. Two longitudinal studies reported data on the relationship of exercise and diet to health status. The Physicians' Health Study I used as an outcome variable the lifetime risk of heart failure from age 40. During the mean follow-up period of 22.4 years, the incidence was 14.5% for subjects consuming fewer than four servings of fruits and vegetables and one serving of breakfast cereal daily. This compared to 12.4% for those who ingested four servings or more of the fruit and two or more of cereal. Subjects who exercised five or more times weekly had a heart failure rate of 11.4%, contrasted with 14.3% among those who exercised five or fewer times per week (Djoussé et al., 2009). A 14-year follow-up of over 80,000 healthy younger adult women from the second Nurses' Health Study found the relative risk of hypertension was .87 for women who exercised vigorously 7 days a week compared to those who worked out less than 1 day per week. Those in the highest quintile of the DASH diet (based on a high intake of fruits, vegetables, nuts and legumes, low-fat dairy products, whole grains, and a low consumption of sodium, sweetened beverages, and red and processed meats) had a relative risk of high blood pressure of .82 compared with those in the bottom 20% (from Forman et al., 2009).

34. Subjects were from the Cache County Study on Memory and Aging. Their standard for healthy nutrition was the 2005 Dietary Guidelines for Americans, referenced above, which emphasizes consumption of fruits, vegetables, lean meats, fish, low-fat dairy products, and high-fiber, whole-grain cereals and breads with relatively few calories. Each subject's diet was rated regarding its quality. Although statistically significant, the average differences in mental test scores between those who more fully complied with the recommended diet and those in the bottom quarter who were far less compliant was small (1.3%). The test was the Modified Mini-Mental State Examination (3MS), a brief screening measure for dementia. Although the proportional difference in decline rates between the healthiest and least healthy eaters was 35%, the absolute difference in the decline rates of 3.4 versus 5.2% for the bottom quarter was not large, in keeping with much of the research of this type [Wengreen, H. J., Neilson, C., Munger, R., & Corcoran, C. (2009). Diet quality is associated with better cognitive test performance among aging men and women. *Journal of Nutrition, 139,* 1944–1949].

35. Subjects with 14 or more mentally unhealthy days during the previous 30 days were defined as having "serious psychological distress." The definition was based on the K6 inventory, designed to identify persons with serious psychological distress using as few questions as possible [from Kessler, R. C., Barker, P. R., Colpe, L. J., Epstein, J. F., Gfroerer, J. C., Hiripi, E., et al. (2003). Screening for serious mental illness in the general population. *Archives of General Psychiatry, 60,* 184–189].

36. This research analyzed interview data from the Behavioral Risk Factor Surveillance System (BRFSS; http://apps.nccd.cdc.gov/HRQOL/index.asp). A total of 35,845 subjects aged 65+ were included. Variables examined were healthy weight (BMI of 18.5 to 24.9), not smoking, less than one alcoholic beverage per day, at least five fruits or vegetables daily, moderate-to-vigorous physical activity weekly, influenza and pneumococcal immunization [McGuire, L. C., Strine, T. W., Okoro, C. A., Ahluwalia, I. B., & Ford, E. S. (2007). Modifiable characteristics of a healthy lifestyle in U.S. older adults with or without frequent mental distress: 2003 Behavioral Risk Factor Surveillance System. *American Journal of Geriatric Psychiatry, 15,* 754–761].

Consume Alcohol Moderately

37. Among the all-male doctors, those who consumed 5–14 drinks per week had a slightly lower relative risk of heart failure (13.1%) during the 22-year follow-up than those (14.2%) drinking fewer than five drinks weekly (Djoussé et al. (2009). Among the all-female nurses, the risk of hypertension was slightly lower for those who consumed alcohol moderately—a drink or two a day—than for the rest of the group, including abstainers. Women who drank more than that were 61% more likely to develop hypertension during the 14-year follow-up period when controlled for other risk factors (Forman et al., 2009). Other research with nonmedical subjects confirmed these findings [Shaper, A. G., Wannamethee, G., & Walker, M. (1988). Alcohol and mortality in British men: Explaining the U-shaped curve. *Lancet, 2,* 1267–1273].

38. Blow, F. C. (1998). *NCADI consensus report: Substance abuse among older adults.* Rockville, MD: DHHS Publication No. (SMA) 98-3179; also a 9-year follow-up study by Thun, M. J., Peto, R., Lopez, A. D., Monaco, J. H., Jane Henley, S. J., Heath, C. W., et al. (1997). Alcohol consumption and mortality among middle-aged and elderly U.S. adults. *New England Journal of Medicine, 337,* 1705–1714.

39. These longitudinal studies were in several countries: *Denmark:* Rasmussen, H. B., Bagger, Y. Z., Tankó, L. B., Qin, G., Christiansen, C., & Werge, T. (2006). Cognitive impairment in elderly women: The relative importance of selected genes, lifestyle factors, and comorbidities. *Neuropsychiatric Disease and Treatment, 2,* 227–233. *France:* Letenneur, L. (2004). Risk of dementia and alcohol and wine consumption: A review of recent results. *Biological Research, 37,* 189–193. *Netherlands:* Ruitenberg, A., van Swieten, J., Witteman, J., Mehta, K., Van Duijn, C., Hofman, A., et al. (2002). Alcohol consumption and risk of dementia: The Rotterdam study. *Lancet, 359,* 281–286. *Sweden:* Huang, W., Qiu, C., Winblad, B., & Fratiglioni, L. (2002). Alcohol consumption and incidence of dementia in a community sample aged 75 years and older. *Journal of Clinical Epidemiology, 55,* 959–964.

40. Some argue that the benefits of wine derive from the flavonoid content and the antioxidant activity, while others believe that wine drinkers follow a healthier diet than beer or spirit drinkers [Commenges, D., Scotet, V., Renaud, S., Jacqmin-Gadda, H., Barberger-Gateau, P., & Dartigues, J. F. (2000). Intake of flavonoids and risk of dementia. *European Journal of Epidemiology, 16,* 357–363; and Tjonneland, A., Gronbaek, M., Stripp, C., & Overvad, K. (1998). Wine intake and diet in a random sample of Danish men and women. *American Journal of Clinical Nutrition, 69,* 46–54].

41. A review was provided by Verbaten, M. N. (2009). Chronic effects of low to moderate alcohol consumption on structural and functional properties of the brain: Beneficial or not? *Human Psychopharmacology, 24,* 199–205.

42. Conclusions about the association between the amount of drinking and mental ability are often confounded by the limitations of cross-sectional studies and design problems such as abstainers and light drinkers being more often female, better educated, and healthier (Verbaten, 2009).

43. This study is based on a national probability sample of 3,005 community-dwelling subjects aged 57–85. See Drum, M. L., Shiovitz-Ezra, S., Gaumer, E., & Lindau, S.T. (2009). Assessment of smoking behaviors and alcohol use in the national social life, health, and aging project. *Journal of Gerontology: Psychological Sciences, 64B,* (suppl 1), 119–130.

Surveys yielding slightly different results include the National Center for Health Statistics, 2010 report on 2007 data, which found that 38.9% of women and 55.6% of men 65–74 used alcohol, and the Drum et al. 2009 study, which found that 52.9% of the females and 64.9% of the males 65–74 were drinkers.

44. The decade in which the data were gathered was 1997 to 2007. Non-age-adjusted proportions of adults 18+ drinking in 1997 and 2007 were 63.4 and 61.4%, respectively. The calculations were based on the number of all adults over 18 in 2007 (227,719,000). In the 2007 population, 2% fewer adult drinkers is 4,554,380 people. The decline among all adults occurred among all major age divisions, and across diverse groups: Whites (from 66% in 1997 to 64.5% in 2007), Asians (from 45.8 to 43.4%), Hispanics (53.4 to 51.1%), and Mexicans (53 to 47.9%). The only slight increase was among African American adults (47.8 to 48.8%). The total number of drinkers fell among the poorest among us (from 46.1 to 44.6% among those below the poverty level) to the wealthiest (from 68.7 to 66.8% for those at 200% or more above the poverty level). From National Center for Health Statistics (2010).

45. In the period from 1997 to 2007, the U.S. Census data on the proportion of heavy drinking (defined as more than five drinks a day from once a year to once a month) among women 65–74 was difficult to estimate accurately. The percentages have ranged from 2.4 to 3.1%, with the 2006 figure of 4.7% deemed unreliable.

46. In this cross-sectional study, 5.2% of the women 65–74 said that they had four or more drinks 4–12 times in the past 3 months. Only 3.3% of the females 57–64 met this criterion for heavy drinking. Although more 3rd Age males than females drank heavily (9.6%), they had a lower frequency of excessive drinking than the 14.6% of men aged 57–64 (Drum et al., 2009).

47. Data for monthly prescription medicine from National Center for Health Statistics (2010). The most recent analysis was from 2003–2006 surveys, which found 90.3% of the women and 88.2% of the males 65+ filling at least one prescription monthly. Since these percentages have been rising, it seems reasonable to assume that the 2010 survey will show more than 90% of elders on prescription medication.

48. MRI studies review by Verbaten (2009). Earlier reviews were in keeping with these findings [Parsons, O. A., & Nixon, S. J. (1998). Cognitive functioning in sober social drinkers: A review of the research since 1986. *Journal of Studies of Alcohol, 59,* 180–190]; *research on dementia* [Smith, D. M., & Atkinson, R. M. (1995). Alcoholism and dementia. *International Journal of Addictions, 30,* 1843–1869]; *mental ability* review using studies of the Haldstead-Reitan battery [Leckliter, I. N., & Matarazzo, J. D. (1989). The influence of age, education, IQ, gender, and alcohol abuse on Halstead-Reitan neuropsychological test battery performance. *Journal of Clinical Psychology, 45,* 484–512].

49. Approximately 1.2% of adults 65+ from the 2001–2002 National Epidemiologic Survey on Alcohol and Related Conditions (NESARC) met the *DSM-IV* (*Diagnostic and Statistical Manual of Mental Disorders, Fourth Edition;* American Psychiatric Association, Washington, DC, 1994) criteria for alcohol abuse and dependence. Based on the 2002 U.S. census, that number would be about 3,458,680. Presuming the percentage of alcohol-abusive and -dependent people 65+ were to remain the same, the 2010 estimate would rise to 3,722,796. Data from Grant, B. F., Dawson, D. A., Stinson, F. S., Chou, S. P., Dufour, M. C., & Pickering, R. P. (2004). The 12-month prevalence and trends in *DSM-IV* alcohol abuse and dependence: United States, 1991–1992 and 2001–2002. *Drug Alcohol Dependency, 74,* 223–234. Also available on NIAA Web site http://www.

niaaa.nih.gov/Resources/DatabaseResources/QuickFacts/AlcoholDependence/abus-dep3.htm (retrieved August 11, 2010).

50. Criteria for alcohol abuse/dependence are adapted from the *DSM-IV* (American Psychiatric Association, 1994). For older drinkers, a consensus report recommended that the categories of heavy drinker, alcohol abuser, and alcohol dependent be collapsed into two categories—at-risk and problem drinker (Blow, 1998).

51. Considerable disagreement exists about the effectiveness of AA and other 12-step programs. A review of eight studies involving 3,417 subjects found that AA improved retention in the treatment, but there were no differences in the number of days drinking or number of drinks daily compared to other programs [Ferri, M., Amato, L., & Davoli, M. (2006). Alcoholics Anonymous and other 12-step programmes for alcohol dependence. *Cochrane Database of Systematic Reviews, 3,* Art. No.: CD005032. DOI: 10.1002/14651858.CD005032.pub2]. A more recent review found that veterans who remained in AA or 12-step programs were twice as likely to be abstinent at 12- and 18-month follow-up. No information, however, is available on those who dropped out of the programs [Kaskustas, L. A. (2009). Alcoholics Anonymous effectiveness: Faith meets science. *Journal of Addictive Diseases, 28,* 145–157].

52. Research in the United States found that 10 to 30% of nondependent problem drinkers reduced their alcohol intake to safer levels following a brief intervention by a physician or other clinician (Blow, 1998). Spanish review by Ballesteros, J., Ariño, J., González-Pinto, A., & Querejetad, I. (2003). Effectiveness of medical advice for reducing excessive alcohol consumption. Meta-analysis of Spanish studies in primary care. *Gaceta Sanitaria, 17,* 116–122.

53. The success rates for middle-aged adults was 59%; for older adults, it was 55%, and for young adults, it was 50% [Satre, D. D., Mertens, J., Areán, P. A., & Weisner, C. (2004). Five-year alcohol and drug treatment outcomes of older adults versus middle-aged and younger adults in a managed care program. *Addiction, 99,* 1286-1297; and Blow, 1998].

Maintain Satisfying Social Relationships

54. From an extensive meta-analysis of studies of over 300,000 subjects, which yielded an average effect size for various social relationship measures of .50. These findings were consistent across age, gender, and initial health status [Holt-Lunstad, J., Smith, T. B., & Layton, J. B. (2010). Social relationships and mortality risk: A meta-analytic review. *PLoS Medicine, 7,* e1000316].

55. *Resistance to disease*: Investigators gave 400 adult volunteers nose drops containing a common cold virus, then waited to see who would be infected. Meanwhile, subjects were asked to indicate if they were close to anyone in 12 different groups of people, such as spouse, family, and close friends. Not surprisingly, about half the subjects developed a cold soon afterward. When researchers looked at the relationship between the number of different groups in which subjects had friends and whether they developed a cold, they found that 61% of those with the least-diverse social networks developed a cold compared to only 34% of those with the most diverse networks. [Cohen, S., Doyle, W. J., Skoner, D. P., Rabin, B. S., & Gwaltney, J. M. Jr. (1997). Social ties and susceptibility to the common cold. *Journal of the American Medical Association, 277,* 1940–1944].

Recovery from heart attacks: Most of the research published has been with patients with cardiovascular disease. Examples are studies by Lisa Berkman [Berkman, L. F. (1995). The role of social relationships in health promotion. *Psychosomatic Medicine, 57*, 244–254]. The number of people subjects said that they could count on were classified into three groups: 0, 1, and more than 2. During the 6-month follow-up, 34% of the females and 44% of the males died. Others have reported similar findings [Coyne, J. C., Rohrbaugh, M. J., Shoham, V., Sonnega, J. S., Nicklas, J., & Cranford, J. A. (2001). Prognostic importance of marital quality for survival of congestive heart failure. *American Journal of Cardiology, 88,* 526–529]. *Life expectancy:* Findings from four of the most representative of these longitudinal studies showed the powerful effect of social connections on health and mortality. These are likely conservative estimates because the data analyses controlled statistically for the confounding effects of other factors that could account for death, such as baseline health, obesity, smoking and alcohol consumption, socioeconomic status, race, physical activity, life satisfaction, and preventive health care [House, J. S., Landis, K. R., & Umberson, D. (1988). Social relationships and health. *Science, 241,* 540–544].

56. Two other studies with slightly different designs failed to find consistently significant associations between positive support and better health. Norwegian researchers found that positive relations with family and friends had little impact on mortality, but social isolation was strongly linked to mortality [Murberg, T. A. (2004). Long term effect of relationships on mortality in patients with congestive heart failure. *International Journal of Psychiatry in Medicine, 34*, 207–217].

57. At the University of Michigan's Institute for Social Research, investigators looking for significant links between social networks and health came up with mixed results. Older subjects who felt that their spouses and children supported and listened to them lived longer than those who felt unsupported and ignored. However, among people with chronic illnesses, those who reported greater demands or criticism from spouses or children survived longer than people with medical conditions who reported lower levels of negative relations [Birditt, K., & Antonucci, T. C. (2008). Life sustaining irritations? Relationship quality and mortality in the context of chronic illness. *Social Science and Medicine, 67,* 1291–1299].

58. A clear treatment of this complex topic of good and bad relationships being both good and bad for health was provided by Birditt and Antonucci, 2008.

59. Subjects were 287 volunteers from the Florida Geriatric Research Program in Clearwater. Self-reported health scores were based on five major questions about decline in the past 5 years: overall health, functional health, energy level, activities limited by pain, and decline in such areas as vision, hearing, and balance. Scores on self-reported cognitive decline in the past 5 years were based on questions of overall mental ability, mental ability compared to peers, and decline in specific abilities such as attention, visuospatial abilities, and reasoning. The independent variables were current social satisfaction, overall social satisfaction over the past 5 years, diversity of social networks, and the number of people subjects could count on for support [Powell, D. H. (2002, November). *Psychosocial correlates of stable or improved health among 3rd Agers.* Paper presented at the annual meeting of the Gerontological Society of America, Boston].

60. *Baltimore, Maryland:* Holtzman, R. E., Rebok, G. W., Saczynski, J. S., Kouzis, A. C., Doyle, K. W., & Eaton, W. W. (2004). Social network characteristics and cognition in middle-aged and older adults. *The Journals of Gerontology Series B: Psychological*

Sciences and Social Sciences, 59, 278–284. *Madrid, Spain:* Zunzunegui, M. V., Alvarado, B. E., Del Ser, T., & Otero, A. (2003). Social networks, social integration, and social engagement determine cognitive decline in community-dwelling Spanish older adults. *Journal of Gerontology: Social Sciences, 58B,* S93–S100.

61. Wang, H. X., Karp, A., Winblad, B., & Fratiglioni, L. (2002). Late-life engagement in social and leisure activities is associated with a decreased risk of dementia: A longitudinal study from the Kungsholmen Project. *American Journal of Epidemiology, 155,* 1081–1087.

62. Gow, A. J., Pattie, A., Whiteman, M. C., Whalley, L. J., & Deary, I. J. (2007). Social support and successful ageing: Investigating the relationships between lifetime cognitive change and life satisfaction. *Journal of Individual Differences, 28,* 103–115.

63. The subjects averaged 61 and had 10 years of education. After controlling for the other variables, loneliness accounted for about 2% of the variance. Size of social networks and support factors explained 23% of the variance in satisfaction with life ratings.

64. See Holt-Lunstad et al., 2010.

65. Both cross-sectional and longitudinal investigators agree that social isolation puts older adults at much greater risk for decline in intellectual functioning. An analysis of the cognitive impact of social isolation is contained in a report by a Johns Hopkins research team [Green, A. F., Rebok, G., & Lykens, C. G. (2008). Influence of social network characteristics on cognition and functional status with aging. *International Journal of Geriatric Psychiatry, 23,* 972–978]; also see Murberg, 2004.

Manage Stress

66. Among their many writings on this topic is Folkman, S., & Lazarus, R. S. (1988). Coping as a mediator of emotion. *Journal of Personality and Social Psychology, 54,* 466–475. This approach to managing stress-related emotions does not exhaust the options. Multimodal or cognitive behavior therapies are frequently used to combat disabling emotions or overcome harmful behavior patterns. For example, Beck, J. S. (2005). *Cognitive therapy for challenging problems.* New York: Guilford; Barlow, D. H. (2002). *Anxiety and its disorders: The nature and treatment of anxiety and panic* (2nd ed.). New York: Guilford; Lazarus, A. A. (1997). *Brief but comprehensive therapy: The multimodal way.* New York: Springer; Goldfried, M. R., & Davison, G. C. (1994). *Clinical behavior therapy* (expanded ed.). New York: Wiley.

67. Observation by Kemeny, M. E. (2003). The psychobiology of stress. *Current Directions in Psychological Science, 12,* 124–129. In one of Selye's first articles about the nature of stress, he did not define the term [Selye, H. (1955). Stress and disease. *Science, 122,* 625–631]. Two decades later, when he did define stress for his colleagues in the Canadian Medical Association, it was brief: "Stress is the nonspecific response of the body to any demand." [Selye, H. (1976). Forty years of stress research: Principal remaining problems and misconceptions. *Canadian Medical Association Journal, 115,* 53–56].

68. Selye, H. (1974). *Stress without distress.* New York: Signet.

69. See Cohen, S. (1996). Psychological stress, immunity, and upper respiratory infections. *Current Directions in Psychological Science, 5,* 86–90.

70. The bomber crews reporting the most physical and emotional disorders were beginners with 1–5 combat missions (28%) and those who had flown more than 30 missions (nearly 50%). Those who had flown 6 to 25 missions had the lowest rate of reported illness, about 18% [Stouffer, S. A., Lumsdaine, A. A., Williams, R. M., Jr., Smith, M. B., Janis, I. L., Star, S. A., et al. (1965). *The American soldier: Combat and its aftermath* (p. 381). New York: Science Edition by Wiley. (Original work published 1949)]. This U-shaped curve is consistent with Hans Selye's general adaptation syndrome (Selye, 1974).

71. The immune system is exceedingly complex. Our natural defense against disease, the job of the immune system is to detect, inactivate, and remove bacteria, viruses, tumors, and other foreign bodies in our system. It plays an important role in the repair of tissue following injury and creates "natural killer" T and B cells, which detect and destroy foreign substances in the body. It also creates specific antibodies to resist diseases such as measles and chicken pox. A succinct description of the immune system is contained in Sapolsky, R. M. (1994). *Why zebras don't get ulcers: A guide to stress and stress-related diseases, and coping.* New York: Freeman.

72. Among many review articles on the effect of stress hormones on intellectual functioning and structure of the brain written by Sonia Lupien and her colleagues is Lupien, S. J., Fiocco, A., Wan, N., Maheu, F., Lord, C., Schramek, T., et al. (2005). Stress hormones and human memory function across the lifespan. *Psychoneuroendocrinology, 30,* 225–242.

73. The hippocampus is especially vulnerable to stress hormones. The adverse effects of repeated stress include suppression of glucose metabolism, dendritic branching, and neurogenesis. Most of the initial studies used laboratory rodents [McEwen, B. S. (1999). Stress and hippocampal plasticity. *Annual Review of Neuroscience, 22,* 105–122]. Later reports included data on human subjects [Sapolsky, R. M. (1999). Glucocorticoids, stress, and their adverse neurological effects: Relevance to aging. *Experimental Gerontology, 34,* 721–732; and Lupien, S. J., & Lepage, M. (2001). Stress, memory, and the hippocampus: Can't live with it, can't live without it. *Behavioural Brain Research, 127,* 137–158].

74. Adapted from Gurvits, T. V., Shenton, M. E., Hokama, H., Ohta, H., Lasko, N. B., Gilbertson, M. W., Orr, S. P., Kikinis, R., Jolesz, F. A., McCarley, R. W., & Pitman, R. K. (1996). Magnetic resonance imaging study of hippocampal volume in chronic combat-related posttraumatic stress disorder. *Biological Psychiatry, 40,* 1091-1099. This is an analysis of the hippocampal volume as shown by the MRIs of 14 Viet Nam veterans with and without posttraumatic stress disorder. For those with the most severe combat exposure the decrease in hippocampal volume was was 26% on the left side and 22% on the right. On average, 28 contiguous 1.5 mm slices were used to derive the volume of the hippocampal complex. Combat exposure severity was assessed by the Combat Exposure Scale, which assessed the number of times each veteran was exposed to one of seven types of combat experiences. Scores ranged from 0-41. Clinical experience found the scale to be a consistent predictor of PTSD symptomatology in veterans [Keane, T. M, Fairbank, J. A., Caddell, J. M., Zimering, R. T., Taylor, K. L., & Mora, C. A. (1988). Clinical evaluation of a measure to assess combat exposure. *Psychological Assessment, 1,* 53–55]. One lingering question is whether the lower hippocampal volume might have preceded the combat experience.

75. Lupien et al., 2005.

76. Report on higher levels of glucocorticoids by Sapolsky, 1994. This has caused some experts to speculate that some of the apparent differences in mental skills like memory among younger and older persons may be partly a function of age [Lupien, S. J., Maheu, F., Tu, M., Fiocco, A., & Schramek, T. E. (2007). The effects of stress and stress

hormones on human cognition: Implications for the field of brain and cognition. *Brain and Cognition, 65,* 209–237].

77. Four-community study analysis by Gatz, M., & Smyer, M. A. (1992). The mental health system and older adults in the 1990s. *American Psychologist, 47,* 741–751. Lower rates of depression and anxiety among elders in contrast to young and middle-aged adults also have been reported in Australia, Canada, and the Netherlands. *Australia:* Henderson, S., Andrews, G., & Hall W. (2000). Australia's mental health: An overview of the general population survey. *Australia and New Zealand Journal of Psychiatry, 34,* 197–205. *Canada:* Bland, R. C., Newman, S. C., & Orn, H. (1988). Period prevalence of psychiatric disorders in Edmonton. *Acta Psychiatrica Scandinavica, 77,* 33–42. *Netherlands:* 3rd Age adults selected from the Longitudinal Aging Study Amsterdam (LASA) for analysis were scored as primarily anxious (4.5%), depressed (5.4%), or both (7.3%). See Bierman, E. J. M., Comijs, H. C., Jonker, C., & Beekman, A. T. F. (2005). Effects of anxiety versus depression on cognition in later life. *American Journal of Geriatric Psychiatry, 13,* 686–693.

78. The test was a research version of Charles Spielbeger's State Trait Personality Inventory [Spielbeger, C. D. (2005). State Trait Personality Inventory. Menlo Park, CA: Mind Garden].

79. Observation that, once aroused, the emotional state of older adults requires a longer period of time to return to normal than those in midlife by Sapolsky, 1994, and by Carstensen and her colleagues [Scheibe, S., & Carstensen, L. L. (2010). Emotional aging: Recent findings and future trends. *Journal of Gerontology: Psychological Sciences, 65B,* 135–144].

80. Among the many publications on the positivity effect by Laura Carstensen are Charles, S. T., & Carstensen, L. L. (2008). Unpleasant situations elicit different emotional responses in younger and older adults. *Psychology and Aging, 23,* 495–504; Carstensen, L. L. (2006). The influence of a sense of time on human development. *Science, 312,* 1913–1915; and Charles, S. T., Mather, M., & Carstensen, L. L. (2003). Aging and emotional memory: The forgettable nature of negative images for older adults. *Journal of Experimental Psychology: General, 132,* 310–324.

81. Samanez-Larkin, G. R., Robertson, E. R., Mikels, J. A., Carstensen, L. L., & Gotlib, I. H. (2009). Selective attention to emotion in the aging brain. *Psychology and Aging, 24,* 519–529.

82. Fung, H. H., & Carstensen, L. L. (2003). Sending memorable messages to the old: Age differences in preferences and memory for advertisements. *Journal of Personality and Social Psychology, 85,* 163–178.

Reflections and Applications

83. Specifically, the mortality rate at average age 75 for these physicians was 21.2%; for those exercising more than five times a week, it was 11.4% (Djoussé et al., 2009).

84. Any three of the lifestyle habits were from a list used in both studies that included exercise, BMI, diet, and alcohol use. The physicians' study also included smoking, and the nurses' research included use of folic acid, acetaminophen, nonsteroidal anti-inflammatory drugs, and aspirin. Any three of the factors reduced the risk of death due to heart failure by 34.6% and reduced by 50% the incidence of hypertension in nurses with BMIs under 30 who exercised vigorously and consumed the healthiest diet (Djoussé et al., 2009; Forman et al., 2009).

85. Reuser, M., Bonneux, L. G., & Willekens, F. J. (2009). Smoking kills, obesity disables: A multistate approach of the U.S. Health and Retirement Survey. *Obesity, 17,* 783–789.

86. Other research findings from Europe, China, and the United States do not agree, concluding instead that excess adiposity reduces the length as well as the quality of life, especially among men. *Europe:* Zamboni, M., Mazzali, G., Zoico, E., Harris, T. B., Meigs, J. B., Di Francesco, V., et al. (2005). Health consequences of obesity in the elderly: A review of four unresolved questions. *International Journal of Obesity, 29,* 1011–1029. *China:* Wang, J., Gao, Y. T., Wang, X. L., Liu, E. J., Zhang, Y. L., & Yuan, J. M. (2005). A prospective cohort study on body mass index and mortality among middle-aged and elderly men in urban Shanghai. *Zhonghua Liu Xing Bing Hue Za Zhi, 26,* 394–399. *United States:* Ajani et al., 2004.

87. National Center for Health Statistics, 2010.

88. Franz et al., 2007.

89. Blow, 1998.

90. For example, Rasmussen et al., 2006; Thun et al., 1998.

91. Blow, 1998.

92. I have found that eliminating "ever" allows the instrument to be more sensitive to concerns about current problem drinking without substantially increasing the number of false positives. Mayfield, D., McLeod, G., & Hall, P. (1974). The CAGE questionnaire: Validation of a new alcoholism screening instrument. *American Journal of Psychiatry, 131,* 1121–1123.

93. Bradley, K. A., Kivlahan, D. R., Bush, K. R., McDonell, M. B., & Fihn, S. D. (2001). Variations on the CAGE alcohol screening questionnaire: Strengths and limitations in VA general medical patients. *Alcoholism: Clinical and Experimental Research, 25,* 1472–1478; and National Institute on Alcohol Abuse and Alcoholism. (1995). *The physician's guide to helping patients with alcohol problems* (NIH Publication 95-3769). Bethesda, MD: National Institutes of Health.

94. Green et al., 2008.

95. Example from Mather, M., Knight, M., & McCaffrey, M. (2005). The allure of the alignable: Younger and older adults' false memories of choice features. *Journal of Experimental Psychology: General, 134,* 38–51.

96. When instructed to attend selectively to both positively and negatively valenced stimuli, older and younger subjects responded comparably. Interventions that instruct older adults to pay less attention to their emotional responses and concentrate on the specific facts when a choice must be made have a strong likelihood of success [Scheibe & Carstensen (2010); Samanez-Larkin et al. (2009)].

97. AARP Elder Fraud Project report. Retrieved August 11, 2010, from http://www.fraud.org/elderfraud/eldproj.htm.

Chapter 5

Working Smarter: Anticipate Cognitive Decline and Minimize Negative Effects

1. When younger (18–22) and older (66–78) volunteers were asked when they felt best and were most alert, age dictated their responses. The older adults outperformed the younger

subjects in the morning when judged by the "hits" (84 vs. 76%) or the difference score when the errors were subtracted from the hits (47 vs. 46%). The major difference was in the afternoon, when the error rate for older subjects rose to 55% from 37% in the morning [May, C. P., Hasher, L., & Stoltzfus, E. R. (1993). Optimal time of day and magnitude of age differences in memory. *Psychological Science, 4,* 326–330].

2. While several studies confirmed the findings by May et al. (1993), a number have not found the same differences in optimal time of day for cognitive performance that puts older adults on a par with those a generation or two younger. Two different Canadian research teams tested older and younger adults and found significant age group differences in memory, especially false memories, across a large array of crystallized and fluid mental abilities, which were not reduced by time of day [Murphy, K. J., West, R., Armilio, M. L., Craik, F. I. M., & Stuss, D. T. (2007). Word-list-learning performance in younger and older adults: Intra-individual performance variability and false memory. *Aging, Neuropsychology, and Cognition, 14,* 70–94: also Brown, L. N., Goddard, K. M., Lahar, C. J., & Mosley, J. L. (1999). Age-related deficits in cognitive functioning are not mediated by time of day. *Experimental Aging Research, 25,* 81–93].

Applying Selection, Optimization, and Compensation

3. Although the meaning is the same, this strategy is also called "selective optimization with compensation." The seminal articles on these techniques are Baltes, P. B. (1997). On the incomplete architecture of human ontogeny: Selection, optimization, and compensation as foundations of developmental theory. *American Psychologist, 52,* 366–380; and Baltes, P. B., & Baltes, M. M. (1990). Psychological perspectives on successful aging: The model of selective optimization with compensation. In P. B. Baltes & M. M. Baltes (Eds.), *Successful aging: Perspectives from the behavioral sciences* (pp. 1–34). New York: Cambridge University Press. Others whose ideas have contributed to this section are Freund, A. M., & Baltes, P. B. (1998). Selection, optimization, and compensation as strategies of life management: Correlations with subjective indicators of successful aging. *Psychology and Aging, 13,* 531–543; and Bender, R. M. C. X. (2005). *Successful aging and selection, optimization and compensation behaviors.* (Doctoral dissertation, University of Hartford, Hartford, CT). *Dissertation Abstracts International: Section B: The Physical Sciences and Engineering, 66,* 3396.

4. Both napping studies were carried out in Japan [Kaida, K., Ogawa, K., Matsuura, N., Takahashi, M., & Hori, T. (2006). Relationship between the habit of napping with self-awakening and generalized self-efficacy. *Japanese Journal of Health Psychology, 19,* 1–9; and Tanaka, H., & Shirakawa, S. (2004). Sleep health, lifestyle and mental health in the Japanese elderly: Ensuring sleep to promote a healthy brain and mind. *Journal of Psychosomatic Medicine, 56,* 465–477].

5. Manning, C. A., Hall, J. L., & Gold, P. E. (1990). Glucose effects on memory and other neuropsychological tests in elderly humans. *Psychological Science, 1,* 307–311; tests of nonmemory functions in older adults found similar improvements with glucose [Allen, J. B., Gross, A. M., Aloia, M. S., & and Billingsley, C. (1996). The effects of glucose on nonmemory cognitive functioning in the elderly. *Neuropsychologia 34,* 459-465].

6. Investigators in different disciplines and in different regions of the world have confirmed the usefulness of the SOC strategy. For example, Yemei, W., Guopeng, C., & Yi, S. (2007). A review on studies of the SOC model of successful aging. *Psychological Science (China), 30,* 377–379; Burnett-Wolle, S., & Godbey, G. (2007). Refining research on older adults' leisure: Implications of selection, optimization, and compensation and socioemotional selectivity theories. *Journal of Leisure Research, 39,* 498–513; Chou, K.-L., & Chi, I. (2002). Financial strain and life satisfaction in Hong Kong elderly Chinese: Moderating effect of life management strategies including selection, optimization, and compensation. *Ageing and Mental Health, 6,* 172–177; Gignac, M. A. M., Cott, C., & Badley, E. M. (2002). Adaptation to disability: Applying selective optimization with compensation to the behaviors of older adults with osteoarthritis. *Psychology and Aging, 17,* 520–524; and Abraham, J. D., & Hansson, R. O. (1995). Successful aging at work: An applied study of selection, organization, optimization, and compensation through impression management. *Journal of Gerontology: Psychological Sciences, 50B,* 94–103.

7. Study by Jopp, D., & Smith, J. (2006). Resources and life-management strategies as determinants of successful aging: On the protective effect of selection, optimization, and compensation. *Psychology and Aging, 21,* 253–265. The relatively resource-rich subjects who applied SOC more often did not differ much from the frequent users. In Hong Kong, researchers found a significant correlation between an SOC questionnaire and life satisfaction and self-esteem in older adults [Chou, K.-L., & Chi, I. (2001). Selection, optimization, and compensation questionnaire: A validation study with Chinese older adults. *Clinical Gerontologist, 24,* 141–152].

8. Example from Baltes, B. B., & Heydens-Gahir, H. A. (2003). Reduction in work-family conflict through the use of selection, optimization, and compensation behaviors. *Journal of Applied Psychology, 88,* 1005–1018. Young professionals using SOC reported more satisfaction with their work and felt greater emotional balance in their lives [Wiese, B. S., Freund, A. M., & Baltes, P. B. (2002). Subjective career success and emotional well-being: Longitudinal predictive power of selection, optimization and compensation. *Journal of Vocational Behavior, 60,* 321–335].

Recognizing That Experience Matters: Captain Chesley Sullenberger of Flight 1549

9. From interview with *CBS Evening News* anchor Katie Couric, January 16, 2009. Additional material about Captain Sullenberger and the saga of Flight 1549 was drawn from other CBS News reporters and from Rick Newman, How Sullenberger Really Saved US Airways 1549. *U.S. News and World Report Flow Chart,* February 3, 2009.

10. Until recently, airline pilots were required to retire at age 60. On December 13, 2007, President Bush signed the Fair Treatment for Experienced Pilots Act, which raised the mandatory retirement age to 65 for pilots flying domestic routes. International flights, however, still require that one of the pilots be under the age of 60.

Active Experience Matters to All of Us

11. Data on processing speed from Salthouse, T. A. (1996). The processing-speed theory of adult age differences in cognition. *Psychological Review, 103,* 403–428; data on processing speed and visuospatial ability from Finkel, D., Reynolds, C. A., McArdle, J. J., & Pederson, N. L. (2007). Age changes in processing speed as a leading indicator of cognitive aging. *Psychology and Aging, 22,* 558–568; and on visuospatial ability from Powell, D. H. (in collaboration with D. K. Whitla) (1994). *Profiles in cognitive aging.* Cambridge, MA: Harvard University Press.

12. More than 50 years ago, Keith Sward compared the aptitude test scores of older and younger professors at Stanford (Stanford, CA) and Berkeley (Berkeley, CA) [Sward, K. (1945). Age and mental ability in superior men. *American Journal of Psychology, 58,* 443–479]. These findings apply to older and younger professors and truck drivers, nuns and executives, architects and nurses, doctors, and pilots. Even when the tasks were not mental tests but real-life situations—playing chess, cooking a five-course meal, or carrying out household chores—the results favored the younger men and women.

13. Knowledge, and the competence that comes with it, usually increases with experience until midlife. Then, it remains stable or declines [from Salthouse, T. A. (2003). Interrelations of aging, knowledge, and cognitive performance. In U. M. Staudinger & U. Lindenberger (Eds.), *Understanding human development: Dialogues with lifespan psychology* (pp. 265–287). Dordrecht, Netherlands: Kluwer].

14. An evidence-based definition of wisdom comes from Baltes, P. F., & Staudinger, U. M. (1993). The search for the psychology of wisdom. *Current Directions in Psychological Science, 2,* 75–80.

15. This is not a new idea. Lao Tsu, the famous Chinese philosopher who lived in the sixth century BCE, believed that humility was essential to wisdom [Grigg, R. (1995). *The new Lao Tsu.* Boston: Tuttle].

Giving Consideration to Cognitive Training

16. Retrieved May 3, 2010, using the terms "cognitive training and aging."

17. These commercial Web sites (reflecting order of appearance of the statements), from which the statements were selected and edited slightly, were accessed August 11, 2010: http://mindsparkebrainfitnesspro.com/?gclid=CJCGqri0pZkCFQJvswodGjRhqQ; http://www.24-7pressrelease.com/press-release/new-study-reveals-happyneuron-online-cognitive-training-exercises-improve-brain-performance-84239.php; http://www.lumosity.com/blog/cognitive-training-and-aging/.

18. Much of the research cited in support of these extravagant claims is based on studies of lab animals raised in enriched environments; the brains of these animals grew larger compared to those of littermates raised in stimuli-deprived cages. The assumption is that these results will generalize to humans. It may also be that normal scientific caution is being compromised by the growing demand for brain fitness merchandise. In the United States alone, consumers will spend close to $100 million this year on these products. The clearest statement I have read about the limitations of the brain fitness assertions is contained

in Aamodt, S., & Wang, S. (2008). *Welcome to your brain: Why you lose your car keys but never forget how to drive and other puzzles of everyday life.* New York: Bloomsbury USA.

19. Johns Hopkins group: Rebok, G. W., Carlson, M. C., & Langbaum, J. B. S. (2007). Training and maintaining memory abilities in healthy older adults: Traditional and novel approaches. *Journal of Gerontology: Psychological Sciences, 62B,* 53–61.

20. Two meta-analyses found significant training effects on test scores: Verhaeghen, P., Marcoen, A., & Goossens, L. (1992). Improving memory performance in the aged through mnemonic training: A meta-analytic study. *Psychology and Aging, 7,* 242–251; and Floyd, M., & Scogin, F. (1997). Effects of memory training on the subjective memory functioning and mental health of older adults: A meta-analysis. *Psychology and Aging, 12,* 150–161.

21. ACTIVE study subjects, averaging nearly 74 years of age, were 2,832 women and men (aged 65–94) who took 10 sessions of cognitive training in six different U.S. centers. Subjects were randomly assigned to one of three abilities that are highly vulnerable to the aging process: processing speed, reasoning, and memory. A fourth group constituted a no-treatment control group. Memory-training techniques included learning mnemonic strategies such as clustering, cued recall, and the method of loci. Before the training began, aptitude tests were administered to all subjects [Ball, K., Berch, D. B., Helmers, K. F., Jobe, J. B., Leveck, M. D., Marsiske, M., et al. for the ACTIVE Study Group. (2002). Effects of cognitive training interventions with older adults: A randomized controlled trial. *Journal of the American Medical Association, 288,* 2271–2281].

22. Improvement was judged by a ≥1 standard error of the mean gain in test scores. These percentages are averages of the immediate posttest and the 1-year follow-up. At 2 years, the differences narrowed but still were statistically significant: for processing speed: trained 73%, controls 37%; for reasoning: trained 53%, controls 35%; for memory: trained 40%, controls 29%.

23. These findings have been verified by many other investigators: *Reasoning:* Boron, J. B., Turiano, N. A., Willis, S. L., & Schaie, K. W. (2007). Effects of cognitive training on change in accuracy in inductive reasoning ability. *Journal of Gerontology: Psychological Sciences, 62B,* 179–186; *Visuospatial:* Baltes, P. B., Dittmann-Kohli, F., & Kliegl, R. (1986). Reserve capacity of the elderly in aging-sensitive tests of fluid intelligence: Replication and extension. *Psychology and Aging, 1,* 172–177. *Working memory:* Jaeggi, S. M., Buschkuehl, M., Jonides, J., & Perrig, W. J. (2008). Improving fluid intelligence with training on working memory. *Proceedings of the National Academy of Sciences of the United States of America, 105,* 6829–6833. *Verbal memory:* Mahncke, H. W., Connor, B. B., Appelman, J., Ahsanuddin, O. N., Hardy, J. L., Wood, R. A., et al. (2006). Memory enhancement in healthy older adults using a brain plasticity-based training program: A randomized, controlled study. *Proceedings of the National Academy of Sciences of the United States of America, 103,* 12523–12528.

24. Among those who first discovered that abilities not selected for training failed to improve were Rebok, G. W., & Balcerak, L. J. (1989). Memory self-efficacy and performance difference in old and young adults: The effect of mnemonic training. *Journal of Developmental Psychology, 25,* 714–721; and Schaie, K. W., Willis, S. L., Hertzog, C., & Schulenberg, J. E. (1987). Effects of cognitive training on primary mental ability structure. *Psychology and Aging, 2,* 233–242.

25. Cognitive placebo effects in analogous research have been most often general rather than specific. To my knowledge, none of the authors of the cognitive training reports

has specified exactly what was said to the subjects before the research started with respect to the goals of the project. For example, were the ACTIVE subjects told that training would improve their processing speed and not their memory? Were the German women told that the study was about the effect of multivitamins on their memory? Since no instructions were reported, the assumption is that subjects were not told which abilities would be influenced by the training. In nearly all cases, the improvement in the placebo groups was global. Examples are Wolters, M., Hickstein, M., Flintermann, A., Tewes, U., & Hahn, A. (2005). Cognitive performance in relation to vitamin status in healthy elderly German women—the effect of 6-month multivitamin supplementation. *Preventive Medicine, 41,* 253–259; and Crews, W. D., Jr., Harrison, D. W., Griffin, M. L., Addison, K., Yount, A. M., Giovenco, M. A., et al. (2005). A double-blinded, placebo-controlled, randomized trial of the neuropsychologic efficacy of cranberry juice in a sample of cognitively intact older adults: Pilot study findings. *Journal of Alternative and Complementary Medicine, 11,* 305–309; also, Bardwell, W. A., Ancoli-Israel, S., Berry, C. C., & Dimsdale, J. E. (2001). Neuropsychological effects of 1-week continuous positive airway pressure treatment in patients with obstructive sleep apnea: A placebo-controlled study. *Psychosomatic Medicine, 63,* 579–584.

26. Follow-up studies of other memory improvement programs 6 months to 5 years after training reported that the gains were still apparent. Follow-ups summarized in Rebok et al., 2007.

27. Experts involved in cognitive training have puzzled over why the improved test scores do not generalize to real life. A number of possible technical explanations include selecting healthy and well-educated subjects who were already performing well on the functional aspects of everyday life, leaving little room for improvement on tests of everyday activities; practice effects that raised the scores of control subjects on functional activities of everyday life; and inadequate length of follow-up (Rebok et al., 2007).

28. University of Michigan researchers were Lustig, C., & Flegal, K. E. (2008). Targeting latent function: Encouraging effective encoding for successful memory training and transfer. *Psychology and Aging, 23,* 754–764.

29. The training was rigorous considering the age of the subjects—30 weekly meetings of 135 minutes each. A limitation of this study is that because of the advanced age of subjects, only 57.9% who completed the training were available for follow-up [Oswald, W. D., Gunzelmann, T., Rupprecht, R., & Hagen, B. (2006). Differential effects of single versus combined cognitive and physical training with older adults: The SimA study in a 5-year perspective. *European Journal of Ageing, 3,* 179–192].

30. Research by Mate-Kole, C. C., Fellows, R. P., Said, P. C., Mcdougal, J., Catayong, K., Dang, V., et al. (2007). Use of computer assisted and interactive cognitive training programmes with moderate to severely demented individuals: A preliminary study. *Aging and Mental Health, 11,* 485–495.

Engaging in Attention Restoration Activities

31. The research by University of Michigan psychologists Stephen and Rachael Kaplan and their colleagues has established a theoretical and empirical foundation for attention

restoration theory [Kaplan, S. (1995). The restorative benefit of nature: Toward an integrative framework. *Journal of Environmental Psychology, 15,* 169–182]. A readable brief history of the benefit of exposure to nature to health, emotional control, and attention is contained in Jaffe, E. (2010). This side of paradise: Discovering why the human mind needs nature. *APS Observer, 23,* 10–15.

32. James, W. (1962). *Psychology: Briefer course* (paperback edition; pp. 230–237). New York: Collier-Macmillan. (Original work published 1892.) This comparison of passive/involuntary attention with active/voluntary attention captures their essential differences.

33. Subjects were University of Michigan students, 38 in the first study and 12 in the second. The walks took between 50 and 55 minutes. The cognitive test was backward digit span, which measures attention and working memory [Berman, M. G., Jonides, J., & Kaplan, S. (2008). The cognitive benefits of interacting with nature. *Psychological Science, 19,* 1207–1212].

34. Students were from the University of California at Irvine: Hartig, T., Evans, G. W., Jamner, L. D., Davis, D. S., & Garling, T. (2003). Tracking restoration in natural and urban field settings. *Journal of Environmental Psychology, 23,* 109–123; also the University of Padova in Italy: Berto, R. (2005). Exposure to restorative environments helps restore attentional capacity. *Journal of Environmental Psychology, 25,* 249–259.

35. Harvard Medical School study by Naghshineh, S., Hafler, J. P., Miller, A. R., Blanco, M. A., Lipsitz, S. R., Dubroff, R. P., et al. (2008). Formal art observation training improves medical students' visual diagnostic skills. *Journal of General Internal Medicine, 23,* 991–997. A limitation of this research is that it is not clear what the individual and joint contributions of the observational exercises and the didactic sessions were to the students' improved observational skills.

36. *Yale:* Dolev, J. C., Friedlaender, L. K., & Braverman, I. M. (2001). Use of fine art to enhance visual diagnostic skills. *Journal of the American Medical Association, 286,* 1020–1021. *University of London:* Kirklin, D., Duncan, J., McBride, S., Hunt, S., & Griffin, M. (2007). A cluster design controlled trial of arts-based observational skills training in primary care. *Medical Education, 41,* 395–401. *Other medical schools* were University of California at Irvine [Shapiro, J., Rucker, L., & Beck, J. (2006). Training the clinical eye and mind: Using the arts to develop medical students' observational and pattern recognition skills. *Medical Education, 40,* 263–268] and *University of Cincinnati* [Elder, N. C., Tobias, B., Lucero-Criswell, A., & Goldenhar, L. (2006). The art of observation: Impact of a family medicine and art museum partnership on student education. *Family Medicine, 38,* 393–398]. Still other programs have given medical students exposure to drawing, dance, and writing with similarly positive results.

37. The quotations about the impact of the art appreciation classes were from University of Cincinnati medical students (Elder et al., 2006).

38. As these articles have found, many different settings have attention restorative powers. A limitation of this research is that they did not include direct measures of attention or other mental skills. All demonstrated positive restorative effects on mood or stress level, which are linked to cognitive function [Korpela, K. M., Ylen, M., Tyrvainen, L., & Silvennoinen, H. (2008). Determinants of restorative experiences in everyday favorite places. *Health and Place, 14,* 636–652; Ouellette, P., Kaplan, R., & Kaplan, S. (2005). The monastery as a restorative environment. *Journal of Environmental Psychology, 25,* 175–188; Scopelliti, M., & Giuliania, M. V. (2004). Choosing restorative environments

across the lifespan: A matter of place experience. *Journal of Environmental Psychology, 24,* 423–437; Korpela, K. M., Hartig, T., Kaiser, F. G., & Fuhrer, U. (2001). Restorative experience and self regulation in favorite places. *Environment and Behavior, 33,* 572–589; and Kaplan, S., Bardwell, L. V., & Slakter, D. B. (1993). The museum as a restorative environment. *Environment and Behavior, 25,* 725–742].

39. Kaplan's theoretical model of attention restoration theory has four components that contribute to the restorative experience: *fascination*, which can be "soft" (gazing at a sunset) or "hard" (watching a cluster of speeding cars jockeying for position at a NASCAR race); a sense of *being away* (a setting that is physically or conceptually different from the usual environment that demands effortful concentration); *extent* (a setting sufficiently rich and complex to engage the mind and promote reflection); *compatibility* (a match between our tastes and capabilities and the kinds of activities available in the surrounding environment) (Kaplan, 1995).

40. To Kaplan's list, I have added two components that are characteristic of recreation—a synonym for restoration: nonobligation and freedom from the requirement of doing well [Powell, D. H. (1983). *Understanding human adjustment: Normal adaptation through the life cycle.* Boston: Little, Brown]. Since *extent* has not had consistent support in surveys about characteristics of the restoration experience, this variable is not included in the delineation of attention restoration activities (Korpela et al., 2008; Scopelliti & Giuliania, 2004).

41. Subjects were drawn from four centers across the United States and averaged 74.8 years of age. Cognitive tests were an abbreviated MMSE (Mini-Mental State Exam) and Trails B. Another explanation for the lower scorers' preference for shopping malls and indoor gyms may be that they were in slightly poorer health and had a greater fear of falling [Prohaska, T. R., Eisenstein, A. R., Satariano, W. A., Hunter, R., Bayles, C. M., Kurtovich, E., et al. (2009). Walking and the preservation of cognitive function in older populations. *The Gerontologist, 49,* (Suppl. 1), S86–S93].

42. Those elements of attention restoration that have received the most validation have been the compatibility between the restoration activity and a person's interests and the feeling of being away from the world of directed attention. Also, there is a dose-response relationship between the amount of mental fatigue and how often people engage in attention restoration experiences. The benefits of restorative activities grow with more frequent practice. Examples of research in these areas are Korpela et al., 2008; and Hartig, T., & Staats, H. (2006). The need for psychological restoration as a determinant of environmental preferences. *Journal of Environmental Psychology, 26,* 215–226; and Ouellette et al., 2005.

Reflections and Applications

43. Two articles that point to the correlation between an engaged and stimulation-rich lifestyle are Hultsch, D. F., Hertzog, C., Small, B. J., & Dixon, R. A. (1999). Use it or lose it: Engaged lifestyle as a buffer of cognitive decline in aging? *Psychology and Aging, 14,* 245–263; and Schaie, K. W. (1993). The Seattle longitudinal studies of adult intelligence. *Current Directions in Psychological Science, 2,* 171–175.

44. From Salthouse, 2006.

45. Ulrich, R. S. (1984). View through a window may influence recovery from surgery. *Science, 224*, 420–421.
46. Korpela et al., 2008.
47. Daffner, K. R., Chong, H., Riis, J., Rents, D. M., Wolk, D. A., Budson, A. E., et al. (2007). Cognitive status impacts age-related changes in attention to novel and target events in normal adults. *Neuropsychology, 21*, 291–300.
48. Example from Samet, E. D. (2007). *Soldier's heart: Reading literature through peace and war at West Point.* New York: Farrar, Straus and Giroux, p. 71.

Chapter 6

1. Amazon.com listed 2,080 books on optimal aging, including "optimal aging" (33); "successful aging" (165); "aging well" (652); and "healthy aging" (1230). The total number overstates the actual figures because many books are listed in multiple categories. A Google search retrieved a total of 117,181,000 sites for these terms, distributed approximately in the same proportions as Amazon.com listings (retrieved May 4, 2010).
2. My personal exemplar of an optimal cognitive ager is Stephen Hawking, professor of mathematics at the University of Cambridge in the United Kingdom. Known for his contributions to the fields of cosmology and quantum gravity, especially in the context of black holes, he has written science bestsellers *A Brief History of Time* and *The Universe in a Nutshell.* Hawking was 65 when he gave the opening address at the 2006 annual meeting of the Chinese Academy of Arts and Sciences in Beijing, though he was disabled by amyotrophic lateral sclerosis (ALS), known in the United States as Lou Gehrig's disease. Almost completely paralyzed and unable to speak, he addressed the audience from his wheelchair with the aid of a computerized voice synthesizer driven by an infrared device that tracked his eye movements (from "Hawking Takes Beijing: Now Will Science Follow?" by Dennis Overbye, *The New York Times,* June 20, 2006).
3. Healthy lifestyle habits include eating sensibly, exercising regularly, maintaining active social networks, and minimizing stress. To this list, the Mayo team adds intellectual stimulation. Among medical conditions with cognitive comorbidities are hypertension, diabetes, hyperlipidemia, and sleep disorders. The Mayo clinic doctors note that these are "possible" strategies because most have yet to be verified by empirical study. [Fillit, H. M., Butler, R. N., O'Connell, A. W., Albert, M. S., Birren, J. E., Codman, C. W., et al. (2002). Achieving and maintaining cognitive vitality with aging. *Mayo Clinic Proceedings, 77,* 681–696].
4. Although they used slightly different terms to describe their successfully aging older adults, subjects on the high end of their continua shared many characteristics with optimal cognitive agers. In a cross-sectional study in Finland, 28% of participants were in the top group ("Cluster 1") on the basis of health, activity level, and cognitive test scores [Ylikoski, R., Ylikoski, A., Keskivaara, P., Tilvis, R., Sulkava, R., & Erkinjuntti, T. (1999). Heterogeneity of cognitive profiles in aging: Successful aging, normal aging, and individuals at-risk for cognitive decline. *European Journal of Neurology, 6,* 645–652]. Two longitudinal studies of subjects drawn from the Health, Aging, and Body Composition (Health, ABC) study, a prospective investigation of community-dwelling older adults living in four different U.S. geographical regions, were carried out to examine the impact

of certain risk factors on their level of cognition as they grew older. Follow-up of subjects in their early 70s at baseline divided 9,704 primarily White women being followed for osteoporosis into three groups on the basis of whether they maintained their level of baseline cognitive function. The "no decline" group was comparable to optimal cognitive agers [Barnes, D. E., Cauley, J. A., Lui, L. Y., Fink, H. A., McCulloch, C., Stone, K. L., et al. (2007). Women who maintain optimal cognitive function into old age. *Journal of the American Geriatrics Society, 55,* 259–264]. Surviving subjects averaged 72 at baseline and 85 at follow-up, 9% of whom could be classified as optimal agers on the basis of follow-up test scores. The second U.S. study followed 2,509 Black and White elders from the Pittsburgh, Pennsylvania, area, age 73 at baseline, for 8 years. At follow-up, the scores of 30% of the subjects qualified them as optimal agers [Yaffe, S. K., Fiocco, A. J., Lindquist, K., Vittinghoff, E., Simonsick, E. M., Newman A. B., et al. for the Health ABC Study. (2009). Predictors of maintaining cognitive function in older adults: The Health ABC Study. *Neurology, 72,* 2029–2035]. A longitudinal study of older Finnish adults classified the agers as "positive" [Uotinen, V., Suutama, Y., & Ruoppila, I. (2003). Age identification in the framework of successful aging: A study of older Finnish people. *International Journal of Aging and Human Development, 56,* 173–195]. Berkman and colleagues investigated differences in high, usual, and impaired functioning among subjects and classified 32.6% in the "high" category [Berkman, L. F., Seeman, T. E., Albert, M., Blazer, D., Kahn, R., Moths, R., et al. (1993). High, usual and impaired functioning in community-dwelling older men and women: Findings from the MacArthur Foundation Research Network on Successful Aging. *Journal of Clinical Epidemiology, 46,* 1129–I140].

Who Are the Optimal Cognitive Agers?

5. American Psychiatric Association. (2000). *Diagnostic and statistical manual of mental disorders* (4th ed., text revision). Washington, DC: Author.
6. Little problem occurred with rating the optimal cognitive agers. Classification was apparent in 93% of the cases. Few of the subjects interviewed met all the criteria, but most had seven or eight of the health-related characteristics and attitudes/behaviors linked to optimal cognitive aging.

Health-Related Qualities Associated With Optimal Cognitive Aging

7. Characteristics in bold print were exhibited by at least 67% of the subjects. Those in regular font were manifested by 33 to 66% of the optimal cognitive agers interviewed.
8. A Baylor Medical School research team compared the cerebral blood flow of active and sedentary retirees. The active women and men with greater cerebral perfusion were over three times more vigorous than the sedentary subjects [Rogers, R. L., Meyer, J. S., & Mortal, K. F. (1990). After reaching retirement age, physical activity sustains cerebral perfusion and cognition. *Journal of the American Geriatric Society, 38,* 123–128]. Two other reports based on thousands of subjects aged 70–80 across the country told the same story [Wessel, T. R., Arant, C. B., Olson, M. B., Johnson, D., Reis, S. D. E., Sharaf, B. L., et al. (2004). Relationship of physical fitness vs. body mass index with coronary artery disease

and cardiovascular events in women. *Journal of the American Medical Association, 292,* 1179–1187; also Yaffe, K., Barnes, D., Nevitt, M., Lui, L.-Y., & Covinsky, K. (2001). A prospective study of physical activity and cognitive decline in elderly women: Women who walk. *Archives of Internal Medicine, 161,* 1703–1708].

9. A study of the relationship between self-rated health and medical and functional ratings of health in six developed European countries found a strong correlation in most areas [see Bardage, C., Pluijm, S. M. E., Pedersen, N. L., Deeg, D. G. H., Jylha, M., Noale, M., et al. (2005). Self-rated health among older adults: A cross-national comparison. *European Journal of Ageing, 2,* 149–158.

10. In contrast to only 34.7% of normal agers, 95.2% of optimal agers said they had no medical problems, and that their functional health was good or very good. Also, 68.1% reported feeling younger than their chronological age, while only 34.9% of normal agers responded similarly (Uotinen et al., 2003).

11. National prevention guidelines do not recommend the annual physical exam for asymptomatic adults [U.S. Preventive Services Task Force (1996). *Guide to clinical preventive services: Report of the Preventive Services Task Force* (2nd ed.). Baltimore, MD: Williams & Wilkins]. A strong argument for the preventive and educational value of the annual physical is presented in an article representing the views of the American Cancer Society, the American Diabetes Association, and the American Heart Association [Eyre, H., Kahn, R., Robertson, R. M., Clark, N. G., Doyle, C., Hong, Y., et al. (2004). Preventing cancer, cardiovascular disease and diabetes: A common agenda for the American Cancer Society, the American Diabetes Association, and the American Heart Association. *Diabetes Care, 27,* 1812–1824]. Others stress the value of the annual physical from the point of view of health-related quality of life counseling and fostering the doctor patient relationship; for example, a study of over 1,000 patients at the Gunderson Medical Foundation clinic in La Crosse, Wisconsin, found that patients who were overweight, obese, smoked, or had excess stress were more likely to expect discussions with their health care provider about these problems than lower-risk patients. Obese and overweight patients were more likely to report being motivated to maintain or lose weight as a result [Stork, L. J., & Rooney, B. L. (2001). Health behavior counseling at annual exams. *Wisconsin Medical Journal, 100,* 29–32].

12. The value to the mind and body of compliance with prescribed medication for hypertension has been demonstrated many times. Two examples are Hajjar, I., Catoe, H., Sixta, S., Boland, R., Johnson, D., Hirth, V., et al. (2005). Cross-sectional and longitudinal association between antihypertensive medications and cognitive impairment in an elderly population. *Journal of Gerontology A: Biological Sciences Medical Sciences, 60,* 67–73; and Murray, M. D., Lane, K. A., Gao, S., Evans, R. M., Unverzagt, F. W., Hall, K. S., et al. (2002). Preservation of cognitive function with antihypertensive medications: A longitudinal analysis of a community-based sample of African Americans. *Archives of Internal Medicine, 162,* 2090–2096.

13. A Finnish study that evaluated 224 older adults similar to optimal agers found that after 8 years subjects retained high scores on scales measuring "zest for life" and "meaning in life." In 1988, there were 93.8% who said that their zest for life had not decreased, and 79.3% said that their life had meaning. Among remaining subjects 8 years later, zest for life rose slightly to 96.2% and finding meaning in life dropped fractionally to 78.5% (Uotinen et al., 2003).

14. Examining data collected over 18 years from the Ohio Longitudinal Study of Aging and Retirement, psychologists found that subjects with more positive self-perceptions of aging at baseline (average age 65) were in better functional health at follow-up than those with more negative self-perceptions [Levy, B. R., Slade, M. D., & Kasl, S. (2002). Longitudinal benefit of positive self-perceptions of aging on functional health. *Journal of Gerontology: Psychological Sciences, 57B,* 409–417.

15. In a 2001–2005 Behavioral Risk Factor Surveillance System (BRFSS) survey, the average number of mentally unhealthy days per month by age group were 3.1 for those 55–64, 2.0 for those 65–74, and 1.9 for those 75+. The BRFSS is the largest telephone health survey in the world. The Centers for Disease Control and Prevention (CDC) Web site provides more information about it (retrieved August 11, 2010, from http://www.cdc.gov/brfss/about.htm).

16. Until very recently, self-appraisal has been generally neglected in aging research. This neglect is rather striking considering that problem-solving self-appraisal has been extensively studied and been associated with positive health-related outcomes [see Hanson, K. M., & Mints, L. B. (1997). Psychological health and problem-solving self-appraisal in older adults. *Journal of Counseling Psychology, 44,* 433–441.

17. See Berkman et al., 1993.

18. Systolic blood pressure, diastolic blood pressure, mean arterial pressure, and heart rate for a group of volunteers were recorded every half hour during the day and hourly at night. Analyses revealed that lower systolic and diastolic blood pressure and mean arterial pressure were related to giving social support. Correlational analyses revealed that participants with a higher tendency to give social support also received greater social support, had greater feelings of self-efficacy and self-esteem, and reported less stress and depression than those with a lower tendency to give social support to others. A limitation of this study is that it was based on college students [Piferi, R. L., & Lawler, K. A. (2006). Social support and ambulatory blood pressure: An examination of both receiving and giving. *International Journal of Psychophysiology, 62,* 328–336].

19. Studies in which older and younger subjects were judged positively or negatively found that the more youthful-appearing women and men were rated as more appealing than their elders. However, these differences were minimized when the comparison was made in a work environment [Kite, M. E., & Johnson, B. T. (1988). Attitudes toward older and younger adults: A meta-analysis. *Psychology and Aging, 3,* 233–244].

20. Not long ago, people who wanted plastic surgery to improve their appearance were viewed as more anxious and depressed and having poorer self-esteem, body image, and interpersonal functioning than matched controls who did not opt for cosmetic procedures [Guthrie, E., Bradbury, E., Davenport, P., & Faria, F. S. (1998). Psychosocial status of women requesting breast reduction surgery as compared with a control group of large-breasted women. *Journal of Psychosomatic Research, 45,* 331–339]. Studies in the first decade of the third millennium, however, found a more accepting attitude about cosmetic interventions. Women 50–70 were interviewed in depth about their opinion on the use of cosmetic activities to improve their appearance as they grew older. Although many articulated the importance of retaining a "natural look," almost all engaged in some means to enhance their attractiveness. While some women argued for an acceptance of the physical realities of growing older, others asserted that an aged appearance should be resisted using whatever "interventions were required and available" [from Clarke, L. H., & Griffin, M. (2007). The body natural and the body unnatural: Beauty work and aging. *Journal of Aging Studies, 21,* 187–201].

Attitudes and Behaviors Associated With Optimal Cognitive Aging

21. The General Motors Institute is now Kettering University in Flint, Michigan.
22. In a Finnish study (Uotinen et al., 2003), 64.8% of those subjects equivalent to optimal agers rated their cognitive capacity as "better than satisfactory."
23. Finnish optimal agers (67.9%) felt "younger mentally" than their contemporaries (Uotinen et al., 2003). Also, results from cross-sectional (Ylikoski et al., 1999) and longitudinal (Berkman et al., 1993) research found that subgroups similar to optimal cognitive agers significantly outscored normal and high-risk subjects on a wide range of cognitive tests.
24. Benign lapses in concentration are common among older adults without objective memory decline [Cargin, J. W., Colie, C. A., Masters, C., & Maruff, P. (2008). The nature of cognitive complaints in healthy older adults with and without objective memory decline. *Journal of Clinical and Experimental Neuropsychology, 30*, 1–13]. Research on word retrieval and tip-of-the-tongue blockages has typically found that 3rd Agers do not recall as well as young and middle-aged adults [Ross, T. P., Lichtenberg, P. A., & Christensen, B. K. (1995). Normative data on the Boston Naming Test for elderly adults in a demographically diverse medical sample. *The Clinical Neuropsychologist, 9,* 321–325]. Given sufficient time, both types of memory problems usually resolve in the oldest subjects [Heine, M. K., Ober, B. A., & Shenaut, G. K. (1999). Naturally occurring and experimentally induced tip-of-the-tongue experiences in three adult age groups. *Psychology and Aging, 14,* 445–457].
25. The point on which both cross-sectional and longitudinal investigators agree is that social isolation puts older adults at risk for greater cognitive decline. An example of the differences in the results produced by cross-sectional and longitudinal studies on the cognitive impact of social isolation is contained in a report by a Johns Hopkins research team [Green, A. F., Rebok, G., & Lyketsos, C. G. (2008). Influence of social network characteristics on cognition and functional status with aging. *International Journal of Geriatric Psychiatry, 23,* 972–978].
26. Edinburgh researchers were Gow, A. J., Pattie, A., Whiteman, M. C., Whalley, L. J., & Deary, I. J. (2007). Social support and successful aging: Investigating the relationships between lifetime cognitive change and life satisfaction. *Journal of Individual Differences, 28,* 103–115.
27. Karen Allen and her colleagues have published several papers on the value of pets to health [see Allen, K., Blascovitch, J., & Mendes, W. B. (2002). Cardiovascular reactivity and the presence of pets, friends, and spouses: The truth about cats and dogs. *Psychosomatic Medicine, 64,* 727–739; also Allen, K., Shykoff, B. E., & Izzo, J. L., Jr. (2001). Pet ownership, but not ACE inhibitor therapy, blunts home blood pressure responses to mental stress. *Hypertension, 38,* 815–820].
28. Growing numbers of seniors operate computers and use the Internet, but the overall percentage is modest. A turn-of-the-century report estimated computer and Internet use at 25 and 8.9%, respectively for nondisabled adults over 65 [Kaye, H. S. (2000). *Computer and Internet use among people with disabilities* (Disability Statistics Report 13). Washington, DC: U.S. Department of Education, National Institute on Disability and Rehabilitation Research]. A later report found that one third of older adults used computers in a retirement community [Carpenter, B. D., & Buday, S. (2007). Computer use among older adults in a naturally occurring retirement community. *Computers in*

Human Behavior, 23, 3012–3024]. A significant number of older adults stop using the computer and Internet. Barriers to continued usage were described as frustration because of complexity and difficulty in operation, changing technology, growing mental and physical limitations, and disinterest [Gatto, S. L., & Tak, S. H. (2008). Computer, Internet, and e-mail use among older adults: Benefits and barriers. *Educational Gerontology, 34,* 800–811].

29. Despite frequent claims about the value of mental exercise, its intuitive plausibility, and a strong desire to believe that it is true, a careful review of empirical studies published in the past five decades found little scientific evidence that mentally stimulating activities alter the rate of cognitive decline [Salthouse, T. A. (2006). Mental exercise and mental aging: Evaluating the validity of the "use it or lose it" hypothesis. *Perspectives on Psychological Science, 1,* 68–87].

30. See Baltes, P. B. (1997). On the incomplete architecture of human ontogeny: Selection, optimization, and compensation as foundations of developmental theory. *American Psychologist, 52,* 366–380; and Baltes, P. B., & Baltes, M. M. (1990). Psychological perspectives on successful aging: The model of selective optimization with compensation. In P. B. Baltes & M. M. Baltes (Eds.), *Successful aging: Perspectives from the behavioral sciences* (pp. 1–34). New York: Cambridge University Press.

31. Research on openness to experience having a positive effect on cognition among older adults by Zimprich, D., Allemand, M., & Dellenbach, M. (2009). Openness to experience, fluid intelligence, and crystallized intelligence in middle-aged and old adults. *Journal of Research in Personality, 43,* 444–454. Differences in the length of time viewing stimuli occurred only among older subjects with superior IQs, compared with 3rd Agers with lower IQs. No differences were found with the target stimuli in these IQ groups among middle-aged and young adults [Daffner, K. R., Chong, H., Riis, J., Rentz, D. M., Wolk, D. A., Budson, A. E., et al. Cognitive status impacts age-related changes in attention to novel and target events in normal adults. *Neuropsychology, 21,* 291–300].

32. A sense of control is a correlate of subjective well-being in the face of declining health and other losses in later life [Lachman, M. E., Röcke, C., & Rosnick, C. B. (2009). The rise and fall of control beliefs and life satisfaction in adulthood: Trajectories of stability and change over ten years. In H. B. Bosworth & C. Hertzog (Eds.), *Aging and cognition: Research methodologies and empirical advances* (pp. 143–160). Washington, DC: American Psychological Association]. In a cross-sectional study of younger, middle-aged, and older (60–75) subjects, there was a significant relationship between control beliefs and cognitive performance in later life [Miller, L. M. S., & Lachman, M. E. (1999). The sense of control and cognitive aging: Toward a model of mediational processes. In T. M. Hess & F. Blanchard-Fields (Eds.). *Social cognition and aging* (pp. 17–41). New York: Academic Press. Research on the relation of a sense of competence or self-efficacy to higher mental ability typically has found that a higher mental ability influences a sense of competence. A classic study is Lachman, M. E. (1983). Perceptions of intellectual aging: Antecedent or consequence of intellectual functioning? *Developmental Psychology, 19,* 482–498. Similar findings were published half a world away 25 years later [Windsor, T. D., & Anstey, K. J. (2008). A longitudinal investigation of perceived control and cognitive performance in young, midlife and older adults. *Neuropsychology, Development, and Cognition, Section B: Aging, Neuropsychology, and Cognition, 15,* 744–763]. The relation between feelings of being useful to others and morbidity and mortality has been reported by MacArthur Study researchers. They found that adults 70–79 who rarely or

never felt useful to others had more illness and higher death rates over a 3-year period than those who felt useful, even when controlled for demographic, health status, behavioral, and psychosocial factors [Gruenewald, T. L., Karlamangla, A. S., Greendale, G. A., Singer, B. H., & Seeman, T. E. (2009). Increased mortality risk in older adults with persistently low or declining feelings of usefulness to others. *Journal of Aging and Health, 21,* 398–425].

Reflections and Applications

33. Pioneer cognitive aging researcher and Georgia Tech professor Christopher Hertzog put it this way: "The enduring challenge for the field is to gain an understanding of who ages successfully and who does not" [Hertzog, C. (2006). Tireless in Seattle: The continuing contributions of the Seattle Longitudinal Study to our understanding of adult intellectual development. *PsycCRITIQUES, 51*(1), 15540138, 20060101.

34. *San Francisco researchers*: Weekly activities of subjects were converted to kilocalories, and the sum was divided by the number of calories required to walk a city block. The researchers discovered that the top 25% of these women averaged walking the equivalent of 175 blocks per week. The females in the next two lower quartiles—the 25% just above and below the middle of the pack—averaged 77 and 28 blocks, respectively (Yaffe et al., 2001). Studies elsewhere produced similar findings. For nearly 4 years, University of Florida scientists followed 936 women in their late 50s who had a clinically indicated angiography. Those who exercised most had fewer medical problems during follow-up. The strenuous exercisers, as defined by MET (metabolic equivalent) activities, exceeded the lowest group by 332% (Wessel et al., 2004). Top-rated older subjects in Boston; New Haven, Connecticut; and Durham, North Carolina, engaged in more than twice the amount of strenuous exercise per year than did the middle group (116 hours vs. 52.3; Berkman et al., 1993).

35. MacArthur studies: Berkman et al., 1993; Daffner et al., 2007.

36. Barnes et al., 2007.

37. Wolfe, T. (1998). *A man in full.* New York: Farrar, Straus Giroux, p. 157.

Chapter 7

1. On January 3, 2011, PubMedCentral, which is the National Library of Medicine's digital archive of biomedical and life sciences literature, found 53 citations for "normal cognitive aging" AND "humans." For the "optimal cognitive aging" and "at risk cognitive aging" AND "humans" the number of references were 1455 and 4659, respectively.

2. This example of the difficulty even experts in the field have defining normal cognitive aging was taken from an excellent clinical summary by Australian neuroscientists Karen Anstey and Lee-Fay Low about normal cognitive changes in later adulthood, modifiable risk factors, and differentiating normal subjects from individuals with dementia [Anstey, K. J., & Low, L.-F. (2004). Normal cognitive changes in aging. *Australian Family Physician, 33,* 783–787].

3. For example, in one study normal agers were those who did not meet the four criteria for mild cognitive impairment [Geda, Y. E., Roberts, R. O., Knopman, D. S., Petersen, R. C., Christianson, T. J., Pankratz, V. S., et al. (2008). Prevalence of neuropsychiatric symptoms in mild cognitive impairment and normal cognitive aging: Population-based study. *Archives of General Psychiatry, 65,* 1193–1198]. Another term is "minor decliners." Over an 8-year period, subjects with a predicted decline in 3MS (Modified Mini-Mental State Examination) scores of less than −1 standard deviation below the mean of 2,509 subjects were classified as minor decliners [Yaffe, S. K., Fiocco, A. J., Lindquist, K., Vittinghoff, E., Simonsick, E. M., Newman A. B., et al. for the Health ABC Study. (2009). Predictors of maintaining cognitive function in older adults: The Health ABC Study. *Neurology, 72,* 2029–2035]. A study led by Deborah Barnes used the same term, defining it as those subjects falling in the middle tertile on the basis of cognitive test scores [Barnes, D. E., Cauley, J. A., Lui, L. Y., Fink, H. A., McCulloch, C., Stone, K. L., et al. (2007). Women who maintain optimal cognitive function into old age. *Journal of the American Geriatrics Society, 55,* 259–264]. A longitudinal study of older Finnish adults classified successful agers as "positive," impaired subjects as "negative," and the remainder as "others" [Uotinen, V., Suutama. Y., & Ruoppila, I. (2003). Age identification in the framework of successful aging: A study of older Finnish people. *International Journal of Aging and Human Development, 56,* 173–195].

4. The estimates for the percentage of subjects in other investigations who have qualities in common with the definition of normal cognitive agers given in this chapter are 53% (Yaffe et al., 2009); 58% (Barnes et al., 2007); 70% (Uotinen, 2003); and 62.5% [Ylikoski, R., Ylikoski, A., Keskivaara,P., Tilvis, R., Sulkava, R., & Erkinjuntti, T. (1999). Heterogeneity of cognitive profiles in aging: Successful aging, normal aging, and individuals at-risk for cognitive decline. *European Journal of Neurology, 6,* 645–652].

Who Is Normal?

5. American Psychiatric Association. (2000). *Diagnostic and statistical manual of mental disorders* (4th ed., text revision). Washington, DC: Author.

6. In about one third of the cases, there was enough overlap with an adjacent group so that these subjects were compared to both groups. Most often, the overlap was between normal and optimal agers. When this occurred, these subjects were scored and placement made on higher number of characteristics exhibited.

Health-Related Qualities Associated With Normal Cognitive Aging

7. See Note 8, Chapter 6.

8. Data from Uotinen et al., 2003. In the 1988 study group of 843 subjects, 65.3% said their functional capacity was the same or worse than their peers.

9. In 2006, there were 56.5% of Americans aged 65–74 who reported that they had not visited a primary care physician or specialist in the past 12 months. For those 75+, the figure was 61.8% [National Center for Health Statistics. (2010). *Health, United States, 2009: With special feature on medical technology.* Hyattsville, MD].

10. Data from the 2008 National Health and Interview Survey showed that 56% of those 65+ reported being diagnosed with two or more of six chronic medical conditions (diabetes, cardiovascular disease, chronic obstructive pulmonary disease, asthma, cancer, or arthritis). These occurred in 59.4% of females versus 51.4% for males [Center for Disease Control and Prevention. (2009). Percent of U.S. adults with chronic conditions. Atlanta, GA: Author. Retrieved August 11, 2010 from http://www.cdc.gov/nchs/health_policy/adult_chronic_conditions.htm].

11. A review by Anstey and Christensen summarized studies showing the adverse cognitive effects of several medical conditions, such as hypertension and diabetes [Anstey, K., & Christensen, H. (2000). Education, activity, health, blood pressure, apolipoprotein E as predictors of cognitive change in old age: A review. *Gerontology, 46*, 163–177].

12. In two longitudinal investigations, normal agers smoked, exercised less, and drank more than those aging optimally (Yaffe et al., 2009; Barnes et al., 2007).

13. Korean and Scandinavian researchers analyzed 7-year longitudinal data on the effect on mortality and morbidity of four risky lifestyle habits (smoking, drinking, being sedentary and obese) from Waves 1 and 4 of the U.S. Health and Retirement Survey. Complete data were available on 10,278 subjects, most of whom were in their 60s at Wave 4. Primary findings were that bad habits such as smoking, remaining obese, and exercising less than three times a week were individually associated with increasing the odds of a disability in activities of daily living from 42 to 68% for subjects in their 60s. In keeping with the results from other studies, moderate levels of alcohol consumption were associated with lower mortality and morbidity [Jung, S-H., Ostbye, T., & Park, K.-O. 2006). A longitudinal study of the relationship between health behavior risk factors and dependence in activities of daily living. *Journal of Preventive Medicine and Public Health, 39,* 221–228].

14. See Uotinen et al., 2003; of the 613 normal cognitive agers, 46.3% said that their health problems imposed limitations on hobbies and other activities.

15. Caregivers of patients with Alzheimer's disease are at particular risk. A research team at Pennsylvania State University looked at the impact of caring for loved ones with Alzheimer's disease and found that higher levels of both objective and subjective stressors were associated with poorer self-reported health, more negative health behaviors, and greater use of health care services [Son, J., Erno, A., Shea, D. G., Femia, E. E., Zarit, S. H., & Stephens, M. A. (2007). The caregiver stress process and health outcomes. *Journal of Aging and Health, 19,* 871–887]. In an Italian study of caregivers in the their mid-50s, 51% said that they were not getting enough sleep, and 55% reported worsening of health [Ferrara, M., Langiano, E., Di Brango, T., De Vito, E., Di Cioccio, L., et al. (2008). Prevalence of stress, anxiety and depression in Alzheimer caregivers. *Health and Quality of Life Outcomes, 6,* 93–97].

16. How caregivers reacted to stress greatly influenced the health consequences of caring for a loved one with dementia. Those who used emotion-based coping strategies were more negatively affected than those who employed problem-based solutions [Almberg, B., Grafstrom, M., & Winblad, B. (1997). Major strain and coping strategies as reported by family members who care for aged demented relatives. *Journal of Advanced Nursing, 26,* 683–691]. It is also true that the behaviors of some patients are more difficult to deal with than others. Those patient actions that raise the caretaker burden of stress include hallucinations, wandering off, abnormal behavior at night, and disruptive actions [Allegri, R. F., Sarasola, D., Serrano, C. M., Taragano, F. E., Arizaga, R. L., Butman, J., et al. (2006).

Neuropsychiatric symptoms as a predictor of caregiver burden in Alzheimer's disease. *Neuropsychiatric Disease and Treatment, 2,* 105–110].

17. Mean mentally unhealthy days (because of depression, stress, or emotional problems) averaged between two and three in the past decade according the Behavior Risk Factor Surveillance System interviews for the 65–74 age group. Females reported a slightly higher proportion—3.4 days to 2.6 for males [Centers for Disease Control and Prevention. Health related quality of life surveillance—United States, 1993–2002. In: *Surveillance summaries,* October 28, 2005. *MMWR* 2005:54(No. SS-4). http://www.cdc.gov/mmwr/ PDF/ss/ss5404.pdf. Retrieved August 11, 2010].

18. The percentage of mentally unhealthy days is greatly affected by income level and education. For example, the percentage of women and men 65–74 feeling serious psychological stress most or all of the time was 1.7% for those at 200% or more above the poverty level compared to 7.6% for those with incomes below it. Relative differences in depressive symptoms also occurred between those with less than a high school education, 12.8% of whom felt sad and 6.7% hopeless some of the time, compared with 5.1% and 2.8%, respectively, for those with a college degree [Pleis, J. R., Lucas, J. W., & Ward, B. W. (2009). Summary health statistics for U.S. adults: National Health Interview Survey, 2008. National Center for Health Statistics. *Vital Health Care Statistics,* Series 10, Number 242].

19. Studies of younger subjects reported that shame and guilt causes some who are obese to feel like failures, which lowers the likelihood of successful weight reduction [Conradt, M., Dierk, J-M., Schlumberger, P., Rauh, E., Hebebrand, J., & Rief, W. (2008). Who copes well? Obesity-related coping and its associations with shame, guilt, and weight loss. *Journal of Clinical Psychology, 64,* 1129–1144].

20. A subgroup of younger women saw exercise as a duty and associated exercise with feelings of guilt and inadequacy [Bulley, C., Donaghy, M., Pyne, A., & Mutrie, N. (2009). Personal meanings, values and feelings relating to physical activity and exercise participation in female undergraduates: A qualitative exploration. *Journal of Health Psychology, 14,* 751–760]. These findings may apply less to 3rd Agers because of their tendency to regulate negative thoughts and affect.

Attitudes and Behaviors Associated With Normal Cognitive Aging

21. Of those subjects in the middle group ("others"), 86.7% did not rate their cognitive capacity as "better than satisfactory" (Uotinen et al., 2003).

22. A study compared clinically verified normal subjects in their mid-70s with younger normals and those with mild cognitive impairment and Alzheimer's disease. When given tests of visual motion perception, verbal and visual memory, and a road map test of spatial navigation, 20% of the older normals exhibited visuospatial impairment [Mapstone, M., Steffenella, T. M., & Duffy, C. J. (2003). A visuospatial variant of mild cognitive impairment: Getting lost between aging and AD. *Neurology, 60,* 802–808]. On the whole, spatial problems were more often experienced by older females than males, although females compensated by driving fewer miles and stayed closer to home [Turano, K. A., Munoz, B., Hassan, S. E., Duncan, D. D., Gower, E. W., Roche, K. B., et al. (2009). Poor sense of direction is associated with constricted driving space in older drivers. *Journal of Gerontology: Psychological Sciences, 64B,* 348–355].

23. To my knowledge, none of the studies that classified 3rd Agers into high, medium, and low groups questioned their subjects directly about whether they were letting nature take its course. The closest question, "Do you feel the weighing of age?" was asked by Uotinen et al. (2003). Those in the middle responded "yes" 51.7% of the time, whereas only 16.7% the optimal ager equivalents replied in the affirmative.

24. Research on the size of social networks has found significant correlations with health and psychological well-being [Melchior, M., Berkman, L. F., Niedhammer, I., Chea, M., & Goldberg, M. (2003). Social relations and self-reported health: A prospective analysis of the French Gazel cohort. *Social Science and Medicine, 56,* 1817–1830; and Uchino, B. N., Cacioppo, J. T., & Kiecolt-Glaser, J. K. (1996). The relationship between social support and physiological processes: A review with emphasis on underlying mechanisms and implications for health. *Psychological Bulletin, 119,* 488–531].

25. A review of seven longitudinal studies that addressed this question found a small connection between social network size and less deterioration of mental ability [Fratiglioni, L., Paillard-Borg, S., & Winblad, B. (2004). An active and socially integrated lifestyle in late life might protect against dementia. *The Lancet Neurology, 3,* 343–353]. An 8-year follow-up study by Uotinen and colleagues found that two to three times the number of older normal agers reported no friends compared with optimal agers at baseline and at end of study: 2.8 and 5.1% for optimal agers versus 9.0 and 11.1%, respectively, for normal agers (Uotinen et al., 2003).

26. See Note 28, Chapter 6.

27. The correlation between the use of elements of SOC and age was −.26 and was affected by available resources, such as health and size of social networks [Freund, A. M., & Baltes, P. B. (1998). Selection, optimization, and compensation as strategies of life management: Correlations with subjective indicators of successful aging. *Psychology and Aging, 13,* 531–543].

28. There have been small but significant correlations between the use of SOC and global intelligence (Freund & Baltes, 1998). However, no data are available about differences in the use of SOC by older optimal, normal, and high-risk cognitive agers or its impact on intellectual functioning. A doctoral thesis found no relationship between SOC and cognition in older adults. It did, however, describe the effect of life circumstances on the use of elements of SOC by adults 65+. For example, better health is associated with increased use of optimization, while poorer health results in more loss-based selection and compensation. More social support results in greater use of optimization and compensation [Bourgeois, S. (2003). Strategies of adaptation to age-related losses in everyday activities of independent seniors. *Dissertation Abstracts International: Section B: The Sciences and Engineering, 63*(10-B), 4890].

29. A comprehensive summary of the cognitive variables that have been included among the executive functions is Jurado, M. B., & Rosselli, M. (2007). The elusive nature of executive functions: A review of our current understanding. *Neuropsychological Review, 17,* 213–233.

30. Meta-analyses of the differences between unimpaired older and younger subjects found very large differences (effect sizes greater than −1.0) for a number of categories and perseverative errors [Rhodes, M. G. (2004). Age-related differences in performance on the Wisconsin Card Sorting Test: A meta-analytic review. *Psychology and Aging, 19,* 482–494].

31. See Note 31 in Chapter 6; also Allemand, M., Zimprich, D., & Martin, M. (2008). Long-term correlated change in personality traits in old age. *Psychology and Aging, 23,* 545–557.

32. To my knowledge, there have been no longitudinal studies that reported data bearing on the question of whether older adults avoided tasks that they had no reservations tackling when younger or healthier. Cross-sectional findings, however, are in agreement that normal older adults are more risk averse and slower to act to a variety of cognitive challenges [Frank, M. J., & Kong, Lauren. (2008). Learning to avoid in older age. *Psychology and Aging, 23,* 392–398; and Deakin, J., Aitken, M., Robbins, T., & Sahakian, B. J. (2004). Risk taking during decision-making in normal volunteers changes with age. *Journal of the International Neuropsychological Society, 10,* 590–598].

Reflections and Applications

33. See Note 17.

34. National Center for Health Statistics, 2010 data showed higher percentages of obese and overweight individuals in the 45–64 age group compared to those 65–74.

35. Most instructions about the nature, regimen, effectiveness, and side effects of medications are given by pharmacists (58.7%), followed by nurses (14.3%). and physicians (6.4%) [Ruppar, T. M., Conn, V. S., & Russell, C. L. (2008). Medication adherence interventions for older adults: Literature review. *Research and Theory for Nursing Practice: An International Journal, 22,* 114–147].

36. A balanced review of the reasons patients do not take prescription medication, which includes why the medication is necessary, and approaches to encouraging adherence to the recommendations of health care providers are contained in Snowden, A. (2008). Medication management in older adults: A critique of concordance. *British Journal of Nursing, 17,* 114–119.

37. Coined by Robert Butler four decades ago, ageism is a form of discrimination similar to racism or sexism [Butler, R. N. (1969). Ageism: Another form of bigotry. *The Gerontologist, 9,* 243–246].

38. An informative review of relevant topics related to ageism, including myths and stereotypes, is contained in Ory, M., Hoffman, M. K., Hawkins, M., Sanner, B., & Mockenhaupt, R. (2003). Challenging aging stereotypes: Strategies for creating a more active society. *American Journal of Preventive Medicine, 25,* 164–171.

39. Palmore noted that people subjected to negative stereotyping may come to believe these negative views and behave accordingly [Palmore, E. B. (1999). *Ageism: Negative and positive* (2nd ed.). New York: Springer].

Chapter 8

1. Over an 8-year period, subjects (with a predicted decline in 3MS scores of more than one standard deviation below the mean of 2,509 subjects were classified as "major decliners" [Yaffe, S. K., Fiocco, A. J., Lindquist, K., Vittinghoff, E., Simonsick, E. M., Newman, A. B., et al. for the Health ABC Study. (2009). Predictors of maintaining cognitive function in

older adults: The Health ABC Study. *Neurology, 72*, 2029–2035]. At 8-year follow-up, 426 older Finnish subjects were classified as "negative" if they responded positively to questions about illness or injury causing problems in daily life or health problems imposing limitations on hobbies or gave negative answers to self-rating questions of functional capacity, memory, learning ability, mental agility, and mood [Uotinen, V., Suutama, Y., & Ruoppila, I. (2003). Age identification in the framework of successful aging: A study of older Finnish people. *International Journal of Aging and Human Development, 56*, 173–195]. Subjects among 4,030 older women and men studied were rated as "impaired" if they scored 5 or fewer correct on the 9-item Short Portable Mental Status Questionnaire or had at least one daily living limitation [Berkman, L. F., Seeman, T. E., Albert, M., Blazer, D., Kahn, R., Mohs, R., et al. (1993). High, usual and impaired functioning in community-dwelling older men and women: Findings from the MacArthur Foundation Research Network on Successful Aging. *Journal of Clinical Epidemiology, 46*, 1129–1140]. Older women's declining mMMSE scores placed them in the lowest tertile over a 15-year period [Barnes, D. E., Cauley, J. A., Lui, L. Y., Fink, H. A., McCulloch, C., Stone, K. L., et al. (2007). Women who maintain optimal cognitive function into old age. *Journal of the American Geriatrics Society, 55*, 259–264].

2. The risk of dementia is greater for older individuals with medical conditions such as hypertension, type 2 diabetes, or elevated serum cholesterol levels. Those at higher risk for dementia are more often sedentary, isolated, or clinically depressed. Examples are Artero, S., Ancelin, M.-L., Portet, A. F., Dupuy, A., Berr, C., Dartigues, J.-F., et al. (2008). Risk profiles for mild cognitive impairment and progression to dementia are gender specific. *Journal of Neurology, Neurosurgery, and Psychiatry, 79*, 979–984; also, Mariani, E., Monastero, R., & Mecocci, P. (2007). Mild cognitive impairment: A systematic review. *Journal of Alzheimer's Disease, 12*, 23–35. *Sedentary*: Podewils, L. J., Guallar, E., Kuller, L. H., Fried, L. P., Lopez, O. L., Carlson, M., et al. (2005). Physical activity, APOE genotype, and dementia risk: Findings from the Cardiovascular Health Cognition Study. *American Journal of Epidemiology, 161*, 639–651. *Socially isolated:* Fratiglioni, L., Paillard-Borg, S., & Winblad, B. (2004). An active and socially integrated lifestyle in late life might protect against dementia. *Lancet Neurology, 3*, 343–353.

3. High-risk cognitive agers include a higher proportion than normal agers of those with AACD or MCI. Ylikoski classified a higher number of subjects similar to those in the high-risk range as having AACD (82%) or MCI (54%), compared to 24 and 14.7%, respectively, of those in the normal group (Ylikoski, R., Ylikoski, A.,Keskivaara,P., Tilvis, R., Sulkava, R., & Erkinjuntti, T. (1999). Heterogeneity of cognitive profiles in aging: Successful aging, normal aging, and individuals at-risk for cognitive decline. *European Journal of Neurology, 6*, 645–652 ; also Barnes, et al., 2007.

4. Neuropsychologists, neurologists, and other experts differentiate between AACD (one of many terms describing the age-related deterioration of mental abilities that is below an expected norm but short of mild dementia) and MCI, which is seen as a transitional state between normal cognitive aging and dementia. The students interviewing these high-risk agers were not qualified to diagnose the presence of AACD or MCI but were aware of the shared clinical characteristics of these two conditions, which included persistent memory problems or other chronically impaired mental skills. See Notes 46–48 in Chapter 3.

5. Estimates of the proportion of subjects similar to high-risk cognitive agers in other studies are Yaffe et al., 2009, 16%; Barnes et al., 2007, 33%: Uotinen, et al., 2003, 12%; and Ylikoski et al., 1999, 9%.

Assessing Individuals at High Risk for Cognitive Impairment

6. American Psychiatric Association. (2000). *Diagnostic and statistical manual of mental disorders* (4th ed., text revision). Washington, DC: Author.
7. When I think of high-risk cognitive agers as accidents waiting to happen, I have in mind people in stories that have appeared in newspapers and other media. Here are four examples: Duhigg, C. (2008, March 2). Tapping homes can be a pitfall for the elderly. *New York Times*; Duhigg, C. (2007, December 24). Shielding money clashes with elders free will. *New York Times*; Kolkata, G. (2007, May 28). Lost chances for survival, before and after stroke. *New York Times*; Kolkata, G. (2007, April 8). Lessons of the heart, learned and ignored. *New York Times*. We interviewed a number of individuals who seemed similarly at risk for adverse physical, economic, or psychosocial events.

Health-Related Qualities Associated With High-Risk Cognitive Aging

8. Compared to their peers, about one third of those similar to high-risk agers said that they felt older than their age mates, while only 8.4% of those similar to normal agers shared that view (Uotinen et al., 2003).
9. For instance, a national sample of women was studied to evaluate whether high activity level reduced the degree of cognitive decline. Using as a unit of measurement the amount of energy it takes to walk a city block, researchers studied the number of equivalent city blocks walked by more than 9,000 older women. The lowest 25%, akin to high-risk agers, averaged only seven blocks weekly. The next-highest quarter, similar to normal agers, walked a mean of 28 blocks (Barnes et al., 2007). A study of Finnish 3rd Agers found that those fitting the criteria for being at risk were approximately half as likely to engage in weekly activities as normal agers—36 versus 68.5% (Ylikoski et al., 1999).
10. Scientists at the Karolinska Institute in Sweden who followed women and men into their 3rd Age of life found that obesity, high cholesterol, and elevated blood pressure all correlated with a higher likelihood of developing dementia. And, the risks increased additively, so that those with these three medical conditions are six times more likely to become demented than their peers without these risk factors [Kivipelto, M., Ngandu, T., Fratiglioni, L., Viitanen, M., Kåreholt, I., Winblad, B., et al. (2005). Obesity and vascular risk factors at midlife and the risk of dementia and Alzheimer's disease. *Archives of Neurology, 62,* 1556–1560]. Another review confirmed both the adverse impact of obesity and type 2 diabetes and their additive nature with respect to the probability of developing dementia [Luchsinger, J. A., & Gustafson, D. R. (2009). Adiposity, type 2 diabetes, and Alzheimer's disease. *Journal of Alzheimer's Disease, 16,* 693–704].

11. In one of the Finnish studies, 38.6% of subjects similar to high-risk agers reported a decreased "zest for life," in contrast to 14.1% of the normal agers. Eight years later, the differences widened, with 43.8% of those at risk saying that they had decreased zest, in contrast to only 14.2% of the normals. Also, because of the selection criteria for classifying high-risk agers in this research, all of the subjects in this lower group reported that illness or injury caused problems in daily living and limited enjoyment of their hobbies (Uotinen et al., 2003).

12. The differences between normal and high-risk agers in the frequency of serious medical conditions were, respectively, as follows: *stroke*, 2.4% for normals compared to 4.6% for the high-risk group; *diabetes*, 6.9 versus 8.4%; *hypertension*, 38.1 and 41.8% (from Barnes et al., 2007).

13. According to the American Heart Association Web site (retrieved August 11, 2010, from http://www.americanheart.org/presenter.jhtml?identifier=4756), the metabolic syndrome is characterized by these factors: abdominal obesity; atherogenic dyslipidemia (high tri-glycerides, low high-density lipoprotein [HDL], and high low-density lipoprotein [LDL] cholesterol); elevated blood pressure; insulin resistance or glucose intolerance (e.g., Type 2 diabetes); prothrombotic state (e.g., high fibrinogen or plasminogen activator inhibitor 1 in the blood); and proinflammatory state (e.g., elevated C-reactive protein in the blood).

14. Data on average number of down days monthly from Behavioral Risk Factor Surveillance System (BRFSS) (retrieved August 11, 2010, from http://apps.nccd.cdc.gov/HRQOL/index.asp). More older women in the lower group reported a high degree of depressive symptoms (8.5%) than those in the middle (5.8%) group (Barnes et al., 2007). In a 2006–2007 national survey, 2.1% of women and men 65+ exhibited evidence of serious psychological distress on the basis of their answers to a short inventory [National Center for Health Statistics. (2010). *Health, United States, 2009: With chartbook on trends in the health of Americans.* Washington, DC: U.S. Government Printing Office].

15. The presence of psychological distress in older adults has been shown to reduce patients' adherence to some recommended prevention measures, such as receiving flu shots and dental checkups, and in women being less likely to have a breast examination [Thorp, J. M., Kalinowski, C. T., Patterson, M. E., & Sleath, B. L. (2006). Psychological distress as a barrier to preventive care in community-dwelling elderly in the United States. *Medical Care, 44,* 87–91].

16. Although the emotional strain can be substantial, most older adults recover from the death of a loved one within 6–12 months. Those who continue to be depressed often have a history of depression prior to the loss [Zishook, S., & Schuchter, S. R. (1993). Uncomplicated bereavement. *Journal of Clinical Psychiatry, 54,* 365–372]. Extended grieving may have a component of anger. The classic reference on pathological griev-ing is Freud, S. (1953–1964) Mourning and melancholia. In J. Stachey (Ed. & Trans.) in collaboration with A. Freud, *The standard edition of the works of Sigmund Freud* (Vol. 14, pp. 237–258). London: Hogarth Press. (Original work published 1917)

17. Data from recent National Health Interview Survey of 225,225 adults in 2008 found 6.9% of individuals 65–74 and 19.2% of those 75+ reported difficulty in executing one or more IADLs (retrieved August 11, 2010, from http://www.cdc.gov/mmwr/preview/mmwrhtml/mm5848a6.htm). Earlier findings from a smaller sample in the 2004 Medicare Current Beneficiary Survey found 11.1% of those 65–74 and 15% of those 75–84 had one or more compromised IADLs (retrieved August 11, 2010, from http://www.cdc.gov/nchs/ppt/aging/aging_english.ppt). As with other surveys, the largest demographic differences

in the percentage of adults with difficulty in executing more than one IADL are between the poor (11.1%) and not poor (2.5%) and those with less than a high school diploma (6.9%) and a college degree (1.9%).

Attitudes and Behaviors Associated With High-Risk Cognitive Aging

18. Procedures used by law enforcement officers when stopping those suspected of driving under the influence (DUI) of alcohol vary widely from one jurisdiction to another. Valerie's experience would not have been unusual for someone stopped for suspected DUI in southwest Florida in 2010. My thanks are extended to Sergeants David Citrone of Florida Gulf Coast University, Thomas Humann of the Collier County Sherriff's Department, and Allan Kolak of the Cape Coral Police Department.

19. The subjective sense of feeling cognitively older than peers was supported by findings reported by Uotinen et al. (2003). More than five times the number of subjects who were classified as high-risk cognitive agers using their criteria said that they felt their mental age was older than their actual years compared to those in the normal- and optimal-aging categories (9.8 vs. 2.8% and 0.7%, respectively). Eight years later, the ratio was more than 6:1.

20. Subtests in a study (Ylikoski et al., 1999) assessing primarily memory functions among at-risk agers that were at least −1.0 standard deviation lower than average included logical memory (Wechsler Memory Scale–Revised [WMS-R]), visual memory (WMS-R), verbal fluency (number of kinds of animals recalled in 30 seconds), and object name recall (Boston Naming Test).

21. Ylikoski et al.'s research among high-risk cognitive agers (see Note 20) also found significant decline in a mix of crystallized and fluid abilities other than memory of more than −1.0 standard deviation: reasoning (Wechsler Adult Intelligence Scale–Revised [WAIS-R] Similarities), visuospatial (WAIS-R Block Design), attention (Trails A), cognitive inhibition (Stroop Test), and finger tapping.

22. For example, Deakin, J., Aitken, M., Robbins, T., & Sahakian, B. J. (2004). Risk taking during decision making in normal volunteers changes with age. *Journal of the International Neuropsychological Society, 10*, 590–598.

23. Difference in size of and satisfaction with social networks was greatest among high-risk cognitive agers. Finnish neuroscientists (Uotinen et al., 2003) found that one in five subjects similar to high-risk agers had no friends, compared to only 5.9% of optimal and normal agers combined. Over twice as many (51.8%) of those at the high-risk level said that they were lonely, contrasted with optimal (20%) and normal (25.5%) agers.

24. Engagement in social and leisure activities is associated with a decreased risk of dementia. Individuals living alone or who had no close relationships had a 60% increased dementia risk compared to those with normal social relationships [Wang, H.-X., Karp, A., Herlitz, A., Crowe, M., Kåreholt, I., Winblad, B., et al. (2009). Personality and lifestyle in relation to dementia incidence. *Neurology, 72*, 253–259; Fratiglioni et al., 2004].

25. For a summary, see Salthouse, T. A. (1991). *Theoretical perspectives on cognitive aging.* Hillsdale, NJ: Erlbaum.

26. See Turano, K. A., Munoz, B., Hassan, S. E., Duncan, D. D., Gower, E. W., Roche, K. B., et al. (2009). Poor sense of direction is associated with constricted driving space in older drivers. *Journal of Gerontology: Psychological Sciences, 64B*, 348–355. About a third

of drivers with MCI who continue to drive have severe visuospatial problems associated with poorer performance on a simulated road test [Mapstone, M., Steffenella, T. M., & Duffy, C. J. (2003). A visuospatial variant of mild cognitive impairment: Getting lost between aging and AD. *Neurology, 60,* 802–808].

27. These symptoms are likely to exist on a continuum from relatively mild impairment to dysexecutive MCI. Subjects with the former may have one or two impaired executive functions (e.g., disinhibition, difficulty shifting set) but score above the threshold for MCI [Kahokehr, A., Siegert, R. J., & Weatherall, M. (2004). The frequency of executive cognitive impairment in elderly rehabilitation inpatients. *Journal of Geriatric Psychiatry and Neurology, 17,* 68–72]. Patients with dysexecutive MCI were described as having recent difficulty with planning, multitasking, attention/concentration, or disorganization. They had significantly lower scores on the majority of executive function tests, increased behavioral symptoms, and left prefrontal cortex atrophy on MRI scans when compared with controls [Pa, J., Boxer, A., Chao, L. L., Gazzaley, A., Freeman, K., Kramer, J., et al. (2009). Clinical-neuroimaging characteristics of dysexecutive mild cognitive impairment. *Annals of Neurology, 65,* 414–423].

28. Examples in Note 7. The breadth of this problem worldwide is discussed in the following articles: Cohen, C. A. (2008). Editorial: Consumer fraud and dementia—Lessons learned from conmen. *The International Journal of Social Research and Practice, 7,* 283–285; also Langenderfer, J., & Shrimp, T. A. (1999). Consumer vulnerability to scams, swindles, and fraud: A new theory of visceral influences on persuasion. *Psychology and Marketing, 18,* 763–783.

Reflections and Applications

29. Examples of large-magnitude differences between subjects similar to high-risk and normal agers in longitudinal studies reported above were as follows: larger percentage with no friends, high risk 9% versus normal 20% (Uotinen et al., 2003); fewer hours of weekly activities, high risk 4% versus normal 17% (Ylikoski et al., 1999); decreased zest for life, high risk 43.8% versus normal 14.2% (Uotinen et al, 2003).

30. See Note 12 in Chapter 6.

31. Anger is a common emotion accompanying depression when individuals believe their lives will be barren without a loved one, a vocation, or an activity no longer possible because of physical limitations. Exploring feelings of resentment can speed the return to normal among people in prolonged grief states (Freud, 1917/1953–1964).

Chapter 9

Older Americans Are in Better Health Now Than at Any Time in History

1. An example is a summary article complied by Nicholas Bakalar, "Americans are Sicker Than They Think, C.D.C. Finds" (Vital statistics. *New York Times,* November 25, 2008),

which highlighted only negative statistics about medical conditions and risky lifestyle behaviors.

2. Unless otherwise noted, all data on health statistics, status and practices in this section are from National Center for Health Statistics. (2010). *Health, United States, 2009: With special feature on medical technology.* Hyattsville, MD. Respondents were asked to rate their health on a 5-point scale: poor, fair, good, very good, and excellent. All age groups from 55 to 84 reported higher percentages of subjects rating themselves in good, very good, or excellent health.

3. The percentage of those aged 65–74 in good health or better rose from 74 to 76.6% during the period 1991 to 2007. The number of Americans 65–74 in 2007 was estimated at 19,370,000. Of that figure, 2.6% is 503,620. U.S. Census Bureau, Statistical Abstract of the United States (2009). *Annual estimates of the resident population by sex and age: 1980-2008.* Washington, DC. <http://www.census.gov/compendia/statab/> Retrieved December 22, 2010.

4. The Swedish study compared three birth cohorts, separated by 5 years (1901–1902, 1906–1907, and 1911–1912) on health measures. Fewer 70-year-olds were feeling unhealthy in the two younger cohorts, fewer reported symptoms, and there were indications of better physical functioning in the younger cohorts. The improvement among women was greater than among men [Wilhelmson, K., Allebeck, P., & Steen, B. (2002). Improved health among 70-year olds: Comparison of health indicators in three different birth cohorts. *Aging Clinical and Experimental Research, 14,* 361–370]. A study of 10 European nations found that the proportions of elderly people with disability were decreasing [Äijänseppä, S., Notkola, I.-L., Tijhuis, M., van Staveren, W., Kromhout, D., & Nissinen, A. (2005). Physical functioning in elderly Europeans: 10 year changes in the north and south: The HALE project. *Journal of Epidemiology and Community Health, 59,* 413–419]. Not every report is in agreement. A small U.K. study found more subjects aged 65–69 reporting fair or poor health in 1996 than a different cohort had reported in 1991 [Jagger, C., Matthews, R. J., Matthews, F. E., Spiers, N. A., Nickson, J. , Paykel, E. S., et al. and the Medical Research Council on Cognitive Function and Ageing Study. (2007). Cohort differences in disease and disability in the young-old: Findings from the MRC Cognitive Function and Ageing Study (MRC-CFAS). *BMC Public Health, 7,* 156].

5. These are proportional changes among adults 65+ from 1995 (smoking), 1997 (drinking), and 1998 (exercising regularly) to 2007. The absolute percentage decreases were from 14.9 to 9.3% (smoking), 48.6 to 46.5% (drinking), and 19.9 to 21.6% (exercising regularly) (National Center for Health Statistics, 2010).

6. These gains occurred in less than a decade. From 1999 to 2006, women and men lowered their serum cholesterol by 6.7 and 8.3%, respectively. In the younger age groups, only middle-aged males (4.2%) reduced their readings [Schober, S. E., Carroll, M. D., Lacher, D. A., & Hirsch, R. (2007). *High serum total cholesterol—an indicator for monitoring cholesterol lowering efforts: U.S. adults, 2005–2006* (NCHS Data Brief No, 2). Hyattsville, MD: National Center for Health Statistics. Retrieved August 11, 2010, from http://www.cdc.gov/nchs/data/databriefs/db02.pdf].

7. In the interval from 1984 to 2004, the disability rate declined from 26.2 to 19%. In 2004, the population of women and men aged 60–79 was approximately 39,659,276. Had these older Americans in 2004 suffered the 1984 disability rate of 26.2% rather than 19%, another 2,855,458 of them would have become disabled. Estimated from U.S. Census Bureau, *Annual Estimates.*

8. Among a quarter century of writings on this topic by James Fries is Fries, J. F. (2003). Measuring and monitoring success in the compression of morbidity. *Annals of Internal Medicine, 139,* 455–459.

9. Demographers at the National Center for Health Statistics analyzed data on 43,000+ subjects from the Medicare Current Beneficiary Survey and calculated changes in total life expectancy from 1992 to 2002. Then, they computed the number of remaining years that a 65-year-old would likely be free of disability at the beginning and end of that decade [Cai, L., & Lubitz, J. (2007). Was there compression of disability for older Americans from 1992 to 2003? *Demography, 44,* 479–494].

10. Experts in gerontology from the Netherlands, Switzerland, New Zealand, and Sweden have been examining the merits of this theory using different methods, and several of these early empirical reports have been favorable. *The Netherlands:* Nusselder, W. J., & Mackenbach, J. P. (1996). Rectangularization of the survival curve in the Netherlands, 1950–1992. *The Gerontologist, 36,* 773–782. *Switzerland:* Paccaud, F., Sidoti-Pinto, C., Marazzi, A., & Mili, J. (1998). Age at death and rectangularisation of the survival curve: Trends in Switzerland, 1969–1994. *Journal of Epidemiology and Community Health, 52,* 412–415. *New Zealand:* Graham, P., Blakely, T., Davis, P., Sporle, A., & Pearce, N. (2004). Compression, expansion, or dynamic equilibrium? The evolution of health expectancy in New Zealand. *Journal of Epidemiology and Community Health, 58,* 659–666. *Sweden:* Hessler, R. M., Eriksson, B. G., Dey, D., Steen, G., Sundh, V., & Steen, B. (2003). The compression of morbidity debate in aging: An empirical test using the gerontological and geriatric population studies in Göteborg, Sweden (H70). *Archives of Gerontology and Geriatrics, 37,* 213–222. Not everyone agrees with the compression of morbidity theory [e.g., Woo, J., Goggins, W., Zhang, X., Griffiths, S., & Wong, V. (2009). Aging and utilization of hospital services in Hong Kong: Retrospective cohort study. *International Journal of Public Health, 55,* 201–207; and Parker, M. G., Ahacic, K., & Thorslund, M. (2005). Health changes among Swedish oldest old: Prevalence rates from 1992 and 2002 show increasing health problems. *The Journals of Gerontology Series A: Biological Sciences and Medical Sciences, 60,* 1351–1355].

11. In most cases, more education and higher income level strongly correlated with more active preventive health care behavior for all adults, including those age 65–74. Racial differences were smaller than educational and income differences for nearly all variables. Among adults with some college, 8.2% were smokers in 2006, compared to 28.8% with no high school diploma or GED (general equivalency diploma). For adults 65+, racial differences in smoking percentages were as follows: White 8.7%, Black 8.5%, and Hispanic/Mexican 5.6%. Income level also mattered: 59.7% of the more affluent females received a Pap smear, in contrast to 44.4% of those living at or below the poverty level.

Healthy Lifestyle Habits That Benefit the Intellect

12. Swan, G. E., & Lessov-Schlaggar, C. N. (2007). The effects of tobacco smoke and nicotine on cognition and the brain. *Neuropsychology Review, 17,* 259–273; and Fagard, R. H., & Nilsson, P. M. (2009). Smoking and diabetes—the double health hazard! *Primary Care Diabetes, 3,* 205–209.

13. Data on a variety of smoking cessation programs from a meta-analysis of 633 studies that included 71,806 subjects. The overall success rate for people in these programs was 25%, with 6.4% stopping on their own [Viswesvaran, C., & Schmidt, F. L. (1992). A meta-analytic comparison of the effectiveness of smoking cessation methods. *Journal of Applied Psychology, 77,* 554–561]. Data on the percentage of adults wanting to quit smoking and the number who have been successful from the 2007 National Health Interview Survey. Among the estimated 86.8 million adults who had smoked at least 100 cigarettes in their lifetime, 52.1% (47.3 million) were no longer smoking at the time of the interview [Centers for Disease Control and Prevention (CDC). (2008). Cigarette smoking among adults—United States, 2007. *Morbidity and Mortality Weekly Report, 57,* 1221–1226]. Additional data from the CDC Web site (retrieved August 11, 2010, from http://www.cdc.gov/tobacco/data_statistics/fact_sheets/cessation/quitting/index.htm).
14. See Note 5, Chapter 4.
15. See Note 15, Chapter 4.
16. See Note 27, Chapter 4.
17. See National Center for Health Statistics. Health, United States, 2010.
18. See Note 33, Chapter 4.
19. See Note 34, Chapter 4.
20. See Chapter 2 Notes (Note numbers given in parentheses here) on the cognitive value of compliance for hypertension (13) diabetes, type 2 diabetes (48), clotting time—prothrombin time and international normalized ratio—for atrial fibrillation (23, 24), CPAP for obstructive sleep apnea (43, 44), and hearing aids (54–56).
21. Studies of compliance vary greatly depending how compliance is defined. A method that has shown promise is to divide subjects into those who take medication 80% of the time and compare them on a dependent variable (e.g., decline in IQ) with those who are adherent less than 80% of the time. For example, Grant, R. W., Singer, D. E., & Meigs, J. B. (2005). Medication adherence before an increase in antihypertensive therapy: A cohort study using pharmacy claims data. *Clinical Therapeutics, 27,* 773–781.
22. See Note 64, Chapter 4.
23. See Note 65, Chapter 4.
24. See Note 79, Chapter 4.
25. See Djousse, L., Driver, J. A., & Gaziano, J. M. (2009). Relation between modifiable lifestyle factors and lifetime risk of heart failure. *Journal of the American Medical Association, 302,* 394–400.

Three Levels of Cognitive Aging

26. These publications were based on longitudinal studies that used a three-level system (e.g., high, medium, low) to classify subjects and included measures of intellectual functioning. The U.S. studies were Yaffe, S. K., Fiocco, A. J., Lindquist, K., Vittinghoff, E., Simonsick, E. M., Newman A. B., et al. for the Health ABC Study. (2009). Predictors of maintaining cognitive function in older adults: The Health ABC Study. *Neurology, 72,* 2029–2035; and Barnes, D. E., Cauley, J. A., Lui, L. Y., Fink, H. A., McCulloch, C., Stone, K. L., et al. (2007). Women who maintain optimal cognitive function into old age. *Journal of the American Geriatrics Society, 55,* 259–264. The two Finnish studies

were published earlier [Uotinen, V., Suutama, Y., & Ruoppila, I. (2003). Age identification in the framework of successful aging: A study of older Finnish people. *International Journal of Aging and Human Development, 56*, 173–195; and Ylikoski, R., Ylikoski, A., Keskivaara, P., Tilvis, R., Sulkava, R., & Erkinjuntti, T. (1999). Heterogeneity of cognitive profiles in aging: Successful aging, normal aging, and individuals at-risk for cognitive decline. *European Journal of Neurology, 6*, 645–652].

27. Baltimore study by Carlson, M. C., Saczynski, J. S., Rebok, G. W., Seeman, T., Glass, T. A., McGill, S., et al. (2008). Exploring the effects of an "everyday" activity program on executive function and memory in older adults: Experience Corps. *The Gerontologist, 48*, 793–801. An example of less-fit 3rd Agers who made greater progress than fitter subjects at increasing their fitness level through exercise is discussed in Ogawa et al., 1992 (see Note 4, Chapter 4).

Clinical Notes for Caregivers

28. See Note 26, Chapter 3.
29. See Note 33, Chapter 5.
30. See Note 35, Chapter 5.
31. See Note 38, Chapter 5.
32. Scopelliti, M., & Giuliania, M. V. (2004). Choosing restorative environments across the lifespan: A matter of place experience. *Journal of Environmental Psychology, 24*, 423–437.
33. These symptoms are less severe than dysexecutive mild cognitive impairment and are more consistent with dysexecutive cognitive impairment. A survey of 52 randomly selected 80-year-old volunteers in rehabilitation found 25% showed two signs of compromised cognitive functions. Of these, only one scored below the threshold for mild cognitive impairment [Kahokehr, A., Siegert, R. J., & Weatherall, M. (2004). The frequency of executive cognitive impairment in elderly rehabilitation inpatients. *Journal of Geriatric Psychiatry and Neurology, 17*, 68–72].
34. According to a report from the Insurance Institute for Highway Safety on April 11, 2010 (Licensing renewal provisions for older drivers. Retrieved August 11, 2010, from http://www.iihs.org/laws/olderdrivers.aspx), there were 27 states that required older people to be retested (usually a vision test) more frequently to retain a driver's license. The age at which more frequent retesting begins varied widely from 54 (North Carolina) to 85 (Texas), with most states indicating between 65 and 75. Frequency of retesting ranged from two (Hawaii) to six (Florida) years for those 80 and under.
35. Comments inspired by Safe Driving for Older Adults (retrieved August 11, 2010, from http://www.ec-online.net/Knowledge/articles/safedriving.html), by Rich O'Boyle, founder and community coordinator of ElderCare Online.
36. A summary of the age-related changes in the regulation of affect by application of the socioemotional selectivity theory (older people being more attracted to people who are emotionally soothing) and the positivity effect in Carstensen, L. L. (2006). The influence of a sense of time on human development. *Science, 312*, 1913–1915.
37. See Notes 81 and 95, Chapter 4.
38. See Note 94, Chapter 4.

38. U.S. report by Gatz, M., & Smyer, M. A. (1992). The mental health system and older adults in the 1990s. *American Psychologist, 47,* 741–751. A Dutch study found 10.2% prevalence of anxiety disorders and 2% frequency of depression [Beekman, A. T., de Beurs, E., van Balkom, A. J., Deeg, D. J., van Dyck, R., & van Tilburg, W. (2000). Anxiety and depression in later life: Co-occurrence and communality of risk factors. *American Journal of Psychiatry, 157,* 89–95].

39. I have treated anxiety disorders with a range of techniques that have included relaxation training, progressive muscle relaxation, hypnosis, autogenic training, systematic desensitization, and thought stopping.

40. See Yaffe, K., Barnes, D., Nevitt, M., Lui, L.-Y., & Covinsky, K. (2001). A prospective study of physical activity and cognitive decline in elderly women: Women who walk. *Archives of Internal Medicine, 161,* 1703–1708.

41. Other prospective studies that reported raw test scores at baseline and follow-up showed only a small difference in the rate of cognitive decline on global dementia screening tests. For example, Yaffee, et al., 2001; also MacKinnon, A., Christensen, H., Hofer, S. M., Korten, A. E., & Jorm, A. F. (2003). Use it and lose it? The association between activity and performance established using latent growth techniques in a community sample. *Aging, Neuropsychology and Cognition, 10,* 215–229; and Ghisletta, P., Bickel, J.-F., & Lovden, M. (2006). Does activity engagement protect against cognitive decline in old age? Methodological and analytical considerations. *Journal of Gerontology: Psychological Sciences, 61B,* 253–261.

Still More to Learn

42. I was a distance runner in college in the mid-1950s. During one preseason physical exam, the team doctor warned me about the dangers of "athlete's heart." Later, I discovered that he was referring to studies carried out at Oxford and Cambridge, as well as Harvard and Yale, in the second quarter of the 20th century, which discovered that varsity letter winners had shorter life expectancies than their sedentary classmates. While these studies lacked the sophisticated designs common in the research of today, the conclusions were hard to ignore. A brief readable summary of these studies is contained in Hayflick, L. (1994). *How and why we age.* New York: Ballantine. In the last quarter of the 20th century, professional opinion began to shift 180 degrees to the conviction that exercise extended life expectancy. In the United States, a key report by Stanford physician Ralph Paffenbarger demonstrated that college graduates who expended at least 2,000 kilocalories weekly following graduation lived substantially longer than their classmates with lower activity levels [Paffenbarger, R. S., Jr., Hyde, R. T., Wing, A. L., & Hsieh, C. (1986). Physical activity, all-cause mortality, and longevity in college alumni. *New England Journal of Medicine, 314,* 605–613; and Paffenbarger, R. S., Jr., Wing, A. L., & Hyde, R. T. (1978). Physical activity as an index of heart attack risk in college alumni. *Journal of Epidemiology, 108,* 161–175].

43. In this cross-sectional study, subjects averaged 69.3 years of age. Prevalent age-related diseases were accepted, but individuals at risk of cognitive impairment due to premorbid factors or evident stroke were excluded, and 3.3% of the unexplained ("unallocated") variance was due to the implicit conservative bias of the method of the R^2

change calculation [Bergman, I., Blomberg, M., & Almkvist, O. (2007). The importance of impaired physical health and age in normal cognitive aging. *Scandinavian Journal of Psychology, 48*, 115–125].

44. Nearly every clinically significant health problem correlated with lower scores on cognitive tests. For instance, individuals with cerebral pathology (silent infarctions, atrophy, and white matter load) did not perform as well on a wide range of tests of mental skills, including processing speed, attention, memory, verbal fluency, flexibility, and visuospatial ability. Among hypertensives, greater cognitive decline occurred in memory and psychomotor speed, while those with cardiac arrhythmias more often had lower scores on dementia screening batteries (Bergman et al., 2007).

45. Nine longitudinal studies of patients with mild cognitive impairment for at least 3 years divided subjects at follow-up into three categories of progression: dementia, stable, and no longer impaired. At the end of the nine studies, the median progression rate to dementia was 44.9% (range 53.9 to 19.2%), median percentage of patients remaining stable was 35.0% (75.8–11.2%), and median for no longer impaired was 16.7% (34.9–5.0%).

Appreciating the Richness of the 3rd Age

46. Rowe, J. W., & Kahn, R. L. (1998). *Successful aging*. New York: Pantheon. These researchers did not view these three characteristics as challenges but rather as the three essential components of successful aging. For the majority who are not optimal agers, however, these are aspirational goals.

47. The characteristics of George Vaillant's men who aged well closely resemble those of Rowe and Kahn (1998). Though Vaillant used five criteria rather than three to define aging well, two of them related to physical health (no disability at 75 and good self-rated health), and the other three overlapped with maintaining high physical and cognitive functions and active engagement [Vaillant, G. E. (2002). *Aging well: Surprising guidepost to a happier life*. Boston: Little, Brown].

48. O'Kelly, E. (with A. Postman). (2008). *Chasing daylight*. New York: McGraw-Hill.

49. The author used slightly different words, with similar meaning, to describe some of the terms used in this section. While he did not use "disengagement" to describe his resignation as CEO and chair of KPMG, his actions involved a similar complete separation from his previous executive life. O'Kelly also used the term *unwinding* to describe meeting people with whom he shared special moments, and not "touching base," which includes revisiting places that once had special meaning and may evoke emotionally charged memories of a younger self.

50. For most older people, the changes in identity are far more gradual than in O'Kelly's case. A theoretical discussion of how this transformation of identity may occur was described by Whitbourne, S. K., Sneed, J. R., & Skultety, S. K. (2002). Identity processes in adulthood: Theoretical and methodological challenges. *Identity, 2*, 29–45. The authors made the point that a developmental challenge in older age is to balance identity assimilation (a tendency for older individuals to interpret experiences in terms of a previous sense identity—e.g., "I have always had an excellent sense of direction") and identity accommodation, which involves gradual changes in the view of self based on a realistic appraisal of new experiences ("This is the second time I've gotten confused driving to my

son's new house. My navigation skills are slipping a little. Next time, I'm going to use Google Maps as a backup.").

51. There has been nearly a century of research on this topic of control. For a balanced historical summary of the ways control and related terms have been conceptualized, see Blazer, D. G. (2002). Self-efficacy and depression in late life: A primary prevention proposal. *Aging and Mental Health, 6,* 315–324. The concept of control has been described in other terms that have considerable overlap. These include competence, hardiness, resiliency, and self-efficacy [White, R. (1972). *The enterprise of living: Growth and organization in personality.* New York: Holt, Rinehart and Winston; Kobasa, S. C., Maddi, S. R., & Kahn, S. (1982). Hardiness and health: A prospective study. *Journal of Personality and Social Psychology, 42,* 168–177; Welch, D. C., & West, R. L. (1995). Self-efficacy and mastery: Its application to issues of environmental control, cognition, and aging. *Developmental Review, 15,* 150–171; and Bandura, A. (1997). *Self-efficacy: The exercise of control.* New York: Freeman]. The common elements included in the concept of control are a sense of agency, a positive attitude, being committed to a task, social supports, and a belief in one's capabilities to accomplish a goal.

52. Longfellow, H. W. (1875). "Morituri Salutamus," Stanza 24.

53. Among 287 members of the 3rd Age Study, the correlations between Speilberger's State Curiosity scale and less physical and cognitive decline were moderately strong, measuring .27 and .30, respectively [Powell, D. H. (2002, November). *Psychosocial correlates of stable or improved health among 3rd agers.* Paper presented at the annual meeting of the Gerontological Society of America, Boston]; research on novel stimuli by Daffner, K. R., Chong, H., Riis, J., Rents, D. M., Walk, D. A., Budson, A. E., et al. (2007). Cognitive status impacts age-related changes in attention to novel and target events in normal adults. *Neuropsychology, 21,* 291–300.

Index

Note *t* indicates tables, *f* indicates figures, and *n* indicates notes.

A

AA (Alcoholics Anonymous), 75–76, 245*n*51
AACD, *see* Age-related cognitive decline
Access, restraint, delete function, 47, 190
Accidents waiting to happen, 158, 271*n*7; *see also* High-risk cognitive aging
Actions to benefit intellect, *see* Strategies to maximize intellect
Activation of doctor within, 15, 16–17, 58, 194–195
ACTIVE research project, 100–101, 236*n*58, 254*nn*21–22
Activities of daily living (ADLs), 175–176, 266*n*13, 272*n*11
Activity levels
    aptitude test performance and, 68–69
    benefiting others (*see* Volunteerism)
    brain and, 68, 238–239*n*16, 259–260*n*8
    case studies, 116
    dementia and, 239*n*19, 273*n*24
    health and, 238*n*14
    high-risk cognitive aging and, 160–161, 177, 271*nn*8–9, 274*n*29
    level of intellect and, 6, 7
    life expectancy and, 279*n*42
    normal cognitive aging and, 136–137, 137*t*
    optimal cognitive aging and, 66–67, 115–116, 130, 186, 188, 195–196, 259–260*n*8
    in retirement, 237*n*8
Adiposity, *see* Obesity
ADLs (activities of daily living), 175–176, 266*n*13, 272*n*11
Adrenalin, 80, 81–82, 94
Advanced Cognitive Training for Independent Vital Elderly (ACTIVE), 100–101, 236*n*58, 254*nn*21–22
Aerobic exercise, 63, 65
AFib (atrial fibrillation), 19–20, 22–24, 178, 216–217*nn*15–24, 227*n*77

Age and mental ability, *see* Age-related cognitive decline; Mental ability and aging
Ageism, 154, 269*nn*37–39
Age-related cognitive decline (AACD); *see also* Mental ability and aging
    case studies, 50, 59
    definition of, 51
    dementia and, 53, 53*t*, 234–235*n*48
    hearing loss and, 29
    high-risk cognitive aging and, 157, 270*nn*3–4
    identification of, 233*nn*37–38
    mild cognitive impairment and, 52–53, 234–235*nn*45–50
    strategies to minimize, 11*t*, 12
Aging, cognitive, *see* Mental ability and aging; *specific levels of cognitive aging*
Aging optimally, *see* Optimal cognitive aging
Aging well, 213–214*n*1, 280*n*47; *see also* Optimal cognitive aging; Successful aging
Airline pilots, 93–96, 94*f*, 95, 252*n*10
Alcohol abuse/dependence; *see also* Alcohol consumption
    AA and 12-step programs, 75–76, 245*n*51
    case studies, 167–169
    driving under influence, 167–169, 273*n*18
    gender and, 74–75, 85
    identification of, 84–85
    overview of, 75, 244–245*nn*49–53
Alcohol consumption
    AA and 12-step programs, 75–76, 245*n*51
    abuse/dependence (*see* Alcohol abuse/dependence)
    aging and, 73, 244*n*46, 245*n*52
    case studies, 139, 142, 167–169
    cohort changes in, 275*n*5
    decrease in, 184
    frequency of, 74, 75, 244*nn*44–46
    giving up, 120
    health and, 73–74, 75, 266*n*13
    hypertension and, 73, 243*n*37
    measurement of, 250*n*92

mental ability and, 243*n*42
normal cognitive aging and, 153–154
prescription medication and, 84
wine drinkers, 74, 120, 139, 243*n*40
Alcoholics Anonymous (AA), 75–76,
    245*n*51
Alzheimer's disease; *see also* Dementia
    Alzheimer's type dementia and,
        233*n*40
    applications and reflections, 50, 58–59,
        61
    burden of caregivers, 266–267*nn*15–16
    case studies, 59–61
    chronic obstructive pulmonary disease
        and, 218*n*31
    diagnosis of, 51–52, 233*n*40
    diet and, 213*n*23
    Lewy body dementia and, 52, 234*n*43
Analogies test, 41
Anger, 158–160, 179, 180, 274*n*31
Annual physicals, 117, 260*n*11
Anxiety; *see also* Stress management
    about mental acuity, 13
    aging and, 81, 249*n*77
    frequency of, 194, 279*n*38
    hypertension effects and, 215*n*10
    management of, 79, 194, 279*n*39
    mental ability effects, 213*n*18
    problem solving and, 97
Apneas, 26; *see also* Obstructive sleep
    apnea (OSA)
Appearance
    hearing aids and, 164
    high-risk cognitive aging and, 159, 161
    optimal cognitive aging and, 6, 121,
        261*nn*19–20
Applications and reflections, *see* Practice
    applications and reflections
Aptitude test performance; *see also*
    specific abilities (e.g., memory)
    activity levels and, 68–69
    aging and (*see* Mental ability and
        aging)
    alcohol consumption and, 74
    atrial fibrillation and, 22–23
    cognitive training and, 100
    crystallized and fluid abilities, 42, 42*f*,
        44–47, 55, 236*n*55
    diabetes and, 28, 221*n*46
    exercise and, 63–66, 65*f*, 237*n*7, 237*n*9
    health and, 280*n*44
    hearing loss and, 222*n*53

high-risk cognitive aging and,
    273*nn*20–21
hypertension and, 21, 215*n*7, 215*n*10,
    240*n*26
obesity and, 240*n*26
obstructive sleep apnea and, 25, 26, 27,
    219*n*38
optimal cognitive aging and, 124–125,
    262*n*23
processing speed and, 40, 228*nn*6–9
Art education and practice, 104–105, 191,
    256*n*36
Arthritis; *see also* Joint pain
    case studies, 165–166
    obesity and, 83
    resentment and, 178
    rheumatoid, 129
Atrial fibrillation (AFib)
    intellect and, 19–20, 22–24, 216–
        217*nn*15–24, 227*n*77
    management of, 178
Attention
    aging and, 45, 46, 82, 109, 250*n*96
    applications and reflections, 190–191,
        195
    atrial fibrillation and, 19, 23
    case studies, 170, 172, 173–174
    chronic obstructive pulmonary disease
        and, 25
    distractions and, 89, 109
    driving and, 192–193
    effortful versus passive, 103
    focus lost, 123, 125
    hearing loss and, 222*n*52
    high-risk cognitive aging and, 273*n*21
    memory and, 104, 190–191
    optimal cognitive aging and, 113
    positivity bias and, 82
    restoration activities, 12, 105–106, 109,
        191, 255–257*nn*31–42
Attention restoration
    applications and reflections, 105–106,
        109, 191
    maximizing intellect and, 12,
        255–257*nn*31–42
Attitudes and behaviors; *see also specific
    topics beginning with attitudes*
    applications and reflections, 177–181
    high-risk cognitive aging, 167–177,
        170*t*, 178–181, 273–274*nn*18–28
    normal cognitive aging, 143–152, 145*t*,
        267–269*nn*21–32

optimal cognitive aging, 112, 118–119, 122–129, 123*t,* 260–261*nn*13–14, 262–264*nn*21–32

Attitudes and behaviors with high-risk cognitive aging
driving dangerously, 174–175, 273–274*n*26
dysexecutive cognitive symptoms, 175–176, 274*n*27
feelings on mental ability, 170, 178, 273*n*19
memory problems, 171, 273*n*20
mental activities, 172–173, 273*n*22
other chronic cognitive problems, 171–172, 273*n*21
social relationships, 173–174, 273*nn*23–24
vulnerable financially, 169, 176–177, 274*n*28

Attitudes and behaviors with normal cognitive aging
cognitive decline accepted, 147, 268*n*23
cognitive status appraisal, 146–147, 267*n*22
communication technology limited, 148–149, 262–263*n*28
feeling mentally average with declines, 145–146, 267*n*21
mental activities avoided, 151–152
mild executive dysfunction, 150, 268*nn*29–30
openness to new experiences, 151, 262*n*31
selection, optimization, compensation, 149–150, 268*nn*27–28
social relationships, 147–148, 268*nn*24–25

Attitudes and behaviors with optimal cognitive aging
activities for sharpness, 127, 263*n*29
benefits of, 261*n*18
case studies, 122–123, 124–125, 126, 127, 128–129
communication technology, 6, 126–127, 262–263*n*28
control and usefulness, 129, 263–264*n*32
mentally sharp, 124–125, 262*n*23
mental vigor and focus, 123–124
minor cognitive problems, 125, 262*n*24

openness to new experiences, 128, 188, 201, 263*n*31
overview of, 112, 123, 123*t,* 188
selection, optimization, compensation, 128
social relationships, 126, 188, 262*nn*25–27

Average cognitive aging, *see* Normal cognitive aging

B

Bariatric surgery, 158–160, 180
Behavioral Risk Factor Surveillance System (BRFSS) survey, 261*n*15
Behaviors and attitudes, *see* Attitudes and behaviors
Being away, 105–106, 257*n*39, 257*n*42
Bereavement
case studies, 163, 164–165, 166, 173–174
depression and, 189, 272*n*16, 274*n*31
Biggest Loser, The (television), 84
Bill paying problems, 166–167, 172–173, 179
Blood clots, 22
Blood pressure, *see* Hypertension
BMI (body mass index), 69–70, 249*n*84
Body mass index (BMI), 69–70, 249*n*84
Bomber crews, 79–80, 248*n*70
Brain
activity levels and, 66, 68, 238–239*n*16, 259–260*n*8
alcohol consumption and, 74, 75
atrial fibrillation and, 217*n*20
cancer of, 199–200
chronic pulmonary disease and, 24–25, 26
diabetes and, 28, 221*n*47
exercise and, 55, 66
hypertension and, 22, 23
mild cognitive impairment and, 274*n*27
neuroplasticity and, 47–49, 231–233*nn*27–36
sedentary lifestyle and, 259–260*n*8
smoking and, 185
stress and, 80, 81*f,* 213*n*18, 248*nn*73–74
Brain fitness merchandise, 98, 99, 253–254*n*18; *see also* Cognitive training

Brain-scanning technologies, 48, 58, 196, 231*n*28
Breast cancer, 56, 117, 167–169
BRFSS (Behavioral Risk Factor Surveillance System) survey, 261*n*15
Burden of caregivers, 141, 165, 266–267*nn*15–16

C

CAGE (cut back, annoyed, guilt, eye opener), 85
Calculation, 42, 42*f*, 113
Calorie use, 67, 68*t*, 238*n*13
Cancer
  brain, 199–200
  breast, 56, 117, 167–169
  pancreatic, 172–173, 179
  prostate, 78, 79
Cardiovascular disease
  alcohol consumption and, 73, 243*n*37
  atrial fibrillation, 19–20, 22–24, 178, 216–217*nn*15–24, 227*n*77
  case studies, 78, 79, 158–160, 162, 180
  cognitive decline and, 22, 23, 215*n*7, 217*n*24, 280*n*44
  diet and, 14, 72–73, 83, 186, 212*n*13, 213*n*22, 242*n*33, 249*n*84
  exercise and, 11, 65, 82–83, 187, 196, 237*n*4, 242*n*33
  hypertension (*see* Hypertension)
  metabolic syndrome and, 164
  normal cognitive aging and, 139
  obesity and, 83
  social relationships and, 76, 245–246*n*55, 261*n*18
Caregivers
  clinical notes for, 190–196, 278–279*nn*28–41
  levels of intellect and, 5–6, 188–189
  stress of, 141, 152–153, 165, 266–267*nn*15–16
Care providers, xv, 190–196, 278–279*nn*28–41
Cars, *see* Parking and finding cars
Case studies
  challenges and passions of 3rd Agers, 14
  healthy habits for mental ability, 66–67, 71–72, 78, 79

high-risk cognitive aging (*see* High-risk cognitive aging case studies)
  mental ability and aging, 50–51, 59–61
  normal cognitive aging (*see* Normal cognitive aging case studies)
  optimal cognitive aging (*see* Optimal cognitive aging case studies)
  source of, xvi
  strategies to maximize intellect, 102–103, 114–115, 125, 127
  therapeutic alliance, 16–17
Cell phone use, 44, 151; *see also* Communication technology; Telephone use
Change
  adapting to, 97–98, 113
  identity and, 15
  motivation for, 179
Chasing Daylight (O'Kelly), 199–200
Checking accounts, 172–173, 179
Cholesterol
  case studies, 134–136, 158–160, 167–169, 172, 180
  dementia and, 271*n*10
  reductions in, 184, 275*n*6
Chronic bronchitis, 24–25
Chronic medical conditions; *see also specific conditions*
  applications and reflections, 177–181
  case studies, 129, 138
  dementia and, 11, 20, 21, 162, 270*n*2, 271*n*10
  disability and, 31–32, 36, 225*n*68
  gender and, 37, 222*n*50, 226*n*75, 266*n*10
  health self-ratings and, 225–226*n*71
  high-risk cognitive aging and, 7–8, 161–162, 163, 177–178, 271*n*10, 272*n*12
  increases in, 183, 184–185
  intellect and (*see* Chronic medical conditions and intellectual functioning)
  normal cognitive aging and, 138–139, 260*n*10, 266*nn*10–11
  optimal cognitive aging and, 19, 213–214*n*1, 260*n*10
  quality of life and, 4
  risky habits and, 274–275*n*1
  smoking and, 185
  social relationships and, 246*n*57

Chronic medical conditions and
   intellectual functioning
   cardiovascular disease, 20–24, 214–
      217*nn*5–24, 227*n*77, 266*n*11
   chronic pulmonary disease, 24–27,
      218–220*nn*25–44
   cognitive decline, 20, 197, 198*f*
   diabetes, 27–28, 220–222*nn*45–49,
      266*n*11
   hearing loss, 28–31, 222–223*nn*50–60
   high-risk cognitive aging, 7–8
   overview of, 11, 19–20, 213–214*nn*2–4
Chronic obstructive pulmonary
   disease (COPD), 24–25, 162,
      218–219*nn*27–34
Chronic pulmonary disease
   chronic obstructive pulmonary disease,
      24–25, 162, 218–219*nn*27–34
   obstructive sleep apnea, 25–27,
      219–220*nn*35–44
Cognition, *see* Intellectual functioning
Cognitive aging, *see* Mental ability and
      aging; *specific levels of cognitive
      aging*
Cognitive decline; *see also* Dementia; Mild
      cognitive impairment (MCI)
   age-related (*see* Age-related cognitive
      decline)
   anxiety and, 194
   applications and reflections, 58–59,
      108, 179
   case studies, 175–176
   chronic conditions and (*see* Cognitive
      decline and chronic medical
      conditions)
   concerns about, 114
   curiosity scale and, 281*n*53
   dementia global screening and, 279*n*41
   driving and, 193
   dysexecutive cognitive impairment,
      278*n*33
   education and, 39–40, 197, 198*f*
   gender and, 198*f*
   health and, 197, 198*f*, 280*n*44
   healthy habits and (*see* Cognitive
      decline and healthy lifestyle
      habits)
   high risk for (*see* High-risk cognitive
      aging)
   normal cognitive aging and, 147,
      268*n*23

optimal cognitive aging and, 44–46,
      125, 130
   quality of life and, 4
   smoking and, 185
Cognitive decline and chronic medical
      conditions
   atrial fibrillation, 23, 217*n*24
   chronic obstructive pulmonary disease,
      24–25
   diabetes, 28
   hearing loss and, 223*n*56
   hypertension, 22, 215*n*7
   obstructive sleep apnea, 26, 27, 220*n*44
   overview of, 20, 197, 198*f*, 280*n*44
Cognitive decline and healthy lifestyle
      habits
   alcohol consumption, 74, 75
   diet, 73, 186
   exercise/activity levels, 65–66, 69
   isolation, 77, 173, 247*n*65, 262*n*25
   mental exercise, 263*n*29
   obesity, 70
   openness to new experiences, 201
   overview of, 10, 13
   social relationships, 77, 147
   stress management, 187
Cognitive inhibition, 47, 90, 190–191
Cognitive placebo effects, 101,
      254–255*n*25
Cognitive training
   generalization to life, 100, 101–102,
      255*n*26
   mild cognitive impairment and, 59
   neuroplasticity and, 232*n*32
   overview of, 98–102, 253–255*nn*16–30
   research on, 100–101, 236*n*58,
      254*nn*21–22
Cohort effects, 184, 227*n*2, 230*n*23,
      275*nn*4–5
Cold virus and social networks,
      245–246*n*55
College attendance, 127
Combat exposure and stress, 80, 81*f*,
      248*n*70, 248*n*74
Communication technology
   case studies, 134–136
   normal cognitive aging and, 148–149,
      262–263*n*28
   optimal cognitive aging and, 6,
      126–127, 262–263*n*28
Compatibility component, 105–106,
      257*n*39, 257*n*42

Compensation, 92; *see also* Selection, optimization, compensation
Competence and optimal cognitive aging, 129, 263–264*n*32
Compliance, *see* Medical advice compliance; Prescription medication compliance
Compression of morbidity, 184, 196, 276*n*10
Compromised mental functioning, 49–54, 53*t*, 233–235*nn*37–50; *see also* Cognitive decline
Computer use, 126–127, 151, 262–263*n*28
Concentration, 262*n*24; *see also* Attention; Working memory
Consumer fraud, 87, 169, 176–177, 274*n*28
Continuing care retirement communities, 85–87, 193–194
Continuous positive airway pressure (CPAP) mask, 27, 220*n*43
Control, cognitive, 64, 65*f*; *see also* Attention; Cognitive inhibition
Control, sense of
   elements of, 281*n*51
   loss of, 199–200
   optimal cognitive aging and, 129, 263–264*n*32
Cooking and multitasking, 44
COPD (chronic obstructive pulmonary disease), 24–25, 162, 218–219*nn*27–34
Coping, 34–35*t*, 35, 79; *see also* Strategies to maximize intellect; Stress management
Coronary disease, *see* Cardiovascular disease
Cortisol, 80
Cosmetic interventions, 121, 261*n*20
Counseling
   benefits of, 179–181, 189
   therapeutic alliance, 16, 213*n*25
CPAP (continuous positive airway pressure) mask, 27, 220*n*43
Cross-sectional research, 39, 227–228*nn*2–3, 262*n*25
Crystallized and fluid abilities
   aptitude test performance, 42, 42*f*, 44–47, 55, 236*n*55
   high-risk cognitive aging and, 273*n*21
   training and, 100
Curiosity and declines in functioning, 201

Cut back, annoyed, guilt, eye opener (CAGE), 85

D

DAT (dementia of Alzheimer's type), 233*n*40
Death, 4, 210–211*nn*6–7; *see also* Mortality
Decision making
   active experience and, 95, 96, 97–98
   aging and, 229*n*15
   applications and reflections, 56–57, 131
   positivity bias and, 85–87, 193–194
   working memory and, 43
Defensive listening, 30
Dementia
   activity levels and, 239*n*19, 273*n*24
   age-associated cognitive decline and, 53, 53*t*, 234–235*n*48
   alcohol consumption and, 74
   of Alzheimer's type, 233*n*40 (*see also* Alzheimer's disease)
   atrial fibrillation and, 22, 216*n*16
   caregiver burden and, 141, 266–267*nn*15–16
   chronic medical conditions and, 11, 20, 21, 162, 270*n*2, 271*n*10
   definition and diagnosis of, 51–52
   diet and, 14, 213*n*23
   healthy habits and, 10
   with Lewy bodies, 52, 234*n*43
   lifesaving interventions and, 4, 210–211*nn*6–7
   mild cognitive impairment and, 53, 53*t*, 58–59, 60, 197–198, 235*n*49, 280*n*45
   obesity and, 70, 83, 240*n*25, 271*n*10
   overview of, 233–234*nn*39–44
   social relationships and, 77, 273*nn*23–24
   training programs and, 102
   vascular, 52
Demographics
   chronic medical conditions and, 36
   dementia risk and, 53
   life expectancy, 226*nn*73–74
   of 3rd Agers, 3, 209*n*2, 275*n*3
Depression
   aging and, 81, 249*n*77
   anxiety and, 194
   bereavement and, 189, 272*n*16, 274*n*31
   brain and, 80

burden and, 141
case studies, 158–160, 164, 173–174, 180
diagnosis of, 112
down days (*see* Down days)
education and, 267*n*18
exercise and, 65
frequency of, 279*n*38
high-risk cognitive aging and, 272*n*14
social relationships and, 165
Developmental hurdles of 3rd Agers, 130–131, 199, 280*n*50
Diabetes
case studies, 118, 143, 158–160, 164, 180
dementia and, 271*n*10
diet and, 186, 221–222*n*49
healthy habits and, 72
high-risk cognitive aging and, 163
intellect and, 27–28, 220–222*nn*45–49, 266*n*11
management of, 178
normal cognitive aging and, 139
obesity and, 83
stress hormones and, 80
Diagnostic and Statistical Manual of Mental Disorders, Fourth Edition (DSM-IV-TR), 112, 134
Diet
cardiovascular disease and, 14, 72–73, 83, 186, 212*n*13, 213*n*22, 242*n*33, 249*n*84
dementia and, 14, 213*n*23
diabetes and, 186, 221–222*n*49
mental ability and, 71–73, 186, 241–242*nn*30–36
resource on, 241*n*32
Digital hearing aids, 223*n*58
Digit symbol substitution, 41, 41*f*
Direct actions for intellect, *see* Strategies to maximize intellect
Disability
declines in, 31–32, 224–225*nn*63–68, 275*n*7
gender and, 37
high-risk cognitive aging and, 158
life expectancy free of, 184, 276*n*9
obesity and, 83
optimal cognitive aging and, 124, 127, 258*n*2
risky habits and, 139, 266*n*13
Disengagement, 199–200, 280*n*49

Disorientation/getting lost, 7, 143–144, 146–147, 273–274*n*26, 280–281*n*50; *see also* Visuospatial abilities
Distractions; *see also* Attention restoration
atrial fibrillation and, 19
attention and, 89, 109
case studies, 147
homemade remedies for, 195
inhibition and, 47, 90, 190–191
memory and, 57
Divided-attention tasks, *see* Multitasking
Divorce case study, 119
Dizziness case study, 138
DLB (Lewy body dementia), 52, 234*n*43
Doctor within, 15, 16–17, 58, 194–195
Down days
case studies, 134–136, 142, 158–160, 180
high-risk cognitive aging and, 158, 164–165, 272*nn*14–15
normal cognitive aging and, 141–142, 267*nn*17–18
optimal cognitive aging and, 119, 261*n*15
Drinking, *see* Alcohol consumption
Driving
alcohol consumption and, 167–169, 273*n*18
applications and reflections, 192–193
case studies, 50, 55–56, 115, 143–144, 146, 174–175
disorientation/getting lost, 143–144, 146–147, 273–274*n*26, 280–281*n*50
giving up, 115
high-risk cognitive aging and, 174–175, 273–274*n*26
improving (*see* Driving strategies)
license retesting requirements, 193, 278*n*34
mild cognitive impairment and, 273–274*n*26
multitasking and, 174–175
Driving strategies
directions memorized, 45, 46, 47
global position system (GPS), 143–144, 193
parking/finding car, 90, 125, 128, 172, 192
route planning, 89–90

selection, optimization, compensation , 128, 192–193
stress management, 12
Driving under influence (DUI), 167–169, 273*n*18
Drug treatment, *see* Prescription medication
DSM-IV-TR (Diagnostic and Statistical Manual of Mental Disorders, Fourth Edition), 112, 134
Dual-tasks, *see* Multitasking
DUI (driving under influence), 167–169, 273*n*18
Dysexecutive cognitive impairment, 278*n*33
Dysexecutive mild cognitive impairment, 175–176, 192, 274*n*27

E

Educational level
    aging and, 197, 198*f,* 280*n*44
    chronic medical conditions and, 36
    cognitive decline and, 39–40, 197, 198*f*
    compromised functioning and, 53
    healthy habits and, 184–185
    instrumental activities of daily living and, 272–273*n*17
    mentally unhealthy days and, 267*n*18
    preventive health care and, 276*n*11
Elective selection, 91
E-mail, *see* Communication technology
Emotion(s)
    adrenalin rush and, 94
    arousal time, 81–82, 249*n*79
    attention and, 250*n*96
    positivity bias and, 193–194, 201
    stress management and, 79, 152–153, 266–267*n*16
    touching base and, 200
Emotional problems, 7, 52, 141–142; *see also* Mental health
Emphysema, 24–25, 139
Employment and technology, 149
Encoding, 47–48, 229*n*18
Energy levels
    high-risk cognitive aging and, 160–161, 177, 271*nn*8–9
    level of intellect and, 6–7
    normal cognitive aging and, 136–137, 137*t*

optimal cognitive aging and, 115–116, 130, 259–260*n*8
Environment and cognitive aging, 54–55; *see also* Living arrangement decisions
Executive functioning
    activity levels and, 68
    aging and, 42, 42*f*
    applications and reflections, 192
    case studies, 150
    diabetes and, 221*n*46
    exercise and, 48, 64, 65*f,* 66
    measurement of, 238–239*n*16
    mild cognitive impairment and, 175–176, 192, 274*n*27, 278*n*33
    normal cognitive aging and, 150, 268*nn*29–30
    obstructive sleep apnea and, 26, 219*n*38
Exercise
    activities of daily living and, 266*n*13
    aptitude test performance and, 63–66, 65*f,* 237*n*7, 237*n*9
    benefits of, 10, 186
    brain and, 55, 66
    cardiovascular health and, 11, 65, 82–83, 187, 196, 237*n*4, 242*n*33
    case studies, 114, 116
    chronic obstructive pulmonary disease and, 25, 219*n*33
    cognitive control and, 64, 65*f*
    diet compared to, 72–73
    executive functioning and, 48, 64, 65*f,* 66
    fitness level and, 278*n*27
    generalization of cognitive training and, 101–102, 255*n*29
    guilt and shame, 142–143, 267*n*20
    health and, 34*t,* 35, 242*n*33, 264*n*34
    high-risk cognitive aging and, 189
    increase in, 184, 275*n*5
    life expectancy and, 279*n*42
    loss-based selection and, 91
    mental ability and, 63–66, 65*f,* 236–237*nn*2–11, 238*n*13, 249*nn*83–84
    mental health and, 73
    metabolic equivalents for, 67, 68*t,* 238*n*13, 264*n*34
    mortality and, 82–83, 249*nn*83–84
    neuroplasticity and, 48, 232*nn*32–33
    type and amount needed, 63–65
    weight loss and, 241*nn*28–29

Extent component, 257*nn*39–40

F

Failure of success, 31; *see also* Life
    expectancy
Faith and health, 35, 35*t*
Fascination, 105–106, 257*n*39
Fatigue, 26, 27; *see also* Sleep
Favorable attrition, 227*n*2
Favorite place prescriptions, 109, 191
50th reunions, 1–2
Fight-or-flight response, 80
Financial issues; *see also* Income
    bill paying, 166–167, 172–173, 179
    health and, 35, 35*t*
    residence decisions and, 85–87, 97–98,
        193–194
    vulnerability to misjudgment, 87, 169,
        176–177, 274*n*28
Fish in diet and dementia, 14, 213*n*23
Flexibility, mental, 23, 150, 201
Flexibility training (exercise), 65
Flight 1549, 93–96, 94*f*
Florida Geriatric Research Program
        (Clearwater, FL)
    comparative health in, 32–36, 33*f*,
        34–35*t*, 225*n*70, 246*n*59
    stress and health in, 81
Flu and stress, 79
Fluid and crystallized abilities
    aptitude test performance and, 42, 42*f*,
        44–47, 55, 236*n*55
    high-risk cognitive aging and, 273*n*21
    training and, 100
*F*MRI (functional magnetic resonance
        imaging), 231*n*28
Forgiveness, 15–17
Fraud, 87, 169, 176–177, 274*n*28
Free choice, 105–106
Freedom from doing well, 105–106,
        257*n*40
Friendships, *see* Social relationships
Functional magnetic resonance imaging
        (*f*MRI), 231*n*28
Functional plasticity, *see* Neuroplasticity

G

GAF (Global Assessment of Functioning),
        112, 134, 158
Gender differences

alcohol consumption, 74–75, 85,
        243–244*n*46
chronic medical conditions, 37,
        222*n*50, 226*n*75, 266*n*10
cognitive decline, 198*f*
health, 275*n*4
hearing loss, 222*n*50
life expectancy, 37
mentally unhealthy days, 267*n*17
spatial abilities, 267*n*22
Generalization of cognitive training,
        101–102, 255*n*29
Global Assessment of Functioning (GAF),
        112, 134, 158
Global position system (GPS), 143–144,
        193
Glucocorticoids, 248–249*n*76
Glucose consumption, 92, 107
GPS (global position system), 143–144,
        193
Gray matter of brain, 48–49, 66,
        232–233*nn*34–35
Grieving, *see* Bereavement

H

Habits, *see* Healthy lifestyle habits
Hallucinations and dementia, 52
Hawking, Stephen, 258*n*2
Health
    aging and, 33, 33*f*, 34–35*t*, 73, 197,
        198*f*, 280*n*44
    better now than ever, 183–185,
        274–275*nn*1–11
    chronic medical conditions and,
        225–226*n*71
    cognitive decline and, 197, 198*f*,
        280*n*44
    cohort effects, 184, 275*nn*4–5
    comparative ratings of, 32–36, 33*f*,
        34–35*t*, 225*n*70
    curiosity scale and, 281*n*53
    definition of, 3, 210*n*3–4
    feeling useful and, 263–264*n*32
    healthy habits and (*see* Health and
        healthy lifestyle habits)
    high-risk cognitive aging and, 157,
        271–272*nn*10–13
    intellect and (*see* Health effects on
        intellectual functioning)
    pre-hypertension and, 20–21
    problem solving and, 261*n*16

qualities with intellectual levels (*see* Health-related qualities)
self-perceptions of aging and, 261*n*14
self-rated health and, 116, 137, 260*n*9, 275*n*2
stress and, 79–80, 81, 187, 248*n*70, 266–267*nn*15–16
Health and healthy lifestyle habits
activity levels, 238*n*14
alcohol consumption, 73–74, 75, 266*n*13
exercise, 34*t*, 35, 242*n*33, 264*n*34
medication compliance, 186–187
openness to new experiences, 201
overview of, 9, 211–212*nn*12–13
pets, 126, 262*n*27
preventive measures, 184, 276*n*11
selection, optimization, compensation, 268*nn*27–28
social relationships, 34–35*t*, 35, 268*n*24
volunteerism, 120
Health-care coverage task, 43
Health care providers, xv, 190–196, 278–279*nn*28–41; *see also* Caregivers
Health effects on intellectual functioning; *see also specific conditions*
applications and reflections, 12–15, 36–38, 226–227*nn*72–77
chronic conditions, 19–31, 214–223*nn*2–60 (*see also* Chronic medical conditions and intellectual functioning)
disability rate and, 31–32, 224–225*nn*63–68
health ratings and, 32–36, 33*f*, 34–35*t*, 225–226*nn*70–71
healthy habits (*see* Healthy lifestyle habits)
measurement issues, 70, 227*n*77
Health Professionals Follow-up Study, 212*n*13
Health-related qualities; *see also specific topics beginning health-related*
high-risk cognitive aging, 160–167, 161*t*, 177–178, 271–273*nn*8–17
normal cognitive aging, 136–143, 137*t*, 265–267*nn*7–20
optimal cognitive aging, 112, 115–121, 115*t*, 259–261*nn*7–20
Health-related qualities with high-risk cognitive aging
applications and reflections, 177–181

chronic conditions or risky habits, 161–162, 163, 177–178, 271*n*10, 272*n*12
down days, 158, 164–165, 272*nn*14–15
energy and activity level, 160–161, 177, 271*nn*8–9
instrumental activities of daily living, 166–167, 272–273*n*17
major risk factors, 163–164, 272*nn*12–13
problems reduce enjoyment, 162–163, 272*n*11
stressful events, 165–166, 178, 272*n*16
Health-related qualities with normal cognitive aging
chronic conditions, 138–139, 266*nn*10–11
comparative health, 137–138, 265*n*8
corrective action lacking, 142–143, 267*nn*19–20
down days, 141–142, 267*nn*17–18
energy and activity level, 136–137, 137*t*
medical checkups, 138, 265*n*9
risky habits, 139–140, 266*nn*12–13
stressful events, 141
Health-related qualities with optimal cognitive aging
appearance conscious, 6, 121, 261*nn*19–20
attitude upbeat, 118–119, 260–261*nn*13–14
awareness of healthy behaviors, 119–120, 261*n*16
energy and activity level, 66–67, 115–116, 130, 186, 188, 195–196, 259–260*n*8
good health, 116–117, 260*nn*9–10
medical advice compliance, 11, 11*t*, 117, 118, 260*nn*11–12
overview of, 188
proactive checkups, 117, 260*n*11
stress management, 78–79, 119, 131, 261*n*15
volunteerism, 120–121, 129, 130, 188, 261*n*18
Healthy lifestyle habits
applications and reflections, 131
cognitive decline and, 10, 13
disability rate and, 32
doctor within and, 58
gender and, 37
improvements in, 154–155, 184–185

for mental ability (*see* Healthy lifestyle habits for mental ability)
mild cognitive impairment and, 54
neuroplasticity and, 48, 232*nn*32–35
optimal cognitive aging and, 10, 11*t*, 188, 195–197, 198*f,* 212*n*13, 213–214*n*1, 280*n*44
overview of, 111, 258*n*3
preventive health care, 184, 276*n*11
Healthy lifestyle habits for mental ability
active leisure, 66–69, 68*t,* 238–239*nn*12–20
alcohol moderation, 73–76, 243–245*nn*37–53
applications and reflections, 82–87, 249–250*nn*83–97
case studies, 66–67, 71–72, 78, 79
eating healthy, 71–73, 186, 241–242*nn*30–36, 249*n*84
exercising, 63–66, 65*f,* 236–237*nn*2–11, 238*n*13, 249*nn*83–84
obesity fighting, 69–71, 84, 239–241*nn*21–29, 269*n*34
overview of, 185–187, 195–197, 198*f,* 276–277*n*12–25, 280*n*44
rationale for, 8–12, 11*t,* 63, 211–212*nn*12–13, 212–213*nn*17–19
social relationships, 76–77, 245–247*nn*54–65, 268*n*24
stress management, 78–82, 81*f,* 247–249*nn*66–82
volunteerism, 189
Hearing aids
compliance on, 30, 164, 223*n*57, 223*n*59
digital, 223*n*58
as optimization, 91
Hearing loss
case studies, 163, 164
gender and, 222*n*50
intellect and, 28–31, 222–223*nn*50–60
Heart disease, *see* Cardiovascular disease
Helplessness, 97
Hereditary factors in mental ability and aging, 54–55, 235–236*nn*51–54
High blood pressure, *see* Hypertension
High-risk cognitive aging
applications and reflections, 177–181, 274*nn*29–31
attitudes and behaviors, 167–177, 170*t,* 178–179, 273–274*nn*18–28

case studies (*see* High-risk cognitive aging case studies)
chronic medical conditions, 7–8, 161–162, 177–178, 271*n*10, 272*n*12
feeling older, 271*n*8, 273*n*19
health qualities, 160–167, 161*t,* 177–178, 271–273*nn*8–17
identification of, 157, 158–160, 170*t* 161*t,* 269–270*n*1, 271*nn*6–7
intelligence and, 8
mental abilities, 189
overview of, 5*f,* 7–8, 157, 269–271*nn*1–5
High-risk cognitive aging case studies
attitudes and behaviors, 167–169, 170, 171, 172–177, 273*n*18
health qualities, 162, 163, 164–167
identification of, 158–160
Hip fracture, 97–98
Hippocampus
neuroplasticity and, 231*n*28
stress and, 80, 81*f,* 213*n*18, 248*nn*73–74
Humility and decision making, 98
Hypertension
alcohol consumption and, 73, 243*n*37
applications and reflections, 154
brain and, 22, 23
case studies, 15–17, 118, 134–136, 158–160, 167–169, 172, 180
definition of, 20, 214*n*5
dementia and, 21, 271*n*10
diet and, 72–73, 83, 242*n*33, 249*n*84
effects of, 13, 227*n*77
exercise and, 242*n*33
healthy habits and, 212*n*13
high-risk cognitive aging and, 163
intellect and, 20–22, 214–216*nn*5–14
medication compliance and, 22, 260*n*12
memory, 240*n*26
stress hormones and, 80
Hypoxemia, 24–25, 26–27, 220*n*40

I

IADLs, *see* Instrumental activities of daily living
Identity
bariatric surgery and, 158–160, 180, 189
change and, 14

redefining, 199
richness of 3rd age and, 280–281*n*50
Immune system, 248*n*71
Income
    alcohol consumption and, 244*n*44
    chronic medical conditions and, 36
    healthy habits and, 184–185
    instrumental activities of daily living
        and, 272–273*n*17
    intellectual deterioration and, 39–40,
        228*n*3
    mentally unhealthy days and, 267*n*18
    optimal cognitive aging and, 188
    preventive health care and, 276*n*11
Inhibition, cognitive, 47, 90, 190–191
Insomnia, *see* Sleep
Instrumental activities of daily living
        (IADLs)
    case studies, 166–169, 172–173, 179
    high-risk cognitive aging and, 166–167,
        272–273*n*17
Intellectual functioning
    aptitude test performance (*see* Aptitude
        test performance)
    case studies, 14, 15–17
    growing importance of, 3–4,
        210–211*nn*3–9
    health effects on (*see* Health effects on
        intellectual functioning)
    healthy habits and, 8–12, 11*t*, 211–
        212*nn*11–19 (*see also* Healthy
        lifestyle habits for mental
        ability)
    intelligence (*see* Intelligence)
    levels of, xiii, 4–8, 5*f*, 188–189, 211*n*10,
        277–278*nn*26–27
    mental ability/general aptitude (*see*
        Mental ability and aging)
    overview of, 1–3, 209*n*1
    strategies to maximize (*see* Strategies
        to maximize intellect)
    working principles for, 12–15,
        213*nn*20–25
Intelligence (IQ)
    aging and, 39, 40*f*, 227*n*1
    compromised functioning and, 52
    crystallized and fluid abilities, 236*n*55
    hearing loss and, 29, 30, 222*n*53
    hereditary factors in, 54–55
    high-risk cognitive aging and, 8
    hypertension and, 22
    loneliness and, 77

mild cognitive impairment and, 54
    openness to experiences and, 263*n*31
    selection, optimization, compensation,
        268*n*28
    social relationships and, 126
    wisdom versus, 125
Internet use, 126–127, 151, 262–263*n*28
Investigations, *see* Research
IQ, *see* Intelligence (IQ)
Irritations and mortality, 246*n*57
Isolation; *see also* Loneliness
    case studies, 162
    cognitive decline and, 77, 173, 247*n*65,
        262*n*25
    mortality and, 246*n*56
    negative impact of, 85
    normal cognitive aging and, 153–154
    social networks and, 187

J

Joint pain, 138, 172; *see also* Arthritis
Judgment, *see* Decision making
Juggling and brain, 48–49,
        232–233*nn*34–35

L

Learning
    applications, 58
    desire for, 82
    gray matter and, 48–49
    memory and, 47, 57, 230–231*n*24
    optimal cognitive aging and, 95–96
Lewy body dementia (DLB), 52, 234*n*43
Life expectancy
    activity levels and, 279*n*42
    demographics, 226*n*73, 226*n*74
    free of disability, 184, 276*n*9
    gender and, 37
    living arrangements and, 97
    obesity and, 240–241*n*27, 250*n*86
    quality of life and, 31
Life satisfaction, 252*n*7; *see also* Quality
        of life
Listening, defensive, 30
Living arrangement decisions, 85–87,
        97–98, 193–194
Loneliness; *see also* Isolation
    case studies, 162, 173–174
    high-risk cognitive aging and, 273*n*23
    IQ and, 77

satisfaction with life and, 247*n*63
social relationships and, 165, 187
Longfellow, Henry Wadsworth, 200
Longitudinal research, 39, 227–228*nn*2–3,
    262*n*25
Long-term oxygen therapy (LTOT), 25,
    218–219*n*32
Losing way/disorientation, 7, 143–144,
    146–147, 273–274*n*26, 280–
    281*n*50; *see also* Visuospatial
    abilities
LTOT (long-term oxygen therapy), 25,
    218–219*n*32

M

MCI, *see* Mild cognitive impairment
Meaning of life, 260*n*13
Medical advice compliance
    annual physicals and, 117, 260*n*11
    benefits of, 186–187
    case studies, 117, 118, 134–136, 139,
        143–144
    diabetes, 28, 221–222*n*49
    hearing aid use, 30, 164, 223*n*57,
        223*n*59
    improving, 37
    level of intellect and, 6, 7–8
    mind-body connection and, 13
    normal cognitive aging and, 142–143,
        267*nn*19–20
    optimal cognitive aging and, 11, 11*t*,
        117, 118–119, 260*nn*11–12
    prescription medications (*see*
        Prescription medication
        compliance)
    psychological distress and, 164, 272*n*15
    weight loss, 241*nn*28–29
Medical checkups/intervention
    health ratings and, 34*t*, 35
    level of intellect and, 6, 7–8
    normal cognitive aging and, 138,
        265*n*9
Medication, *see* Prescription medication
Melancholic grieving, 165; *see also*
        Bereavement
Memory
    activity levels and, 68
    age-related cognitive decline and, 51,
        233*n*38, 234–235*n*48
    aging and, 42, 42*f*, 43–44, 45–47, 48,
        229*nn*13–17, 251*n*2, 262*n*24

attention and, 104, 190–191
case studies (*see* Memory case studies)
cohort effects, 230*n*23
compromised functioning and, 52
diabetes and, 28, 221*n*46, 221*n*48
dual tasking and, 229*n*18
exercise and, 66
glucose intake and, 92
hearing loss and, 29, 30, 223*n*56,
    223*n*60
high-risk cognitive aging and, 171,
    273*n*20
hypertension and, 240*n*26
hypoxemia and, 220*n*40
learning and, 47, 57, 230–231*n*24
mild cognitive impairment and,
    236*n*58
neuroplasticity and, 47–48, 232*n*30
obesity and, 70, 186, 240*n*26
optimal time of day and, 90
parking/finding cars, 7, 90, 172
processing speed and, 228*n*6
senior moments and, 1–2
stress hormones and, 80
tip-of-the-tongue blockage (*see* Tip-of-
    the-tongue memory blockage)
training, 99, 100, 101, 236*n*58, 254*n*22,
    255*n*26
working memory, 43, 45, 46, 171,
    229*nn*13–17
Memory case studies
    compromised functioning, 50–51, 60
    high-risk cognitive aging, 170, 171
    normal cognitive aging, 143–144,
        145–146, 147, 149–150, 170,
        268*nn*27–28
    optimal cognitive aging, 125
Ménière's disease, 163
Mental ability and aging
    anxiety and, 213*n*18
    applications and reflections, 55–61,
        236*nn*55–59
    aptitude test performance (*see* Aptitude
        test performance)
    attitudes and behaviors and (*see*
        Attitudes and behaviors)
    case studies, 50–51, 59–61
    chronic conditions and (*see* Chronic
        medical conditions and
        intellectual functioning)

compromised functioning, 49–54,
53t, 233–235nn37–50 (see also
Cognitive decline)
control and, 263–264n32
declines from interviews, 44–47,
230–231nn21–26
declines from research (see Mental
ability and research findings)
education and, 197, 198f, 280n44
emphasis recent on, 4
health and, 33, 33f, 34–35t, 73, 197,
198f, 280n44
healthy habits for (see Healthy lifestyle
habits for mental ability)
hearing loss and, 29, 30, 222–223n54
hereditary factors in, 54–55,
235–236nn51–54
high-risk cognitive aging and, 171–173,
273nn21–22
hormones and, 80, 248–249n76
intelligence (see Intelligence)
mental health and, 81, 249n77
mortality and, 70
neuroplasticity, 47–49, 231–233nn27–
36, 236n57
new learning and, 82
optimal cognitive aging and, 196, 197,
279n41
optimal time of day, 90, 106–107,
250–251nn1–2
overview of, 39–40, 40f, 227–228nn1–
5, 253n12
selection, optimization, compensation,
268n27
strategies to maximize (see Strategies
to maximize intellect)
vision impairment and, 28–29
Mental ability and research findings; see
also specific abilities
analogies, 41
aptitude test performance (see Aptitude
test performance)
attention, 45, 46, 82, 109, 250n96
decision making, 229n15
digit symbol substitution, 41, 41f
executive functioning, 42, 42f
intelligence (IQ), 39, 40f, 227n1
memory, 42, 42f, 43–44, 45–47, 48,
229nn13–17, 251n2, 262n24
MicroCog, 39–40, 40f
multitasking, 43–44, 229–230nn17–20

overview of, 40–43 41f, 42f,
228nn6–12
processing speed, 40–42, 41f, 45–46
reasoning, 41, 42, 42f, 125
visuospatial abilities, 42, 42f, 45, 46,
95, 267n22
Mental challenges, 34t, 35, 92
Mental distress, see Psychological distress
Mental flexibility, 23, 150, 201
Mental health; see also Depression
counseling and, 179–181, 189
dementia and, 52
down days (see Down days)
frequency of, 261n15
healthy habits and, 73
high-risk cognitive aging and, 158
normal cognitive aging and, 7
stress and, 141–142, 248n70
Mental vigor, 92, 123–124; see also
Strategies to maximize intellect
Metabolic equivalents (METs) for exercise,
67, 68t, 238n13, 264n34
Metabolic syndrome, 164, 272n13
METs (metabolic equivalents) for exercise,
67, 68t, 238n13, 264n34
MicroCog, 39–40, 40f, 42, 42f
Middle-old, 209n1; see also 3rd Age of Life
Mild cognitive impairment (MCI); see also
Cognitive decline
age-related cognitive decline and,
52–53, 234–235nn45–50
brain and, 274n27
case studies, 50–51, 59–61
dementia and, 53, 53t, 58–59, 60,
197–198, 235n49, 280n45
driving and, 273–274n26
dysexecutive mild cognitive
impairment, 175–176, 192,
274n27
high-risk cognitive aging and, 157,
270nn3–4
intelligence and, 54
memory and, 236n58
mental lapses and, 51
nonimpaired state from, xiv
training programs and, 102
visuospatial abilities and, 273–274n26
Mind, see Brain; Mental ability
Mini Mental State Exam (MMSE), 214n4,
239n19, 242n34, 265n3
Minor decliners, see Normal cognitive
aging

Miracle on the Hudson, 93–96, 94*f*
MMSE, *see* Mini Mental State Exam
Modifiable lifestyle habits, *see* Healthy
    lifestyle habits
Morning people, 90; *see also* Optimal time
    of day
Mortality
    alcohol consumption and, 73–74,
        266*n*13
    exercise and, 82–83, 249*nn*83–84
    feeling useful and, 263–264*n*32
    obesity and, 70, 240*n*23, 250*n*86
    risky habits and, 139, 266*n*13
    social relationships and, 76,
        245–246*nn*54–57
Motivation to change, 179
Multi-infarct dementia, *see* Vascular
    dementia
Multitasking
    aging and, 43–44, 229–230*nn*17–20
    avoiding, 89
    case studies, 134–136, 145–146, 147
    driving and, 174–175
    optimization and, 91
    proofreading error and, 56

N

Names, memory for, 45, 46, 47
Napping, 107
National Health Interview Survey (NHIS),
    210*n*4, 214*n*2, 266*n*10
National Long Term Care Survey (NLTCS),
    210*n*4, 224*n*64, 224*n*65
Nature (outdoors), 103–104, 108, 257*n*41
Nature (heredity) in cognitive aging,
    54–55, 235–236*nn*51–54
Navigational problems; *see also*
    Visuospatial abilities
    case studies, 50, 55–56
    driving, 143–144, 146–147, 280–281*n*50
Negative social contacts, 76
Neurocognitive scaffolding, *see*
    Neuroplasticity
Neuroimaging, 48, 58, 196, 231*n*28
Neuroplasticity
    mental ability and, 47–49, 231–
        233*nn*27–36, 236*n*57
    research directions, 49, 58, 196,
        233*n*36, 236*n*57
New learning, *see* Learning

NHANES III (Third National Health and
    Nutrition Examination Survey),
    210*n*4
NHIS (National Health Interview Survey),
    210*n*4, 214*n*2, 266*n*10
NLTCS (National Long Term Care Survey),
    210*n*4, 224*nn*64–65
Non-insulin-dependent diabetes mellitus,
    see Diabetes
Nonobligation component, 257*n*40
Normal cognitive aging
    age-related cognitive decline and, 51
    anxiety and, 194
    applications and reflections, 152–155,
        269*nn*33–39
    attitudes and behaviors with, 143–152,
        145*t*, 267–269*nn*21–32
    case studies (*see* Normal cognitive
        aging case studies)
    chronic medical conditions and,
        138–139, 260*n*10, 266*nn*10–11
    definition of, 133, 264–265*n*2
    health qualities with, 136–143, 137*t*,
        265–267*nn*7–20
    identification of, 134–136, 137*t*,
        265*nn*3–6
    overview of, 5*f*, 6–7, 133–134,
        264–265*nn*1–4
Normal cognitive aging case studies
    attitudes and behaviors, 143–144,
        145–146, 148–149, 150, 151, 152
    health qualities, 136–138, 139, 142
    identification of, 134–136
Numbers, memory for, 45, 46, 47
Nuture (environment) in cognitive aging,
    54–55, 235–236*nn*51–54

O

Obesity
    activities of daily living and, 266*n*13
    aging and, 269*n*34
    annual physical and, 260*n*11
    baby boomers and, 186
    bariatric surgery and, 158–160, 180
    case studies, 139, 143, 159
    dementia and, 70, 83, 240*n*25, 271*n*10
    fighting, 69–71, 84, 239–241*nn*21–29,
        269*n*34
    frequency of, 69, 70, 83, 186
    guilt and shame with, 142–143, 267*n*19
    high-risk cognitive aging and, 177–178

life expectancy and, 240–241n27,
250n86
memory and, 70, 186, 240n26
metabolic syndrome and, 164
mortality and, 70, 240n23, 250n86
normal cognitive aging and, 153
obstructive sleep apnea and, 27,
220n42
Observational skills and art, 104–105, 191,
256nn35–36
Obstructive sleep apnea (OSA), 24–27,
219–220nn35–44
OctoTwin Study, 54
O'Kelly, Eugene, 199–200
Omnidirectional hearing aids, 30
Openness to new experiences
level of intellect and, 6, 7
normal cognitive aging and, 151,
262n31
optimal cognitive aging and, 128, 188,
201, 263n31
Optimal cognitive aging
active experience and, 95, 107
activity levels and, 66–67, 115–116,
130, 186, 188, 195–196,
259–260n8
applications and reflections, 57,
129–131, 264nn33–37
attitudes and behaviors with, 112,
118–119, 122–129, 123t, 260–
261nn13–14, 262–264nn21–32
case studies (see Optimal cognitive
aging case studies)
chronic medical conditions and, 19,
213–214n1, 260n10
cognitive decline and, 44–46, 125, 130
cognitive restoration and, 108
concerns with, 55
effort required for, 195–196, 279n41
as exemplary, 202, 258n2
health qualities with, 112, 115–121,
115t, 259–261nn7–20
healthy habits and, 10, 11t , 188,
195–197, 212n13, 280n44
identification of, 112–115, 258–259n4,
259nn5–6
importance of, xiii–xiv
intellect and, 3–4, 6, 123–124, 210n5
learning and, 95–96
mental lapses and, 56, 57
middle age and, 152–153

overview of, 5–6, 5f, 111–112, 258–
259nn1–4, 280n47
as proactive choice, 202
selection, optimization, compensation
and, 92
stress management and, 78–79, 119,
131, 261n15
Optimal cognitive aging case studies
attitudes and behaviors, 122–123,
124–125, 126, 127, 128–129
healthy habits, 116–117, 118–119
identification of, 113–115
Optimal time of day, 90, 106–107,
250–251nn1–2
Optimization, 91; see also Selection,
optimization, compensation
OSA (obstructive sleep apnea), 24–27,
219–220nn35–44
Overweight adults, 9, 139; see also Obesity

P

Pancreatic cancer, 172–173, 179
Parking and finding cars
case studies, 125
improving, 128, 192
memory and, 7, 90, 172
Parkinson's disease, 52
Pet(s), 126, 262n27
PET (positron emission tomography), 48,
231n28
Pharmaceutical treatments, see
Prescription medication
Physician's Health Study I, 212n13, 242n33
Physician's study on aging
as empirical data base, xvii, 209
MicroCog and, 39–40, 40f, 228nn4–5
Placebo effects (cognitive), 101,
254–255n25
Plasticity, see Neuroplasticity
Plastic surgery, 121, 261n20
Positive thinking, 35, 35t
Positivity bias
adverse effects with, xiv
attention and, 82
decision-making and, 85–87, 193–194
emotions and, 193–194, 201
stress management and, 187
Positron emission tomography (PET), 48,
231n28
Post-traumatic stress disorder (PTSD),
248n70, 248n74

Practice
annual physicals, 117, 260*n*11
applications and reflections (*see*
Practice applications and
reflections)
art observation and, 104–105, 191,
256*n*36
clinical notes, 190–196,
278–279*nn*28–41
compliance (*see* Medical advice
compliance; Prescription
medication compliance)
favorite place prescriptions, 109, 191
improving healthy habits, 154–155,
184–185
questions about intellect and, 3, 13,
38, 50
research gap with, xv
selection, optimization, compensation
and, 91–92, 107
Practice applications and reflections
clinical notes, 190–196,
278–279*nn*28–41
health effects on intellect, 12–15,
36–38, 226–227*nn*72–77
healthy habits, 82–87, 131,
249–250*nn*83–97
high-risk cognitive aging, 177–181,
274*nn*29–31
intellectual functioning, 12–15,
213*nn*20–25
mental ability and aging, 55–61,
236*nn*55–59
normal cognitive aging, 152–155,
269*nn*33–39
optimal cognitive aging, 57, 129–131,
264*nn*33–37
strategies to maximize intellect, 58,
257–258*nn*43–48
Pre-hypertension, 20–21
Prescription medication
alcohol consumption and, 84
for Alzheimer's disease, 60–61
for atrial fibrillation, 23, 217*n*23
for chronic obstructive pulmonary
disease, 218*n*30
compliance with (*see* Prescription
medication compliance)
health and, 34*t*, 35
hypertension and, 22
for mild cognitive impairment, 59
rate of use, 244*n*47

for weight loss, 71
Prescription medication compliance
applications and reflections, 154
benefits of, 11, 186–187
case studies, 134–136, 162, 167
high-risk cognitive aging and, 7–8, 178
hypertension and, 22, 260*n*12
improving, 37
instructions about, 269*n*35
measurement of, 226–227*n*76, 277*n*21
optimal cognitive aging and, 118
reasons for lack of, 269*n*36
Preventive health care behavior, 184,
276*n*11
Problem drinkers, *see* Alcohol abuse/
dependence
Problem solving, 95, 97, 261*n*16
Problem- versus emotion-based coping,
79, 152–153, 266–267*n*16
Processing speed
activity levels and, 68
aging and, 40–42, 41*f*, 45–46
applications and reflections, 56
aptitude and, 40, 228*nn*6–9
diabetes and, 221*n*46
exercise and, 64, 65*f*
measurement of, 238–239*n*16
problem solving and, 95
training techniques, 100–101, 254*n*22
Prostate cancer, 78, 79
Psychological distress
declines in, 225*n*67
definition of, 242*n*35
diet and, 73
high-risk cognitive aging and, 164,
272*nn*14–15
Psychomotor speed, 219*n*38; *see also*
Processing speed
Psychosocial adjustment; *see also*
Social relationships; Stress
management
hearing loss and, 29, 30, 222*n*52
optimal cognitive aging and, 11–12,
11*t*, 212*n*17
PTSD (post-traumatic stress disorder),
248*n*70, 248*n*74
Public speaking, 150
Pulmonary disease, *see* Chronic
pulmonary disease

Q

Quality of life
  hearing loss and, 29
  intellect and, 3
  life expectancy and, 31
  living versus dying focus, 202
  medical conditions and, 4
  normal cognitive aging and, 134,
    142–143, 267nn19–20
  obesity and, 70–71, 250n86
  selection, optimization, compensation
    and, 93
  social relationships and, 126, 147–148
  stress and, 33, 34–35t, 35–36, 141

R

Race
  alcohol consumption and, 244n44
  chronic medical conditions and, 36
  life expectancy and, 226n73
  obesity and, 239–240n21
  preventive health care behavior and,
    276n11
Reasoning
  aging and, 41, 42, 42f, 125
  training techniques, 100, 254n22
Religion and health, 35, 35t
Research
  attention restoration and, 256–257n38
  characteristics of cited, xv
  cross-sectional and longitudinal, 39,
    227–228nn2–3, 262n25
  empirical data base, xvii, 209
  future directions for (see Research
    directions)
  normal cognitive aging and, 133
  patient-provider collaboration and, xv
  task demands and, 230n20
Research directions
  attention restoration activities, 106
  dementia and mild cognitive
    impairment, 60
  health effects on intellect, 38
  healthy habits for mental ability, 87
  mental ability and aging, 57–58
  neuroplasticity, 49, 58, 196, 233n36,
    236n57
  overview of, xv, 196–198,
    279–280nn42–45

reasons for successful aging, 129–130,
    264n33
  strategies to maximize intellect,
    107–108
Resentment, 178, 274n31
Resource on diet, 241n32
Retirement
  activity levels in, 122, 237n8
  for airline pilots, 95, 252n10
  case studies, 148–149, 151
  continuing care communities and,
    85–87, 193–194
  high-risk cognitive aging and, 163
  optimal cognitive aging and, 118
  selection, optimization, compensation
    and, 149–150
  social relationships in, 148–149, 165
  volunteerism during, 129
Retrieval from memory, 47–48, 229n18,
    262n24
Reunions, *see* 50th reunions
Reverse mortgages, 177
Rheumatoid arthritis, 129
Risky lifestyle habits
  chronic medical conditions and,
    274–275n1
  high-risk cognitive aging and, 161–162,
    177–178, 271n10
  normal cognitive aging and, 139–140,
    266nn12–13

S

Satisfaction with life
  case studies, 158–160, 163, 180
  living versus dying focus, 202
  social networks and, 247n63
Schweitzer, Albert, 15, 194–195
Sedentary lifestyle
  aptitudes and, 63, 66, 68–69
  brain and, 259–260n8
  life expectancy and, 279n42
Selection, optimization, compensation
    (SOC)
  applications and reflections, 91–92, 107
  driving and, 128, 192–193
  maximizing intellect and, 11t, 12,
    90–93, 213n19, 251–252nn3–8
  normal cognitive aging and, 149–150,
    268nn27–28
  overview of, 90–93, 251–252nn3–8
Self-esteem, 252n7

Self-rated health (SRH)
    chronic medical conditions and,
        225–226*n*71
    comparative, 32–36, 33*f,* 34–35*t,*
        225*n*70
    decline, 44–46
    health and, 116, 137, 260*n*9, 275*n*2
Senior moments, 1–2, 46, 60
Sensory impairments, *see* Hearing loss;
        Vision impairment
Severe psychological distress, 73, 242*n*35
Shifting set (flexibility), 23, 150, 201
Simplified living, 34*t,* 35
Singing, 128
Sleep
    caregiver stress and, 266*n*15
    case studies, 134–136
    cognitive impairment and, 26, 27
    obstructive sleep apnea and, 25–27,
        219–220*nn*35–44
Sleep apnea, 25–27, 219–220*nn*35–44
Smoking
    activities of daily living and, 266*n*13
    case studies, 134–136, 139, 143–144,
        162, 164
    chronic obstructive pulmonary disease
        and, 24
    decrease in, 184, 275*n*5
    demographics and, 276*n*11
    effects of, 13
    mental health and, 73
    overview of, 185–186
    quitting success, 9, 155, 186, 277*n*13
SOC, *see* Selection, optimization,
        compensation
Social isolation, *see* Isolation
Social relationships
    alcohol consumption and, 74
    appearance and, 159
    benefits of, 12, 212*n*17, 261*n*18
    cardiovascular disease and, 76,
        245–246*n*55, 261*n*18
    case studies, 114, 148, 164–165
    chronic medical conditions and,
        246*n*57
    decision making and, 98
    health and, 34–35*t,* 35, 268*n*24
    as healthy habit, 76–77,
        245–247*nn*54–65
    high-risk cognitive aging and, 8,
        173–174, 273*nn*23–24, 274*n*29
    monitoring, 85

normal cognitive aging and, 147–148,
        268*nn*24–25
    optimal cognitive aging and, 126, 188,
        262*nn*25–27
    repopulating networks, 12, 187
    selection, optimization, compensation,
        268*nn*27–28
    volunteerism and, 120
Socioeconomic status, *see* Income
Sound amplification devices, *see* Hearing
        aids
Spatial abilities; *see also* Visuospatial
        abilities
    declines in, 236*n*55
    exercise and, 65*f,* 66
    gender and, 267*n*22
    processing speed and, 228*n*6
Speed, *see* Processing speed; Psychomotor
        speed
SRH, *see* Self-rated health
Stimulation, *see* Cognitive training;
        Strategies to maximize intellect
Strategies to maximize intellect; *see also*
        specific strategies
    active experience, 95–98, 253*nn*11–15
    applications and reflections, 58,
        257–258*nn*43–48
    attention restoration, 12, 105–106, 109,
        191, 255–257*nn*31–42
    case studies, 102–103, 114–115, 125,
        127
    cognitive training, 59, 98–102, 232*n*32,
        236*n*58, 253–255*nn*16–30
    defensive listening, 30
    experience matters, 93–96, 252*nn*9–10
    memory, 57, 60
    overview of, 111
    research directions, 107–108
    selection, optimization, compensation,
        11*t,* 12, 90–93, 213*n*19,
        251–252*nn*3–8
    stress management, 34–35*t,* 35
    tip-of-the-tongue memory blockage, 57
    working smarter, 89–90, 250–251*nn*1–2
Strength training, 63, 65
Stress
    brain and, 80, 81*f,* 213*n*18, 248*nn*73–74
    of caregivers, 141, 152–153, 165,
        266–267*nn*15–16
    case studies, 134–136
    decision making and, 85–87
    definition of, 79, 247*n*67

directed attention and, 103
health and, 79–80, 81, 187, 248n70
high-risk cognitive aging and, 165–166,
    178, 272n16
management of (see Stress
    management)
mental health and, 141–142, 248n70
optimal cognitive aging and, 188
quality of life and, 33, 34–35t, 35–36,
    141
Stress hormones, 80, 248nn73–74
Stress management
benefits of, 12, 187, 212n18
emotion- versus problem-based, 79,
    152–153, 266–267n16
health and, 33, 34–35t, 35–36
as healthy lifestyle habit, 78–82, 81f,
    247–249nn66–82
neuroplasticity and, 232n32
optimal cognitive aging and, 78–79,
    119, 131, 261n15
Strokes
atrial fibrillation and, 22, 23, 216n16
case studies, 59–61
dementia and, 52
high-risk cognitive aging and, 163
Successful aging; see also Optimal
    cognitive aging
components of, 198–199, 213–214n1,
    258–259n4, 280n46
factors important to, 3–4, 210n5
research challenges of, 264n33
Sullenberger, Chesley, 93–96, 94f, 107
Surveys of health, 3, 210n4, 214n2,
    266n10
Survival, see Mortality

T

Task difficulty and aging, 41, 43
Technology
case studies, 134–136
employment and, 149
normal cognitive aging and, 148–149,
    262–263n28
optimal cognitive aging and, 6,
    126–127, 262–263n28
Teeth grinding, 119
Teetotalers, 74; see also Alcohol
    consumption
Telemarketing fraud, 87; see also Financial
    issues

Telephone use
attention and, 172
cell phones, 44, 151
cognitive decline and, 77
Texting, see Communication technology
Therapeutic alliance, 15, 213n25
3rd Age of life
challenges and passions of, 14
definition of, 2–3, 209n1
demographics of, 3, 209n2, 275n3
developmental hurdles of, 130–131,
    199, 280n50
hard work of, 195–196
optimal aging and, xiii–xiv
richness of, 198–202, 280–281n46–53
3rd Age Study (Clearwater, FL), xvii, 44
Third National Health and Nutrition
    Examination Survey (NHANES
    III), 210n4
Time passage, 201
Time pressure, see Processing speed;
    Psychomotor speed
Tip-of-the-tongue memory blockage
aging and, 45, 46f, 262n24
memory and, 230nn21–23
review on, 236n56
strategies for, 57, 195
Tobacco use, see Smoking
Touching base, 200–201, 280n49
Tough love interactions, 76
Training, see Cognitive training; Strength
    training
Travel/trips; see also Driving
case studies, 50, 55–56, 129, 143–144,
    151
health and, 34t, 35
losing way/disorientation, 143–144,
    146–147, 273–274n26,
    280–281n50
strategies for, 12, 45, 46, 47, 89–90
12-step programs, 75–76, 245n51
Twin studies, 54–55, 235n51
Type 2 diabetes, see Diabetes

U

Unwinding, 199–200, 280n49
Usefulness, 129, 263–264n32
Usual cognitive aging, see Normal
    cognitive aging

V

Variance, calculation of, 279–280*n*43
Vascular dementia, 52
Verbal meaning, 236*n*55
Verbal memory, 45–46
Veterans and stress, 79–80, 81*f,* 248*n*70,
    248*n*74
Vigor, intellectual, 92, 123–124
Vision impairment, 28–29, 225*n*67
Visuospatial abilities
    age-related cognitive decline and, 51
    aging and, 42, 42*f,* 45, 46, 95, 267*n*22
    case studies, 55, 171
    disorientation/getting lost, 7, 143–
        144, 146–147, 273–274*n*26,
        280–281*n*50
    high-risk cognitive aging and, 171,
        273*n*21
Volunteerism
    benefits of, 14, 213*n*23
    health and, 34*t,* 35
    mental ability and, 189
    optimal cognitive aging and, 120–121,
        129, 130, 188, 261*n*18
    3rd Age of life and, 2
Vulnerability
    to financial misjudgment, 87, 169,
        176–177, 274*n*28
    high-risk cognitive aging and, 8

W

WAIS (Wechsler Adult Intelligence Scale),
    42–43, 227*n*1
Walking, 102, 103–104, 256*n*33, 257*n*41
Walking the knife's edge, 131
War veterans and stress, 79–80, 81*f,*
    248*n*70, 248*n*74

Wechsler Adult Intelligence Scale (WAIS),
    42–43, 227*n*1
Weight loss; *see also* Obesity
    bariatric surgery, 158–160, 180
    benefits of, 83–84
    case studies, 158–160, 159, 164
    exercise and, 241*nn*28–29
    guilt and shame, 142–143, 267*n*19
    life expectancy and, 240–241*n*27,
        250*n*86
    obstructive sleep apnea and, 27,
        220*n*42
    quality of life and, 70–71
Well-being, 36, 263–264*n*32, 268*n*24; *see
    also* Quality of life
White matter of brain
    activity level and, 68, 238–239*n*16
    atrial fibrillation and, 23
    diabetes and, 28, 221*n*47
    hypertension and, 22
Wine drinkers, 74, 120, 139, 243*n*40
Wisdom, 98, 125
Witch doctor treatment, 15
Word pair memory, 48
Work and technology, 149
Working memory
    aging and, 43, 45, 46, 229*nn*13–17
    case studies, 171
Working smarter, *see* Strategies to
    maximize intellect

Y

Young-old, 209*n1*; *see also* 3rd Agers
Youthfulness and appeal, 261*n*19

Z

Zest for life, 260*n*13, 272*n*11, 274*n*29